JOSEPH LISTER

1827–1912

Joseph Lister

1827-1912

RICHARD B. FISHER

MACDONALD AND JANE'S · LONDON

FIRST PUBLISHED IN GREAT BRITAIN IN 1977 BY
MACDONALD AND JANE'S PUBLISHERS LIMITED,
PAULTON HOUSE,
8 SHEPHERDESS WALK,
LONDON N.1.

ISBN 0 354 04145 2

PRINTED IN GREAT BRITAIN BY
REDWOOD BURN LTD.,
TROWBRIDGE AND ESHER

To Don Baker

CONTENTS

ILLUSTRATIONS

1

UPTON PARK

'. . . the baby has been today unusually lovely,' Isabella Lister wrote to her husband on October 21, 1827. With an archaic turn of phrase to express a timeless maternal sentiment, she provided the first written record of their fourth child other than the registration of his birth on April 5, six months before.

As the second son he had been named Joseph after his great grandfather and his father. John, the first son, was named after his grandfather and great-great grandfather. This Quaker custom of repeating Christian names from generation to generation can make genealogical research difficult. Isabella Sophie, born between John and Joseph, bore not only her mother's name but her maternal grandmother's. In each of the four families that descended from the seven children of Isabella and Joseph Jackson Lister, moreover, there was a Joseph Lister, not because of admiration for the brother who was to make surgery safe by defeating infection, but as a sign of affectionate respect for Joseph Jackson.

He received the news of his infant son while he was at Gloucester, probably on business to do with the City of London guild of which he was a member. Isabella's note was a postscript to a letter by their eldest child, Mary, that set forth the quiet current of life at home from her seven-year-old viewpoint.

In 1826 on the advice of Samuel Gurney, the Quaker banker who lived at Ham House in Ham Park to the west of Upton Lane, Joseph Jackson Lister bought the property to the east of the Lane known as Upton Park in the parish of West Ham, Essex. Upton Park meandered from Waltham and Wanstead to the north via the hamlet of Upton to Plaistow and the Thames at Blackwall. To the west were the Hackney marshes and to the east, Barking Creek. Today Ham Park remains as West Ham Park but Upton Park is occupied by a church and school and Upton House has been replaced by an ugly council block called Joseph Lister Court. The area is typical of the two-storey terraces that sprawled across London's industrial east in the early years of the twentieth century. It is a lower-middle-class multi-racial community.

In 1841 only 12,738 people lived in the whole of West Ham Parish. It was still largely open country. Transportation was by horse along the mud tracks that passed for roads, and by river. The marshes and the Thames foreshore abounded with butterflies, birds and small animals. Both Mary and John reported to their father in Gloucester that a stag had been captured at Upton. At Samuel Gurney's orders the animal's horns had been cut off, and it had been kept 'in the cow house,' wrote John, 'he is like a goat only a great deal larger'. Mary added that he was to be 'let . . . go back to the forest . . . that they might have the pleasure of hunting it again. There are 6 more of this kind in the forest, which is a wild red deer.'

Even then Plaistow and its Essex hinterland did not consist solely of country parks and suburban villas. There were small working farmers, leaseholding yeomen for the most part, shopkeepers and artisans in the small towns and the servants to the new residents. The Lister children had a nanny. There was a cook named Rhoda when Joseph was five, and at about the same time Isabella had a personal maid named Rebecca. Joseph at school learned from Mary that Elizabeth Fry, the prison reformer who was Samuel Gurney's sister,

wishes to have a meeting with the servants of friends' families and those in the neighbourhood and Mamma means to let all of ours go which I think will be very amusing for us who stay at home and almost like the day when we were at Shanklin the servants all went to Black Gang Chine.

These people lived on their employers' premises, but many of them came from families in the neighbourhood. Plaistow was an old community where the new middle class had recently settled. There were even pirates: 'A prominent object on the river bank,' wrote one old resident in 1891, 'was a jibbet, on which the bodies of cattle lifters, pirates, etc, hung till they rotted away.' The Lister children could not escape entirely the harshness of Britain in the midst of the industrial revolution.

John was at school in Tottenham in 1838. 'The early part of my summer holydays was occupied with the trial of some boys who had robbed our out house at school and taken several cricket bats and balls carpenters tools and pairs of skaites and shoes,' the sixteen-year-old boy recorded in his diary. He and Edmund Gurney were witnesses at the trial:

they were all found guilty and the two who had sold the balls by name William Ashton & Richard Jenkinson were sentenced to seven years transportation; the others William Well & Thomas Newland to 9 months hard labour.

Such incidents occurred closer to home. In August of the same year Mary wrote to Joseph that two boys had been caught stealing in a neighbour's garden. The culprits were local people and not street boys from London.

Yet if Upton Park was something less than Eden, it offered a fair simulacrum of an English rural paradise. The 69 acres were level and wooded. The house was a rambling structure with a Queen Anne façade of weathered brick. It was then over a century old and had been frequently extended. 'I am writing in the study with the folded windows open to the garden,' Joseph Jackson wrote to Joseph; '& the temperate warmth & stillness, and the chirping of birds & hum of insects, the bright lawn & aloe & the darker spread of the cedars & chequered sky above, altogether tempt to idle enjoyment that I must not indulge in.'

A stream crossed by an ornamental bridge flowed through the garden. There were apple trees and an array of beech, oak, elm and chestnut. During the summer of 1855 the American aloe or century plant unexpectedly flowered. Joseph had begun the practice of surgery in Edinburgh, and during his Christmas holiday at Upton he wrote a 'case history' of the bloom:

the whole constitution of the aloe appears to have been remarkably affected with a tendency to flowering, and just as the part above ground, instead of producing, as usual, a few leaves, shot forth this year a stem with a multitude of flower buds, so the underground portion of the plant, instead of sending out, as usual, a few . . . sprouts terminating in leaf-buds, this year produced many . . . ending in flower-buds and destitute of leaves.

The cedars near the house became almost as important to the inhabitants as the walls themselves. After a heavy snowfall had damaged the trees Joseph Jackson apologized to Joseph:

I ought not to have left it to Mary to tell thee of the disaster to our Cedars, but I think it will please thee to hear that seen from the side of the house it still retains much of the appearance with which thy early recollection would be associated.

His father referred to Joseph's supporting impression of being 'in thy right place' at Upton. It was a feeling for family as well as place.

The Lister family originated in West Yorkshire around the town of Bingley, a centre of the early cloth industry. There was a Joseph Lister at Alerton near Bingley, a non-conformist, who wrote an autobiographical account of the Civil War battle of Bradford and Leeds which had been won for Parliament in 1642 by Fairfax. The first certain ancestor of the Joseph Lister born in 1827, however, was Thomas Lister, a maltster and farmer of Bingley. In 1705 he married Hannah Lister, the daughter of a yeoman and probably a cousin. The couple joined the Society of Friends.

Their eldest son, Joseph, was born the next year. At the age of fourteen he left home to make his life in London. He became a tobacconist in Aldersgate, and in 1728 married Mary Gray, the daughter of a wool factor, also a Quaker.

John Lister, their youngest son, was the surgeon's grandfather. He was born in 1738, reputedly in one of the houses that lined old London bridge. He died in his ninety-ninth year when his grandson, Joseph, was ten. A great grandson described his 'slight, antique figure, brisk and lively in his manner, dressed in a long coat with knee breeches, silk stockings and low shoes with silver buckles. He wore a cocked hat and his long silvery hair was tied back with a black ribbon'. This fine Quaker gentleman told his grandchildren blood-curdling stories about the heads of traitors, presumably rebel Scots, set on pikes on the roof of the Gateway Tower. At Kendal in Cumbria where he had been sent to school, he saw the Young Pretender marching through the streets at the head of the small force that was to grow into an army on the road to Culloden.

John Lister returned from school to an apprenticeship as a watchmaker. His artisan-employer was Isaac Rogers who had become a member of the Bakers' Company and a citizen of the City of London. Citizenship brought with it the right to do business in one's own name, to be registered and insured and to participate in the City government. But citizenship could be obtained only through membership in one of the City companies or guilds, and there was none for watchmakers. The reason for the selection of the Bakers' guild and not that of, let us say, the Barbers' may have been quite simply a matter of money. When Joseph Jackson Lister's nephew, Richard Beck, became his partner in 1821, he entered the Bakers' Company because even at £45 its fees were among the lowest. Nevertheless, from 1759 John Lister conducted his own business in Bell Alley, Lombard Street, and became a member of the Bakers' Company and a citizen of London on February 4, 1760.

In 1766 he abandoned watchmaking in order to take over his father's tobacco business. Two years before he had married Mary Jackson at the Gracechurch Street Meeting House in the City. She was the daughter of Stephen Jackson, wine merchant, of Lothbury. Her family had not been happy about the marriage. 'If thou wilt have thy Johnny,' she reported them as having said, 'thou wilt have him to nurse.' He was a slight young man allegedly in 'feeble health', but he outlived his wife by thirty years. There may have been another reason for her family's doubts, the difference in the economic status of prospective bride and groom. Only five years after his marriage, however, John Lister acquired his father-in-law's successful wine business.

John and Mary Lister had two daughters. The youngest, Elizabeth, married an Ipswich merchant named Beck. One of their sons, Richard, became partner with his uncle, Joseph Jackson, in the wine business. Richard's nephew, Marcus Beck, lived with his cousin Joseph when he studied medicine in Glasgow. He became one of Joseph's most outspoken defenders during the difficult early days of the antiseptic method. These practical relationships are early examples of that Quaker cousinhood which characterized Lister's family life. The same traditional spirit underlay the otherwise commonplace life of John's eldest daughter, Mary. A spinster, she cared for her father in his Stoke Newington home until his death.

Seventeen years after the birth of Elizabeth Lister, in 1786, John and Mary had a third child whom they named Joseph Jackson. He was destined to have a noteworthy career of his own as businessman, Quaker leader, paterfamilias, scientist and humanist.

A few months before his sixth birthday Joseph Jackson Lister had been sent to a Quaker school at Hitchin, Hertfordshire, where there were relatives named Lucas. His first letter, preserved and appropriately labelled by his 'Honred Parents' begins: 'It is with much Pleasure I sit down for the first time to hand you a few lines'. A year later he wrote a letter in French on which his father noted, 'JJL's usher only corrected two words in the above.' His curriculum included Latin, mathematics and penmanship, which also meant spelling. In the latter discipline the boy was at first less successful. When he was ten, his father wrote to him enclosing nine books 'for the instruction and benefit of the youth of the present generation'. He then noticed with dismay the inadequacy of Joseph's copying and spelling, and concluded: 'we intended to have sent thee a plumb cake, had we heard a better account but shall now leave it till another time.' From his Master, however, the boy received a copy of *The Power of Religion on the Mind* 'as a Reward for his Improvement in Writing 1793'. Three copybooks headed 'Specimens of Handwriting' in an elaborate copperplate cursive and dated 1794, 1795 and 1797 reveal that his efforts are not only legible, as they always remained, but remarkably beautiful.

In February 1798 when he was eleven, Joseph Jackson went to Rochester School where he stayed for a year before being sent to a third Quaker school belonging to one Thomas Thompson at Compton, Somerset, near the Dorset border. After two years at Compton he returned to London to become an apprentice in his father's wine business. There is no record of his last years at school, but judging from his later research and his catholic interests, he must have been an above average scholar. Nor do the early letters leave much room to doubt the father's lively interest in his son's education. It is surprising, therefore, to find him entering business at fourteen. The £20 fee that John Lister had paid at Rochester three years before was certainly not trivial, and it is possible that the family fortunes had declined, however temporarily. Perhaps the war with France made peculiar difficulties for the wine trade. Or possibly like other young men Joseph Jackson Lister simply wanted to get on with 'life', and lost patience with school. He continued to read the Latin classics for pleasure and knew French and German. His later work on lenses sharpened his mathematics. Some correspondence with Richard Abbott, a mathematician, indicates that miscellaneous maths problems amongst Joseph Jackson's papers were probably related to his later role as a school visitor.

On April 18, 1807, when Joseph Jackson was eighteen, John Lister made over to him his 'Goods Household Stuff Utensils, Brass pewter Bedding contained in my House situated in and being No 42 Lothbury excepting one

Desk standing on the floor in the Accompting House'. The deed was written 'in consideration of the faithful services of and parental affection that I owe to my Son'; it also made Joseph Jackson a co-partner in the business. John Lister's generosity was to be repeated in Joseph Jackson's dealings with his children, and there is ample evidence that his famous son, Joseph, made frequent money gifts to nieces, nephews and dependents too.

The wine business prospered. After the death of his wife, in 1808, John Lister retired to Stoke Newington. When the Bank of England absorbed the premises in Lothbury in order to enlarge, Joseph Jackson rented a house nearby at 5 Tokenhouse Yard. The cellars were used as wine vaults, the ground floor as offices and warehouse, and the proprietor lived in the upper floors. In 1821 Joseph Jackson Lister became part owner of a ship which his wife's brother commanded. He invested in various other limited companies, and appears to have been contemplating a coal mining venture in the Llanelly valley, though how far he pursued this interest is not known.

The premises in Tokenhouse Yard were rented at £30 a year from the Gracechurch Street Meeting of which Joseph Jackson was a member as his father and mother had been. Despite considerable price inflation during the early years of the century, the rent remained the same at least until 1856.

The Gracechurch Street Meeting was one of the oldest in London. Its members included bankers such as the Gurneys and the Barclays and merchants such as the Tindalls and the Harrises. Their businesses were located in the City, and until the dispersal of the more prosperous families to the new suburbs they lived on their business premises. The Listers, Harrises, Tindalls and Barclays were then or later became related by marriage.

Gracechurch Street Meeting had a high proportion of prosperous members because of its location in the City, but within the Society of Friends it was by no means unique in this. The Society was singularly well-suited to the sober puritanical industriousness which the Victorians formalized and stereotyped in the ethic of work and probity. Quakers believe absolutely that one must render unto Caesar what is Caesar's and unto the Lord what is the Lord's. Excepting military service, they accepted the authority of the state as well as its class structure. Their Rules of Discipline prescribe both the duties of master and man and the relationship between them. Yet though they accepted state authority, they rejected all religious authority, not only that of the Established Church but also within their own body. Church government was conducted by Monthly Meetings composed of all the adult members of meeting houses in contiguous areas. The Monthly Meeting elected members to Quarterly Meetings in London, Yorkshire and other larger regions, and the Quarterly Meetings in turn sent delegates to an Annual Meeting in London. Priests they had none. Ministers and elders were elected by members of the congregation. Women enjoyed a greater measure of equality than in any other western religious body. They could be elected as ministers and elders. There was a Woman's Monthly Meeting at the same time as the men's, but at this point custom interposed itself: it was an unwritten rule that in the event of a conflict between the meetings, the men prevailed. Financial matters were also a male prerogative. The Society avoided dogma while adhering to a faith that is fundamentalist in all but expression.

To speak in meeting required that the speaker undergo a virtual religious experience, according to their rules, and usually implied the intention to become a minister. On the other hand religious enthusiasm was frowned upon, as Joseph Lister later learned, no less than too casual observance. There were two meetings on Sunday and one in midweek. Friends were expected to attend all three. If they did not, their Friends would call on them to make formal enquiries. Both Joseph Jackson Lister and his wife made such visitations. At home a strict religious atmosphere excluded jewellery and ribbons and ostentation in furnishings and entertainment. The archaic forms of address, thee and thou, like the austere clothing, were meant to symbolize not merely sobriety, the negative recognition of frippery and forms, but the positive assertion of the individual soul. George Fox, founder of the Society of Friends, had carried to its logical conclusion the Puritan insistence that though salvation might be predestined, success in this life was a sure sign of election. Success, his church held, is to be measured in piety, good works and the elevation of one's personal fortunes.

Joseph Jackson Lister tempered his religion to external needs. 'My impression is that less stress was laid on doctrine,' wrote a grandson, 'and I believe that (he) . . . had, at the time of the expected invasion of England by Napoleon, gone through some training as a volunteer.' He was nevertheless an active Friend. At that time the London Society was governed not only by the Quarterly Meeting but also by a Six-Weeks Meeting. This assemblage, introduced because of the need in London for more frequent discussion of Society property, discipline and government, was even then carried on almost solely because it had been instituted by Fox himself. Joseph Jackson frequently represented Gracechurch Street Monthly Meeting at the Six-Weeks Meeting. In 1815 he acted as its clerk and was also appointed to its Committee of Accounts. He continued to attend the Six-Weeks Meeting from time to time on behalf of the Ratcliff and Barking Meeting after he settled in Upton, nearby. He served as clerk of the Ratcliff and Barking Meeting and as their representative to the Quarterly Meeting.

Like London, Ratcliff and Barking consisted of several scattered meeting houses in that part of Essex that is now the industrial east end of London. The Listers belonged to the Meeting at Plaistow. It had been built in 1819, replacing an earlier meeting house. There were two services on Sunday and one on Thursday to which the Listers went with the Barclays and the Gurneys who had preceded them in the neighbourhood. Samuel Gurney's sister, Elizabeth Fry, attended Plaistow Meeting when she was not travelling on one of her frequent missions. John Bright, the Corn Law reformer, often came to this Meeting. According to one observer, writing many years later, there were 'seldom less than twenty carriages, nearly all of them with a pair of horses . . . on a Sunday morning'. The Plaistow Friends, like their co-religionists, refused to pay rates to the Established Church, 'and once a year Mr Cogan . . . went in his official capacity and seized a piece of silver plate from Mr Samuel Gurney, at Ham House, and Mr Joseph Lister, at Upton House.' Yet the Quakers were the principal supporters of the first school in Plaistow.

Amongst Joseph Jackson's religious duties he seemed to set greatest store by his role as a school visitor and trustee. He was for many years trustee of the Quaker school at Croydon and was followed in that position by his youngest son, Arthur. On at least one occasion in January 1828 he visited Sidcot School near Bath where the Superintendent, William Batt, was his cousin. About 1815 Joseph Jackson also became a visitor at Ackworth School near Pontefract in that part of west Yorkshire whence his family had come a century before. Ackworth was established in 1779, like the school at Kendal attended by John Lister, for the hundreds of Friends' families scattered through rural England 'who had literally no opportunity of obtaining for their children any mental education but that of the simplest and rudest village schools', according to an historian of Ackworth. Joseph Jackson visited until his death in 1869. There, he met his wife.

Isabella Harris, junior, was twenty when Joseph Jackson Lister first came to Ackworth. Her mother, Isabella Harris, senior, was the principal mistress or governess of the school. She was responsible for administration of the Girls' department from 1803 until her retirement in 1827. The daughter of William and Mary Bull of Dublin, Isabella, senior, became a Quaker when she was fifteen. Her father's business is unknown, excepting that it provided an opportunity for 'much exposure to the wickedness of the world', according to the Quaker Meeting at Ackworth. In 1778 Isabella, then twenty-one, married Anthony Harris, two years her senior. The Harrises had been farmers at Broughton, Lincolnshire, but Anthony went to sea where he prospered. He became a master mariner, a Quaker, a teetotaller and a staunch opponent of slavery. Anthony Harris may have met his future wife on a voyage to Dublin. Her marriage did not 'at first abate her natural love of gay company'. The couple settled at Maryport. In 1795 Anthony sailed from Maryport for Waterford, the first stage of a journey that was to take him amongst the north Atlantic whale herds to collect verdigris, it is said. This voyage was intended to make his fortune. Instead the ship foundered. With his pregnant wife he left six young children, Isabella junior, being the sixth.

The widow moved to Cockermouth, near Maryport, and thence to Holme in Nottinghamshire, probably as a governess. She first spoke in meeting there and was elected as a minister by the Holme Monthly Meeting. After her retirement as principal mistress at Ackworth, she lived in Stockton on Tees with her children. She continued to help out at Ackworth from time to time until her death in 1832, shortly before Joseph Lister's fifth birthday.

Isabella, junior, had been sent to Ackworth as a student while her mother was still at Holme. In 1813 she became reading and writing mistress on the Ackworth staff. Under her guidance reading amongst the girls achieved its 'highest excellence', according to the school's historian. At that time reading meant elocution, an art form that was widely admired. A leading British elocutionist of the day, Lindley Murray, is said to have considered Isabella's reading 'of a very high order'. When she left the school, a Committee of the trustees expressed their appreciation for her services 'in endeavouring to instruct the Children in the paths of Virtue and Religion, and to promote the peace and harmony of the Family' as well as for her teaching, and awarded her 'an acknowledgement to the value of Twenty Guineas'.

Isabella's professional career came to an end on July 14, 1818, the day she married Joseph Jackson Lister. Almost nothing is recorded about their courtship, not even its length. There is one tiny ray of light however, an abridged edition of Locke's *Essay Concerning Human Understanding* inscribed: 'J.L. to Isa Harris, Jnr.' It is not the sort of gift that foolish young lovers might exchange. They were married at Ackworth.

Isabella continued to perform the duties of an active Quaker when her growing family and her slowly deteriorating health permitted. She represented the Ratcliffe and Barking Woman's Meeting at the Quarterly Meeting, and for at least two terms she was Clerk of the Ratcliffe and Barking Woman's Meeting. In 1853 she was appointed an elder. She also did good works in the neighbourhood, visiting Friends who were in need of help.

Like so many mothers and wives of the famous, however, Isabella Lister remains a shadowy figure even in her own home. She gave birth to seven children between 1820 and 1832, when Jane was born. The longest hiatus, a period of four years between the birth of her second daughter, Isabella Sophie, in 1823 and of Joseph in 1827, may be explained by her already uncertain health. In 1838 she suffered from 'erysipelas of the face'. Three years later Joseph Jackson took his wife and their two eldest daughters to the spa at Leamington for two months because Isabella suffered from lassitude, yellow skin and a swollen face. The symptoms suggest that she had hepatitis with the early signs of heart disease. Curative trips to the inland spas became frequent and were supplemented by holidays at the seashore. By 1857 she suffered severely from rheumatism in her hands and legs. Nevertheless, 'Mamma holds up much as usual—tried with pain but cheerful,' wrote her husband. A grandson remembered her as 'a dear, dignified old lady, dressed in the subdued, harmonious colours of the Quaker garb, and a muslin cap of the proper cut' who took 'exception to some full "bell sleeves" of one of my sister's as "superfluities".' A few months before she died in 1864, Joseph

Jackson wrote to his son that, despite erysipelas, she 'often enjoys her food (which she takes between the regular meal times) and especially her porter'. According to her husband, Isabella was the correspondent more often than he was, but the surviving evidence suggests that it was his fondness speaking. Only a handful of her letters remain, and she seems quite pale in the light of her husband's extraordinary vividness.

In the summer of 1824 during the four-year interim in her child-bearing, Isabella Lister went on holiday with her three children in Hastings. Joseph Jackson came down from London when he could, using the public coaching service. After one such visit on July 15, 1824, he described the homeward journey in a letter to his wife:

... the storm ... was one in extent & duration such as I do not recollect to have ever witnessed before and presented to us for hours a scene truly aweful & sublime—I watched its gradual approach from the sea for some miles on the road in company with another inside passenger who like myself had chosen the open air ... but we were both driven in long before we reached Battle by the violent rain The flashes of lightning surrounding us on all sides dividing as it flew from cloud to cloud into a number of vivid forked branches or darting perpendicularly in ragged lines to the ground. It continued thus incessantly for between one & two hours raising in me as I think a near thunderstorm always does a solemn feeling of present danger which we are utterly helpless to avert—yet I could not keep my eyes from this most magnificent sight while my companions covered theirs & after a little while I believe went to sleep . . . The colour of the lightning varied from violet to yellow & red & sometimes illuminated a huge map of cloud from behind sometimes shot in full view before them—after a while the violence of the storm drifted off to the Northwest the rain abated . . . till I think between 4 & 5 this morning & while they were thus playing in the west and north the moon appeared in a clear sky from the edge of the clouds . . . & to complete the singularity of the scene the hedges . . . were studded with the mild green light of the glowworm . . .

At about this time Joseph Jackson began the research that gives him an independent place in the history of science. He continued to be active in his business, but the partnership with his nephew, Richard Beck, freed him for other work. In 1824 he began to grind lenses, applying his mathematical interests to the curvatures required in microscopes. There is a story that his curiosity was aroused by an imperfection in the glass of one of his study windows that magnified the landscape as he peered through it. However that may be, his first published paper in 1827 was written with a close friend, Dr Thomas Hodgkin. Hodgkin was also a Quaker and physician to Guy's Hospital, London, where he described the cancer-like disease of lymphatic tissue which was given his name in 1865, the year before he died. In 'Some Microscopical Observations of the Blood and Animal Tissues' Lister and Hodgkin accurately described the peculiar, convex, disc-like shape of healthy human red blood cells and their tendency to collect together like a stack of dishes, called rouleaux, when exposed to air,

In 1830 the *Philosophical Transactions* of the Royal Society published a second paper by Joseph Jackson Lister. It dealt with the properties of an achromatic microscope lens, one which would overcome the troublesome iridescence and consequent blurring that had limited the usefulness of microscopic observation of very small objects seen in white light. The achromatic lens transmits white light without breaking it into a rainbow. Lister ground his own lenses, even making some of the grinding tools that he required, but he did not actually manufacture a microscope. At first he supplied lenses and later the data for their manufacture to instrument makers, among them another son of his sister Elizabeth Beck. His improved instrument was universally adopted and made possible the new science of bacteriology, in the birth of which Joseph Lister played a major role.

Joseph Jackson Lister was elected to be a Fellow of the Royal Society in 1832. Amongst his papers is a list of the names of those whom he wished to receive copies of the paper on the achromatic lens. They are, in the main, Fellows of the Royal Society and include Sir John Herschell, the astronomer, Herschell's friend Charles Babbage, the economist, and Dr Hodgkin. Herschell became one of Joseph Jackson's close friends and, like Hodgkin, visited the family socially. Joseph Jackson attended Royal Society meetings often. In 1834 he published a third paper, 'The Structure and Function of tubular and Cellular Polypi and of Acidia', in the *Philosophical Transactions*. A fourth on the limits of the microscope was read to the Royal Microscopical Society in 1837 but was not published until 1913.

Joseph Jackson continued his research for another eight years, until about 1846. In that year his eldest son, John, died at the age of twenty-four probably of a brain tumour. From his diaries and family accounts it seems clear that John had been a scholar with a strong 'practical' side, like his father. He had already entered the wine business. In 1841 he was recovering from smallpox. Three years later his younger brother, Joseph, wrote to their mother: 'we cannot hope for John to be well yet, although the way in which he bore his late unfortunate operation was, I think, encouraging'. He had had several teeth pulled, perhaps in an attempt to combat early symptoms of the tumour. At the beginning of 1845 he wrote a letter to welcome Mary Lister's future husband, Rickman Godlee, to dinner at Upton Park. It was in pencil rather than the more usual ink and in a large but legible hand. In it John said, 'my little perception of light continues to be rather more trouble than use to me. I have taken to spectacles again lately I hardly know what for'. He also referred to 'my machine' to hold and possibly to light his notepaper. That summer, a letter from Mary to her fiancé reveals the full horror of John's illness:

. . . this is a most awful day to us—we were gathering flowers for Bessie when we heard a grievous noise and found that he had fallen on the steps and was utterly unable to move his legs—the men carried him in and laid him on the sofa—where he was 1st <u>very</u> red & we had to undo his stock and shirt collar—he is not sensible but his pain is intense. He has been sick several times . . . poor dear fellow he is so sweet but it is so heartrending to hear him—'Oh hold my forehead while I die' etc etc. . . . Since this he has been worse. . . .

He died on October 23, 1846.

Death from disease, undiagnosable and incurable, was a relative commonplace. The Quakers, like all other sects, counselled the expectation of early and sudden death. The fact that all seven Lister children survived into adult life is itself remarkable. Yet a brain tumour can be more destructive than other cancers because it almost inevitably attacks the personality. The sufferer wastes in growing darkness, mounting pain and madness.

After John's death Joseph Jackson's life contracted. He wrote no more papers, and although he continued to work with the microscope, he made no further improvements in it. However the Society of Friends still occupied him. In 1848 he not only served on a committee to raise funds for relief of Irish potato famine victims, but he also observed their conditions for himself. His second daughter, Isabella Sophie, married an Irish Quaker named Thomas Pim in that year, and after visiting the Pims, Joseph Jackson wrote from County Clare to his other son-in-law, Rickman Godlee: 'It is painful in passing through the counties of Mayo and Galway to see the fragmentary garments and the worn starved look of the poor.' The long letter gives a detailed account of the povery-stricken countryside. Its liberal tone characterized his thinking.

In respect to politics and business he was completely a man of the new middle class. He was scandalized when a nephew married 'their servant girl', though his strictures were directed against the nephew who had 'no means in purse or brain, I fear, of maintaining her'. In 1848 he wrote to Joseph: 'I have just been reading . . . in today's Times a speech of Lord Ashley's on the extraordinary race of children taught at the "ragged schools" of London. I called them a race rather than a class for it is a sad picture of a tribe of young savages in the midst of our high civilization.' It is not surprising to find in a letter of July 11, 1865, that Joseph Jackson had 'this morning been giving my vote for the 4 Liberals'. But neither religion, politics, nor business absorbed him completely. Fortunately, he had his friends, his family and Upton Park.

After their marriage Joseph Jackson and Isabella Lister moved into the apartments at the top of 5 Tokenhouse Yard where the wife supplanted a housekeeper named Rebecca Scotton. Mary, their eldest child, was born there in 1820, but before the birth of their second child, John, two years later, they left the City for a suburban house near John Lister in Paradise Row, Stoke Newington. The four younger children were born at Upton, first Joseph followed by William Henry, Arthur and Jane. It was a closeknit family even by the standards of the time. Three of the children bought houses near

Upton after their marriages, Mary Godlee in the same parish, Arthur in the new suburb of Leytonstone and Jane at Woodford when she married Smith Harrison, a successful Quaker wholesale merchant. While he lived in Scotland, Joseph returned to Upton almost every Christmas along with his brothers and sisters and their growing families, and he visited frequently in the intervals.

The family organized shelves and cabinets for their collections of fossils and other specimens in a room on the first floor that came to be known as the Museum. Attached to the house was a greenhouse where camellias and fuschias thrived. At the Wanstead flower show in September 1838, Mary told Joseph, 'we got prizes for the fuschias, mulberries, greengages, and apples of last year.'

Domestic animals seemed to merge into pets. There were chickens and horses, a cow and calves (but no mention of a bull), carrier pigeons, goldfish in the pond and dogs. In 1842 Joseph Jackson wrote to Joseph, 'the rage in this house just now seems to be the love of cats.' On the wild side there were rabbits, rats, deer and silkworms! Naturally this multitude came into conflict from time to time. Mary thought it worthwhile to inform Joseph that 'Spot found a nest of wild rabbits the other day in the bed below the terrace; he killed one and the men four and one got away. He was in disgrace the other evening for flying at Parlezvous but he did not really hurt her.' Something of the child's view of this populous world appears in a letter from the eleven-year-old Joseph to his father: 'How are all the animals, and the two calves. I forgot to ask how Charlotte Milne and her child are.'

The smaller children played the games that were once the currency of family life: hide and seek, thread the needle, Puss in the corner and blind man's buff in two variations—French and common. They rode, skated, played cricket and bowls. There were parties with neighbours, and the Quakers forbade neither dancing nor drink.

Their reading included the Latin authors. Joseph Jackson heard each child read in the mornings while he was dressing. One of his earliest gifts to Joseph, probably for his sixth birthday, was a four-volume work called *Evenings at Home or the Juvenile Budget Opened* by Dr John Aiken and Anna Letitia Barbauld. The books contain fables, fairy tales and natural history. Religious books made up a significant part of the family library. Joseph Jackson had bought a volume published by the Society of Friends, *Memorials concerning Several Ministers*, and had marked an account of Mary Pennington, a distant relative of his and of William Penn. For Joseph's sixteenth birthday his mother gave him a Bible 'with references'. He wrote to her by way of thanks that it was 'beautifully bound'.

Gifts of books were frequent. Joseph's twenty-first birthday present from Isabella Sophie, William Henry, Arthur and Jane was another edition of the Bible, *The English Hexapla*. On the occasion of William Henry's twenty-first,

Joseph, Arthur and Jane gave him a new atlas by John Betts. Many years later as a Christmas gift to Lord Lister, his nieces and nephews considered *The Great Rift Valley* by J W Gregory to be appropriate.

It is noteworthy in a family with such varied interests and abilities that in their letters and diaries there are no references at all to music and drama and almost none to fiction, poetry and painting. Jane, the youngest, wrote little stories for a time. When Joseph was six, he received a pious letter from his Aunt Mary Lister, Joseph Jackson's eldest sister, which contained two stanzas beginning:

> Let Innocence be thy defense!
>   Nothing that's evil do!
> In what is right, place thy delight!
>   And God will it ensue.

She quoted them, she said, because they 'were repeated by thy Grandfather as he was retiring to rest, one night last week'. Apart from poesy addressed to or in praise of Joseph Lister, the great surgeon, the only other poem amongst the Lister papers is a curiosity. Erasures and crossouts show that it is a rough draft. It was written in pencil on a scrap of paper, without date or signature, but the handwriting could be that of Joseph Lister during his young manhood, and the subject would have interested him.

> Who does not know the dire torpedo's fate
> Its power noted by deserved names
> Tis soft indeed and moves with swimming slow
> Its form scarce gliding o'er the sands below.
> But nature in its sides a poison fixed
> A deadly cold, which in its marrow mix'd
> Freezes the life blood of all living things
> And draws a chilling horror through its limbs.
> Nature delighted with its fronds it sways.
> And conscious of its lot its art displays.
> Expanding lengthways in the seaweed lies
> And joyful in success begins to rise,
> Confiding in his power and, strange to say,
> So without hurt he feeds on living prey
> For if incautious in the mouth he took
> The bait neath which there lurked a treacherous hook
> He would not rage, nor, biting with his jaws
> But still more closely to the line he draws
> And een though captive mindful of the past
> Pours from his poison'd being a nauseous blast.
> Through the thin line behold the power creeps.
> To—the lonely man it leaves the deep.
> From out the lowest depths a horror dread
> Shines forth, and, gliding up the hanging thread,
> Passes with secret cold the jointed rod,
> And smears the captor's hand with clotted blood.

The fisher throws the hurtful load away,
And, having lost his rod, restores his prey.

The powerful naturalism adds horror to an incident Joseph could easily have seen. Though the poem is unique, his nephew and official biographer assumed that Joseph wrote it.

Despite their silence on painting, several members of the family were talented artists. Joseph Jackson painted respectable landscapes and drew finely delineated portraits of his wife and children. He often used a new invention, the camera lucida, which permits the artist to trace his subject as it is reflected by means of a glass on to the paper. He made sketches of a monogram using his initials, and on one letter from Joseph, Jane, Arthur, William Henry and their nanny, Lucy Wilkinson, to Joseph Jackson in 1838 this seal appears in red wax:

Mary painted a lovely watercolour of Upton showing the back of the house in summertime with its colonnaded porch, the greenhouse against the south wall and part of the garden. She also drew landscapes during holidays and sketches of members of her own family. Arthur, who became an accomplished amateur mycologist, illustrated his collections and papers. Joseph's artistic gifts may have surpassed them all.

When they were not sketching, gardening, studying, reading or attending to domestic chores, the Listers wrote letters. Not that they were exceptional in this. Large, literate families were woven together by letters. Without telephones and motor cars, indeed before the railway, there was no other means of communication when the family was separated. Perhaps for this reason letters were saved so that they can be read today not only for information, but also as evidence that there was an art in letter writing, a gift that was not evenly distributed. Joseph Jackson's letters range from the impressionistic to the practical with an expressive facility that sets them apart, in a class with Chesterton and Thomas Arnold. Very few of Isabella's letters survive, and those that do are short, pious and uninformative. Mary Lister's are meticulous, warm and embracing. With one or two exceptions, insufficient to judge the writers, no letters from John, Isabella Sophie or Jane have been found.

Scarcely more survive from William Henry, but they give a personal impression. The fifth child, he was born eighteen months after Joseph on October 30, 1828. That he was no scholar became apparent early. 'Billy seems quite comfortable,' wrote Joseph when his younger brother arrived at Grove House School, Tottenham, in April 1843, 'but I am sorry to say, he is not in the upper room, and I think he feels himself a little degraded, especially in

Latin, Greek and French, but there are so many boys, older, and more forward in Mathematics than he, that it cannot be helped.' William Henry had more to say than the others about the animals at Upton, however, and in 1852 he wrote to Mary Godlee's husband about the early days of his apprenticeship to a farmer. The next year he was working on a farm in Yorkshire. He later became a partner in this venture, or he may have had his own sheep farm for a time. Perhaps because his health was deteriorating, he entered the business of Forster and Fison, Wool Merchants, whereupon the company changed its name to Fison and Lister. By 1859 he was suffering with tuberculous haemorrhages. In October he embarked on a voyage to Australia, possibly to join Rickman Godlee's eldest brother who had a sheep ranch near Adelaide. On October 28 he died and was buried at sea.

Short though his life was, William Henry seems to have found his place. Joseph wrote to his father about a conversation with William Henry just before his brother had sailed in 1859. Joseph described 'his humble but decided trust that he was being and would be cared for by his Heavenly Father'. Naturally his illness depressed him, but he had the courage to try for renewed health in the dry Australian outback. What he lacked in intellect, he possessed in wit. When Joseph announced his engagement, William Henry thanked him for his letter which had arrived 'most unexpectedly', implying very much the opposite. 'I suppose the light ethereal substance of love would not sink among the grosser waves of arduous study, however agitated by thy utmost efforts but would ever float on the surface . . . I am writing gammon, but I was intending to say that tho' I expected the event I did not expect the honour of so full and delightful an announcement of it from thy own overstressed pen'. The slight note of acerbity is rare in the Listers' letters, and the self-mockery unique.

Arthur was the only brother to survive into old age, and his life became increasingly intertwined with Joseph's, especially after the death of their father. Yet they all received strength from the family. Its formal relationships provided a frame within which its members functioned. Each of them found love and solace with each of the others. William Henry's acknowledgement of Joseph's engagement raises an eyebrow principally because it throws into relief the otherwise unbroken surface of family affection. Any moments of conflict that did occur melted in the warm waveless sea of mutual respect. The Becks, the Godlees, the Rickmans, the Lucases—all the aunts and uncles and cousins added depth to the sustaining waters, but it was the immediate family that gave each member a name and place. They seem to have recognized Joseph's potentialities very early.

2

THE
COMING OF
THE RAILWAY

WHEN JOSEPH LISTER was born, in 1827, the communications between the towns and farms of Britain were by rivers, canals and dirt roads. The Eastern Counties Railway, later the Great Eastern, did not open formally until June 18, 1839, but the line to Romford, north of Upton, was very much an object of interest and attention at Upton House. 'They are getting on famously with the railroad and it was very curious as we were returning' from tea at a neighbour's house 'to see the fires in different parts to light the men—for they work both day and night,' Mary wrote to Joseph in September 1838.

The main line between London and Birmingham passed near Hitchin in Hertfordshire where the Lucas relatives lived. In June 1838 John recorded a visit to Hitchin: 'we went down 3 times to see the railroad, the mail train which passed at $10\frac{1}{2}$ looked very grand in the dark'. He described a derailment in which no one was hurt, but the engine, 'Leviathan', was half buried in the bank. That August Joseph was sent to the school at Hitchin which his father and eldest brother had attended.

Joseph Jackson evidently undertook the entire early education of his children, but only the boys were sent away to school. Before his sixth birthday Joseph was writing very self-assured letters. To his father's sister he wrote:

Upton 6th Month. 20th. 1833

My dear Aunt Mary

I am very much pleased to write thee a letter and to tell thee about our bees. Thomas Nutt came here yesterday and brought a hive of bees into the Dining-room and put a sort of lantern with some Sack in the paper into a green bag with the hive hung over it which made the bees tipsy and they all dropped into it we picked out the Queen which John killed and then they were all carried into the Box. I have made thee a little bag which I hope thee will like. I have in my garden a Sweet William and some Scarlet runners and I bought a watering pot and a trowel to dig in it. All my Brothers and Sisters and I send our love to Grandpapa and thee. I remain thy affectionate nephew

Joseph Lister

Although the Upton gardens dominated a letter to his mother a few months later, he concluded: 'Again I must tell thee that I have got to the Death of Henry the seconed in English History. I remain thy affectionate son. Joseph.'

He was eight when Mary wrote to authorize his use of her large Latin dictionary because Joseph had found 'John's little Dictionary' inadequate for the exercises he was doing: '. . . only do not dirty it,' she instructed, adding kindly, 'I do not mind thy using it while I am here' visiting the Hitchin relatives 'if thee would like it'. By the time the eleven-year-old boy was sent away to school, he had had the benefit of a firm educational foundation added to the solid support of his close-knit family.

Still, it was unusual for boys to be kept at home for so long, especially when they were considered to be 'forward' academically, as Joseph was reported to have been. Probably the reason was his stammer. To a sensitive boy the affliction must have been a serious embarrassment. Throughout his life it tended to appear when he became tense or excited, but at other times it was no more than the slightest hesitancy in his otherwise low and musical voice. Nevertheless, he was always conscious of the stammer and was said in later life to have referred to it as a 'severe thorn in the flesh'. The stammer was undoubtedly associated with Lister's aloofness, and it may also afford a key to the one major crisis in his early life. Of course it affected his outlook when he first left home. 'He says he does not stammer at all', wrote Mary to John soon after Joseph had gone to Hitchin, 'and the boys do not even know that he does so, as Master did not tell any one'.

Hitchin School was then known as Isaac Brown's, after the incumbent Master. Most of the students boarded in the town. Joseph lived with William Lucas, Junior. The arrangement reduced the strangeness of being away from home, as did the presence among his fellow students of earlier friends and another cousin, Samuel Capper.

Mary, who had come to visit the Lucases, told their parents: 'They have their hair combed twice a week but never washed so I am going to get him a small-tooth comb which he wants'. Joseph Jackson offered more spiritual help: 'It is a new scene thou hast entered upon, and thou wilt . . . find in it new troubles and new pleasures, but if thou keep to that which is right and try to give satisfaction to thy master I trust thou wilt find thyself very comfortable'. Two months later he returned to the subject: 'thou will remember my advice about the right kind of boys to be intimate with etc. and keep up to what thou knowest to be right', but that was the last letter of its kind. Joseph Jackson may have felt that he had been unnecessarily concerned about Joseph's inexperience. Despite new surroundings and the changes in diet and hygiene, the boy wrote:

I am happier than I expected to be, as I know S. Capper, R. Shewell and R. Smith. I am in the upper room, in the third Class. I shall be glad if you can send me a Virgil, a Caesar, and a Latin and French Dictionary, if they can be spared. I shall only need two towels. I went to Cousin William Lucas Senior's at half-past twelve on sixth-day morning, to spend the afternoon with William and Richard Beck. . . . After dinner we played about in William Lucas's Barn and after tea had a game at trap-bat-and-ball. Perhaps you would like to hear how much school we have. We get up at six, and have two, or very nearly two hours before breakfast and another quarter of an hour at half past eleven; we go down from school to dinner, have half an hour after dinner, and an hour and a half after school in the afternoon; we have supper at half past six, bread and cheese and beer on fourth and seventh days, and bread and butter and milk and water on other days. You have not yet told me how the calf gets on. Tell W. H. that if he likes he may have my bow and arrow. Master says he thinks there is no need of making any alteration in my box. . . .

In the Quaker calendar first day was Sunday so that fourth day was Thursday and seventh day, Saturday.

It may have been in an attempt to ward off homesickness that his brothers and sisters and the nanny, Lucy Wilkinson, began to write an occasional joint letter to Joseph. They gave it the appearance of a newspaper with a columnar layout and a masthead name: *Upton Journal*. There were six numbers, followed by two unnumbered 'issues' between September 8, 1838, a month after Joseph's departure for Hitchin, and March 8, 1839. The contents suggest the esteem with which they regarded Joseph's abilities as well as their instinctive admiration for a classical education. For example, the ten-year-old William Henry wrote: 'We are glad to hear that thee are translating Anacharsis which I wish I could do, and Mamma thinks that thee are improved in writing'. As to Virgil, 'how thou wilt enjoy the long sounding words in some of the lines', wrote Mary.

English grammar, spelling and writing were more of a problem. He complained that there were too many exercises to do for someone who wrote as slowly as he did. The next year he continued in Latin, reading Sallust as well as Virgil, and did French and Greek too. Early in 1840 he reported himself 'in the first class in greek and doing homer', the lack of capitals indicating some continuing uncertainties in English. By the end of his stay at Hitchin he had read Sophocles, doing '100 lines for a lesson', and Horace's Satires and Cicero's Orations.

He was sufficiently well-grounded in mathematics to begin geometry just before his twelfth birthday, and he asked for a case of drafting instruments. The next year he wrote about the practical work as a surveyor that he was encouraged to carry out near the school. Hitchin apparently offered no regular courses in science or natural history, but the students were taken to hear visiting lecturers. 'A man of the name of Cooper gave three very interesting lectures at the Sun on botany . . . to all of which we went', Joseph wrote to his mother, a month after he had come to school. 'On 7th day we went a walk with the lecturer in search of shells.' A few months later he heard two lectures on electricity and a third on galvanism, at the end of which the lecturer 'brought in a dead rabbit, and made it kick by means of the galvanic battery'. The curriculum seems to have been neither too onerous nor too stimulating.

His master was satisfied with Joseph's progress and with his general conduct, though he added to one report: 'He is full of spirits, which sometimes cause him to outstep the rules of order and bring him a little into disgrace'. To absorb their spirits, the boys played 'Prisoner's Base and trap-and-bat, and cricket in the playground'. Joseph confessed to John that he was 'not at all expert' at cricket. There were also excursions, like a visit to Woburn Abbey with Mary. He went for walks with his schoolmates and asked for paper so that he could sketch. He asked for 'a few more shillings' to be brought by his mother when she visited, and then reported to her that he had 'been keeping accounts as Papa wished me to; but have not had much to put down in it as I have not spent much'.

By the end of 1840 Joseph had exhausted the resources of Hitchin School. Before his fourteenth birthday Joseph Jackson sent him to another Quaker school, Grove House in Tottenham, where again John had preceded him. Joseph approved the change:

What a nice school this is, in comparison to Hitchin. I have a desk in the upper room, have a bed-room to myself, and everything is so comfortable, and what we have to eat is so good that it seems almost like home after Hitchin. As yet I have got much better into school, than I expected, for as yet nobody has taken into his head to bother me, and I am getting so used to it now, that if they do not begin soon they will not be able to. I am much further on in learning in comparison with the other boys than I expected so altogether I am very comfortable.

The touch of arrogance that colours this letter cannot hide his discomfort at the thought of hazing.

At Grove House Joseph met for the first time boys with whom he was to maintain connections as his own career expanded. John Hodgkin, a nephew of his father's friend Dr Thomas Hodgkin, followed Lister to University College where they lodged together. Hodgkin became an historian of modern Europe. William Fox entered medicine, and William Forster became a Liberal Member of Parliament and served in the Cabinet. These more permanent acquaintances reflect his own maturity rather than any special quality of the Grove House student body.

His bent toward the sciences was now given greater scope. According to his nephew and official biographer, Sir Rickman J Godlee, himself a noted surgeon, Joseph first made known his interest in surgery 'when quite a child'. He devoted part of the summer holiday in 1841 to the dissection of a sheep's head, the drawing of a human skeleton, and the labelling of the cranial bones and the bones in the hand. To his father he wrote: 'With John's help, I managed to put up a whole skeleton, that of a frog, and it looks just as if it was going to take a leap'. It is probably this skeleton which provided the model for a beautiful drawing in light blue, grey, brown and white washes. His interest in anatomy went hand in hand with his drawing. He asked his mother if he could buy a sable brush 'as I had to borrow one all last half and the boy of whom I used to borrow it left, and I am just going to shade another man to shew the rest of the muscles'. The first of his drawings to be preserved is a beautiful pencil sketch of yellow and blue crocuses for 'Sister Mary on her 1$\overline{5}$ birthday, 3^{d} mo.$\overset{th}{10}$. 1835'. A year later he gave his father a watercolour of holly, the red and yellow berries bright against green leaves. Like the frog's skeleton and the dozens of drawings done to illustrate his research Common-place Books, case notes and travel diaries, these early works reveal an interest in the reality of space, form and colour on paper as well as a notable skill. It is almost as though his drawing provided the reason for the anatomy. At Tottenham, however, Joseph wrote four essays on 'The Human Structure—Osteology' and another on 'The Similarity of Structure between a Monkey and a Man'.

During his first term at Grove House he heard two lectures on 'Chymestry', 'which were very interesting'. The next year he took charge of the limited laboratory facilities provided by the school, 'washing the bottles which were a filthy mess not having been cleaned since John was at school'. This letter to Mary was written in great haste. At the bottom are several large ink blots followed by a PS : 'We never make blots'. On May 18, 1843, he gave a lecture on chemistry to the students at Grove House. It dealt with laughing gas, then still a chemical oddity of interest as an adjunct to parlour games.

Although the curriculum at Grove House included modern languages and the classics, 'little time was wasted on Latin verses', according to Godlee. In 1840 Lister acquired *Lectures on Astronomy* by Reverend H Moseley, and while he was still at Grove House volumes on trigonometry and differential and integral calculus. On the other hand, after he had matriculated at University College, Joseph bought Aeschylus' *Prometheus* in Greek with a Latin translation which he annotated, and a history and grammar of *The English Language* by R G Latham.

In the summer of 1843 Joseph spent two weeks on holiday with Mary, William Henry, Arthur and Jane at Dover. The three boys returned to school, Arthur to Hitchin and William Henry and Joseph to Grove House. Mary, John, Isabella Sophie and Jane accompanied their parents on a journey to Belgium and along the Rhine.

These family holidays are the first, excepting the sojourns at Harrogate and Hastings required by Isabella's health, for which there is documentary evidence. They begin a practice that Joseph and the others continued throughout their lives. The Listers were prosperous, and adventurous enough to season the diet of English vacations with occasional holidays abroad.

In the autumn of 1844 Joseph visited the Lakes, probably on an extended walking tour. During the summer of 1845 the family took a house at Dorking in the Surrey countryside as much because of John's health as Isabella's.

Joseph joined them during part of their stay. In September, however, he and William Henry were at Folkestone on their own. The weather had not smiled, and they asked their mother for permission to stay on. She consented to a few more days. Joseph replied:

We most gladly accept . . . for the two fine days we have had . . . seem to have almost driven away Billy's cold, and mine also (for I had taken a slight one either just before or just after our arrival here). Besides, the wet weather almost took away the first 3 or 4 days of this week . . . We have this morning before breakfast enjoyed our 2nd bathe, for we have been prevented by the very great roughness of the sea from going in. . . . The morning till dinner time we spend quietly, first sketching, (I a view of the harbour, and W. H. one of the aqueduct) and then walking about on the pier watching steamers etc . . . one can do just as one likes here, they have not yet made a Brighton of it. After dinner, also, we continued our sketches, and since tea we have been walking along the shore . . . where we have seen what is exceedingly beautiful . . . on striking the water, with a stick etc. we saw it sparkle most beautifully with phosphoric light, this we understand is occasioned by thousands of little phosphorescent worms. We asked one sailor what the insects were, when he informed us that they were water-burns; the next man we asked said that the tide was 'brimming', and afterwards that the 'sea was firing'.

The following August Joseph made up a party of six—Mary and Rickman Godlee, Rickman's sister, Lucy Godlee, his brother Burwood and Burwood's wife—for a trip up the Rhine and a tour of Switzerland. They travelled to Cologne by train, by river steamer to Mainz and Mannheim, by train to Heidelberg, and by omnibus to Strasbourg where Lucy and the men climbed up the cathedral spire for the view. 'Joe seems enjoying himself very much and makes himself very useful,' wrote Mary. 'He has undertaken the luggage at the railways—getting the tickets for it, seeing it weighed and getting it safe to the Hotel in the evening.' After an eleven-and-a-half hour journey by diligence from Basle to Lucerne, Rickman and Joseph fell victim to the traveller's complaint: 'we are almost afraid the sour wine does not suit us,' Mary said. They went on by boat to Weggis, and thence took horses to the Rigi because the two invalids 'did not incline to walk'. For the next four days they walked and rode horseback with guides across the St Gotthard Pass into the Valais. 'Bella and Jane would have been amused to see our cortege 7 horses in a line . . . our carpet bags strapped behind on a small pad and our cloaks spread over the saddle and round our legs and a guide to each lady holding on to the horse tails', Mary reported to her father. At Interlaken they met Dr Hodgkin and his wife with other friends. And they discovered that their luggage, left at Lucerne to follow them, had gone missing. 'We are sorely tried having come out with light provision for one week. poor Joe thro a misunderstanding with his nightshirt only!' She said that neither Joseph nor Rickman had fully recovered from their complaints, though the 'dear little Dr' had mixed some medicine for them. They planned to be at Chamonix the following week. It was a journey that Joseph Jackson had made before his marriage, and they gratefully used his guidebook.

The next August, 1847, Joseph climbed Snowdon with William Henry and Arthur. In September he joined the family at Folkestone and stayed on alone after they had left. He was now twenty and a student at University College London. Various friends were also taking holidays in Folkestone. 'Yesterday after meeting Mary Waterhouse invited R. C. Ransome and myself to dine with them at Sandgate,' he wrote to William Henry. 'Anne Marsh and the Styleses etc . . . came in to tea.' Mary Waterhouse was a Quaker minister and a friend of the Godlees. The others appear to have been Joseph's contemporaries. It sounds like a pleasant, late summer break, enjoyed by a young man in the full bloom of youth, but the events of the next six months show that Joseph's life was far from one dimensional. He also displayed an interest in his mother's charitable activities while he was at Folkestone. Isabella subscribed to a girls' school there, and on September 17 Joseph 'attended the annual examination':

There was nothing very particular about the actual examination, except that it was pleasant to see about 100 poor fishermen's daughters assembled neat and clean, and to hear them spell correctly, repeat many texts of Scripture, and the higher classes read fairly, and answer questions in tables. They seem to do capitally with their needles, the Pavilion especially provides them abundance of work, and I understand from Anne Marsh that these girls have altogether made as much as 14£ in one year in this way. But the most interesting part to me was the distribution of the rewards . . . The committee examine the children monthly, and if a child has behaved in an unexceptionable manner she receives a certain number of tickets. These are however forfeited by bad conduct, and a daily register is kept for putting down bad marks to the children when bad conduct requires it. Before the annual examination the good tickets of each child are reckoned up and they receive rewards in clothes in proportion to their numbers. The full number of tickets for those in a higher class is greater than can be got by a girl in a lower class, and so, as the value of the rewards is always according to the number of the tickets, this affords a stimulus to them to get into higher classes as well as to excell in their own. The reward, too, is no mean one; some of them get clothes to the value of as much as 12s, gown-stuff, flannel, stockings, pocket handkerchiefs, etc, and it is so managed that not one goes without something . . . Then they are allowed to bring what they have got to school with them and make it up into clothes . . . The distribution of a couple of large buns to each girl terminated the occasion.

In 1843 when Joseph was sixteen the decision was taken that he should enter university. He was the first of his family to do so. To begin with he attended a junior class of Botany at University College. He may have required the course to matriculate in the University of London of which University College is a part, but he was also very young to be accepted as a university student. In any case he completed the course in 1844 with a Second Certificate of Honour. During the course he also began a collection of plants found in the neighbourhood of Upton. Although he continued this collection for only four years, he brought back wild flowers from most of the expeditions he made in later life and carefully preserved them.

Between April and June 1844 Joseph also attended University classes in Greek and Mathematics. During the next academic year, from October through June 1845 he continued his Greek, winning the 'Sixth Certificate of Honour' in the Senior Class. He also continued mathematics, though his instructors felt that he prepared too few exercises. In the Senior Class of Latin he won the 'Third Certificate of Honour'. To the classics he now added Natural Philosophy, winning a first certificate and a first prize in the experimental class. His prize was a copy of Charles Hutton's *Recreations in Mathematics and Natural Philosophy,* translated from Ozanam. Thereupon in August 1845 he was allowed to matriculate.

University College had opened its doors on October 1828 and was incorporated within the University of London, the degree-granting authority, eight years later. The College had built the Palladian structure on Gower Street which now houses its administrative offices. It was 'somewhat ostentatiously non-sectarian,' according to Godlee, and well it might have been. The religious tests continued to exclude dissenters from Oxford and Cambridge, and excepting the Scottish universities there was nowhere else Lister could have gone. There were only two faculties in 1844, medicine and art, and the former was the larger, though according to one historian of the University, 'Both were in decline in Lister's time'. University College Hospital had been opened as the North London Hospital in 1834, in Gower Street, across from the College.

Inasmuch as Lister intended to enter medicine, the relative importance of the medical faculty of the University of London was a positive advantage. All the more interesting, therefore, that he matriculated in the arts faculty. It was a most unusual course for a prospective British surgeon to follow.

Whereas medicine had for centuries customarily been taught in universities, surgery had no such intellectual pretensions. Physicians were often educated men who could read and write the classical languages. Thus at the end of the sixteenth century William Harvey wrote his great paper on the circulation of the blood in Latin. The Hippocratic Oath itself states: 'I will not cut persons labouring under the stone, but will leave this to be done by men who are practitioners of this work'.

Excepting a few great anatomists such as Ambroise Paré, surgeons had been barbers. They also pulled teeth and on occasion removed musket balls or amputated limbs, if there was no other way to save a life. They were often illiterate and their knowledge of anatomy scarcely broader than their interest in physics. Even John Hunter, said to be the greatest British surgeon before Lister, had come to London from his native Glasgow with only one clear-cut plan: to take up a position as a clerk that had been offered to him by his eldest brother, William. William Hunter ran his own anatomy school in Covent Garden for the training of surgeons. Before his death in 1793 John Hunter had transformed surgery. He displayed remarkable dexterity as an operator,

34

but his influence grew out of the almost accidental training in therapeutics and anatomy that he gained from his brother even before he had finally decided on his own career.

It was not until 1743 that the surgeons of Paris ended their guild association with the barbers. Two years later the Company of Barber-Surgeons in London was replaced by the Company of Surgeons. In 1800 this Company became the Royal College of Surgeons, with power over the admission of applicants to the profession within a seven-mile radius of the capital. In this way the surgeons acquired a corporate status similar to that which Henry VIII had given physicians when he incorporated the Royal College of Physicians in 1518.

The Apothecaries Act of 1815 required formal teaching and a period of internship for anyone practising medicine, and the act defined medicine as the performance of surgery as well as the administration of drugs. The right of admission to the various medical professions was left in the hands of the respective Royal Colleges and the Society of Apothecaries. At first, fellowship in the Royal College of Surgeons was possible only after examinations open to candidates who had qualified through hospitals in London, Edinburgh, Aberdeen or Dublin, but after 1832 anatomy schools in provincial towns with voluntary hospitals were also recognized. Finally, in 1843, the charter of the Royal College of Surgeons was amended to give it control over examinations for applicants who wished to practise anywhere in England.

Nothing better demonstrates the inferior position of surgeons than their relative poverty. Until 1848 no major hospital paid a surgeon, nor were there private beds in any London hospital. The surgeon was an honorary staff member. The position gave him prestige as well as an opportunity to apply his skills to diseases and accidents suffered by the hospital governors and their social circle. There were a few wealthy surgeons, the more noteworthy because of their rarity. Sir Astley Cooper, a President of the Royal College of Surgeons and surgeon at Guy's Hospital, achieved eminence a generation before Lister. He is said to have had an income of £15,000 a year, and his butler was accused of making £600 a year by showing in patients out of turn. Surgeons who did not have university appointments often acted as physicians too, in order to make a living.

Historically, the distinction between physicians and surgeons had been based on their respective functions and the distinction in education, organization and class had followed. The physician considered himself to be a diagnostician. He knew how limited his powers were. Other than opium to kill pain, quinine to control the shakes and various substances to open the bowels, he had almost no drugs. The fashionable city physician if not his less prosperous country brethren left it to the surgeon to apply the counter-irritants and the leeches or cups which Lister and many of his colleagues continued to use until the 1880s. Because of his education and class, however, it was the physician who fixed the boundaries between his practice and that of the surgeon. The surgeon coped with the fractures and the accidents, the abscesses and degenerative changes brought about by venereal disease and tuberculosis.

A surgeon faced three fundamental problems with each of his patients. The first to be solved was haemorrhage, the second was pain, and the third, infection. The invention of the ligature, a thread, wire or length of animal tissue that could be used to tie a blood vessel, is usually attributed to Paré. Before the ligature only a hot iron to occlude the vessel by burning it could stop bleeding. It was a very uncertain technique, especially with large arteries. Any substance applied like a ligature to living tissue has serious limitations: thread and wire may cut through the vessel, and animal tissue such as catgut (sheep or horse intestine but not that of a cat) may slip. In either case a secondary haemorrhage occurs after the wound has been closed so that the bleeding escapes notice until it is too late. Before Lister, moreover, any ligature could be a source of infection. Thus the blessing brought by Paré was mixed. No wonder he said with proper humility: 'I dressed him, but God healed him'. Yet some lived who would otherwise have died. The ligature extended the surgeon's range. Nevertheless, to apply the knife was a counsel of last resort. The patient knew that whatever his pain at the moment, an operation meant unrelieved agony. Successful surgeons like John Hunter were men of enormous dexterity and often possessed great physical strength. Speed triumphed. A leg might be amputated in thirty seconds. Indeed, one surgeon is said to have performed a triple amputation in twenty seconds: the diseased leg, his assistant's thumb and the patient's genitals. James Syme, Lister's teacher and father-in-law, could remove a diseased jaw bone in under five minutes. Despite such acrobatics, the patient's suffering continued until his insulted nerves stopped their screams, or until he fainted. The surgeon too had to stiffen his will before the torture he was bound to inflict.

The word anaesthetic was suggested by the American doctor Oliver Wendell Holmes, who also proposed that washing the midwives' hands and instruments with soap and water might reduce the incidence of childbed fever. Curiously, this creative physician is remembered chiefly as the author of a charming memoir called *The Autocrat of the Breakfast Table*. Holmes's word applied at first to ether, the effectiveness of which had been demonstrated by William Thomas Green Morton, a Connecticut dentist who tried to hide the nature of the agent with dye and perfume so that he could patent it. He was permitted to demonstrate his discovery, including a breathing apparatus, a necessary last minute repair to which almost obliged him to abandon the test, by John Collins Warren, senior surgeon at the Massachusetts General Hospital in Boston. Warren removed a tuberculous gland from the neck of a twenty-three-year-old house painter named Gilbert

Abbott on October 16, 1846.

News of Morton's success reached England on December 12. Within the week ether had been administered twice in this country, at the house of a Dr Boott on Gower Street near University College, and at the Dumfries and Galloway Royal Infirmary in Scotland. The first public trial was undertaken on December 21 by Robert Liston, a Scotsman who had become Professor of Surgery at University College and senior surgeon at University College Hospital. Liston's ether inhaler was devised by an Oxford Street chemist named Peter Squire, and the anaesthetist was Dr William Squire, a nephew. Liston had two cases that day, a leg amputation and the removal of an ingrown toenail. The amputee was a butler, Frederick Churchill. The operation took place in the usual manner in front of students as well as the surgical assistants. Liston is said to have begun the trial by saying: 'We are going to try a Yankee dodge today, gentlemen, for making men insensible'. The operation was completed with the speed for which Liston was famous, and the surgeon said: 'This Yankee dodge, gentlemen, beats mesmerism hollow'.

One month later, in January 1847, James Y Simpson, Professor of Midwifery at Edinburgh University, used ether to ease the pain of childbirth. Simpson had been sniffing gases to compare their anaesthetic effects, and in March he published a paper on chloroform. The following November, chloroform was first used in surgery by Simpson, who collaborated with his colleague James Miller, the Professor of Systematic Surgery.

When Liston demonstrated the value of ether at University College Hospital, Lister was a student in the arts faculty. Fifty years later he told the British Association: 'I witnessed the first operation in England under ether'. There is no better evidence that his decision to become a surgeon was already firmly taken a year before he received the BA degree. He may have attended Liston's clinical lectures regularly, if unofficially, perhaps with the help of his fellow lodger, Edward Palmer, a medical student and one of Liston's assistants.

Palmer was to play an important, if not an entirely benign role in Lister's life during his university career. Just before Joseph's seventeenth birthday his father allowed him to take up residence at 28 London Street, near University College. On April 2, 1844, Joseph wrote to his mother: 'I have attended the lectures hitherto, and like them much, and notwithstanding Papa's fears, have found quite enough to employ my time after 3 o'clock. I am getting pretty much settled in here, and anticipate a pleasant residence here'. Edward Palmer also lived at 28 London Street. He was eight years Lister's senior, 'one of my dear Uncle Dr Hodgkin's many protégés', wrote John Hodgkin who became a fellow lodger, 'a young man in straightened circumstances but with a real enthusiasm for the surgeon's profession'.

Hodgkin recalled that the joint-lodging arrangement had been adopted partly to permit Palmer to meet his expenses, which suggests that his rent may have been paid by Joseph Jackson Lister and John Hodgkin's father. On December 23, 1847, when Joseph and Edward Palmer had moved to 2 Bedford Place, Ampthill Square, Joseph Jackson wrote to Joseph:

It has given me pleasure to learn from thee this morning the arrangement thou hast made which promises to retain thee in the present lodgings on nearly the same terms as before, while it is very advantageous to thy expected companion—I am not surprised at thy host's acceding to the terms he has, but I am well pleased that you are not obliged to seek a new place among strangers—I think it is not unfair for your landlady to expect the 14/– on the agreement you made—nor would it be unfair to ask J. H. to pay it all—but to ask only the half of him is the handsomest thing and what I would be content with.

Even though Joseph may have understood the referrents for his father's nouns and pronouns, the letter is unusual for its grammatical inexactitude. The 'expected companion' must have been John Hodgkin, 'J. H.', five years Joseph's junior. He came to the University from Grove House school when he was just fifteen. Probably 'thy host' is Palmer. Hodgkin called him 'bear leader', and says that he settled with their landlady. Perhaps he had rented the flat both because he was senior, and because he was expected to act as a kind of housemaster to Lister. In that case Palmer may have felt that John Hodgkin's arrival was not only an unwarranted drain on his time but also more responsibility than he was being paid to carry. He may have wished to withdraw himself, or he may have asked to be allowed to take in other boarders to pay his rent. Had Palmer done either, Lister and Hodgkin might well have had to seek other quarters. It is not possible to guess what terms Palmer accepted, but if Hodgkin was the new man, it would have been reasonable to expect him to pay all of any premium due to the landlady. These minutiae are important only because of their bearing on Joseph's nervous breakdown.

Meanwhile Palmer was his companion as well as his host. Shortly after Joseph had left home, Joseph Jackson called, but his son was out. To his mother Joseph wrote:

I must . . . express my sorrow that Papa had the trouble of calling here yesterday for nothing. When he called, E. Palmer and myself were not at lecture but going a very nice walk to Hampstead Heath and church over Primrose Hill; which we enjoyed thoroughly. We started about $8\frac{1}{2}$ and came back about $\frac{1}{4}$ to 11. It is about 9 miles there and back; we walked fast all the way, and had a fine run on the heath when we got there.

Between his matriculation in August 1845 and his graduation in December 1847 with the degree of Bachelor of Arts 'In 1st division at the Pass Examination', Joseph continued along the academic lines prefigured by his junior courses: Greek, mathematics—in which he performed 'diligently' despite an occasional insufficiency of exercises, and natural philosophy with astronomy. Excepting mathematics, he seems to have attended no classes during the academic year 1846–1847, but in January he bought *A Manual of Elementary Chemistry* by G. Fownes. In July 1847, furthermore, he won a silver medal as first prize for an essay in chemistry. During the autumn term of 1847, before he received the BA degree, he had also been permitted to begin the study of anatomy. According to University College records, he continued to attend the course 'regularly' during the early part of 1848.

His extra-curricular activities seem to have been extremely infrequent. In 1844 he told his mother that he had attended 'the ethological society yesterday which I enjoyed very much'. According to Godlee, he 'worked very hard in rather gloomy surroundings'. Neither the London Street flat nor the second residence in Ampthill remain, but the gloom to which Godlee referred may have been social as well as physical. Hodgkin said that Lister had no close friends. His most frequent companions were his two fellow lodgers.

Hodgkin referred to Palmer as 'that curious being'. 'Poor Palmer,' he wrote, 'though a good and I suppose a clean man was a peculiar rather tiresome person and not I should think a very suitable companion even for Lister.' 'Edward Palmer was undoubtedly an odd man, but I do not think his oddity was specially connected with his religion, though he was of course a "plain Friend". He was very fond of the word "individual" which he pronounced "indivitchual".' Hodgkin continued, in order to elucidate his belief that Palmer was different: 'Though, as I said, he was a "plain Friend" his heart was in surgery. When he had finished his academical course, he set himself up as a surgeon. Then I believe he had a disappointment in love which unhinged his mind and he died I believe under care'.

Hodgkin recalled one evening when Palmer instructed Joseph in 'the art of putting on a bandage and my leg was the one which had the honour of being chosen for the demonstration'. He also gave this vignette of Lister as an intense introverted twenty-year-old medical student:

He was not one who loved strife or debate—not even when I knew him the friendliest discussion or the brightest repartee. His friends always felt his power, but it was silently exerted power. He lived in the world of his thoughts, modest, unmasterful, unassuming, but it was not—at least as I remember him—in his nature to lay his mind along side of yours in order that you and he might beat out truth together.

3

BREAKDOWN

BY EARLY 1848 Lister had begun the study of anatomy, and he had written a prize-winning essay in chemistry. Yet his formal classwork seems to have been remarkably limited. During the entire academic year 1846–1847, according to the records kept by University College, he attended only a mathematics class. What else occupied him, and why should he have left the flat in Ampthill Square abruptly in March 1848?

He was probably attending Liston's surgical lectures. It seems unlikely that he went only once, in December 1846, for the sole purpose of witnessing the trial of ether as an anaesthetic. Whatever Palmer and Liston himself thought might happen at the trial, an epoch-making event is rarely recognized in advance. At best they would have been sceptically hopeful. Palmer might have told Lister that something unusual was to be tried, but the young arts student would not have been asked to attend the demonstration unless he had been doing so with some regularity, and with Liston's approval.

He may also have attended other classes in the medical faculty. An arts undergraduate would have found difficulties in entering medical courses formally, but concessions may have been made to Lister's accomplishments in the classics as well as to his declared interest. Informal attendance at lectures leaves few documents, however, and there is no other clear evidence. We know only that he had the time and, presumably, the wish to begin his medical studies as soon as he could.

There was another aspect of Lister's life at this time that engaged both his intellect and his emotions. He became deeply religious. Indeed, he displayed that most un-Quakerlike attribute, religious enthusiasm.

Of the period at the end of 1847 when he joined Lister and Palmer at Ampthill Square, Hodgkin wrote: 'He was probably at this time passing through some religious conflict of soul. We used always to walk into the City on Wednesday evening to attend the Friends Meeting which was held (largely for the benefit of students) at Gracechurch St.' Hodgkin denied that Palmer was responsible for 'intensifying any tendency toward the morbid-religious' in Joseph's mind, but Palmer's seriousness would not have *counteracted* Lister's.

His health may also have played a role in the evolution of his religious disposition. Apart from an occasional cold he seems to have had little illness. 'When I was an infant I was profusely dosed with calomel for croup,' he said in 1864, and added that he was occasionally bled. From Hitchin he reported an outbreak of 'Blister' pox in 1838, and from Tottenham, chicken pox, four years later, but there is no indication whether he caught either of these childhood diseases. At Grove House, thanks to a cold, he had been brought his breakfast in bed, 'and three or four times have stopped in there till eleven o'clock', he told his parents. Though he may have escaped childhood diseases, he seems always to have shared his family's concern, bordering on hypochondria, for general health. It was easily explained by his mother's illnesses, to say nothing of poor John.

John had died after a dreadful illness in October 1846. He had had smallpox. Had it contributed to his headaches and the blindness that followed? In the light of modern knowledge it seems very unlikely, but to the medical science of the day inexplicable symptoms following an identifiable disease would almost certainly have been associated with it.

In September 1847 Joseph was on holiday in Folkestone, a relaxed and pleasant social interlude. By December, when Hodgkin moved into the Ampthill Square flat, he was 'passing through some religious conflict of soul'. Sometime during the autumn of 1847 Joseph too had smallpox. It was a mild case and seems to have left no noticeable scarring on his face. But one might reasonably suppose that the disease frightened him. One possible response to the fear of disease and death is a search for security in religion.

'The story about Lister's taking part in open air services is to the best of my knowledge quite mistaken,' wrote John Hodgkin. To the Quakers, open air services smacked of revivalism, perhaps even pantheism. Hodgkin's denial was written to reassure R J Godlee that Joseph's aberration had not been quite *that* serious. Yet there is this revealing paragraph in a letter from Joseph Jackson to Joseph a few months later, after Joseph's emotional conflicts and intellectual turmoil had taken their toll.

Dost thou remember the lines of the clerk of St Lawrence I. Wt. on his little church? 'Though the building is but low & small, we may be near to heav'n as at St Paul' & to have a meeting occasionally with the sky alone for our covering in a 'high place' has its impressive solemnity—

Perhaps if Joseph had not actually taken part in an open air service, he had expressed a wish to do so. In any case Hodgkin concluded that portion of his memoir with a recollection that may have been less reassuring to Godlee: 'The only thing approaching it that I remember is that when he was boating on the river with . . . William, he wanted to have some religious talk with the boatman but was dissuaded'. Had he been proselytizing, or even worse, had he been preaching?

For there is no doubt that in his mind he had taken the crucial step that would make preaching possible. Again the information comes from Hodgkin:

I shall never forget the amazement & fear with which I saw him stand up in the silent meeting & utter the words 'I will be with thee & keep thee: fear thou not' . . . at that time, for so young a man 'to speak in meeting' was looked on as something awful, ascetic, something which quite cut him off from his contemporaries & from the world of common men. I am afraid that the influence of his family, naturally anxious for his success as a student was brought to bear to prevent a repetition of the occurrence: at any rate I do not remember ever to have heard him 'speaking in meetings' again.

In the light of what happened, the attitude of Joseph's family to this evidence of religious enthusiasm is at least as important as his behaviour. He must have been fully alive to the momentousness of his act. He adhered to tradition by speaking in words from, or paraphrased from the Bible. He must have known that the man or woman who spoke in meeting usually did so with the intention of becoming a minister. He must have read the words from the Rules of Discipline under the heading 'Advice to the Young' that describes his feelings:

The youthful mind, in its love for the cause of religion, is readily led into action. Here is a fresh call for watchfulness. A benevolent desire to promote the Lord's work in the earth and to serve their fellow-men, may have imperceptibly led some from a close and frequent examination of the state of their own hearts.

Lister's self-examination had evidently revealed that surgery did not satisfy his whole soul. His purpose had weakened, become infirm. '. . . our earnest concern for all . . . is that they whose field of usefulness is principally within the limits of our own society, may be faithful to their call'. Lister's family believed that his 'benevolent desire to promote the Lord's work' would not best be served 'within the limits of our own society'. He was terribly unsure; he wanted to please his family, who expected so much from him, and yet he knew that the decision must ultimately be his to make.

Those members of his family who might have tried to influence his decision were his mother, his father and his brother-in-law, Rickman Godlee. Given the habits of his life and his love for these people, he would naturally attempt to accept their advice. They advised that he should cool his ardour. On the other hand they were devout and active Quakers, wholly committed to the Society. Did their disapproval not conflict with their expressed beliefs? Were his mother or his father or his brother-in-law—or any of them, for perhaps there were even differences amongst those he loved—were they saying to him: we admire your sincerity, but your 'field of usefulness' is surgery; to pursue your present course jeopardizes your service as a surgeon, and you will make a fool of yourself. And suppose that beneath the conflict with his beloved family and beneath the religious enthusiasm lay doubt: what had medicine done for John? What would it do for him if his attack of smallpox evolved into a brain disease as John's had done?

Such speculation is justified only by the facts about what did happen. In March 1848 Joseph had a nervous breakdown. It is not surprising. The stutter had presaged the explosion. It may have reflected a conflict at the root of his being between the shy boy who wanted to live at home and draw, and the brilliant boy who was being guided systematically into a career that satisfied only a part of him. Conflict and loss of certainty, disease-induced physical weakness, hard work, loneliness, death, an apparent discrepancy between the words and deeds of those whom he loved and trusted—such a combination of circumstances is a recipe for schizophrenia. In Lister's case the pressures produced a severe and extended depression. His exact symptoms are not known, but he could not work, and he lost all his drive and motivation. He left the University, and for more than a year he seems to have done almost nothing. In the early weeks of the illness he may have been suicidal.

The phrase 'nervous breakdown' is not an anachronism. It was used by Godlee, Lister's nephew, who heard what had happened from his mother and father. There is no reason to assume that adolescence was any easier in 1847 than it is today. Perhaps it is always harder for the talented. At almost the same time, in 1843, the twenty-one-year-old Francis Galton, who was to become the first statistician of heredity, was in his third year at Cambridge. He underwent a severe breakdown, comparing 'his illness to a mill working inside his head so that he could not banish obsessive thoughts,' wrote a modern biographer. Florence Nightingale was seven years Lister's senior. In 1837 when she was seventeen, she had a vision in which she was 'called' to nursing. The opposition of her family confronted her with a choice between doubting her call and doubting her worthiness, because, 'If she were worthy her light would so shine forth that her parents could not fail to perceive it,' according to her biographer, Cecil Woodham-Smith. Nightingale suffered an extended hysterical illness. Half a century later the fifteen-year-old Albert Einstein underwent a mental disturbance so severe that he was permitted to take six months away from school. Lister, too, possessed abnormal talent, and perhaps an abnormal sensitivity.

On June 7, 1848, he had just arrived at Ilfracombe, a beautiful village on the steep Bristol Channel shoreline of Somerset. Joseph Jackson wrote to his 'very dear' son:

I do entertain a hopeful trust that this excursion may be permitted to be the means of restoring both thy bodily and mental powers. Wilt thou give my love to thy kind companion and say that I hope you will both be careful, while enjoying exercises that it does not extend to fatigue.

The 'kind companion' was 'thy friend Edwd. Palmer'. It was Palmer who had notified their arrival at Ilfracombe, and who reported that Joseph had not been resting well 'which he lays to your taking a late tea—'. No matter the peculiarities he had revealed, Palmer had either gained or retained Joseph Jackson's trust. Because Palmer was too poor to pay for a walking holiday in Somerset, it seems probable that Joseph Jackson had given them—or more probably, given Palmer—funds for them both. Certainly he was now nurse as well as chaperon: 'If as I gather from Edward's note this morning he is likely to have another fortnight at his own disposal,' Joseph Jackson wrote on June 16, 'I would recommend you taking advantage of it to visit some other localities in the West—perhaps to see some of the mining operations of Cornwall or the character of the south coast of Devon'. There can be little doubt that Joseph Jackson differed radically from John Hodgkin's judgement, written seventy years later, that Palmer was 'not I should think a very suitable companion even for Lister'. Joseph Jackson was grateful to Palmer, evidently with reason, because the older man displayed some selflessness in nursing his disturbed companion. If Joseph Jackson had disapproved of Palmer, he could have arranged for Joseph to travel with William Henry or Rickman Godlee, as he did a month later.

Or was there a commitment between Edward Palmer and Joseph which Joseph Jackson recognized? Had there been, he might have feared that any interference could only worsen Joseph's condition. At the least Joseph's religious enthusiasm had drawn quiet support from Palmer at a time when Joseph Jackson had opposed him. Does Joseph Jackson's perception that Palmer's support stood in stark contrast to his own criticism explain the quotation from St Lawrence, Isle of Wight which he sent to Joseph in June? Could there have been overtones in the relationship between Palmer and Lister that caused Palmer eagerly to set aside his work for a month? Could Lister have felt doubt or even guilt about that relationship which was exacerbated by his discovery that there was a flaw in the consistency of his father's faith? Palmer himself, 'though a good and I suppose a clean man', was to die during a mental disturbance. And yet Joseph Jackson's approval of Palmer is simply too obvious to require such a devious explanation. In urging Joseph to extend his holiday, he concluded: 'it would be pity not to give full extent to a journey undertaken expressly for health and that combines with it so much pleasure'.

He was encouraged, he said, by having received regular letters from Joseph himself full of the usual details of excursions and scenery. But the fondly desired cure proved to be elusive. At the end of June Joseph accepted an invitation from a prosperous Irish Quaker, Thomas Pim, to spend some time travelling in Ireland, and to use Pim's home in Dublin as his base. The invitation evidently included Rickman Godlee and William Henry Lister, who accompanied Joseph, but it was certainly directed to the restoration of

Joseph's health. 'I do feel the kindness of our friend Thos Pim's invitation from which your present trip has sprung,' wrote Joseph Jackson on July 1, while the travellers were crossing the Irish Sea from Liverpool; 'he seems fully disposed to make it agreeable to you and I do not doubt you will enjoy the cheerful hospitality of his family where I expect you will have a specimen of true Irish openheartedness'. Rickman Godlee may also have gone to Ireland on Society business or in connection with his law practice because he returned in about two weeks. William Henry stayed on with Joseph.

Where was Palmer on this occasion? Perhaps he could afford no more time away from his work. The fortnight he had had 'at his own disposal' was just ended. The clue to Joseph's state appears in the opening paragraph of his father's letter of July 1:

In thinking of you as engaged in what promises to be an agreeable & beneficial excursion for you all, I can hardly forbear expressing to thee the pleasure with which I look back to our cheerful parting, in connexion with the very interesting & tender interview thou hadst with thy dear mother and me before it. I have compared it to the sunshine after a refreshing shower, following a time of cloud—and I trust the remembrance of our conversation may be permitted to dispel from thy thoughts some phantoms of the dark—that thou will become fully aware of what is certainly true—viz that the things that sometimes distress thee are really only the results of illness, following too close study—and also that it is indeed a mistake proceeding from the same cause, to believe thyself required to bear burthens on account of the states of others, while in fact thou hast to suspend even the pursuit of thy own proper avocations—and believe us, my tenderly beloved son, that thy proper part now is to cherish a pious cheerful spirit, open to see & to enjoy the bounties and the beauties spread around us :—not to give way to turning thy thoughts upon thyself nor even at present to dwell long on serious things. Thou wilt remember how strongly Dr Hodgkin cautioned thee on these points as dangerous to thy mental as well as bodily health—

Palmer remained a part of Lister's life for the time being. In August 1850 he was the first to supply eagerly-awaited news of Joseph's examinations for Honours in Anatomy and Physiology, but he wrote to Rickman Godlee. Joseph just missed the first place, though he won a gold medal, and Palmer concluded: 'Sharing with you in the high gratification which these well merited evidences of real attainment must give and desiring that the next examination may yield still higher success, believe me to remain Thine Sincerely Edward Palmer'. Five years later Lister, in Edinburgh, received a note from Sampson Gamgee, his fellow student at University College Hospital, thanking him for the 'privilege' of an invitation he had received 'through Palmer to attend a soiree at Dr Hodgkin', Palmer's benefactor at Guy's. The links had grown tenuous and finally broke.

Meanwhile the Irish journey continued through July 1848. On the 11th there was a fire at 5 Tokenhouse Yard caused by a carelessly-placed candle, but fortunately the damage was slight. Though Joseph Jackson wrote to Rickman Godlee the next day, 'I smell of fire wherever I go', he began the letter by welcoming Godlee 'and my dear Joseph and W. Hy. to Belfast after your visit to the Causeway'. He hoped 'that your expectations have been not disappointed and your geological ideas extended by that wonderful basaltic development'. With Isabella, their two unmarried daughters and Arthur, Joseph Jackson went to Bangor on holiday, whereupon Joseph and William Henry travelled from Dublin to Holyhead by steamer to greet their family in Wales. With them came their Irish host, Thomas Pim, and a few days later the three travellers returned to Ireland accompanied by Joseph Jackson and Isabella Sophie. The return voyage was so rough, according to William Henry, that 'Dear Papa . . . went to the top of the paddle-boxes with only one expectation but was most agreeably disappointed they wrapped him up in a waterproof coat shawl etc and he went quietly to sleep there on 2 cushions . . . at 7 we went down to dinner . . . Joe had to cut up a tough duck and had to go out for some fresh air before he could begin, and . . . I made a very good dinner.' With his sons as guides Joseph Jackson saw Dublin, and then they travelled west though Killarney. This was Joseph Jackson's first impression of the effects of the potato famine and could not have made for a cheerful journey.

From July 22, 1848, for a year, the record is almost blank. In November 1848 Isabella Sophie married Thomas Pim at the Plaistow Friends Meeting House, and the couple settled in Kingstown. Early in 1849 Joseph travelled in the German states with a cousin, Anthony Harris, the eighteen-year-old son of Isabella's eldest brother. Joseph's letters from Hanover and Hamburg are formal travel accounts with little life of their own, and no medicine. In Hanover he stood one morning looking at a highly decorated gable end on one of the houses 'with its curious carving, when a gentleman . . . began telling me that it was the oldest in Hanover, and very curious, and then asked me whether I would like to see the King's horses, for we were near the palace of his Majesty the Duke of Cumberland (our Queen's uncle as I daresay thou knowest) . . . I could not get into the palace itself, as it has been lately closed against visitors since a disturbance made by either democrats or mob in the town'. It is his only recorded comment on the revolutionary disturbances that swept Europe during 1848 and 1849.

Joseph's life appears to have stood still. He did not re-register at University College. Excepting the trip abroad, he seems to have gone to ground at Upton.

It may have been during this year that he studied anatomy on his own. In 1860 he replied to an enquiry from his uncle about Marcus Beck's preparation for medical training: 'it is of great consequence that he should get a thorough acquaintance with the bones . . . I therefore strongly urge him to do what I did . . . viz. to procure a set of bones, which may be purchased in London easily enough (not articulated, but separate), and devote a good two or three hours each day to going steadily over them with a trustworthy book such as the last edition of Quain's Anatomy'. In 1852 Lister attended Sir Richard Quain's lectures on anatomy at University College.

Not until the fall of 1849 did he register for classes again, but despite an intensive academic year, ending with considerable success, he was still not entirely well. On November 1, 1850, the Medical Committee of University College Hospital appointed Lister as Dresser, a junior assistant, to John Erichsen, the hospital's senior surgeon. Lister declined the appointment 'on account of ill-health'. He was reappointed three months later and accepted. Yet as late as May 8, 1852, Joseph Jackson wrote to Rickman Godlee that he had received a 'cheerful note from Joseph whom I hope you will see tomorrow. He seems well satisfied to have returned to his study, and to be taking it in moderation'. It was then four years after the breakdown, and although this letter may have referred to a passing cold, its tone harks back.

At the least Lister could not or did not cope with his normal academic environment from March 1848 until January 1851. So extended an illness inevitably had far-reaching effects in his later life. Before the breakdown he displayed as much breadth of interest and activity as his background permitted. Thus he drew and painted very well to illustrate a variety of subjects. After his illness his life became compartmentalized and his talents curiously compressed: wild flower collecting and later, bird watching became holiday preoccupations, recorded by only the most perfunctory drawings, whereas Lister continued to make paintings of pathological conditions displayed by patients which have a bizarre and morbid beauty.

The intensity of his religious commitment dissipated forever, but a shadow of it reappeared in his attitude toward surgery: 'If the love of surgery is a proof of a person's being adapted for it, then I am fitted to be a surgeon', he wrote in 1853, 'for thou canst hardly conceive what a high degree of enjoyment I am from day to day experiencing in this bloody and butcherly department of the healing art'. Dramatic overstatement was not amongst his weapons so these words are oddly chosen to praise his profession. Like most people Lister had to believe in the value of what he had undertaken, but he sought a moral imperative where none may have been required. Early in 1855 he wrote to his father:

. . . though at first I have sometimes been almost ready to shrink from them, yet I have braced myself up with that kind of reflection that if I do not do this now how shall I be fit to do my duty as a surgeon hereafter, & then when I have undertaken such operations, as it were on principle, I have always got through them to my own satisfaction or even pleasure.

It is as though he was using moral imperatives to hide from himself a deep ambivalence about his profession. His religious faith on the other hand became stylized both in expression and ritual observance.

Hand in hand with this closing of the doors between rooms went a loss of emotional vitality—a flattening of affect. That a serious adolescent should display the isolation described by Hodgkin is perhaps not surprising, but Lister never emerged from it. Gone were the apparently carefree friendships that he had enjoyed at Folkestone in the autumn of 1847. Although the number of his close relationships may have been no fewer than was customary amongst his contemporaries, Lister had the greatest difficulty in accommodating himself comfortably to the acquaintances and near-friends who peopled his life. He remained fixed in the emotional amber of his adolescence. No doubt such rigidity protected him against the rages that had threatened. Rigidity underlay his persistent fixation on detail which made him both a great man and one who could be singularly blind to general principles. Rigidity gave him the strength to persevere and took away the vital capacity to perceive the strength—and the weakness—of opposition.

Lister could seldom acknowledge his own achievement without a backward glance at his antagonists. At the same time he exaggerated their weight and failed to distinguish amongst them. His tactlessness was the obverse of his aloofness, and both reflected the close control that he imposed over his emotional life.

Slowly, Joseph resumed his university career. In the autumn of 1849 he registered for botany and for the pre-clinical subjects, anatomy and physiology, that had been interrupted in 1848. Between May and July 1850 he again registered for practical chemistry which he attended 'very diligently and successfully'. His lecture notes indicate that the course dealt extensively with the fermentation process and the role that yeast played in it. The process was still very incompletely understood. Pasteur's work in the field, which was to provide a foundation for Lister's antiseptic system, had scarcely begun. In the anatomy and physiology courses Lister won honours, and in the first examination in medicine which completed the botany course, a gold medal.

His professor of physiology, William Sharpey, played a major role in his life during the next few years. Sharpey came from Montrose and had studied medicine at Edinburgh University. As did many others then, he went to Paris to complete his training. There he met another Edinburgh graduate, James Syme, the Scottish surgeon, and they became close friends. Sharpey returned to teach in Edinburgh, but in 1836 he was appointed the first Professor of Physiology at University College. In a day when experiment still took second place to authority in many quarters Sharpey insisted on the importance of observation. He was evidently a large man in more than the intellectual sense; according to one of his Edinburgh students:

I recollect his demonstrating to his class the working of a new spirometer, consisting of a number of cells which expanded one after another when breathed into. He took it up while speaking, made a hardly perceptible inspiration, blew into the bag till every cell seemed ready to burst, then, without pause, and apparently with his superfluous breath, quietly remarked: 'This instrument seems to have been designed for people of ordinary development'.

Sharpey admired and liked Lister. He personally wrote to Joseph, who was 'at present a good way off', that he had won the gold medal in anatomy.

Lister began his residency at University College Hospital in October 1850. He registered for courses in comparative and pathological anatomy, surgery and medicine, taking a first certificate and gold medals in the two anatomy classes and third certificates and second silver medals in surgery and medicine.

Between May and July 1851 Lister took notes at clinical lectures by several doctors, perhaps the best known of whom was William Jenner, Professor of Pathological Anatomy and later President of the Royal College of Physicians. He also attended Erichsen's lectures in clinical surgery. John Eric Erichsen had been born in Copenhagen in 1818. He was appointed Professor of Surgery at University College upon the resignation of none other than James Syme in 1848. Erichsen appreciated Lister's abilities and gave him a testimonial when he applied for the Regius Professorship at Glasgow and on other occasions, but he never fully accepted the value of antiseptic surgery.

Although Lister turned down the first appointment as Erichsen's dresser in November 1850, he acted informally as deputy for his colleagues who became dressers and occasionally wrote their case notes for them. Then in January he took the proferred post. His first notes on a case under his charge are dated February 5, 1851. Erichsen's house surgeon, Henry Thompson, was Lister's immediate superior. He recalled his dresser as 'a shy Quaker . . . He was too shy and reserved to be more than an acquaintance. I remember that he had a better microscope than any man in the College'. At the end of April Lister was appointed to be Erichsen's house surgeon for the term beginning September 1, 1851. His predecessor, Watkin Williams, was unwilling to complete his term, however (he later became a judge), and Lister actually began in June. He served until February 1852.

The usual term for a dresser was three months and for a house surgeon, six months. Each of the two surgeons at University College Hospital had four dressers and one house surgeon assigned to him. These men were selected by the Committee of Management 'from the most proficient students of the College and Hospital,' according to the form completed by applicants. Amongst other duties a dresser was required to take a case history for each patient, to write the case notes and the prescriptions 'dictated by their Principles', to prepare diet tables and assist at post mortems. All dressers attended their superiors every weekday morning between 10.00 and 12.00, and one dresser of each surgeon was in attendance in the surgeon's wards all day for a week.

The house surgeon was the dressers' immediate superior. He was required to visit all patients under the care of his surgeon every morning, to supervise the admission of every patient, the daily reports of cases, daily diet sheets and the ward journals, to attend the visits and clinical lectures of his superiors, to take responsibility for admission, discharge and casualty records, and for post mortems. 'The Senior House-Surgeon, on his predecessor's vacating office', furthermore, 'receives from the Resident Medical Officer all the Surgical Instruments belonging to the Hospital.' House surgeons were already qualified to practise surgery whereas dressers were not. After their election and before commencing their terms of office, house surgeons were required to attend Assistant Surgeons at University College Hospital, but in Lister's case only a month separated election from the start of his term.

The house surgeons and dressers lived in the Hospital. Godlee, who also served as a house surgeon at U.C.H., called Lister's residency a 'pleasant club life' and contrasted it with his earlier living arrangements. Amongst his contemporaries were Watkin Williams, Henry Thompson, who became a successful surgeon, William Flower, later President of the Royal College of Surgeons, and William Roberts, who became Lister's friend and supporter and physician to the Manchester Royal Infirmary. Sampson Gamgee also became a surgeon. He helped Lister with at least one of his cases during 1851, and they continued to be professional friends until 1874, when Gamgee attacked antiseptic surgery. George Buchanan became Lister's colleague at the Glasgow Royal Infirmary, where they continued a friendship begun at University College Hospital. Buchanan later became a member of the Local Government Board. In December 1853, soon after Lister had gone to Edinburgh, Buchanan wrote him a cheerful gossipy letter about University College Hospital, which he signed 'Yours affectionately'. Buchanan also noted in his letter that 'The Medical Society is flourishing. It received your donation, and ordered a cordial vote of thanks'.

Lister is said to have joined both the Debating Society and the Medical Society in order to overcome his stammer. He was making the effort to expand both his activities and his circle of acquaintances.

The Medical Society of University College maintained a library and museum in which were displayed medical specimens. Its members were students, and the Society's minutes give every indication that although they met ostensibly to listen to and discuss papers on medical subjects, their favourite activity was parliamentary disputation. In January 1851 at the Annual General Meeting Lister was elected one of the two secretaries. He was not yet a member, and his election was understandably preceded by an extended discussion of its legality. Lister's minutes were incomplete and untidy, but he was probably no worse than others. In November he became treasurer and the next year one of the two Presidents. While he was secretary, a proposal came before the executive committee to expel the homeopaths from membership. Homeopathy is a school of medicine that uses as drugs substances which are supposed to create in healthy people the symptoms of the disease they treat. It was more often practised on the continent because the British medical profession quickly closed ranks against it in a movement which prompted the action of the Medical Society. Lister strongly favoured the Society motion. It was carried by a two to one majority but was reintroduced at a later meeting 'which ended in disorder', according to an historian of the Society. Despite the antipathy of official medicine in most countries, homeopathy persisted. Forty-five years later Lister was again involved with the issue.

Although he showed no mercy to homeopaths, he tried to prevent the expulsion of a member who was in default on fines and had refused to answer the secretary's letters. This time Lister lost. When he was President, the Annual General Meeting refused to confirm the minutes of a meeting on some legalistic ground, despite Lister's ruling that confirmation signified only the accuracy of the record, a matter that was not in dispute. In addition to such trivia, however, he read papers before the Society on the microscope in medicine and on hospital gangrene.

The paper on hospital gangrene probably reported the occurrence of this commonly-fatal post-operative plague in specific cases under Lister's care when he was house surgeon. According to William Watson Cheyne, who was Lister's house surgeon in Edinburgh and in London, his first case died of the disease. In 1852 the treatment that he described could have been only that attempted under Erichsen's guidance. He scraped away the decaying flesh and tried to cauterize the wound with an acid. But once the infection was established, it was almost impossible to eradicate unless it occurred in a limb that could be amputated.

Lister's father had taught him the value of the microscope, and he was encouraged in its use by Professor Sharpey. Amongst his papers is a note on the mantle and fringe and the dissection of the eye of a 'Squid scarcely dead'. In his precise manner he dated the note, '11.23.1850—Hastings'. A year later he drew a tumour 'excised by Mr Erichsen during my House Surgeoncy', as well as cells from the tumour 'examined microscopically'. After he completed his house surgeoncy, a further note dated '3/30/1852 past midnight' reported: 'I have this night dissected a Lamprey . . . caught in the Thames', and was followed by microscopic drawings, using the camera lucida, of lamprey brain and medulla cells. The drawings and their labels are clear and precisely detailed, and reveal great skill in the preparation of slides.

Throughout 1851 and 1852 Lister continued to dissect and sketch animals, probably in the context of his comparative anatomy course. There is a beautiful labelled drawing in black ink and red and black pencil of the main blood vessels of a tench. Watercolour drawings accompany his dissection of a lobster. At Torquay in March and April 1852 he dissected and sketched star fishes. Microscopic studies with drawings of muscle tissue from the leg of a 'daddy long legs', and of corneal cells from the eye of a boiled lobster are dated July and September 1852, respectively.

On July 14, 1851, Lister did a large painting of a man's head and torso, his arm resting on a chair back. The sleeve is rolled up revealing several sores. Such full-colour clinical drawings, which he did repeatedly during his school years and occasionally after he had begun to practise, are vividly informative in a way that could not have been surpassed before colour photography became possible.

The painting of a man's arm may have been done to illustrate one of a long series of case histories that Lister prepared between May and July 1851 to submit in a competition for 'morbis inspectis descriptisque meruit' (the meritorious observation and description of morbid conditions). The patients were mainly medical rather than surgical.

One John Foster, aged about forty, had failed in business: 'In former times he lived tolerably well, meat every day, with about 2 pints of beer per diem ... used to wear flannel next the skin ... till four years ago when he left it off and took to washing all over every morning with a wet towel'. Ann Balcomb, a servant, aged thirty-six, 'Has lived well, meat and a pint of beer daily, never exposed to weather . . .' William Larecy, aged fifty-six, 'followed the occupation of a painter from his boyhood. His regular number of hours for work was 10 hours, but sometimes he made it 15 hours. . . . He lived pretty well, generally meat every day'. Not only do the case histories reveal a great deal about the living conditions of the lower orders in London at the time of the Crystal Palace Exhibition, but they also illuminate several aspects of medical knowledge.

Thus Mr Larecy 'had good health, with the exception of an attack of colic (painter's colic probably) about 9 years ago: more severe than his present attack.' The pain in his abdomen was not diagnosed on this occasion, and Mr Larecy was discharged. Two cases of scurvy were treated with potash because it was believed that this mineral, common to lemon juice, milk and other antiscorbutics, was the element required to cure the disease. Vitamin C, ascorbic acid, was unknown, but one of the two cases was also fed lemon juice. Both recovered! A diabetic was treated by reduction of his sugar intake through a controlled diet and with yeast.

A large number of the cases are venereal. A twenty-one-year-old jour- neyman shoemaker was unmarried 'but has been a good deal addicted to venery. When only 15 years old he formed a connexion with a female, and sometimes at this early age had connexion 3 or 4 times a day'. He had been hospitalized with 'chancre' and 'clap'—syphilis and gonorrhea. A fifty-six- year-old Irish labourer was diagnosed as being epileptic although: 'The fornications and the painful spots on the thighs would lead one to suspect incipient cerebritis', the last stages of syphilis. A gardener with epilepsy and syphilis had also a skin disease which could have been round or pin worm. When barely sixteen, he had 'joined a community who called themselves Pythagoreans, who professed no religion, but lived in very primitive style ... As is also frequent in epileptic patients, he has had strong inclination to venery; but somewhat remarkably, although only 25 years of age, he has for nearly 12 months passed, felt no disposition this way.' The confusion between epilepsy and the seizures of tertiary syphilis is hardly surprising given the total ignorance of cause.

In the case of another patient who did seem to have had epilepsy, Lister described the two theories of the disease then current. One held that it was a disease of the spinal cord because muscular activity during fits looks like a reflex action, and the brain is not involved in reflexes. The second theory had been advanced by a German physiologist, R A Kölliker. He had not been able to find the beginnings of nerves in the spinal cord because he had been looking at nervous trunks within their white sheaths rather than at the tiny neurons, the cells of which visible nerves consist. On the basis of his observation Kölliker assumed that nerves must pass from the brain through the cord to the extremities, and that reflexes must involve the brain. Lister accepted Kölliker's hypothesis because he thought it was the best description of what he observed in this patient. About twenty-five years later a British physiologist named Hughlings Jackson described the focus of electrical disturbance in the brain where the epileptic seizure originates. His research had only been possible because Lister had enabled surgeons to open up the brain.

Lister described two cases of hysteria in his competition series. One seems to have been a genuine hysterical case, although the outcome is not given. The other, with symptoms that included failure to menstruate and localized pain, was treated for about a month by 'galvanizing', or applying an electric current, in this case to the soles of the feet. The twenty-three-year-old housemaid was later diagnosed as having 'disease of the spine', spinal tuberculosis.

The patients were not under Lister's care because he had not yet qualified, but the case notes were intended to reveal his capability as a medical observer. A sixty-four-year-old man had jaundice, which meant that he also had hepatitis. The liver disease had been diagnosed, however, not because of his colour, but because there was excess 'biliary matter' in his urine. Along with the bile acid, moreover, there was too much sugar. Lister wondered whether sugar was 'a normal constituent of the bile'. (It is not.) He asked A W Williamson, recently appointed Professor of Chemistry in University College, but 'I found he was not prepared to give me a clear answer. I therefore obtained sheeps bile from 2 different sources and applied to both the sulphate of copper and caustic potash tests, but in neither was there any evidence of sugar'. He then tried to reason out the cause of the appearance of sugar in the man's urine, adducing evidence from the work of the great French chemist, Claude Bernard. It is not possible to be sure whether the patient had diabetes, which could have contributed to his hepatitis, or whether the liver disease had caused a general disturbance in his metabolism, nor is it now important. Lister refused to accept his Professor's ignorance. He turned instead to original observation and when that failed, to reasoning on what he took to be relevant observation by an acknowledged authority. He won the Fellowes Gold Medal at the end of the competition.

In the same year Lister also won the Longridge Prize for 'Greatest Proficiency in the 3 years immediately preceding in sessional examinations for Medical Honours and creditable performance of duties of offices at the Hospital'. The prize amounted to £40, a large sum, though not one which Lister really needed. The prizes were prestigious, and Godlee wrote about the 'deadly earnest with which these honours were contested' not only amongst the University College Hospital students, but in some instances amongst the London teaching hospitals. To Lister they may also have reinforced his judgement that the course he had chosen was correct.

During the academic year 1851–1852 Lister attended lectures in midwifery, ophthalmological surgery and medical jurisprudence. Wharton Jones, the Professor of Ophthalmological Surgery, was a shy and retiring eccentric whose influence Lister acknowledged along with William Sharpey's. In 1846 Jones had published a paper describing for the first time the amoeboid movement of leucocytes, one kind of white blood cell, outside the blood vessels, a discovery of immense importance to the understanding of natural immunity which was to concern Lister in later years. It was his approach to surgery that Lister appreciated as a student, however.

The course in medical jurisprudence was taught by William B Carpenter, a biologist and physiologist who resisted vigorously the deterministic implications that he saw in Darwinism and the approach to the body as a complex biophysical machine. Whether this tendency underlay their differences, it is impossible to say, but Carpenter was less impressed than his colleagues by Lister's abilities. In November 1852 he wrote Joseph an unusual apology concerning his standing in physiology and comparative anatomy.

Dear Sir

I feel that you will be much disappointed at finding yourself lowest upon the lists for Honours ... and I think it is as well to let you know the reason ... It was not because you expressed on one or two points, opinions different from those which I have advocated ... with an independence which I am always glad to see; but because as answers to my questions, your papers were so defective ... Whether this defect was the result of a want of systematic knowledge, or the consequence of the injudicious employment of your time ... I have no positive way of knowing; but I fear that the former must be partly the case, since you were obviously very imperfectly informed upon the second question of the afternoon paper ...

Lister rejected his Professor's assurance that independent thought was welcome. He wrote in response to an inquiry from Rickman Godlee: 'Dr Carpenter has placed me last in his list of 5. But I care but little comparatively for this, for I find from conversing with him that it is just a question of whether you have or have not read his book'. Now and in the future he displayed surprising indifference toward the arguments of those who differed with him, cloaked by a somewhat superior humility, the profound sigh of Christian resignation. Inasmuch as he believed himself capable of meeting contrary opinion with evidence that any reasonable man ought to accept, it followed that those who did not accept it sought to persecute him. Scarcely a unique solecism, this mildly paranoid disposition had not appeared before his illness and may have been one of its products.

His annoyance with Carpenter was the more absurd because he had also just won first Honours, a Gold Medal and a Scholarship worth £100 for the results of his second examination in medicine. He concluded the letter to his brother-in-law: 'In surgery I have got the scholarship: in very active competition. The other things are not yet out'. With these examinations he completed the requirements for the MB degree. Although he had been registered for the four years that University College demanded, he had completed his work in three.

On December 6, 1852, he sat the anatomy and physiology examinations at the Royal College of Surgeons, and on the 8th, the pathology and surgery examinations. On the 9th he became a Fellow and was, therefore, fully qualified to practise surgery.

At this point it looked to Lister's friends as though his career took a brief detour. 'For a short time the allurements of medicine seem to have been even stronger than those of surgery,' wrote Godlee. It was not a detour, but at most a jog in the straight surgical line, involving a temporary emphasis on pathology and medicine which were to prove of the greatest value to him. In February 1852, eleven months before sitting his examinations at the Royal College of Surgery, he accepted an appointment as clinical clerk, the equivalent of dresser on the medical side, to the senior Hospital physician, Dr Walter H Walshe. Many students who intended to specialize in surgery followed a similar course; today, it is mandatory.

Lister was living at 25 Harrington Square, having moved into a flat after finishing his house surgeoncy. In addition to the dissections he had begun to do original research. A manuscript note dated April 9, 1852, says that at 11.30 am, he placed 'spermatic fluid from a cock' ... 'on No 1 ovarian ovum, a large one', and fifteen minutes later, on a second egg. He was attempting 'artificial impregnation of ovarian ova' outside the animal, an achievement that required another century of work in the biology of reproduction. The experiment seems to offer nothing of interest to a surgeon, but his contemporaries often said as much of Lister's research.

He turned to the microscopic structure of muscle. This work led to his first two published papers. They appeared in the *Quarterly Journal of Microscopical Science* in January and June 1853. Kölliker, the German physiologist whose theory of nervous connections to the brain had impressed Lister, published new findings on the structure of muscle tissue. Sharpey probably called Lister's attention to his work. In August 1852 he obtained from an operation by Professor Wharton Jones a fresh portion of human iris, the pigmented ring of muscle which regulates the size of the pupil. He teased the tissue apart under water with needles, and then examined it with the microscope. There were two views of the fine structure of the iris, an argument between William Bowman, British oculist and physiologist, and Professor Kölliker about the exact structure and behaviour of the muscle cells. Without realizing that Kölliker had already extended his research so as virtually to prove his own position, Lister described iris cells to the effect that he supported Kölliker. He sent the German physiologist a copy of the paper and received a note of thanks. Lister was complimented on it by Richard Owen too, a friend of Joseph Jackson's, who was a zoologist, Curator of the Hunterian Museum and later of the British Museum of Science in South Kensington.

From the notes on his research it appears that Lister had begun to work with iris tissue that was less fresh. His microscope seemed to reveal pigment granules in the lens as well as in the iris. Lister told Wharton Jones who said that he had made a new observation, but two days later after he had the fresh iris, Lister was 'disposed to believe that the pigment I saw was derived from the iris which was somewhat injured'.

His second paper also arose out of work by Kölliker. 'Observations on the Muscular Tissue of the Skin' introduced a useful technique for making vertical sections of the skin thin enough to be suitable for a microscope slide. 'By compressing a portion [of the scalp] between two thin pieces of deal and cutting off with a sharp razor fine shavings of the wood and scalp together, moderately thin sections may be obtained.' The paper confirmed Kölliker's supposition that muscles capable of erecting a hair exist in hair follicles on all parts of the body. The technical innovation was the first of many that Lister's experimental originality required of him.

The physiology of the skin and indeed of the iris has relevance to surgery, but it was nevertheless unusual to find a scarcely qualified surgeon 'wasting time' on esoteric microscopy. It was even more unusual at the time that observations by a twenty-four-year-old medical student were of sufficient interest to warrant their publication.

From February to July 1853, after qualifying as a surgeon, Lister served as physician's assistant to Dr Walshe, the medical equivalent of house surgeon. On May 4, 1853, he was officially presented by Professor Sharpey for the Chancellor's Scholarship and Medal in Surgery and for the degree of Bachelor of Medicine in the University of London.

Lister's willingness to extend his education suggests that he had neither the need nor the will to fix his course yet. Even his physiological research may have reflected drift despite its immense importance in setting Lister's foot on the path of experimental medicine. He faced no financial compulsion to enter practice or to seek an academic appointment. His father was quite willing to support him. He continued his academic career in part because it postponed the need to act decisively. His illness had left him physically strong enough but psychically weak, unable to commit himself. When he finally did make the ultimate commitment, in Edinburgh, it was under the guidance of another strong personality, the surgeon James Syme. But if there were negative factors that influenced his behaviour and seemed to his friends to make him hesitate at the post, there was also an overwhelming imperative: an independent curiosity. Lister was never disposed to accept a thing because he was told the thing was so. He carried out his own dissections. The microscope gave him the power to probe beneath the surfaces his knife revealed. He always saw surgery as the magnet surrounded by lines of force within which he did his work. 'Physick', he understood better than his contemporaries, had no boundary lines but extended equally in every direction. Already in 1853 he deserved the epithet ascribed to him by the *Medical Examiner* twenty-four years later: 'the apostle of the surgery of thought'.

4

'THE CHIEF'

JOSEPH COMPLETED HIS TERM as Physician's assistant to Dr Walshe at the end of July 1853. In August he and his brother, Arthur, went to Ireland to visit the Pims. When the trip was mooted in July, Joseph wrote to his mother: 'It would be very pleasant to do so, and perhaps another opportunity may not soon occur'. He had already taken the step that was to determine the course of his life.

It was a decision that arose from his indecision. He had discussed his career with Professor Sharpey, who recognized that the young man was drifting, though within the confines of medicine. Sharpey must also have been aware of Lister's relative financial independence. He himself had studied in Edinburgh, going on to Paris. In Edinburgh, furthermore, lived Sharpey's oldest friend, James Syme, 'generally acknowledged to be the most original and thoughtful surgeon in the country—many said in Europe,' Godlee wrote. Sharpey suggested to Lister that he complete his studies by attending Syme's clinical lectures and demonstrations and observing how he handled patients in his wards. After a month in Edinburgh, Sharpey recommended that Lister should go on to the continent for visits to the schools in Paris, Bologna and the German cities. The suggestions suited Lister's needs, and Sharpey wrote a letter of introduction to Syme for him.

Joseph explained to his father the course Sharpey had helped him to take: 'Syme is, I suppose, the first of British surgeons'. A contemporary, Joseph Bell, who had been one of Syme's assistants, called him 'the originator of nearly every improvement in surgery in the century', an overstatement that confirms Syme's status in his profession. One of the operations he invented, an amputation of the foot above the heel designed to control the ravages of tuberculosis of the ankle, is unique amongst the operations described in a surgical textbook by Sir Charles Illingworth published in 1972. It alone is designated by the surgeon's name: Syme's operation.

When Lister came to Edinburgh, Syme was fifty-three. He had been born in Edinburgh, the son of a successful lawyer who lost his money during the formative years of his two sons. They were forced to make their own ways during the early and most difficult periods of their careers. Nevertheless they received good educations. David Syme became a lawyer. James preferred chemistry at first. In 1818 he sent a communication to the *Annals of Philosophy* describing how naphtha, distilled from coal tar, served as a cheap solvent for caoutchouc. Soon afterward, a Glasgow manufacturer called Macintosh took out a patent for a cloth waterproofed by soaking it in the same solution. Syme also studied anatomy, and gave his first anatomy lecture at a private school of medicine in Edinburgh. In 1823 he performed his first public operation before students. Three years later Syme decided to devote himself exclusively to surgery. He published a paper on wound treatment followed by one that dealt with a subject that was to absorb Lister as it had many of their professional colleagues: inflammation. His lectures on surgery at a private institution, the Brown Square School, attracted up to 250 students and was the largest surgical class to have been seen in Edinburgh.

When Syme failed to obtain an appointment to fill a vacancy in surgery at the Edinburgh Royal Infirmary, he determined to open his own school, in a mansion called Minto House on what is now Chambers Street. It was a courageous act by a man without a personal fortune, but Syme made it succeed. In 1833 he was appointed to the Chair of Clinical Surgery at the University of Edinburgh. He surrendered control of the school to his three assistants, Dr John Brown and Drs Peddie and Cornwall, continuing to act as a consultant to Minto House.

Ironically, in 1841 when his career was already well established, Syme and his brother inherited a large sum from an uncle. James continued to receive an income from Minto House until February 1848 when he made one of his few professional mistakes. Robert Liston died suddenly at the end of 1847. Probably through Sharpey's intercession, Syme was offered Liston's chair in Clinical Surgery at University College. After much heart searching, he accepted, resigning his consultancy as well as his Edinburgh professorship. He remained in London only four months, and at the University three, resigning on May 10, 1848.

The reasons are not entirely clear, but blame no doubt lies with the university authorities as well as with Syme. Between the time when he accepted the post in Clinical Surgery and his arrival in London, Samuel Cooper resigned the chair of Systematic Surgery. Clinical differs from Systematic in that the former deals with cases that appear from day-to-day in the wards whereas the latter is organized around a theoretical structure. There is no reason why the two approaches cannot be dealt with simultaneously, and they often were. In fact a school sometimes created a second position—Clinical or Systematic—so as to accommodate within its faculty an eminent surgeon whom it wished to appoint when the incumbent professor was thought to be either less competent or less prestigious. At University

College, however, the number of medical students was actually declining during this period, and it is possible that the governors decided to economize by combining the two chairs. Remarkable though it may seem, they appear not to have consulted Syme. He felt that he had been employed to present Clinical lectures, and that he was being asked to add the Systematic lectures to them. There is also evidence, on the other hand, that the University College students did not take to the dour, homely little Scotsman, which could not have improved his satisfaction with the job. There was some feeling that Cooper's professorship should have gone to his son-in-law, Thomas Morton, instead of to Syme. Fortunately, Edinburgh University had not yet filled Syme's former position and welcomed him back to it.

Lister had left University College in March 1848 because of his breakdown, and he had not met Syme. He arrived in Edinburgh in September 1853, settled in lodgings on South Frederick Street and presented himself with Sharpey's letter. A relationship evolved quickly between Lister and Syme which grew and deepened until Syme's death in 1870. Syme became his father-in-law, but far more important was the intellectual and spiritual dominance over the young man that he achieved. 'Thirty years afterwards,' wrote Hector C Cameron, Lister's house surgeon and assistant in Glasgow, 'his students were still accustomed to a little pause in his demonstration and then, almost as though speaking to himself, he would add reflectively, "Just another of the many things I learned from Mr Syme" '. To Lister Syme represented authority, seriousness and perhaps above all, certainty.

He was supposed to have remained in Edinburgh for a month, but at the end of October he decided to stay on. He wrote to his sister, Mary: 'Syme has his own views based on great experience with a sound judgement and a very original mind'. He cited the broadening of his experience as enough reason for staying, noting that the Royal Infirmary had 200 beds and offered that much greater variety amongst its cases than the sixty beds at University College Hospital. He planned to spend the winter where he was, 'though my doing so should make my visit to the continent exceedingly short'. He had decided, possibly with his father's advice, to set a limit to the period of his training, whatever was to follow.

A few days after his letter to Mary, Lister was appointed as Syme's 'supernumerary clerk', a post in which he repeated the duties of a house surgeon. The position was not part of the normal surgical staff. Syme seems to have invented it to give Lister some status until he could be appointed Syme's house surgeon in January. The measure of Syme's influence is Lister's acceptance of a position normally held by a student when he had been a Fellow of the Royal College of Surgeons of England for almost a year. On the other hand Lister's role in this rapidly evolving relationship is equally interesting. Syme had presumably read his papers on muscular tissue and no doubt appreciated Lister's originality. Perhaps he was flattered by the rapt attention of a graduate of University College, but he must have been deeply impressed indeed to have created a position for a twenty-five-year-old graduate with no experience, and then to appoint him as house surgeon in preference to his own students.

Edinburgh University is the third oldest in Great Britain, and one of the six universities whose medical graduates could automatically sit the examinations of the Royal Colleges. Its medical school has always thrived, in part because like the other Scottish universities but unlike Oxford and Cambridge, religion was not a condition of admission. Scottish church history was too confused by conquest, for the Church of England, known locally as the Episcopal Church of Scotland, to have been able to confirm its monopoly. Dissent was tolerated, if not encouraged, two centuries before the laws of England and Wales embodied similar justice. This reduced by one the irrelevant barriers to training in the professions.

They were further lowered because a greater democracy prevailed in the selection of the student body. Fees and the standard of accommodation were lower than at the great English universities, and in any event the Scottish institutions had never functioned as the well-nigh exclusive preserves of the wealthy and the aristocracy. By custom crofters' lads worked beside the sons of lairds. 'And what a strange mixed company the thirteen or fourteen hundred students of Glasgow College make up!' wrote one of them at this time, explicitly extending his observations to Edinburgh as well:

Boys of eleven or twelve . . . men with grey hair, up to the age of fifty or sixty; great stout fellows from the plough; men in considerable numbers from the north of Ireland; lads from country houses in town, who wish to improve their minds . . . English dissenters, excluded from the Universities of England . . . young men with high scholarships from the best public schools; and others not knowing a letter of Greek and hardly a word of Latin . . .

The new industrial working class in Glasgow did not begin to filter into the University until much later in the century, but it is not surprising that at about the same time in Scotland women too first broke into medical training, much to Lister's dismay.

Edinburgh being a small city with a population under 200,000 in 1851, its medical faculty and its medical facilities were geographically concentrated. The University building, designed by Robert Adam, sits a few hundred yards from the Palladian Royal Infirmary and is almost the same distance from the Royal College of Surgeons of Edinburgh. Minto House was also near at hand to the west, and all of the private medical schools clustered close to the University. By contrast the London medical facilities were widely scattered, as were the hospitals of the metropolis, and the private medical schools were associated with the hospitals. In Edinburgh the University exercised a salutary influence on the standards of education in the private medical schools, which in turn benefited the University. Teachers who were qualified and recognized by the University, whether or not they were associated with a private institution, could hire a lecture room nearby and give an 'extra-mural' or 'extra-academical' course which was accepted in lieu of attendance at the equivalent University course. The practice kept University professors on their toes if only for fear of losing their students and their fees, still paid directly to the professors by the students, and it also provided a reservoir from which faculty vacancies could easily be filled. Most of the extra-mural lecture rooms were located for simplicity of access in the immediate environs of the Edinburgh Royal Infirmary, in two-storey houses built around the High School Yard.

The Infirmary, the first in Scotland, was opened in 1729. A century later the Surgical Hospital moved from its original location to the former High School; the old building continued in use as the Edinburgh Lock Hospital. In 1879, soon after Lister left Edinburgh for London, the Royal Infirmary moved to its present site on Lauriston Place. The Old Infirmary became the Fever Hospital, and when modern medicine reduced the need to separate infectious cases, the building was taken over by the University.

It was into this building that Lister moved when he became Syme's house surgeon in January 1854. There is a splendid photograph taken at the time, the first of Lister to survive, showing him at the centre of a group of six young men, the house surgeon surrounded by his dressers. They called him 'The Chief'. At 5 feet 11 inches Lister was above average height, but in the photograph he is seated. Wavy brown hair cut full and hazel eyes set off a broad forehead, high cheek bones, a small straight nose and a generous mouth, though with rather thin lips. He is dressed simply in black trousers, a black stock and high white collar, but the black coat does not appear to be his customary cutaway. His hands are large, though his sister-in-law said many years later that they were delicate and graceful. His shoulders are erect and his expression serious without dourness. He was an unusually handsome man with great presence.

His companions are either touching him or looking at him. David Christison was the son of Syme's old friend Sir Robert Christison, Professor of Materia Medica at Edinburgh. David became a Fellow of the Royal College of Physicians of Edinburgh, but his principal interest was archaeology. He and Lister remained friends, and they both died in the early months of 1912. Alexander Struthers qualified later in 1854 and died in January at Scutari. Patrick Heron Watson also served in the Crimea but returned to act for twenty-six years as surgeon at the Royal Infirmary. George Hogarth Pringle practised surgery at Parramatta, New South Wales, until his death in 1872, aged forty-one. He had adopted Lister's antiseptic methods even before they were fully described in print, which suggests that he maintained a correspondence with his former Chief. John Kirk had before him perhaps the most adventure-filled career of the seven men. From 1858 to 1863 he served as a surgeon and naturalist on Livingstone's second expedition. Three years later he was appointed medical officer to the Consulate at Zanzibar and later became Consul. Kirk was also the survivor of the group, dying in 1922. John Beddoe was an Englishman and received some medical education at University College, London. He went as surgeon to the Bristol Royal Infirmary. After retiring from medicine in 1890 he continued with a second career in the anthropology of the British Isles.

Despite the rigid pose of their group photograph, a degree of informality prevailed between these young men and their Chief, who was only a year or two their senior. It was common knowledge that Lister was courting Syme's eldest daughter, Agnes. After a staff dinner on May 15, 1854, J H Pringle sang a parody written by Beddoe, Christison and Watson to a popular music hall tune, 'Vilikins and his Dinah':

> Tis of a wine merchant who in London did dwell
>> He had but one hoffspring, an unkimmon fine young swell.
> His name it was Joseph, five & twenty years old,
>> A microscopist clever & surgeon so bold.
>
> As Joseph was val-i-kin the Hospital one day
>> He met with his guv-ner, who to him did say—
> Go dress yourself, Joseph, in drab coat so gay,
>> For you'll meet at dinner my daughter today.
>
> Oh guv'ner excuse me, Already I've dined,
>> And to court your fair daughter I don't feel inclined:
> Miss Syme & her fortin I'll gladly give o'er
>> So she'll have to stay single a year or two more.
>
> 'Go bold understrapper', the surgeon replied,
>> If you will not make that young 'oman your bride,
> Ill make over to Broadbent the post as you're in,
>> And give no compensation to you, not a pin—
>
> As Syme was a stalking the Hospital around
>> He seed Joseph Lister lyin dead upon the ground
> With a sharp-pointed bistoury a lyin by his side
>> And a billet doux a statin t'was by hamorrhage he died—
>
> He took up the vessels a dozen times o'er
>> But twasn't no use, cause he wasn't no more.
> And then with much whiskey his grief did assuage
>> For Joseph cut off in the flower of his age.
>
> Now all you young surgeons take warning by 'im
>> And never don't by no means disobey Mister Sim;
> And all young maydings what hears this sad history.
>> Think on Joseph, Miss Syme, & the sharp-pointed bistoury.

The parody contains several points as sharp as any bistoury's. Syme was not one to be casually thwarted, though it was said that Lister was the only man with whom he never quarrelled. Though the courtship with Agnes Syme was sufficiently public to make such a parody permissible, more than a year passed before Lister presented himself formally to the Symes as a suitor for their daughter's hand.

John Beddoe remained closer to Lister than the others, supporting him during the controversies of the 'seventies. One of the foundations of their friendship was an incident graphically described in Beddoe's memoirs that had nothing to do with medicine. Beddoe was a practised mountain climber. Lister had done little climbing, but he loved walking and joined Beddoe one Sunday for a climb on the Salisbury Crags. The Crags are a long line of sheer cliff face forming the westward edge of the saddle known as Arthur's Seat. 'A broad fissure cuts back into the rock from top to bottom, and is called the Cat's (?Wild Cat's) Nick,' wrote Beddoe. He led the ascent.

I suppose much experience of the place had made me careless. A large fragment came away in my hands, and the stone and I both fell upon Lister. He was looking up at the time, and squeezed himself cleverly against the face of the cliff; but the huge stone struck him on the thigh with a grazing blow, and then whirled down the talus below with leaps and bounds, and passed harmless through the middle of a group of children who were playing hopscotch at the bottom right in its way.

Lister was badly bruised, but no bone was broken. I went off at once to the Infirmary and procured a litter and four men, wherewith I returned to Lister. As our melancholy procession entered the courtyard of the surgical hospital, there met us Mrs Porter, the head nurse then and for many years after. She wept and wrung her hands, for Lister was a universal favourite.

'Eh, Doketur Bedie! Doketur Bedie! A kent weel hoo it wad be. Ye Englishmen are aye sae fülish, gaeing aboot fustlin upo' Sawbath.'

I do not suppose Lister ever whistled on Sunday. I am certain I did not . . . but we had suffered from the national offence. We were both in bed for a fortnight . . .

Lister's closest associate in 1854 was Syme himself. According to Godlee, Syme described their relationship as that of surgeon and consultant surgeon, and he allowed Lister to select some of the patients in the wards as his own. However, he was not licensed to practise in Scotland, and Syme did all the surgery. Lister watched, and learned. A quarter of a century later he described with evident satisfaction how he had held his University College friend Sampson Gamgee 'spellbound outside the gate of the infirmary one evening during my house-surgeoncy in Edinburgh, as I related to him' the details of draining and dressing a wound as performed by Syme.

The social connection with Syme also grew, based no doubt on Lister's interest in Agnes. Syme had a country house at Loch Long to which he and Mrs Syme took Lister in October. The invitation implied 'indeed that thou art still in full favour with thy superior', Joseph Jackson wrote.

Joseph Jackson may have thought that Joseph's relations with Syme had been strained by Lister's attempt to get an appointment that would have taken him back to London. It was the first of five such attempts, extending over the next twenty-three years. Although his motives shifted as the years in

UPTON HOUSE near Stratford in ESSEX.

1. Lister's birthplace. A copper engraving made about 1800 by an unknown artist.

2. Probably Isabella Lister, Joseph's mother. Silhouette made by her husband.

Scotland passed, there is little doubt that in 1854 he wanted to return because London was his home. If it is an overstatement to say that he was homesick, the fact is that he missed his family. His term as Syme's house surgeon was nearing an end, and whatever Syme's own preferences he wanted to help Lister in his career.

In August Joseph asked Rickman Godlee to find out for him who sat on the Committee that managed the Royal Free Hospital. 'For I much want Syme to know something about them before I leave him that I may talk over with him the prospects of my becoming the [illegible] on the staff at the Royal Free. He seems to think it likely that the 3rd surgeon would be a person of thorough respectability and of skill, but young because he does not think they could appoint a person to a higher office than the present surgeons, and no man of celebrity would choose to become Junior Surgeon with Royal Free just now. But I am more and more conscious that such an appointment would be of the greatest advantage to me.' By the end of September the opening seemed no longer to be available because he wrote again to his brother-in-law: 'By the way I never thanked thee directly for thy very kind attentions with regard to the Miserable Free Hospital'.

Less than a month later a second opportunity arose to return to London. The Society of Friends was establishing a new hospital at Poplar in the midst of the emergent slums near the London docks. But Joseph Jackson found that this post did not really exist: 'Yesterday I sent thee hastily the rough rules of the Poplar hospital,' he wrote,

those relating to the surgeons appeared to me framed expressly with a view to the posts being filled by medical men of the neighbourhood, rather than those in the higher grades of the profession . . . although 14 beds are to be prepared, they consider the establishment to be more deserving the name of a Dispensary than an hospital & that the main occupation of the Surgeons would be attending to and visiting out-patients . . .

Then it appeared that the Royal Free appointment was after all still available. Lister consulted Syme during November, and Syme wrote to Sharpey about the suitability of this elusive position. Sharpey's reply, dated December 1, 1854, reveals the strains in the medical establishment into which Lister wanted to move. There were three surgeons at the Royal Free Hospital. The Senior was William Marsden, the second John Gay, and the third Thomas Wakley, Junior. His father, Dr Thomas Wakley, medical practitioner and Member of Parliament, had founded *The Lancet* in 1823 as a personal instrument of reform within the medical profession, particularly in London. One of his first targets was the eminent surgeon of Guy's Sir Astley Cooper, whom Wakley rightly charged with nepotism, a pretty common practice at the time. As a Member of Parliament for a north London constituency, furthermore, Wakley had been sympathetic to the Chartists, who campaigned with near-revolutionary zeal during the early years of

Victoria's reign for universal manhood suffrage, annual Parliaments and various other radical reforms that have since become commonplaces of our political structure. Inevitably, Wakley's fervour brought him into conflict with the medical traditionalists, many of whom asserted with some justice that scandal sells periodicals, and abhorred *The Lancet* accordingly.

In December 1853 John Gay, the second surgeon at the Royal Free, had been forced to resign. Gay had supplied data for a biography of himself that contained several inaccurate 'puffs', for which he was not responsible. It also criticized the Hospital. The Committee of Governors of the Royal Free had taken the view that Gay had done too little to counter these inaccuracies.

Thereupon the London medical establishment split in two. On the one hand there stood the Wakley faction who held that Gay's enforced resignation was justified. Although they claimed complete disinterest, there can be no denying that young Wakley inherited Gay's position as second in the Royal Free surgical hierarchy. Opposed to the Wakleys, and *The Lancet*, were a competing journal, the *Medical Times,* and a substantial number of London medical men who attacked the unjustified interference with a surgeon by a lay body, especially in the light of the fact that Gay had served the Hospital for seventeen years. Sharpey supported the Gay faction.

In his letter to Syme, Sharpey summarized the pros and cons of the junior surgeoncy, the position that Wakley Junior would vacate when he moved up to fill Gay's post. He felt:

That Lister beside being accomplished in his profession is a person of great moral firmness and would know well how, properly, to conduct himself in any probable emergency caused by casting in his lot with evil persons.

On the other hand he said:

The new Surgeon will be thrown much more in with young Wakley—and I fear they would not be long without a misunderstanding in which case there will be endless and distracting disputes before the public—or else Lister's retirement. I cannot imagine Lister concurring with Wakley in his line of proceeding. Nor can I believe that Lister would submit to be kept down for fear he should eclipse young Wakley—but also I cannot conceive Old Wakley allowing any new man to gain reputation at the expense of his son. Puffing enough and to spare, in the Lancet at first, and so long as there was no occasion to call forth Lister's honest independence—but depend on it there would be a change of tone before long.

Sharpey thought Lister would do better not to apply for the job, but he concluded: 'I shall not think one iota the worse of him if he should see fit to follow a different opinion from what I have given'.

On the day after Sharpey wrote to Syme—that is, on December 2—Lister asked Rickman Godlee to enquire 'as thou didst before' of the Secretary of the Royal Free, whether the surgical post might be open to him. 'Only this time,' he said, 'my name must be mentioned, with as many particulars about me as the Secy seems to desire. I wish much that the Poplar affair had not intervened to deter our taking this step: but I hope we may yet be in time if the appointment turns out to be as I suspect it will a desirable one. The great question is, can I act independently there if appointed? I believe I can, & if not, why there is but resignation, which, as Dr Sharpey says, will do good to me if on good grounds in the eyes of the Profession.'

Syme had given Sharpey's letter to Lister, and they had discussed its contents. The incident reveals how sensitive young men had to be to the opinions—and the feuds—of their elders. Perhaps the medical profession has changed very little in this respect, but the language in which these feuds erupted has certainly moderated. Sharpey wrote about 'evil persons' and 'untrustworthy persons'. A few months later Lister became involved in the first of a long series of public arguments, this one on Syme's behalf, which was conducted in tones so strident that it became little better than a slanging match. Diagnosis and therapy were so uncertain and so unscientific that the loudest voice often seemed to prevail. Lister was alive to the political pitfalls, but he also appreciated Sharpey's observation that there was, 'No immediate or early chance of an opening elsewhere'. When the Royal Free position was first mooted in August, he had written to Godlee: 'And thou mayest be sure Rickman the office of full surgeon to an Hospital in London with a good number of beds, is a thing that can only rarely be obtained by a young man like me'.

Nor was it to come so easily to Lister. He had 'made an extraordinary blunder', Rickman Godlee wrote to Joseph Jackson. 'The last day for sending in applications and testimonials was the 27th Ulto. and the day of actual election is tomorrow the 6th'. That same day Joseph Jackson wrote to his son:

Thou art now at liberty to pursue without interruption the plan which thou hadst framed as the right one—to remain to the end of the 1st mo.—or to leave earlier as thou mayst think best & then to take a survey of some of the medical schools of the continent—and if practice & fame should not await thee on thy return, they are not so essential to thee as to many who embark in the profession . . .

One senses a hint of impatience, and there is something farcical in the startings and stoppings Joseph had undergone, at least since August. Yet Joseph Jackson knew that his son had still to find his way.

He had been writing reports of Syme's clinical lectures for publication. The first had appeared in the *Monthly Journal of Medical Science*, a local magazine, in January 1854. Joseph Jackson queried the time he was devoting to these articles. Joseph replied that he thought Syme's 'many original views' should be publicized, adding, 'I am really doing him some substantial service in return for his kindness'. The first paper dealt with Syme's operation for the removal of a kind of bone tumour and included some microscopic observations of its cellular structure made by Lister. An operation on carbuncle was reported in July, again with microscopic work by the writer, and in August Lister described Syme's use of the actual cautery, application of a hot iron as a counter-irritant against pain and swelling. A report on the removal of a tumour of the jaw in November also described the proper use of chloroform.

His occasional articles based on Syme's lectures became weekly reports in *The Lancet* during the early part of the year. In March he described the operation called tenotomy, Syme's amputation. The article provoked a response from Mr William Adams, then assistant surgeon to the Royal Orthopaedic Hospital, London, who declared that Mr Syme's operation was impossible. Lister answered briefly to the effect that the technique was nevertheless being used. Adams replied and called forth a two-page rebuttal which included the following passage: 'If Mr Adams shows so little respect for the word of another, he must not be surprised if his own statements are occasionally not read without some hesitation'. With the same lack of moderation he enlarged the indictment by alleging 'the mistrust with which orthopedic specialists are, I fear, pretty generally regarded by the profession in Great Britain'. Joseph Jackson commented:

I dare say it is a good answer to thy antagonist . . . & I suppose he has given occasion for something of personality that I think I observe in thy tone & which in public discussion it is in general desirable to avoid—but I shall be <u>glad</u> if this matter drops without further rejoinder & reply—It is easier to enter the lists than to leave them unscathed—& he for whom thou hast come forth as the champion is abundantly able to defend himself or to attack his foe—

The rebuke was well-deserved, though Lister's language was not remarkably intemperate by the standards of the day. His tone reflected not only his eagerness to defend his benefactor, however, but also his impatience with opposition.

With the end of his term as house surgeon, in January 1855, Lister no longer had a formal position in Edinburgh. He could now have gone on to the continent according to his original plan, as his father reminded him in December. That he did not do so may have been due in part to the growing dominion over his thoughts of Agnes Syme.

Syme's support seems momentarily to have faltered. The man next in line to Syme at the Royal Infirmary, Dr Mackenzie, had died of cholera in the Crimea toward the end of 1854. Lister proposed to Syme that he should continue Mackenzie's lectures on surgery and apply for the vacant assistant surgeoncy. According to Godlee, Syme 'threw cold water on the scheme'. Without his agreement, Lister had no hope of obtaining the post because he was known as Syme's protégé. But his benefactor soon came round. Perhaps it had become apparent to him that Lister was now seriously interested in his daughter, or she in him. Lister's Fellowship in the Royal College of Surgeons of England did not entitle him to practise in Scotland, so on April 21, 1855, he was elected a Fellow of the Royal College of Surgeons of Edinburgh.

The assistant surgeoncy depended on a decision by the managers of the Royal Infirmary which would not be taken until late that summer, but there was now no reason why Lister should not enter private practice. On April 23 he took fashionable lodgings at 3 Rutland Street, about a mile from the Infirmary in the New Town across the road from Syme's consulting rooms. A few days before he had received Joseph Jackson's considered approval of this move into 'premises that are in their character and their furnishings thoroughly respectable and suited to thy professional position'. His father thought the rent 'rather high'—he was paying it!—'according to the idea I had formed of Edinburgh', but Joseph Jackson approved his taking lodgings 'with a very respectable person, in preference to thy taking a house with the encumbrance of servants'.

I thought it right to place to the credit of thy account with me on the 1st of this month £300—the same allowance as last year & I have also credited thee with £135 for interest making together £450—After awhile I hope the first of these sums will be considerably more than replaced by professional income—but I must not expect this at present & it is a real pleasure to me to be able thus to make thy position easy in the interval.

Joseph Jackson was not given to hyperbole. He undoubtedly felt keenly the pleasure he described, but he added nevertheless, 'Pray remember when thou comst up to bring thy account book with thee'. It was not until September that Joseph received his first fee. The patient had a dislocated ankle which Lister treated under chloroform. Joseph Jackson wrote: 'thy success . . . & the condition of the patient we take as a good augury'.

Soon after he had moved into the Rutland Street rooms, Joseph went to London to attend the wedding of his brother Arthur. Three years Joseph's junior, Arthur had also attended Hitchin and Grove House schools. At the age of sixteen he had been apprenticed to a firm of manufacturing chemists. In 1853 Arthur bought a partnership in a firm of Bradford wool merchants operated by the Tindalls, a branch of the Quaker family who had been members of the Gracechurch Street Meeting in London. Through this connection he met Susannah Tindall. In September 1854 Joseph told Rickman Godlee that he had enquired of 'Papa tonight about the Arthurian affair'. On 2nd May, 1855, it was climaxed by their marriage.

Lister went on to Paris to observe surgical practice there, and according to Godlee, 'with the object of performing operations on the dead body'. The supply of bodies for dissection and the teaching of anatomy was still unsatisfactory in Great Britain. The Anatomy Act of 1832 had at last put an end to the dreadful careers of the 'resurrectionists', the grave robbers, who often worked in illicit collaboration with the private medical schools. It had also removed the incentive that underlay the horrifying murders such as those perpetrated by Burke and Hare in Edinburgh during 1827 and 1828, in order to maintain a supply of human bodies. But the Act favoured the larger medical institutions as against the smaller, and although a Fellow of the Royal

College of Surgeons could obtain a licence to practise anatomy, private individuals pursuing their own research found it almost impossible to do so. During his Paris visit Lister devoted up to three hours a day to dissection. He rose at 7.00, visited a hospital between 8.00 and 10.00, ate breakfast, wrote notes on his observations between 10.00 and 12.00, operated from 12.00 to 2.30 or 3.00, and relaxed during the remainder of the day. In July he was back in Edinburgh. The proposed continental tour had been reduced to the month originally planned for the apprenticeship to Syme.

Joseph broke his return journey with a visit to the newly-weds in Bradford. A day or two after the end of this brief visit Arthur wrote, 'However thee decide as to the best way of proceeding I do hope thee will get the bother off thy mind pretty soon so as to be able to set to at the lectures with comfort'. The 'bother' was Agnes Syme. A week later Lister asked for her hand and was accepted.

He had returned to take up his duties as assistant surgeon at the Royal Infirmary. They included responsibility for the Edinburgh Lock Hospital, the institution to which advanced venereal cases were sent. In the main, however, he performed the same tasks that he had undertaken as a house surgeon excepting that now he could have patients of his own.

It was a patient at the Infirmary who gave him the first of those acknowledgements most coveted by a doctor. Mr Syme had successfully excised a carious elbow joint in a young girl who lived in a village near Edinburgh. After she had gone home, Lister received a letter from a man whose uncle was the Minister in the village:

... the success of Mr Syme's operation—the recovered use of the limb, and your own personal kindness to her when a Patient in Hospital, became the subject of conversation in the Parish, both from her own statements and also from the observations of friends who had visited her when in the Infirmary ...

So favourable was the gossip indeed that the village contributed £50 to the Infirmary Fund.

At last it must have seemed to Lister that he had properly begun his life's work. With the engagement to Agnes Syme, his domestic uncertainties had been resolved. He now had an official position at the hospital and private practice lay just ahead. He was about to begin his first course of extra-mural lectures, having taken over Dr Mackenzie's lease on a lecture room. In September 1855, to prepare for these lectures, Lister began the research that was to preoccupy him in one form or another for the rest of his active life. For four years he had been making occasional notes on the process of inflammation. The new experiments were carefully designed to discover the first stages in the process.

Inflammation is still defined superficially by four classical symptoms: heat, redness, swelling and pain. To the pre-Listerian surgeon these symptoms commonly heralded the advent of suppuration or putrefaction, the words then applied to a local or a generalized infection, respectively, either of which might end fatally. Because the germ theory of disease lay in the future, the notion of infection did not yet exist. Lister and his contemporaries knew that inflammation around operative wounds need not lead to suppuration, the formation of pus, but when it did, their careful excision or repair might come to nothing, the meticulous control of bleeding and the merciful blotting out of pain notwithstanding. Many people hoped that by describing the natural history of the earliest symptoms of suppuration—inflammation—they could learn to control the process itself. They possessed only the microscope to enlarge their world, and a very limited understanding of the body's chemical behaviour. Not even the cellular structure of living matter had been demonstrated. Their observations were confused and superficial seen from the standpoint of the complex chemical cascade that underlies the appearance of inflammatory symptons, which is still only partially understood. Nevertheless, like all scientists, they had to begin with what they knew. If Lister's observations in his first concerted venture into pathological research miss the point despite their precision and originality, they none the less prepared his mind for the great discovery that lay ahead.

He knew that one of the phenomena that seemed invariably to precede inflammation was the slowing of blood flow through the capillaries. Joseph Jackson Lister, in the paper he wrote with Thomas Hodgkin, had described how red blood cells behave just prior to clot formation: the concave cells fit themselves together into stacks or rouleaux. To observe the next steps it was necessary that the tissue remain alive and that it be possible to watch the blood vessels through a microscope. Previous workers had used two tissues thin enough to permit the passage of light, the bat's wing and the web of a frog's foot. Lister's Professor of Ophthalmological Surgery, Wharton Jones, won the Astley Cooper Prize of the Royal College of Surgeons for an essay describing his work on the frog's foot. James Paget, surgeon at St Bartholomew's Hospital, London, adopted the bat's wing as his experimental model at about the same time. Lister gave no reason for his choice, but it was probably because of Wharton Jones's influence that he too began work with the frog's foot.

Observation had shown that inflammation followed some insult to normal tissue, a burn, a cut or an abrasion. Research workers customarily performed experiments in which they applied various irritants to the living transparent tissue and watched the effects through the microscope. By 1856 Paget, Jones and several others, continental as well as British, had agreed that after the application of a noxious agent, retarded capillary blood flow may follow, even when the arteries dilate, despite the fact that dilation might be expected to produce increased blood volume and faster capillary flow. The explanations differed. Wharton Jones had concluded that the stopping of red blood cell movement in the capillaries leading to formation of rouleaux and inflammation was caused by contraction of arterioles, the vessels intermediate between arteries and capillaries. Using milder irritants such as warm water on the frog's web Lister reached the conclusion that contraction of the vessels led to the exclusion of red blood cells from the capillaries, not their arrest, because blood serum, the substance (for Lister) that remained after the red blood cells had been removed, continues to flow. This was his first independent finding in the attempt to understand inflammation.

Joseph Jackson, who was always mindful of the suitability of intelligent self-promotion as against strident dispute, commended the experiments on the frog's web, 'so simple & yet so positive in their results', and suggested: 'If they settle a disputed point . . . the introductory lecture wd seem a good occasion of giving this publicity'.

Joseph's first extra-mural class met on November 7, 1855, at 10 am in response to a printed notice: 'Mr Lister, F.R.C.S. Eng. and Edin., will commence a course of Lectures on the Principles and Practise of Surgery at No. 4, High School Yards'. 'Old Jerusalem', as this particular room was popularly known for some arcane reason, immediately faced the Infirmary gate. Lister estimated that about fifty students attended the lecture although it competed with three other extra-mural classes. It was to last an hour, and he read it from twenty-one foolscap pages, all but three of which had been written between 4 am and 10 am.

Despite Joseph Jackson's advice he did not discuss inflammation but settled for traditional content. He began by praising the capacity of medicine and especially of surgery to relieve human suffering. Anatomy, he said, is the study which necessarily precedes surgery, and Lister recommended it despite the 'offensive effluvia'. 'Disease', he continued, 'is but a modification of the state of health; and every such derangement has its own special structure and fixed laws of action and development, which are just as much objects of scientific investigation as healthy anatomy and physiology'. This definition is of the utmost significance. It links the Hippocratic belief in the existence of a state of normality called health to the modern emphasis on mechanism, the 'special structure and fixed laws of action and development' which Lister did so much to elucidate by means of 'scientific investigation'. He then set forth the principle 'that, as a general rule, disorders of the human frame are accompanied by a salutary effort of Nature to rectify them; those attempts must be carefully watched, for it is in aiding or imitating them that your treatment most commonly consists'.

He explained that surgery could provide more immediate benefits than physic in the aiding of Nature. 'I am well aware that there are many medicines the beneficial effects of which are palpable; nothing can be more certain in science than the soothing effects of Morphia, the antiperiodic influence of Quinine, or the aperient property of Castor oil . . . Chloroform itself is a medicine. But unfortunately this obviously beneficial action is not met with in the majority of drugs.' Excepting these few, physic could comfort the patient at best.

Surgery was more easily understood by the untrained layman, and this fact assured the surgeon 'a much larger amount of gratitude, which is the purest the patient can present'. Surgery could be more beneficial than physic, moreover, because it was easier for the surgeon to avoid quackery. His intervention required that he deal with material flesh and bone whereas the physician dealt all too often with imaginary phenomena.

A good surgeon possessed unusual attributes. Of course he had to wish to benefit others, but he also had to be aware that his craft required him to cause pain. Such a man must be warm-hearted, sensitive and anxious. He must love truth and his profession, and he must possess the ability to focus his attention solely on the operation then in progress. Lister concluded by recommending as a text Syme's *Principles of Surgery*, giving suitable acknowledgement to its author.

It was a competent performance. According to the performer, the audience 'applauded vehemently'. There were five lectures to be given each week—his later ones were delivered from notes—and after the first three meetings, students were required to pay a fee of four guineas. Seven pupils registered. Joseph Jackson knew that his son did not find it easy to speak in public, not least because of his tendency to stammer, and on November 21 complimented Joseph for 'so numerous a class for a beginner and able to pour out to them thy instruction without embarrassment'. By the middle of December the number of students had risen to a very respectable twenty-four though the number included his dressers and clerks.

Notes on the remaining 113 lectures in the course show that they continued to follow a standard syllabus. The second and third meetings further defined disease and described the microscope and its uses. Lectures IV to IX dealt with the circulation of the blood and the watery fluid called lymph. In Lecture VII he described one of his earlier experiments on inflammation; he had applied mustard to his own arm and watched the results. The discussion of inflammation *per se* began with lecture X and continued through XIII, on November 23, the notes for which are headed boldly: '<u>Agnes</u>' <u>birthday</u> <u>(21st)</u>'. He described counter-irritants and other external means of fighting inflammation, the types of diseases, cancers and tumours and diseases of the arteries. The second half of the course was devoted to clinical surgery, though without practical operative demonstrations. The headings included amputations, piles, stone, syphilis, gonorrhea—very nearly the limits imposed on surgical intervention by the prevailing knowledge. For the last four days of the course, from April 15 to April 18, 1856, Lister gave two lectures a day, morning and afternoon, in order to complete the work before the great event then pending, his marriage.

In a letter to Arthur soon after the lectures began he described a typical day: 'I go to bed about 10 and get up by alarum at 5.30, light my fire (laid the evening before) and my coffee boils while I dress. I take it and a bit of bread: work for 3 or 4 hours, and off to my 10 o'clock lecture when my mind is brimful of it. Then I have the afternoon for the Hospital: and for preparation in various ways, such as dissection of tumours, etc, and then my evening is all my own for reading, or occasionally dining out (at Millbank I hope).' Millbank was Syme's home. It was an exciting period of intensive hard work as research worker, surgeon and lecturer, with the promise of his love affair leavening the dough.

Yet the pattern established by the tardy completion of his first lecture persisted. 'But was it not running too great a risk and tempting failure,' Joseph Jackson asked in the letter congratulating Joseph on his early performances, 'to delay so late its preparation? An example of what is to be avoided hereafter?' It was not to be avoided. Not only did he jot down his notes at the last minute, but he often arrived late. 'His unpreparedness, and the habit of leaving the finishing touches to the last moment, became even more marked in later life', wrote his nephew. 'The last few hours before the delivery of an address were often times of great mental and even physical stress'. This lateness, verging on the neurotic incapacity to finish a task in time, seems to have emerged with Lister's first regular professional engagements. His professors at University College gave no indication that they had noticed it. Was it related to the uncertainties reflected in the curious post-breakdown protestations of his love for surgery? Similar delays often occurred with his writing and in keeping to the times fixed for engagements to meet patients and their doctors. Yet in other respects Lister was as meticulous in his work as in his deportment.

In December 1855 he was elected to membership in the Royal Society of Medicine of Edinburgh, and organisation of young graduates and senior students. He was required to mark his election by presenting a dissertation on a subject of his own choosing. His choice underlines with vigorous strokes the traditional character of his therapeutics. 'On the Mode in which external applications act on internal parts' is a masterly review of the theory behind such diverse and dubious practices as cupping, venesection or blood-letting, leeching, hot fomentations, the actual cautery and the use of mercurial and iodine ointments as vesicants and counter-irritants. These treatments were important because they represented the only known means of combating inflammation. Lister described a syphilitic patient whom he had treated at University College Hospital for severe inflammation of the eye:

... as the man's general health was rather low, I omitted general blood letting, and proceeded to cup the temple—No sooner had the first glass been applied, and had drawn up the yet unscarified integument as a red hemispherical mass, than the patient, to my surprise, exclaimed that his vision was much clearer, and that his pain was greatly diminished; and though I could hardly believe my eyes, the sclerotic injection appeared decidedly less. I proceeded to take a few ounces of blood, as I had intended; and from this time forth the inflammation, which had been so rapidly advancing, steadily abated, and in the course of the same afternoon the pupil became much larger and more regular.

The patient's improvement could have been produced by a dozen causes, hysteria and the strange course of syphilis among them, but not by the cupping as such. After defending its theoretical foundations, Lister admitted that there were arguments against blood-letting: 'at all events theory can be adduced on the one side as much as on the other'. During the next decade he quietly abandoned cupping, venesection and leeching as well as hot fomentations, but he used blisters and other skin-irritants throughout his practice. To explain their use he said in 1881, 'that when two parts are nervously in sympathy with each other, if we excite a great action in the nerves of one we may distract action from the nerves of the other'. The hypothesis is essentially the same as that which he stated before the Royal Society of Medicine in 1855. Refined and related to the complex nervous mechanisms that carry sensations of pain, but are still poorly understood, the hypothesis could stand as an explanation for the use of electrical stimulators to combat intractable pain in the last quarter of the twentieth century.

5

AGNES

AGNES SYME was born on November 23, 1834, at 2 Forres Street in St Stephen's Parish, Edinburgh. Her mother, Anne Willis, was the daughter of a Leith merchant, the sister of a schoolfellow of James Syme. She died six days before Agnes's sixth birthday following the birth of her ninth child. Five had died in childhood and two subsequently, leaving only Agnes and her younger sister, Lucy.

The next year Syme remarried. His second wife, Jemima Burns, had five children three of whom survived. Neither Agnes nor Lucy seem to have had much contact with their half brothers and sister after the death of their father. Agnes had survived a life-threatening illness in early childhood, but there are no clues to its nature. Her long convalescence was the origin of a close friendship with her father's associate at Minto House, Dr John Brown, who became her confidant.

Born in 1810 Brown had begun his medical career as Syme's student. He was evidently a competent doctor, but his reputation was based on some volumes of medical essays and several stories. In 1858 he published 'Rab and His Friends'. Rab is a sheep dog who comes with his master, a stone mason, when they bring his mistress to the Edinburgh Royal Infirmary to undergo an operation. The surgeon is Mr Syme. She appears to be recovering well, but then, as was so often the case, blood-poisoning claimed her. Rab and his master watch helplessly as she dies. What the story lacks in literary merit, it makes up for in its evocative description of conditions in the hospital where Syme and Lister worked, and in its bald account of the fatalism that accompanied every operation. Brown was obviously a warm-hearted, witty man with a wide circle of friends. In London, in May 1866, he took Syme to meet Thomas Carlyle, and the relationship that evolved led Carlyle to write a condolence letter to Syme when Jemima Burn died in 1869. To the end of his life Brown maintained a playful, avuncular role with Agnes Syme. In his notes to her he would refer to Lister as 'Josephus', but he committed no such barbarism when he wrote to Lister, whom he addressed as 'My dear Friend'.

While Agnes was still a child, Syme moved twice, first to a house on Charlotte Square and then to the estate called Millbank on the southwestern outskirts of Edinburgh. The view across the gardens to the Pentland Hills is still lovely. Syme built greenhouses and a conservatory. In the former he grew pineapples and bananas, and in the latter, fine specimens of orchids. Many of the foreign visitors who came to see one of Europe's foremost medical schools also came to Millbank. Years later Professor Kölliker, the author of the hypothesis on muscle tissue that Lister had supported with his early research, recalled how he first met Lister at Millbank. For Syme's young assistant also became a frequent guest.

By March 1854 Joseph's parents had become aware that he was interested by Miss Syme. In a letter dated March 25 Joseph Jackson wrote: 'thy dear mother tells me she has been persuading thee not to allow thy other engagms to absorb thee too entirely to our loss ... I do not know how some apprehensions of hers that I told thee of have been awakened, and I try to assure her they are groundless, that most probably no thought has entered thy mind to warrant them or thy judgement would at once have dismissed it as incongruous ... And what I once suggested I will venture to repeat—that it may be well to be on thy guard that in the friendly intercourse to which thou art kindly invited, nothing in thy deportment may give any ground for suspicion that thou has an intention beyond it.' On the evidence of the parody sung by his dressers at the staff dinner in May, he had not yet decided himself what course he wished to follow. It seems likely that what most exercised Isabella's concern was the difference in religion between the Listers and the Symes. But there can be no doubt that Isabella's intuition was better informed than her husband's.

Agnes Syme was a tall, slender girl, well proportioned but plain with dark hair pulled back loosely across her ears and formed into a bun or chignon accentuating small, regular features. Her plainness was made the more evident by the comparison with her beautiful younger sister, Lucy. Joseph described Agnes to Rickman Godlee:

... in the case of my precious Agnes the outward appearance as I have often said before is not at all showy, but there is in her countenance an ever varying expression that artlessly displays a peculiarly guileless, honest, unaffected, and modest spirit, & a very amiable and at the same time sprightly though sobered disposition, while there is no lack of sound and independent intelligence; and on rare occasions, though to me not now so rare as formerly, her eye expresses the deep feeling of a very warm heart.

Lest this somewhat measured analysis seem too cool, he continued, 'Therefore to me her face has become dearer than thee might at first sight suppose. But thee will say I am talking nonsense!' At twenty-eight he was still naive and innocent.

That Agnes had an 'independent intelligence', there is no doubt. Of the greatest importance to her through the married years that lay ahead was the training, much of it probably accidental, that she had received from her father. She was as much at home in the laboratory as in the drawing room, perhaps rather more so, and she found nothing too distressing when she acted on occasion as her husband's assistant in the dissecting room and the slaughter house. What is more, once at least, when she was closer to fifty than forty, she helped Lister in experiments to determine safe quantities of chloroform for anaesthesia by breathing the gas herself.

Of more immediate concern during their courtship were her firm religious views. The Symes had become members of the Episcopal Church of Scotland. The Episcopal Church is the established Church of England and had strong claims in the professional class. Agnes had no intention of abandoning her church.

This meant that if they were to marry, Lister would have to leave his. Seven years before he had been so deeply convinced a Quaker that his family had interfered to calm his passion. Now he was concerned first to determine that if he should become an Episcopalian, his father would not be so distressed as to withdraw his financial support. Immediately upon his return to Edinburgh from Paris he wrote to Joseph Jackson candidly explaining his intentions and asking about his prospects: he had to know what they were before calling on the girl's father. The exact terms of Joseph's letter are unknown, but his father replied:

Thy inquiry in the letter I received last evening is indeed but a reasonable one & deserves to receive a prompt & candid reply—In the first place I may say that believing, from all thou hast told me, that thy affections are fixed on a really virtuous & amiable young woman, I would not allow the circumstances of her not being within our society to affect my pecuniary arrangements for thee—or to alter the expectations given thee some time ago.

Though freed of financial concern, Lister was not entirely relieved. 'I was particularly pleased with thy remark about her religious views & think with thee that she is a friend in all essential points,' wrote William Henry on a reassuring note. Yet Joseph's doubts, and perhaps his guilt, persisted. On October 18 Joseph Jackson wrote: 'Thy last letter . . . restores the openness between us that I feared had been interrupted'. Now that Joseph had explained his 'increased preference for the Ch. of Engld services', though his father thought he might have misunderstood one of her ordinances, neither he nor Isabella wished him to 'attend the worship of "Friends" for the sake of our feelings'. Joseph Jackson recognized how the appearance of conflict between his parents and his fiancée might affect Joseph, and recommended that for the present he avoid any further religious discussion with Agnes. He also suggested that Joseph resign from the Society of Friends rather than wait for them to disown him formally as the Rules of Discipline required. 'It might even, if thy feelings should at some time alter again, make it more easy to return'. Perhaps the most striking aspect of this exchange was not that Agnes's faith was much stronger than his—after Lister's breakdown that may be scarcely surprising—but that he should have doubted for a moment Joseph Jackson's tolerance and flexibility. Yet his father had let him down once before.

In any case, in the first letter on finances Joseph Jackson went on to describe what he did have in mind: he would continue the £300 per year which Joseph had received for the last two years. With the £150 annual interest from his own property, the couple would have £450 per year. In addition he was prepared to give them £1000 'to purchase furniture'. If his professional income should permit Joseph to take less than £300, Joseph Jackson proposed to 'substitute for it as I have done in Arthur's case an increase to thy capital—but not yielding equal intt.' He supposed Syme would make a settlement on Agnes, but suggested that if Joseph's suit was accepted he and Syme should pursue these arrangements further.

During February 1856 an exchange of letters between Joseph Jackson and Syme indicate that they were both prepared to act reasonably, if cautiously. Joseph's property, his father wrote, amounting to about £3300, 'is mostly derived from me & is in my hands', to which he would add £4000 'on his marriage', including the £1000 'for furniture & a journey', leaving a principal sum that would produce £300 a year.

Syme replied that he proposed to make over securities worth £2000 to Joseph and a further £2000 in settlement on Agnes. Neither father felt the other was being overly generous. Syme wrote of the couple's resultant income that it would 'be hardly adequate'. Joseph Jackson sent the correspondence to his son with a covering note in which he observed: 'I do not know how far the sum Mr S. gives equals thy expectation. I had hoped for rather more, but he knows best his own circumstances'. These hard-headed business transactions make it clear that *none* of the principals took money, investments or property lightly.

Syme had been satisfied by Joseph's recital of his material circumstances, and Agnes presumably, by his romantic and spiritual condition. William Henry's letter of congratulations referred to Joseph's doubts apart from the matter of religion. Perhaps he felt that sudden onrush of uncertainty, the panicky, self-torturing 'what have I done?', that afflicts people when they have made an irrevocable decision. A week later Joseph could write to Rickman Godlee in a new tone: 'since the making & acceptance of my offer, I have been from time to time favoured, as I have assuredly believed, with a rather remarkable & to me unexpected sense that I am in my right place in this matter'. But then there emerges the quiet counterpoint of doubt. 'Without some measure of this feeling I should I believe be miserable, notwithstanding Agnes's love, and what may appear to the World the bright prospect before me. As it is however, I feel able at times, & ought I believe to do so more constantly, to rejoice with true thankfulness for what I am assured are present services bestowed; and on the other hand to look forward with some degree of trustfulness for the future, and to pluck up a little courage with reference to the mass of laborious duty that lies before me, as yet almost untouched, as a teacher of Surgery, and to hope that, this step being rightly made, the rest of my path through what I perhaps too much anticipate as a very shady and rough world, may be also safely directed.' Such tortuous expression is not the effect of a pusillanimous concern with money, not even with the trappings of faith. Lister's depressive illness had left a permanent mark on him. Whatever of pomposity his behaviour conveyed, it served to cloak and protect a fearful core.

Joseph Jackson had been in Edinburgh early in 1854 to visit his son, and in September 1855 he returned with Jane. Isabella was too 'weak' to make the trip. They were guests of the Symes, and the purpose of the visit was to meet Agnes. His letter to Joseph immediately after returning to Upton acknowledged this objective and stated, rather too formally, that the three days 'have given her a high place in our regard' 'in association with thee'. He had asked Agnes to come to Upton to meet Isabella '& other members of our family', but she had refused. Her mother had evidently put her foot down, though Agnes was permitted to go away on another visit in November. When she returned, possibly from the home of a Scottish relative, Joseph Jackson warned Joseph: 'She must not engross too much of thy time'. He had been more successful in arranging a visit by the senior Symes to Upton, and they came for a few days in October.

Joseph went home for Christmas 1855 and returned to his classes and his courtship. 'The picture . . . of thy reception at Millbank on the evening of thy arrival & thy "eating tea", with Agnes to hand it thee at the farther end of the drawing room, was a charming little sketch,' wrote his father. Feeling the oppression of five lectures a week, Joseph had complained that there was not time for proper courtship. Joseph Jackson counselled patience: 'thou wilt remember that life is to all a chequered scene & not to be discouraged'.

Lister's next task was to find a suitable house, his own flat being unsatisfactory for the married state. He soon settled on 11 Rutland Street, a granite-faced Georgian house in the same terrace as his present quarters. It had belonged to Syme's friend and associate, Dr Peddie. With three floors and a basement, it had nine principal rooms and the rental was £85 per annum on an extendable three-year lease. He described the appointments to his mother:

. . . there are two sitting rooms on the ground floor, one of them being the dining room, the other the study, or consulting room. The first floor has two rooms; one the drawing room, the other a full-sized, good bedroom. The 2nd floor has, if I recollect rightly, three good bed rooms; one of these used to be Dr Peddie's nursery, and is well provided with a sink with taps for hot & cold water. In one part of the house is a little room with good baths shallow and [illegible], & in the basement is a capital kitchen, servants' room, scullery, laundry, larder and cellars . . . The cupboard-room is excellent in all parts of the house. Further there is no smoking of chimneys . . .

Thereupon, Agnes and her mother fixed the wedding day at April 23. Joseph complained to his father of the delay, and Joseph Jackson replied: 'my preference like thine would be for the earlier, but thou wilt see that there are reasons why the fixing it should be left to the ladies discretion'. The wedding gifts began to arrive: from Thomas and Isabella Pim a black marble clock with inkstand 'fitted for a dining room' in Joseph Jackson's opinion; from Arthur and Susan a dessert service. The Banns were sworn in the Church of St Cuthbert's, the Parish Church for both Millbank and Rutland Street, on April 21, and the wedding took place in the Syme's drawing room two days later. Lucy Syme recalled that the ceremony was performed at Millbank 'out of consideration for any Quaker relation . . . who, it was thought, might prefer not to go to a Church'. R J Godlee wrote that the Symes wished to have the wedding at home because it was 'more convenient and the young couple approved'. The clergyman was the Reverend George Coventry, BD, Vicar of St Peter's, Roxburgh Place. The witnesses were James Syme, Syme's friend, John Macvicar, and William Henry Lister. At the wedding meal Dr John Brown gave a congratulatory speech. One of Lister's house surgeons, who had not been present, reported that Brown said: 'Lister is one who, I believe, will go to the top of his profession, and as for Agnes, she was once in heaven for three or four days when she was a very small child, and she has born the mark of it ever since'.

The honeymoon journey lasted for four months and enabled Lister at last to visit the great medical schools of Italy, Austria and Germany. According to his nephew the trip began in the English Lakes, but there is a charming story reported many years later by a 'minister's wife who was a lady's maid in the house' belonging to Agnes's uncle at Kinross where they went first from Edinburgh. 'He rigged up a room . . . and started some experiments with frogs' which escaped, causing consternation in the house. 'At a certain hour of the day,' furthermore, 'he put his services at the disposal of the poor of the village and parish, and when he left the blessings of the whole community followed him'. This bit of hagiography could have arisen from a later visit, but whatever the facts, Joseph and Agnes arrived at Upton in May for her first visit. Later that month they crossed the Channel to Brussels. Their journey down the Rhine and through Switzerland followed much the same route as Joseph's holiday with the Godlees a decade before, but he and Agnes went on to Milan. The huge hospital there did not appeal to him, though he was well received by the medical faculty at Pavia. After visiting Turin, Genoa and Pisa, Joseph wrote that they were oppressed by the superstition of 'that lovely but melancholy land' where the Risorgimento had as yet made the lives of the peasants only a little more uncertain. They spent a longer time at Florence while Joseph worked in the laboratory of Philip Pacini, Professor of Anatomy at the University, who had read Lister's papers on muscular tissue. Syme had a friend on the faculty at Padua, and at Bologna Joseph was shown the pathological museum. They sailed from Venice to Trieste and travelled by diligence to Vienna.

In the Austro-Hungarian capital they were the guests of Professor Rokitansky, a great pathologist who was then Dean of the Medical Faculty and Rector of the University. He had been a visitor to Upton in 1842 and no doubt his hospitality was arranged by Joseph Jackson. Agnes described the enormous evening meal they were given at the Rokitansky's home: 'But the supper itself was not so remarkable as the Germans' enjoyment of it,' she wrote. The Professor showed Joseph over his museum of pathological specimens. Apparently Lister's interest in the subject of inflammation prompted no discussion between them of the now-neglected attempts by Rokitansky's former colleague, Ignatz Semmelweis, to end the ravages of childbed fever in the Viennese maternity wards more than fifteen years before. Another generation passed before Lister even heard the name of the man whose work anticipated his and failed.

From Vienna Joseph and Agnes went on to Prague, Dresden, Berlin and Leipzig. In Berlin and Leipzig Lister had introductions to ophthalmological surgeons from his University College professor, Wharton Jones, but he had shown interest in eye surgery in Venice and Vienna too. Also at Leipzig he saw teaching methods at the general hospital and reported: 'The students are made to find out the disease of newly admitted patients for themselves, & give their reasons & the treatment they would adopt . . . the two house surgeons themselves perform every operation that requires to be done during the last month of the summer session, the surgeons only standing by & directing & assisting them'. The tour continued through Erlangen, Munich and Nuremberg. At Wurzburg Joseph was disappointed to find that Professor Kölliker was away, but they hurried on to Frankfurt, Heidelberg and Tübingen. The object of each stop was the hospital, the medical museum if any, and practitioners where it was possible to talk to them. The last few days of this remarkable wedding tour were spent at Stuttgart, Strasbourg and Paris. In mid-September they returned to Upton and to Edinburgh at the beginning of October. On October 15 Joseph Jackson wrote: 'We are thinking of your being to day engaged in really settling in your house as your home & Agnes taking for the first time upon her the regular household cares—but I do not imagine she will find these a burthen'.

It had evidently been assumed by Lister, as well as by Syme, that his re-election as assistant surgeon to the Royal Infirmary was a foregone conclusion and did not require his presence in Edinburgh during the summer. On July 16 however, Syme wrote to Joseph: 'There has been an attempt on the part of some . . . ladies to prejudice the Managers in favour of Watson—which I have endeavoured to counteract—But I rather think it would be in order if you were to send them—the Managers—a letter to say that you intend to be a candidate—and will then submit testimonials which you hope will be satisfactory etc'. Patrick Heron Watson, Syme's former dresser and Lister's assistant, later became Professor of Surgery at the University. With Lister on the continent Syme may have collected the testimonials for him, possibly with Joseph Jackson's help. According to custom in the Scottish universities they were presented in a printed booklet. They came from Sharpey, Erichsen, Graham, who had been Lister's Professor of Chemistry, Dr Robert E Grant, Professor of Comparative Anatomy at University College, Syme himself, Dr John Hughes Bennett, Professor of the Institutes of Medicine at Edinburgh, Dr Samuel P Spasshatt, Resident Physician at the Edinburgh Royal Infirmary, Dr Allen Thomson, Professor of Anatomy at the University of Glasgow, Philip Pacini of Florence and Joseph Jackson's old friend Richard Owen. On October 13 the Managers unanimously elected Lister.

His second series of extra-mural lectures began a month later with only eight students. However as late as January 31, 1857, Joseph Jackson noted the acquisition of a new student, so the number grew.

Meanwhile Lister had entered upon a period of intensive experimental work which occupied every moment not given to his patients and the lectures. During the next three years Lister published fifteen papers, all of them describing original research. Nine appeared in 1858! Not until the three years from 1869 to 1871, after the introduction of antiseptic surgery, did he even approach such an astonishing total. Of the thirteen papers published during the post-antiseptic period, furthermore, the majority were defensive, although they usually contained details of new techniques introduced to improve his method. Had Lister maintained and extended the output that he achieved in the early years of his marriage, had he found the time at least to prepare his lectures for publication, he might have had fewer problems when he came to the major work of his life, the introduction and confirmation of the antiseptic treatment. But he never wrote a book. Papers were often delayed because he felt he was not yet ready to publish. A sound principle indeed—not to rush into print—but many people, not least his father, felt that he overdid it. As early as January 1857, Joseph Jackson wrote:

I am ready to ask what new points . . . render requisite still further experiments with the poor frogs—my wish would rather be that it may be well digested compressed & revised by the time when prof Sharpey recommends it being presented . . .

This was the first of a long series of similar comments from his father urging that he publish his increasingly interesting results. Lister was a man of detail, precision and hard work, but he found generalization difficult. He preferred the slog up the mountain to the view from the summit. Here no doubt was another legacy of the nervous breakdown which followed the collapse of his first great commitment. Yet this pedantic man was fated, it seemed, to pursue research which would eventually embroil him in a fight that this time he had the strength to win.

In the event experiments on the frogs led almost immediately to two papers, a preliminary statement of his observations on the development of inflammation and an extension of his work on the structure of muscular tissue. The latter paper was read on December 1, 1856, to the Royal Society of Edinburgh by Lister's former assistant, David Christison. Lister was not then a member. Its content had originated with his observations of arterioles, the smallest arteries, in the frog's web. Kölliker's description of involuntary muscle cells had been criticized because, it was argued, he had had to tease apart tissues with needles to get at the cells, as had Lister in his earlier work on the iris. Therefore, it was said, Kölliker had described artefacts, things that appeared because of his own experimental techniques, rather than real muscle cells. Lister now pointed out that the involuntary muscle cells in the arterioles of the frog's web were exactly as Kölliker had described them and that no separation of the tissues had been required. During November, moreover, he had extended his observation to the outer muscular coating of pigs' intestines, thus showing that these cells occurred in mammals as well as frogs.

Useful though the paper was, it was a by-product of Lister's central concern with the early evidence of the inflammatory process. He had been looking at the blood vessels with inflammation in mind, so to speak, when he noticed the muscle cells in the arterioles. However, his first paper on inflammation grew out of the work begun a year before in preparation for his extramural lectures and extended in the six weeks after he had settled at 11 Rutland Street.

His laboratory was in one of the ground floor rooms. In each of the houses he occupied, one room served a similar purpose. Not only did this arrangement make it easier for him to work far into the night or early in the morning, but it also enabled Mrs Lister to help him more easily. It was by no means unusual for research to be conducted in the scientist's home. Equipment was relatively simple. Joseph Jackson Lister, needing almost nothing except a microscope, could observe the red corpuscles and contribute data about them which marked him as a talented amateur. Indeed, separate laboratory facilities were almost non-existent. Medical schools had their dissecting rooms, but there was no technical reason why anatomical research could not be conducted on a decent table in the back parlour. Lister managed to perform complex bacteriological experiments at home, involving more and more glassware and related equipment, but to observe blood flow in the frog's web he, too, needed only a microscope.

He read a paper 'On the early stages of inflammation, as observed in the Foot of the Frog' to the Royal College of Surgeons of Edinburgh on December 5, 1856. His father, who was present, wrote that the 'large room was well filled'. The manuscript, the first written in Mrs Lister's hand as well as Lister's, was characteristically unfinished. About a third of the paper had to be delivered extempore. Joseph Jackson added, 'Joseph, whom I had left with uneasiness between 5 and 6 . . . & who then seemed almost worn down, was so refreshed after his dinner at home that he showed no embarrassment in delivering his subject'.

Though his audience was drawn from 'the medical and scientific world of Edinburgh', he felt it necessary to distinguish between the red and white corpuscles of the blood and to devote nine pages to arguments which show that the heart is the only means of propulsion of the blood although the calibre of the blood vessels affects the rate of flow. The fact that the major paper on inflammation published eighteen months later contained far less elementary physiological data suggests that Lister may have underestimated his auditors on the first occasion.

Joseph Jackson remained in Edinburgh until December 8. Joseph described the pleasant visit to his mother and added:

We do not yet quite feel to have made up our minds about going southward at Christmas. The only doubt I feel is whether it is good for Aggie to be moving about so much. But we shall certainly come if we can. She, dear sweet darling as she is, sends her dearest love to you all . . .

Why should he have wondered 'whether it is good for Aggie to be moving about so much'? The obvious answer, that she was pregnant, leaps to mind. But they did spend that Christmas at Upton.

A similar side-long reference appeared once again in a letter from his father to Joseph dated January 27, 1869, eight months before Joseph Jackson died: 'Thy last & that of Agnes to Mary are especially touching describing your state of anticipation & at the same time the sweet composure & resignation of the object of your care—How would I desire though hardly hoping that anything like it might be mine in the close to which I often look forward—But, for thy Father in law I truly feel', and then, because of age and perhaps emotion the fine, legible handwriting becomes quite unreadable. Mrs Syme had just died, and Joseph's mother had been dead for four years. Joseph Jackson had been made a grandfather several times over, but not by his eldest surviving son, his dear Joseph. Agnes was now thirty-five and the time to begin a family was passing. It was not to be. Perhaps her early illness had destroyed her capacity to bear children. In all other respects she seems to have been a strong and active woman, but there is nothing surprising in that. It is unfortunately impossible to comment on Mrs Lister's attitude toward children, other than to observe that she is most unlikely to have been conscious of any preference to remain childless. There is more information about Joseph. His letter of December 8, 1856, to his mother, makes no attempt to suppress his pride and love. As to Lister's attitude to children, one niece wrote: 'My uncle was like a boy among us at the big family gatherings, throwing himself with whole-hearted enjoyment into all the games, however childish, that we played'. One wonders why she did not mention her aunt.

By all accounts Lister's favourite patients were children. Mrs Lister is the source of one story. 'There is a little girl in the Infirmary at present whose knee Joseph excised,' she wrote to Mary Godlee in March 1868. 'She is abt 9 years old I think. Yesterday she said to Joseph "you might do the operation on the doll"! Joseph asked what was wrong with the doll, & she said it had "a sair knee" & the bran was coming out.' The story was elaborated by one of Lister's house surgeons : Lister 'received the case, shook his head ominously, for it was very serious . . . asked for a needle and cotton, and carefully and securely stitched on the limb, and with quiet delight handed her back to her mother. Her large brown eyes spoke endless gratitude, but neither uttered a word.' There is no reason to doubt that Lister regretted his childlessness, but he appears to have combined with it sympathy for his wife which strengthened the bond between them.

In the letter to his mother that hinted at Aggie's first pregnancy, Joseph also referred to his continuing research. 'Thee may tell Papa . . . that I have called this afternoon on Mr Goodsir, and that he said to me then that he considered that I had proved the cause of the stoppage of the blood corpuscles in the early stages of inflammation as clearly as anything could be proved by induction.' The cause, he said, was the release of fibrin, a substance that appears in the blood and causes clotting. It is the last to appear of some twelve chemicals that are formed sequentially in the process of clotting, but it was the first to be identified. Fibrin appears, and the red blood cells become adhesive as his father had discovered, when the blood is 'in the vicinity of ordinary solid objects', or—and this was the essential point—when it is 'near inflamed tissues'. He had watched through the microscope as he had applied various irritants to the frog's web, beginning with hot water, in September 1855. Nothing had been done from October 1855 until September 1856. Once they had settled at 11 Rutland Street and the experiments had begun in earnest, he used first mustard and then croton oil as irritants. Now Mrs Lister's handwriting is more evident than her husband's in the detailed laboratory notes. Acetic acid and oil of cantharides were applied, followed by chloroform. On October 29 and 30, the effects of 'chloroform on web & galvanism on frog's blood' were noted by Mrs Lister, who took Joseph's dictation second by second across seven foolscap pages. The work had to make way for lectures in November, but began again intensively after the two papers had been presented in December. On the 16th Lister observed the process of coagulation in 'Human Blood 11.PM Blood drawn from my own finger about 5 minutes ago . . .' The writing was Mrs Lister's. They did not leave for Upton until Christmas Eve, and the laboratory notes begin again on January 3. On the 19th he instituted an experiment to show 'Effects of heat & Inflam on pigment cells' in the frog's web. And so the notes continue meticulously day by day through February and March 1857, as Lister used cold, ammonia, mechanical violence, turpentine and drying to compare the effects of each irritant on the behaviour of the blood, the vessels and the pigmented specks in the interstitial cells. During April he devoted a series of experiments to the influence of the nerves on the contraction of the arteries:

On the 16th April, a large frog being put under chloroform, the entire brain was removed about 3 o'clock p.m. without injury to the cord. After this operation, the arteries, which had previously been pretty full size and transmitting rapid streams of blood, were found completely contracted, so that the webs appeared bloodless except in the veins, and continued so for some minutes. At 3 hours 10 minutes an artery selected for special observation was dilating, having already attained to a diameter of $1\frac{1}{2}$ degrees, and the circulation was returning in the web. At 3 hours 15 minutes the vessel measured 3 degrees, but 2 minutes later was $2\frac{1}{2}$ degrees, and half an hour afterwards exhibited the spontaneous changes in calibre commonly seen in arteries in health, the limits observed being $1\frac{1}{3}$ degrees and 2 degrees . . . At 4 hours, a small part of the spinal canal having been laid open, the anterior sixth of the cord was removed . . . At 4 hours 3 minutes, when the web was first looked at, the artery was contracted to absolute closure and the web exsanguine; and this state of things continued till 4 hours 7 minutes . . .

And so on until 6.40 pm when 'the blood had ceased to move in consequence of the feebleness of the heart'. The laboratory notes continued through May and then sporadically with the last observation on the influence of the nerves on the contraction of blood vessels in June 1859.

Three closely related papers recorded the results of this intensive work. All three were published in the *Philosophical Transactions* of the Royal Society during 1858. They had been drafted and first presented to Professor Sharpey as one paper. Both John Goodsir of Edinburgh and James Paget, the London surgeon, to whom the papers were sent for expert comment and criticism, recommended that it be published as three separate papers: 'An Inquiry regarding the Parts of the Nervous System which regulate the Contractions of the Arteries', 'On the Cutaneous Pigmentary System of the Frog', and the focal study 'On the Early Stages of Inflammation', which was also the longest and the last to be published.

The first to appear presented evidence that the calibre of the arteries in the frog's web was at least partially under nervous control. In order to study the relationship it had been necessary to immobilize the animal and to irritate the spinal cord, techniques which Lister thought it desirable to apply because the means by which blood vessels responded to irritation seemed to him important for the understanding of the inflammatory process. In fact he was covering much the same ground as E F W Pflüger, a Professor at Bonn, whose paper was published at about the same time. Sharpey had told Lister about Pflüger's work even before Lister undertook his own experiments, but Lister saw no account of the German's work until November 1857. Paget had also asked in his referee's report that Lister extend his observations to include those reported by M Brown-Sequard, a French physiologist, on nervous control of blood vessels in mammals, but excepting the experiments on pigs' gut which had a different purpose, Lister seems never to have done so. In any case tests on mammals would have added little because nervous control over blood vessels has limited bearing on the inflammatory process.

His work on the nature and behaviour of pigment was both more original and still less relevant to his central theme. Lister saw that the onset of inflammation was always accompanied by colour changes in the web. He managed to determine that the pigment consists of 'very minute dark granules or molecules' contained within cells—no slight contribution given that the cellular nature of living matter was still no more than a theory, and that he had no dyes or fixatives with which to 'hold' the cells. 'The extreme delicacy of the cell-wall makes it very difficult to trace it among the surrounding tissues', he wrote. He observed that the pigment molecules seemed also to be under nervous control, and as in the case of the arteries he believed that the control was exerted 'by the cerebro-spinal axis'. Pigment mirrored the activity of the blood vessels, and of the blood, he believed, though it is the slowing of the blood flow that actually initiates inflammation.

He saw changes in the pigmentation and even in the calibre of blood vessels long after amputation of the limb above the web he was observing, or death of the limb, and he concluded that somehow local nervous mechanisms assumed control under these circumstances. In other words he assigned a vital principle to living matter which persisted locally for some time after death. 'The idea suggested by the facts is that the tissues begin to suffer from want of fresh supplies of the vital fluid, and resent the injury, as it were, by a struggle'. The phrase 'vital fluid' meant blood, but even so, the statement might have earned the approval of his University College Professor of Medical Jurisprudence, Dr Carpenter. Vitalism, the belief that life embodies a unique force absent from non-living matter, was almost universal in the mid-nineteenth century, and persists at the periphery of biology even in the late twentieth to explain the 'central mysteries' such as inheritance. Lister knew nothing about the astonishing biochemical life of a cell which can continue as long as essential nutrients are available. He had no knowledge of the blood-borne messengers from the brain, hormones, that also regulate the calibre of blood vessels and the movement of pigment. He conceived of the nervous system as a structure mechanically analogous to the cardio-vascular system: brain = heart, cord = large arteries, and so on. The analogy is false and obscures the difference between reflex behaviour and that under central direction. Yet Lister did observe that the frog's skin colour responds not to light shone on the skin but to light on the frog's eyes.

James Paget wrote in his referee's report that the most valuable part of the paper 'On the Early Stages of Inflammation' described the observation of pigment. They 'give the best, or only, visible proof yet discovered that . . . the tissues external to the blood vessels are independently and even primarily affected by the stimulus applied'. Lister's purpose had been to determine whether John Hunter was right in his opinion that inflammation is 'active in its nature, and consisting in an exaltation of the functions of the affected part, or whether it should not rather be considered as a passive response to diminished functional activity'. The behaviour of the pigment and of the blood vessels demonstrated that Hunter had been right in his judgement, Lister believed. What was more, his observations demonstrated a relationship between the tissues, the vessels and the blood which is relevant to coagulation and clotting in healthy as well as inflamed tissue.

During November 1857 he extended his observations to the fine, hair-like cilia covering the frog's tongue. Sharpey had done some work on the effect of irritants on these cilia. In December Lister reported that the tissue responded like any other. Although all tissues were controlled by the nervous system, he thought, they also possessed the capacity to respond independently to an irritant. If the irritant was neither too strong nor applied for too long, the tissue would cease to show inflammatory changes and recover its normal aspect. It now began to emerge that there are different kinds of inflammation. Lister could not yet make explicit distinctions. In this paper he maintained that direct inflammation was actually essential to proper healing because it produced the fibrin and blood clot, but inflammation 'induced indirectly is both unnecessary and injurious'. Within five years he was teaching his students that there was direct inflammation produced by irritants and 'inflammation brought about through the mediation of the nervous system'. In both cases his evidence supported the Hunterian view that inflammation embodies an active response by the tissues.

Lister always believed that these three papers were his most important ones. 'If my works are read when I am gone,' he said in 1905, 'these will be the ones most highly thought of'. A surprising remark by one of the greatest medical innovators of all time, but Lister died believing that his observations on inflammation had merely been reinforced by the discovery of the role played by bacteria. Bacteria were another kind of irritant, or if they were not themselves, then it was the toxins they produced which caused direct inflammation. In 1881 after the germ theory had been all but proven, he described how direct inflammation caused by improper surgical procedure but free of bacteria would disappear when the procedure had been corrected. Conversely, inflammation mediated by the nervous system could not be easily corrected and was, therefore, often fatal. Almost twenty years later he repeated much the same hypothesis.

It contains an element of truth. Yet neither Lister nor any of his contemporaries grasped the essential fact that inflammation is symptomatic of a disease, but it is not a disease itself. To the contrary inflammatory reactions—heat, swelling, pain and redness—are healthy responses by healthy tissue to counteract disease processes. Thanks in part to Lister's contributions medical men had begun to perceive by the 1880s that disease was not merely a collection of symptoms, as they had been taught for almost 300 years, but that it had a treatable cause. A runny nose can presage a cold in the head, measles, pneumonia or schizophrenia, but these are each different diseases with different causes. Doctors saw the symptom, inflammation for example, but in general failed to recognize that it could not be treated or 'cured'. The vigorous originality of Lister's work on inflammation may actually have perpetuated their misunderstanding.

As the research with irritants continued during the early months of 1857 Lister entered a new phase of his teaching career. On February 26 he performed his first two public operations, an amputation of the great toe and an operation for hernia. In a letter the next day to his father he referred to his 'debut' and went on: 'I felt very nervous before beginning, but when I had got fairly to work, this feeling went off entirely & I performed both operations with entire comfort. And I also explained the operations & cases to the students without embarrassment. Altogether I felt very thankful at the way I was able to acquit myself. Everybody congratulated me afterwards & the students cheered very warmly.' A few days later, after a much more complicated operation to remove a tumour which went well, he wrote to his youngest sister, Jane, that he had 'again felt a good deal' but: 'Just before the operation began, I recollected that there was only one Spectator whom it was important to consider . . . & this consideration gave me increased firmness'. Whatever his early hesitancy Lister came to depend on clinical lectures as the best way of imparting information accurately and efficiently.

With the research, the lectures and the patients Lister was extremely busy. Mrs Lister accepted the task of writing the letters that kept the family informed. Welcome as her letters were, Joseph Jackson wrote, 'yet we hope thou wilt not quite lay upon her the keeping up our correspondence'.

In May they went to Upton where Joseph performed experiments on blood flow in the bat's wing. On June 18, 1857, he read all three papers on inflammation in their original form before the Royal Society. The research as well as the lectures continued into July, and in August he and Agnes went to Ireland, no doubt to stay with the Pims. It was Agnes's first visit. At the end of August Lister delivered a paper before the British Association meeting in Dublin. 'On the Flow of the Lacteal Fluid in the Mesentery of the Mouse' is slight by comparison with the work on inflammation in the midst of which it appeared, but Lister considered it of sufficient importance to agree to its inclusion in his *Collected Papers*. The paper was based on two experiments conducted during 1853 when he was working on muscle tissue. It is perhaps most interesting because of his technique: he had fed mice indigo with a meal. Microscopic examination of part of the intestine showed the indigo was not absorbed. Lister interpreted this as evidence that solids cannot be absorbed, nor can they until they have been either largely dissociated into their constituent molecules or emulsified, but indigo consists of indigestible fat-based molecules. The paper reveals both the catholicity of his interest, and his appreciation that publication could help his career as his father frequently emphasized.

Lister returned from Dublin as Syme's assistant, to take charge of Syme's wards and those of the junior surgeon at the Royal Infirmary while they were on holiday. At Syme's suggestion, furthermore, Lister continued to treat patients in his wards after Syme's return.

Following the British Association meeting there were pleasant visits at Millbank with Sharpey, and with Professor Kölliker whom Lister now met for the first time. Joseph and Agnes along with Kölliker then spent a few days as the guests of Dr Allen Thomson in Glasgow. Lister repeated some of his experiments with frogs for Kölliker.

His extra-mural lectures began again in November while he was studying the effects of irritants on the movement of cilia on the frog's tongue. The first student who appeared at the first meeting arrived ten minutes late, and only seven more turned up during the remainder of the hour. At no time in this session did he have more than eleven students.

On November 28 Lister wrote to Sharpey:

There is one point on which you began to speak to me one evening at Millbank, but the conversation was in some way interrupted . . . You objected to my making use of such an expression as implied that the tissues in a state of health exercise an active influence over the blood in their vicinity, keeping the corpuscles from becoming adhesive . . . I must contend for activity somewhere, either in the blood or the tissues . . . if the tissues are merely negative in their operation in health, the blood must have a positively active power.

The mechanisms that cause the blood to clot, or conversely, those that keep it liquid was the second major line of Lister's research. Of peculiar concern to the surgeon from the negative standpoint of haemorrhage, the positive role of the blood as a transport for nutrients and oxygen to the tissues and for the removal of wastes had also long been appreciated. It was clear from the appearance of the blood vessels that inflammation spread along them in some forms of blood poisoning, and that the changes in the vessels was followed by formation of blood clots within them. The clot quickly displayed the odour and grey-green colour of putrefaction, and it was quite impossible to dissociate the problem of blood coagulation from that of inflammation.

The complex chemical events that take place when coagulation occurs are analogous to the cascade of events that produces the symptoms of inflammation. More than a century after Lister's work the releasing trigger is not clear, though it is probably the same substance which initiates the inflammatory cascade, and its effects depend in part on the tissue—whether blood or flesh—in which it is released.

In the eighteenth century three theories of blood clotting attracted

91

attention: it occurred in the presence of air, when cooling took place, as with gelatine, or when the blood came to rest so that it stiffened. All three had been abandoned, but it could still be argued that blood tended to remain liquid within the vessels because they caused it to retain a liquefying substance. Sir Charles Scudamore proposed carbon dioxide as the liquefier, but in 1857 Dr Benjamin Ward Richardson won the Astley Cooper Prize of the Royal College of Surgeons with an influential paper. He proposed that blood remain liquid because it contains a small amount of ammonia. Ernst von Brücke, Professor of Physiology at the University of Vienna, who had also entered a paper, had supported the earlier findings of Cooper himself that 'the vital action of the vessels' inhibited the blood's natural tendency to coagulate. The issue between the liquefiers—Richardson and Scudamore—and the 'solid state' men—Cooper and now von Brücke—had thus been fairly joined when Lister turned his attention to coagulation as a subject distinct from inflammation.

'On Spontaneous Gangrene from Arteritis and the Causes of Coagulation of the Blood in Diseases of the Blood-vessels' was read before the Medico-Chirurgical Society of Edinburgh in March 1858. He had examined the amputated legs of sheep and cats and found that the blood stayed liquid in the vessels up to six days after death, but still coagulated, though more slowly, after the vessels were opened. With the evidence before him he concluded that ammonia in the blood, if any, is less important than the coating of the vessels in preventing coagulation. 'How can the fact that the wall of the vessel is inflamed determine, on simple chemical principles, the evolution of ammonia from the blood within it?' he asked. Richardson's ammonia hypothesis might apply to blood outside the body, he said, but not to blood within healthy vessels. In hardened arteries coagulation of the blood could be expected and for the same reason: the vessel wall had lost its vitality. The example and the reasoning were wrong, but they led him to the right conclusion. Lister aligned himself with the 'solid-state' men, arguing that the condition of the blood vessels determines whether coagulation will occur.

During the summer term from Easter to the end of July 1858, Lister introduced a new extra-mural course of lectures on surgical pathology and operative surgery which he taught in the Royal Infirmary. Seven students enrolled.

He had continued the research on blood coagulation. On April 4, for example, he observed the behaviour of blood in a horse, obtained from the New Veterinary Hospital, and read a further communication to the Medico-Chirurgical Society three days later. In June he amputated the leg of a woman injured in a railway accident and noted that some blood in the limb remained fluid four days later. On August 30th he hastily scrawled notes on two experiments he wished to perform:

First try the effect of putting a piece of silver wire for a time in the vein (of a sheep's foot) containing blood & see if this leads to coagulation of the blood, the wire being removed before coagulation occurs.

Then, if so, the wire for the same time or longer in an empty portion of a vein &, after withdrawing the wire, let some blood in the vein, & see if this blood coagulates. Thus would be readily determined either the wire remains an influence in the blood only, or in the tissue of the vein also.

He also published two brief case histories in the *Edinburgh Medical Journal* in August and December 1858, both relating to the blood vessels. The first was of no special interest, but in the second he noted that clots compensate for the thinning walls in an aneurism, a condition often associated with tuberculosis, in which the artery wall weakens and bulges under the pressure. He had found fibrin deposited within the thinned walls and not in the form of clots. It was a subject of great importance. As one of Lister's later students wrote, 'he worshipped the blood'.

While the observations on coagulation went on, he had returned to another aspect of his work on inflammation, the nerves. The previous year, Pflüger, and another German, Edward Weber, proposed separately that some nerves instead of exciting the muscles to which they lead, inhibit their movement. This was particularly true, they said, of a major nerve leading both to the heart and to the intestines, the vagus. During June and July 1858 Lister, assisted by his wife and two associates, studied the activity of nerves in the rabbit's intestine. In two letters he described the work to Sharpey who replied on July 31, complimenting him on the 'very pretty experiment of cutting the nerves' to the intestine, to determine which controlled activity in a given portion of the gut. Sharpey also suggested that Lister translate the difficult German word *Hemmungs* as inhibitory, thus contributing an important word as well as a major concept to the vocabulary of biological science.

The later summer weeks were spent at Upton where Joseph worked on the paper summarizing these experiments, which he read to the Royal Society on August 13. He and Agnes returned to Edinburgh and to another contest. Lister's reappointment as assistant surgeon at the Royal Infirmary was again opposed by Patrick Heron Watson, again unsuccessfully.

Though his hospital practice was thus assured, his private practice did not thrive. Agnes succinctly summarized it as 'poor Joseph and his one patient'. He was away too often with his family and preoccupied too much with his research to maintain a successful practice, and he could gain surgical experience in the Infirmary. Perhaps it was for much the same reasons that the Listers had very little social life. They were often at Millbank and entertained Joseph's associates, but otherwise they seldom left their work.

Research related to blood coagulation continued during the last months of 1858 so intensively that he may have missed out the annual Christmas journey to the south. The pressure of work was beginning to make itself felt. On

March 2, 1859, he demonstrated before the Medico-Chirurgical Society the first of his contributions to surgical technology, a special needle to sew stitches called sutures. At the end of the month he apologized to Sharpey for his delay in writing 'a few concluding words that will not occupy more than about a page of the transactions' for his paper on the inhibitory nerves. He continued:

but from mere dulness, consequent on my being, I think, rather fagged at the close of the session, together with the fatigue of my lectures & hospital work, I have day after day failed in accomplishing it . . . if all be well, will get it down tonight or at latest tomorrow.

Almost his only relaxation was the walk he took after breakfast in Princes Street Gardens. According to William Turner, his friend and former fellow student at University College, he used the walk to prepare for writing. He 'mapped out in his mind the logical sequence . . . and even the composition of the more important sentences, before he sat down at his desk to write'. It was not always a terribly efficient method of composition for Lister, but he continued the morning walks throughout his active life.

On March 26 Agnes wrote to Mary Godlee about a new friend of Joseph's who had begun to attend his lectures. R Hamilton Ramsay was a nephew of Lord Belhaven, a prominent Glaswegian, and connected through Belhaven with the Duke of Hamilton. Ramsay was older than Lister, who was then thirty-two, but had not yet settled on a profession. It was at least in part due to Lister's influence that he became a doctor. The relationship that developed between the two men was stronger than a mere professional friendship. Lister's nephew, writing with a Victorian vocabulary, said that it was 'rather romantic', and Agnes referred to Ramsay as Joseph's 'bouquet friend'. Early in June Joseph went with Ramsay to Lord Belhaven's home at Wishaw and then to visit friends of Ramsay's near Glasgow. During his 24-hour journey Agnes stayed with her father at Millbank. Ramsay became an intimate friend of Lister's family. Isabella Lister sent him quince jam from the Upton produce. Mary Godlee sent him a poem written by a Godlee aunt. Arthur and Susan Lister went to 'lunch at Mr Ramsays to meet some people we knew nothing about'. That was in August 1866. Two years before, Ramsay had served as Lister's house surgeon in Glasgow, and then he had found a practice at Torquay. Joseph Jackson wrote to Joseph: 'I have only to wish him the success that I think he deserves—He is now staying with Arthur, called here after being at our meeting yesterday & seemed quite well . . . I think you will rather miss his society with its abounding friendship & devotedness . . . and I wish his place as assistant at thy operations may be filled to thy satisfaction'. It appears from Joseph Jackson's next letter that Joseph had sold shares to raise a loan to Ramsay, probably to help him buy the practice. Although Lister was often generous, this is the only occasion on which he is known to have gone to such lengths. Ramsay's connections may have proved useful during Lister's early years in Glasgow, but the loan indicates a response not only to Ramsay's need but also to his devotion. He appears to have been as intimate with Lister as Edward Palmer had been, but after Ramsay moved to Torquay, the relationship seems to have faded. No correspondence with Ramsay exists. Lister's family was once again drawn into the relationship, although the tone of Arthur's sniffy comment on 'people we know nothing about' raises an eyebrow. Perhaps Ramsay appeared to them to be a useful sycophant, and they understood his friendship with Joseph as poorly as we do.

On May 13, 1859, Joseph Jackson answered an enquiry from Joseph about becoming a Fellow of the Royal Society. He knew little about the procedure, he said, and suggested that Joseph ask Professor Sharpey. Joseph Jackson thought his son was too young to be elected, and without saying as much he warned Joseph against disappointment. What with delays coincident upon the application, Lister was not a candidate for election until the next year. In June 1860 there were 417 candidates to fill fifteen places, and Lister was elected.

The vote, despite his youth, was a tribute to the originality of his research, perhaps the most important of which had been presented in papers before the Royal Society. His interest in inflammation and coagulation of the blood continued, both because of their importance in surgery and characteristically because the experiments were immediately useful. According to Godlee, he always tried to give his students more than 'mere theories'. On the day that Joseph Jackson had answered his query about the Royal Society, Lister showed his class an experiment designed to elucidate nervous function. He chloroformed a rabbit and exposed its intestines. Although the intestine normally displays constant motion of its walls, those before the class did not because the chloroform had affected brain centres that controlled the muscles. Then Lister applied a galvanic current to the rabbit's spinal cord, and the intestinal muscles moved. He thus demonstrated a distinction between muscular contractility and the co-ordinating power of nerves.

Further experiments on coagulation were conducted with Mrs Lister's help during April and again in June, 1859. On one of the pages of laboratory notes, Lister wrote: 'Change of lymph into pus'. He had made the observation on a compound fracture patient at the Infirmary. Because the change reflected the process of bacterial infection, the observation was relevant more to suppuration than to coagulation, as Lister would be almost the first to realize.

The nerves rather than the blood were the subject of his next paper. As is often the case in science, the research arose from a newly-discovered technique, a carmine tissue stain that was first demonstrated by a London surgeon, Lockhardt Clarke, in Edinburgh. Lister suggested to William Turner that they jointly use the stain to study the nature of the white matter in the spinal cord. With the carmine it was possible to show that the nerves in the white matter were surrounded by protective sheaths, brown when stained but white in nature, and they proposed correctly that the sheaths act as insulators.

July brought Lister important news. James Adair Lawrie, Regius Professor of Surgery at Glasgow University, was very ill and would have to retire. Lister had two friends on the Glasgow faculty, Allen Thomson and William Gairdner, the Professor of Medicine. Thomson told Syme that the question of Lawrie's successor was being actively canvassed within the faculty. On August 1 Lister wrote to his father. He thought that he would apply for the post. Although he would regret leaving Edinburgh and Mr Syme, he said, the advantages of the Chair were significant. 'In the first place it would give me at once a clear emolument of £400 to £450 per annum. Secondly, it would in all probability lead rapidly to extensive private practice . . . Thirdly, I should in all probability be very soon appointed one of the Surgeons to the Infirmary, through the influence of the Medical Faculty of the University (so says Dr Thomson in a letter to myself). And lastly, the having held that appointment would give me, it appears, an almost certain claim to any Surgical Professorship here that might fall vacant, supposing that I felt disposed to leave Glasgow at all. And again, if any really desirable appointment should offer itself in London, my chance of success would be much greater than if I were a candidate in my present position'. After some further words indicating his preference for London, 'my natural place', he concluded:

Please write as soon as thee conveniently can & tell me what thee think of the matter: for Mr Syme and Dr Christison being both in London could exercise influence with the authorities there, if I gave them carte blanche to do so: but this I, of course, have not done without communicating with thee.

Lawrie's Chair was a Regius Professorship, and therefore, within the gift of the Government, and more particularly, the Home Secretary. Syme and Dr Christison were members of the General Medical Council, newly established by the law of 1858 to coordinate and direct medical services in Great Britain, and were ready to use the opportunity afforded by the Council meeting in London to advance Lister's case from an official platform. There were seven applicants, two from Edinburgh and the others from Glasgow. The political element in the selection became clear when Glasgow's two MPs circularized the city's medical profession early in January, asking which candidate each doctor preferred, adding: 'we shall decide . . . which of the candidates we shall recommend to Sir George Lewis', the Home Secretary. The doctors were outraged, and even the *Glasgow Herald* observed that this 'may be a very easy way of solving a difficulty; but it is a queer way of appointing a Professor of Surgery'. The University's Academic Senate protested strongly.

3. Joseph Jackson Lister. Self-portrait, about 1835.

4. *The legend in pencil below the silhouette was written by Lister's father who made the silhouette. It reads: "Joseph L 2.11.1830 aged 2y. 10m. 16d.".*

Sharpey, Erichsen, Syme and Richard Owen again wrote letters for Lister. They were joined by Kölliker, Professors Christison and Goodsir of Edinburgh and Paget from London, and by four of Lister's contemporaries. William Turner and William Baly had been his friends at University College and now worked in Edinburgh and London, respectively. Joseph Bell, a member of an Edinburgh family long established in medicine, had attended Lister's summer course and praised 'the teacher's thoughtfulness . . . and his enthusiasm'. Frederick Gourlay, a military surgeon, had attended the winter course and also wrote of Lister's 'untiring zeal and enthusiasm' as a teacher. No doubt his competitors presented their printed testimonials containing similar praise, but Lister's support carried much weight. He himself believed that the politicking MPs had helped him, though he did not explain how.

The official notification of his appointment reached him from Lewis's Private Secretary on January 28, 1860. With understandable excitement, he wrote to his father the next day: 'It made us almost intoxicated with gladness, doubled or trebled, I doubt not, by the long period of suspense which had preceded it. Indeed I never remember having experienced before such great and unmixed satisfaction at any intelligence.'

Experiments had begun again on December 22 with the heading in Mrs Lister's hand: 'Coagulation. (Ammonia Theory false)'. Lister had indeed just published a 'Notice of further Researches on the Coagulation of the Blood' in which he had said: 'Speaking generally . . . the theory which attributes the coagulation of the blood to the escape of ammonia is fallacious'. No doubt it was in response to this article that Lister received a friendly letter from Dr Richardson, the originator of the ammonia theory, criticizing aspects of Lister's technique. In a long reply written on December 17 Lister described an experiment which in his view obviated Richardson's objection. He had shown that cold, though it might delay the formation of fibrin, did not halt the release of ammonia from the blood. Notes of the work on coagulation continued intensively during January and sporadically until May.

The research notes for December indicate that Agnes and Joseph remained in Edinburgh for Christmas 1859. It was the second year that they had not spent the holiday at Upton. In part the decision may have been taken because of the Glasgow contest, but it may also have seemed sensible not to make the trip again. They had gone to Upton in October. William Henry had died at sea, and Agnes and Joseph had attended the memorial meeting for him at Plaistow.

6

PROFESSOR LISTER

AFTER THE INTENSE ACTIVITY of the preceding three years, it is astonishing to discover that from 1860–1867 Lister published only four papers. Two of these were chapters in a textbook, *A System of Surgery*, edited by Timothy Holmes and required little original research. Yet the early Glasgow years were the most productive of his life. He began them as a relatively unknown surgeon entering upon his first teaching position as a member of a university faculty. He returned to Edinburgh nine years later as a controversial, if not yet a famous man.

Lister was fortunately able to rent a suitable house, a great problem in Glasgow. It was one of a splendid terrace of late Georgian houses, 17 Woodside Place, then on the western edge of the city. In 1860 the university was still situated almost a mile to the east in the centre of the old city near the Royal Infirmary and the Cathedral. It was surrounded by slums as filthy and corrupt as any in Europe.

The population of Glasgow had more than doubled in the first twenty years of the century. In 1850 it passed that of Edinburgh. A decade later almost 400,000 people crowded into the small, gloomy city. Their prosperity grew out of the American trade, and was subject to the vagaries of the market for tobacco, sugar, molasses and cotton.

Founded in 1843 the University had established a strong reputation in the sciences. Among Lister's faculty colleagues was Sir William Thomson, Professor of Physics, later Lord Kelvin. In the medical faculty he joined his friends Allen Thomson and Dr Gairdner. There were 311 students registered in the Medical School in 1860, about 100 more than at Edinburgh, but Glasgow lacked the extra-mural facilities available in the Scottish capital. From 1861 the University offered a four-year course for a degree of Bachelor of Medicine. Students customarily enrolled in a course by paying their three-guinea fee to the professor. The historian of the University estimated that the Professor of Surgery could have expected an income of about £320 per year from all sources, a good £80 less than the figure Lister had given his father.

He took upon himself the cost of renovating the lecture theatre assigned to the Professor of Surgery. It included a retiring room adjoining the theatre, where Lister kept models, preparations and drawings. New seating was installed, and the two rooms were completely redecorated, with Mrs Lister's advice. At the time of his inaugural lecture in May she wrote to Isabella Lister:

How nice it looks. All so clean and fresh and bright—the green baize on the three doors and the diagram-frame setting off the oak colouring, and the bright little brass handles on the doors setting them off; and the very handsome slate on a frame on one side and the skeleton nicely mounted on the other. Some plates are hung on a diagram frame and some preparations are on the nice oak-table . . .

The 'civilizing effect' of this housewifery on the students was evidently remarkable. 'It is recorded that all took their hats off, which was unusual . . . They did not even scratch their new desks,' wrote Hector C Cameron, one of them, though not in this first class.

Formal induction to the Glasgow University faculty, or more precisely, to membership of the Senatus Academicus, required the performance of a ritual about which Lister 'learned to his consternation', Cameron wrote. A Latin oration was required of the candidate. On this occasion, surprise added to the usual procrastination meant that he finished the speech, dictionary in hand, on the train journey from Edinburgh to attend the Senate meeting on March 9, 1860. No record of the oration remains except its title: *De Arte Chirurgica Recte Erudienda*. He then signed an obligation not to act contrary to the interests of the Church of Scotland, and returned to Edinburgh by the 5 p.m. train.

In the eight weeks remaining before their removal to Glasgow Lister wound up his hospital duties, completed his winter lecture course and conducted new experiments relating to coagulation. With Mrs Lister's help he examined blood remaining in the vessels of amputated sheep's feet. The last work in Edinburgh recorded in the research notes was dated May 1 and required the body of a house mouse.

Toward the end of April Joseph went to Upton for a brief visit, returning to a climactic week before his departure for Glasgow. His students congratulated him on his new position and presented a silver flagon in appreciation of his efforts on their behalf. Some of them also attended a noisy and convivial dinner given by his professional associates. Lister thanked them in his first non-professional speech. It delineates the bland public persona that he had already adopted. He expressed his appreciation to 'the medical practitioners of Edinburgh' for so honouring him. 'I feel too that the appointment on which you have so kindly met to congratulate me, however undeserved on my part, is an honourable one and just such as might have been most the object of my ambition, as opening up to me a wider path in that profession which I dearly love.' He regretted leaving Edinburgh because of her beauty, wit and generosity, and also because of the freedom to work and teach which he had enjoyed. He had friends there, and 'I may perhaps be pardoned for making a passing allusion to the domestic ties which bind me to your city, more especially as one of them has been a source of inestimable advantage to me professionally: I need hardly say I allude to the illustrious Professor of Clinical Surgery.' A Latin tag concerning the search for truth led him into a brief peroration on the importance of professional honesty, and he concluded by repeating his thanks. Yet despite his own formality the occasion had drawn from Lister a description sufficiently vivid to produce this response from Joseph Jackson: 'We are amused at such a learned (&, as we are ready to imagine, grave) company of the faculty recreating themselves with songs at the close'.

Joseph and Agnes settled at 17 Woodside Place early in May, and he began his professional career in Glasgow with a summer lecture course. Cameron said that his first lecture was attentively received. 'They laughed, too, in the right places and when Lister, indulging for once in a form of humour which was for him unusual, described the stumps after an amputation as so good that their owner might have been able to dance the Highland fling upon them, they abandoned themselves, wholeheartedly, to mirth and laughter'. Opinions about Lister's lecture style differ. Another house surgeon, John Rudd Leeson, later said, 'there was never a witticism or light moment'. R J Godlee, on the other hand, wrote that the lectures he heard in Edinburgh at the same time used 'deliberate and clear language, without show or ornament, but rendered piquant by a very slight stammer and an occasional flash of quiet humour'. In 1894 during a non-academic speech to medical students at Glasgow, on the one occasion when a stenographer made notes of the audience reaction, there was laughter eight times and applause eighteen, not including the applause when he finished. As to the content of the lectures he did not stress the particular condition or the details of diagnosis, although he naturally described these clinical aspects of the case. He sought in each case, 'Some fundamental lesson'. This is evident in his notes for his Glasgow lectures on the Principles and Practice of Surgery. They were made on the backs of 4-inch by 1-inch cards of admission to his class and contain headings which are necessarily generalizations not dissimilar from those of his Edinburgh course. Even in the clinical lectures, with the patient in the theatre before the students, Lister tried to teach from the particular to the general. The one great exception, after he had introduced the antiseptic system, was the dressing of wounds, every detail of which was important. But even these details acquired meaning from the germ theory of wound infection.

In 1871 his subject for a clinical lecture was a woman with a large leg ulcer. 'He touches granulating surface of sore and cuts but with scissors, making it bleed, but patient not inconvenienced,' a student noted. 'Thus showing granulations lack sensory nerve ends, but still give protection.' James Alexander Russell, who became Lord Provost of Edinburgh, wrote that in 1870 he had gone to hear Lister lecture 'and was so entranced that I used my lunch hour for some three sessions in attending his lectures and going round his wards with him . . . although I had no intention of becoming a surgeon. To hear him thinking aloud, hunting for fallacies in an experiment was a pure delight.' Yet the French surgeon Lucas-Championnière, one of Lister's first and staunchest defenders, maintained with others like Leeson that he was not a good speaker. All agreed that his voice was light and pleasant, some said musical, and he spoke slowly to avoid the lurking stammer. No doubt reactions varied, in part according to the auditor's expectations.

In August Joseph Jackson and Isabella made the journey to Glasgow in a ' "saloon" carriage of the Gt Northern Railway.' Isabella found the journey very fatiguing but recovered quickly in Joseph's 'excellent house at the West End, airy, with a space of lawn & trees in front', wrote Joseph Jackson to his nephew Edward Beck.

In the same letter Joseph Jackson reported Joseph's advice to Beck's son, Marcus, who wished to become a surgeon. He could not expect to live on surgery alone, but if he wanted to live by his profession, he should prepare for General Practice. In the event Marcus Beck became a student in Glasgow University at the age of seventeen and lived with the Listers from the autumn of 1860 until he was graduated in 1863.

While Joseph's parents were visiting Glasgow, an incident occurred that provides a rare insight into his non-professional family life. Amongst Lister's books there is one by Mrs Ellen H Raynard entitled *The Missing Link*. In language that touches the outer limits of Victorian propriety the book describes evangelical work by Bible Society women in the London slums. The book is inscribed: 'Agnes Lister with JL's dear love' and dated September 10, 1860. There were other books of an evangelical nature belonging to Agnes, but this gift may have reflected her dismay at the raw poverty that was so much more evident in commercial Glasgow than in the Parnassian city of her birth. At about the same time Lister borrowed a volume of Melville's sermons for 1856 from the University Library. The next year Agnes herself borrowed the 1857 volume, along with a book of poetry by Elizabeth Barrett!

Marcus Beck wrote to his mother in February 1861 that he was to attend a faculty conversazione with the Listers. On these occasions the guests walk about and talk while various professors exhibit aspects of their work. Lister was going to show the circulation in a frog's web under certain irritants. Mrs Lister was to attend as well, but when Lister applied for a ticket for Marcus, it was refused because of crowding. Beck said that Uncle Joseph proposed to 'take me just the same as one of his family . . . It will be a very swell concern and almost all the best people of Glasgow will be there'. It was uncharacteristic for Lister thus to disregard social rules, but he had an obligation to his young cousin which took precedence.

Beck evidently enjoyed the company of the Professor. 'After lunch . . . he and I went a walk instead of going to church. We walked by the canal to the west of Glasgow' and 'came across a heap of some sulphuret of iron for burning to make sulphuric acid I suppose and in it we found some most beautiful crystals of quartz and what we supposed to be native iron. We brought home some specimens'.

With the warm weather Agnes and Joseph, accompanied by Lucy Syme, Dr Ramsay and Marcus went on an excursion to Loch Lomond. Marcus described the occasion:

We started about 4 o'clock & reached Ballock at the end of Loch Lomond at 5. There we embarked & steamed about 70 miles up the lake to a place called Tarbet . . . When we reached Tarbet which is situated exactly opposite Ben Lomond we set out for a walk but were driven in by rain & had dinner & tea and went to bed. Next morning however it was very fine & as the day went on it became dreadfully hot . . . After breakfast we went to the Free church & then came back & got some sandwiches & rowed across the lake & leaving the ladies below . . . the professor Mr Ramsay & I began to ascend the mountain. A very little way up we came to a cottage where we got milk to drink & a stick each & left our waistcoats behind & then started again much invigorated . . . It was rather stiff work part of the time but the view was most glorious. We took it very easy & botanized & found some rare specimens . . .

The rest of the letter has been lost, but the image of the three men, one eighteen and the other two about thirty-four, finally abandoning their waistcoats during a hot climb up Ben Lomond provides a key to the style of Lister's recreations.

Meanwhile Lister's winter lecture course had begun in November 1860. Lister said that it was attended by 'the 4th year's men . . . as well as those of the 2nd and 3rd'. It had been 'an unusually large' class. Indeed 182 students registered, and it was said to have been the largest class in general surgery in Britain at the time. He presented his lectures, including the large drawings and the preparations illustrating his subjects, without an assistant, until some years later, when Hector Cameron performed the duties of arranging the exhibits during the summer course. So successful was the first winter class that when it was over, the students 'adopted the very unusual course', wrote Cameron, of voting an address of appreciation which ended with the hope that he would be appointed Surgeon to the Glasgow Royal Infirmary. The address was presented by J B Russell who became the first full-time Medical Officer of Health in Glasgow. The students also made him Honourary President of their Medical Society.

Lister's application for a post at the Infirmary had been rejected in 1860, before the beginning of his winter lecture course. Lister was very much annoyed. He had been advised by Professor Thomson that election would be all but automatic. That the Infirmary Board of Directors held quite a different view of the relationship between their hospital and the University became clear to Lister during the canvass of the Directors which the application required. The chairman of the Board at the time was David Smith, a boot-and-shoemaker. Lister explained to him that as Professor of Surgery in the University he wished to be able to illustrate his theoretical statements in the hospital wards. ' "Stop, stop, Mr Lister," said Mr Smith,' according to Cameron; ' "that's a real Edinburgh idea. But our institution is a curative one. It is not an educational one".' Mr Smith's opinion was idiosyncratic, especially when there was only one hospital in a University town, but it was neither unique nor totally indefensible.

Under the charter granted to the institution by George III there were twenty-five directors. They were the Professors of Anatomy (Dr Thomson) and Medicine (Dr Gairdner)—which established a connection between hospital and University of course—the Member of Parliament for the constituency, the Lord Provost of Glasgow, two religious officials, the President of the Faculty of Physicians and Surgeons (the Glasgow medical society), eight representatives of public bodies and ten who were elected by the contributors and subscribers. The Board had no official chairman, that function being performed by the Convener of the House Committee. In 1860 Mr Smith had the support of a majority against Lister's appointment, and they may also have approved his opinion of the Infirmary's role.

The Glasgow institution was the newest of the six Scottish Royal Infirmaries, Edinburgh's being the oldest. Like the English and Welsh hospitals established by private persons under royal charter, or by the authority of a public body such as Parliament, they were voluntary general hospitals. Many of them refused to admit pregnancies unless the woman came for some other reason, such as a fracture. The mad and those with smallpox, venereal disease, 'itch, or other Infectious Distemper' were usually confined to special hospitals. Nor would the voluntary institutions accept incurables or the dying. They were established for the treatment of a relatively small proportion of the general population, those who were too poor to afford private medical treatment at home or in the home of a doctor. Neither could these patients be servants, for then their masters were responsible for them, nor could they be paupers. Paupers were defined as such by the Poor Law Commissioners, and under the Act of 1837 they went to workhouses where they were also cared for, in a manner of speaking, when they fell ill. Admission for those who did qualify for the voluntary hospitals was free or nearly so. In Edinburgh those who could afford it paid 6d a day. Soldiers paid 4d if they were on duty, and their subsistence was met by the superior officers. The method of admission varied. In England the prospective patient had to be recommended by a subscriber to the local hospital. In Scotland in addition to the subscribers, the Clergy and the Hospital Managers might also recommend for admission. Staff members admitted their own patients when they thought it desirable to do so, and emergencies were treated without exception.

In England and Wales in 1861 there were 11,848 beds in voluntary hospitals of which 3662 were in the nine large London hospitals. Inasmuch as the population was about twenty million, the voluntary hospitals provided less than one bed per 1000 of population. Their purpose, in short, *was* curative, as Mr Smith had said, and then for a very clearly defined minority.

Yet though he spoke within the letter of the Royal Charter, the sheer momentum of medical growth to meet the demands of an urbanizing, industrializing society had long since made the position academic, not to say obstructive. Even before the end of the private medical schools in the 1840s all of the great London hospitals had opened their wards to their students or those of their staff who were also members of medical faculties. In no other way could they have continued to obtain the services of eminent men such as Astley Cooper or James Paget. They paid no salaries, or virtually none, and neither the prestige of hospital staff positions nor the opportunity they afforded to become physician or surgeon to members of the governing boards and their friends could provide an adequate income. Lister never received a salary, neither from the hospitals nor from the universities where he taught, nor did any of his colleagues. Middlesex Hospital, founded in 1745, was the first to have a medical school as one of its departments, and Charing Cross, founded in 1821, was the first 'teaching hospital'. Forty years later there were twenty-three voluntary teaching hospitals in England and Wales and 130 voluntary general hospitals.

Despite the restrictions they imposed on admissions, the voluntary hospitals provided wonderful educational material, especially in the cities. Newly-compacted masses of filthy, half-starving workers, often sleepless from the noise or the vermin that surrounded them, seldom washed, often disabled by drink, provided a breeding ground for infectious disease. Cholera had struck Glasgow most recently in 1848. Plague, smallpox, the venereal diseases and the less dramatic but far more universal scourge, tuberculosis, affected an unknown but growing number. Other infectious diseases such as malaria and typhoid fever were less clearly identified, but the 'febrile contagions' were well recognized although their causes remained a mystery. In addition to the fevers there were the unrecognized effects of the fevers, the sores and madness of syphilis, the ricketty bones due to tuberculosis or vitamin D deficiency or both, the abscesses, the varicose veins and the growths, benign and malignant, that made up a large part of Lister's work. The rarity of statistics is in part a side effect of the confusion in classification of diseases. As late as 1859 each hospital had its own list of afflictions. One of Florence Nightingale's earliest campaigns, with the help of Paget and Sir James Clark, sought to standardize the names given to symptoms and collections of symptoms. But one of the most rapidly growing categories of hospital admissions was accident cases. In the large cities such as Glasgow most of the patients worked in the docks, warehouses and factories twelve or more hours a day. Factory legislation requiring guards on machinery was not passed until 1844 and then only for textile mills. As industrialization advanced, accidents increased, both on the shop floor and from the machinery of transport. A heavy dray could do as much damage to a drunken man's leg as could the wheel of a steam locomotive. Compound fracture cases provided Lister with his first tests of antiseptic treatment.

To most of the hospital practitioners of the day their hospital patients held a position in the scale of creation analogous to that of the central American Indians caught by the Spanish conquest: they were not animals because they had souls, but being savages they could not expect salvation. The doctors and surgeons were Christian gentlemen in the Dickensian sense, and they would certainly not have described the 'deserving poor' in this way, but they tended to treat them as lingual and therefore much more useful, experimental animals.

Only the great reformers managed to rise above the general level of conduct displayed by their peers toward their socially inferior patients. Nightingale and Lister, who seem never to have met, made over the hospitals of the world, the former from the administrative and the latter from the medical standpoints. They acted from professional rather than social motives; they meant to improve the service they each were professionally competent to provide. In no sense did they mean to alter the relationships between the classes, nor did any revolutionary fervour to elevate the downtrodden drive them. It would be more in accord with their self-images though not an accurate description of their motives, to say that their reforms were intended to return the workman to his lathe, to maintain what Karl Marx had called a few years before 'the reserve army of labour'.

In a paper on radical wrist surgery published in 1865, Lister said of a fourteen-year-old sewing machine worker:

Constant attention being subsequently paid to supporting the wrist and bending the fingers, she progressed steadily, though slowly. Thus seven weeks after the operation, the hand no longer drooped when the arm was extended horizontally . . . About this time, as she had never learned to write, the nurse of the ward taught her the art, which, being a clever girl, she soon learned; and half a year afterwards I received from her a letter, well-written with the affected hand, requesting a certificate of soundness for the satisfaction of her old employer, who was about to re-engage her. In August 1864 I saw her again. She was then employed at the sewing machine, earning 10s a week, with the expectation of 11s before long, as she was considered one of the best hands at the work . . . Lastly, in December 1864, I learned that the hand was still constantly increasing in strength, and that she was on her full wages.

Nightingale referred to the soldiers at Scutari as her children. Lister also looked upon his patients, and not just the minors who made up so large a minority amongst them, as difficult children. Another case in the paper on wrist surgery was that of a forty-year-old Glasgow millworker, Elizabeth M'K:

Seven weeks after the operation the limb was almost healed and promised a most satisfactory result, when, being an ignorant woman, and mistaking our efforts to maintain the flexibility of the fingers for attempts to break them she ran away from the hospital, and did not show herself again for nearly five months, during which time she had kept the fingers extended and motionless upon the splint she took out with her.

A few years later a young man who refused to leave his dressing alone, a very serious offence after the introduction of antiseptic methods, 'was discharged for misconduct'. The King's College Hospital ward journal for 1884 records the case of a sixteen-year-old boy recovering well from an operation to reduce varicose veins in his scrotum who was 'Discharged for using obscene language'. As to patients who remained in hospital for a long time Lister once remarked: 'Who knows, it may be that whilst here they may have a chance of learning something of the meaning of the word Gratitude'. He was quoted by one of his house surgeons who went on to say: 'It is really remarkable how seldom a hospital patient expresses gratitude; I think the poor are fatalists and take things as a matter of course'.

According to the standards of his day Lister's attitudes and behaviour toward his patients was exemplary. His duty was to cure them if possible, and to ease their pain if it was not. Their duty was to do as they were told. In London he operated on the fractured knee of a sixty-two-year-old man about whose later condition he wanted information. He wrote to a Birmingham surgeon who located Lister's former patient and arranged for him to go to London where Lister wished to display the man before his clinical class. The former patient's expenses were to be paid, but the Birmingham colleague described his condition, 'In case he should not keep his appointment'. To his audience Lister concluded the account by saying: 'Happily our patient has kept his appointment, so that we are able to see him today'. In fact patients could not be brought before the clinical class without their consent, nor could the surgeon operate without the patient's agreement, assuming the patient was competent in the surgeon's opinion to make a decision.

Leeson described another incident:

One day the instrument clerk so far forgot himself that he brought the instrument tray into the theatre—uncovered!

Lister . . . instantly threw a towel over the tray, and . . . said in slow, sorrowful tones: 'How can you have such cruel disregard for this poor woman's feelings? Is it not enough for her to be passing through this ordeal without adding unnecessarily to her sufferings by displaying this array of naked steel? Really, Mr—I am surprised at you.'

There is no corroboration of the house surgeon's recollection, but surely if Lister had been as concerned for the patient as he was for the proper conduct of his junior, he would have withheld the censure until the patient had been anaesthetized.

During his lectures in 1864 Lister told the students that 'grand words' such as anorexia (loss of appetite) might usefully be employed 'to prevent the patient knowing what you mean besides which, they are somewhat shorter'. 'Every patient, even the most degraded, should be treated with the same care and regard as though he were the Prince of Wales himself', he said with a fine display of his ambivalence toward them. By 'most degraded' he undoubtedly meant venereal cases. He never referred to patients as 'the case' in their presence but as 'this good woman' or 'this good man'. He applied the Golden Rule: 'Put yourself in the patient's place. What would you wish to have done were you in his case?'

He always accompanied serious operative cases back to the ward and assisted their transfer from stretcher to bed, 'himself taking the head', wrote Leeson. He would arrange sandbags and hot water bottles 'accompanied by invariable warnings of the necessity of their being covered by flannel, and how patients recovering from anaesthesia had been burnt if this were omitted. Finally, with almost womanly care he would replace the bedclothes'. During his ward rounds Lister usually did his own dressings, at least in all doubtful cases. According to another doctor he would never leave the patient without asking, 'Now, are you quite comfortable?' and he would end by adjusting the pillows. These people, temporarily in his charge, were to be cosseted and cared for. Most of them accepted their status willingly. One man said to Leeson: 'When the Professor enters the wards I feel as though God Almighty Himself had come in'.

Lister was elected Surgeon to the Glasgow Royal Infirmary on August 5, 1861, after what his nephew characterized as a 'troublesome canvas'. His relations with the hospital Managers were never cordial, but they were not much better with the Managers of the Edinburgh Infirmary after he returned there.

Originally a hospital with 136 beds, the Glasgow Infirmary had gradually enlarged until, in 1861, a new Surgical Hospital was opened as part of the U-shaped complex of buildings, adding 144 beds for a total of 572. Of these about 160, in separate wards, were reserved for fever patients, those, in the main, with infectious diseases. The Infirmary had now almost as many beds as St Bartholomew's, the largest in London. The number of operations performed, including amputations, rose over the decade from 294 in 1862 to 350 in 1869.

At the time of his appointment Lister's term was limited to two consecutive five-year periods. From the managerial standpoint the arrangement may have been useful in maintaining standards, but it denied the appointee a sense of security. At Edinburgh such appointments were permanent. However, Lister and his friend William Gairdner, the Professor of Medicine, were the first two Glasgow Infirmary staff members to benefit from a change in the rules making their appointment good until retirement age, usually sixty-five.

Lister was one of four surgeons. Each had three large wards, a female ward and two for men, one for accidents and major operations and the other for chronic conditions. In addition each had a small ward for special cases. Lister's chronic male ward was in the old Infirmary, but the female ward and the male accident ward were in the new Surgical Hospital. This building consisted of four stories and a basement with two large wards on either side of a central staircase. The wards were 'spacious and lofty, and in the centre of each are two open fireplaces, in a column which runs straight up to the roof,' Lister wrote. The windows were regularly spaced with the beds placed between them. WCs opened off the wards. Ward 24, Lister's male accident ward, was on the ground floor to the left of the entrance as one faced the building. The female ward, number 25, was one flight up in the opposite wing.

In the interval between his appointment and the beginning of the winter term, Lister went to Upton. The trip was delayed by a case, probably at the Infirmary. 'The delay,' Joseph wrote to his father on September 22,

seems to have had good results so far as my work is concerned. For I yesterday made some observations which seem of much importance with reference to the administration of chloroform; which observations I should probably not have been able to make had I been at Upton . . .

The observations were made by means of an instrument recently invented, by which the vocal cords of the larynx (the vocal apparatus) can be inspected with great ease considering their apparently inaccesible position.

The laryngoscope was one of the new diagnostic tools that made it possible to look at previously hidden places in the body. His observations on chloroform were undertaken in connection with the chapter 'On Anaesthesia' that he was writing for Holmes's surgical textbook.

Chloroform was always the anaesthetic Lister preferred, but in 1848, soon after his breakdown, his sister, Isabella Sophie, wrote to him about her experience having a tooth pulled under chloroform. She had been staying in London with the Godlees and went to a dentist named Mr Robinson on Gower Street. Joseph must have replied that she had been risking her life because Isabella Sophie wrote again that she had learned from Arthur about another patient of the same Mr Robinson who had died under chloroform. However this exchange occurred before Lister had had surgical experience and very soon after the introduction of chloroform by Simpson. Six years later Lister reported that he had used chloroform without complications in three cases requiring the removal of tumours of the jaw. In the paper 'On the Early Stages of Inflammation' he classed chloroform with alcohol and opium as 'specific irritants—of the nervous centres'. In a footnote to the chapter for Holmes he set down the reasons why he preferred chloroform to other anaesthetics: it was not inflammable like ether, and therefore it was safer when artificial light was necessary. It protected the heart and blood vessels against the shock of surgery, and it gave the patient 'mental tranquility'. The last two benefits derive equally from any anaesthetic, but Lister always maintained that chloroform was the safest.

Revisions of the chapter appeared in the 1871 and the 1883 editions of the book. There had been no deaths from the use of chloroform in either the Edinburgh or the Glasgow Royal Infirmaries between 1861 and 1870, Lister wrote for the first revision. He stressed that the patient's safety was best secured if his breathing was carefully and continuously observed. The pulse could be safely ignored because the first embarrassment under chloroform was always audible in stertorous breathing. From 1855, when he first recommended its use in the report of an operation by Syme, until the 1880s, Lister preferred to administer chloroform with 'a simple folded handker-chief' as a mask. The simpler the better, he maintained and entrusted the task to an assistant who was told to pour it on a towel, 'no matter how much', admitting plenty of air and watching the breathing. During an operation in 1874 according to the house surgeon then assisting Lister, 'respiration stopped for a few seconds and Lister at once showed his anxiety,' the patient's tongue was pulled forward out of his throat and soon all was well. Lister's serenity returned: 'A false alarm, gentlemen; better a thousand false alarms than one death'. In 1870 he wrote that he felt apprehension about the use of chloroform only with the aged and infirm.

Some modification in his attitudes and practices took place between the second and third editions of Holmes's book. In 1870 he had recommended nitrous oxide for tooth extraction and some short operations, and ether when it was essential to avoid vomiting, as after abdominal surgery. The ward journals frequently refer to post-anaesthetic vomiting, however, and in the 1883 revision he prescribed no solids and recommended tea or beef tea about two hours before the operation 'to stay the storm'.

In 1873 William Watson Cheyne wrote in his notes of Lister's lectures: 'No deaths this session from chloroform. This winter there has been a great outcry against chloroform and it has been said to be criminal for medical men to use it and sulphuric ether has been coming into fashion instead'. Their experience in Edinburgh suggested to Cheyne that chloroform 'can't be so deadly as the English papers say'. The British Medical Association had set up a committee to look into the problem, but it did not report until 1880. Based on animal experiments a synthetic gas, ethidine dichloride, was recom-mended for clinical trial by the committee, but it proved to be more dangerous than chloroform. Ether was found to be the safer.

Lister then tried further tests. His first moves were clinical. During April and May 1882 he performed several operations under ether. Satisfied apparently that he had given this gas a fair trial, he reverted to chloroform on May 19, and on the 24th tried a new inhaler which seemed to work well.

In July the tests moved into the laboratory in his London house. A few months before, a French surgeon, Paul Bert, had published experiments designed to establish the dose-response curve of chloroform, the amount that was required to anaesthetize the patient, and the amount that would depress respiration fatally. Bert's experiments had been conducted on mice. Lister was convinced that smaller proportions of chloroform to air than Bert had used were safer but still effective. His first tests were conducted on chaffinches, but when he returned to the subject in November, humans took their place. The guinea pigs were Lister and his wife. They dampened pads of gauze with measured amounts of chloroform and observed the effect when the pad was held at different distances from their faces for different periods of time.

The 1883 revision continued to recommend chloroform with the customary precaution of watching carefully the patient's breathing. 'There can, however, be no doubt that any agent capable of producing anaesthesia must, if continued in operation for a considerable time, exercise a lowering effect upon the whole vital powers.'

The other chapter by Lister in Holmes's textbook was 'On Amputation'. It was more technical than the chapter on anaesthetics, dealing, for example, with methods for undercutting the flesh and skin so that suitable flaps remained to cover the stump. Between 1858 and his move to Glasgow he had evolved one such technique for the difficult amputation through the joint at the hip, and this was described. It was the first of several contributions Lister made. The chapter also described the silver-wire suture needle that he devised in 1859 and another original implement, an aortic tourniquet. This was a screw device that could temporarily halt the flow of blood through the major arteries. The tough muscular walls of these vessels defied temporary closure and more permanent ligatures were impossible: either they damaged the walls or, if they were left in place too long, the patient died. Yet it was sometimes necessary to bypass swellings called aneurisms that occurred in arteries because of pressure against a point in the wall weakened by disease. Lister first used his tourniquet during an operation performed by Mr Syme at the Edinburgh Royal Infirmary. The date was probably June 13, 1860, after Lister had moved to Glasgow but before he had a surgical post. In December 1862, notes in Mrs Lister's hand record three amputations at the thigh in which the tourniquet had been successfully used. In February 1864 and again in January 1866 Lister took a series of more than one hundred sets of measurements from patients, and from cadavers, to determine the relative distance between the aorta, the midline, the vertebrae and the umbilicus. His purpose seems to have been to improve the tourniquet by standardizing its dimensions. The notes on one adult male cadaver, incidentally, state categorically: 'No umbilicus'! The chapter on amputation was also revised twice, but the nine years between the first and second edition saw one absolutely basic change in operative procedure, the introduction of antiseptic methods, and the 1871 revision bore little resemblance to the 1862 chapter.

The Listers went to Upton in August 1862, in the interval between the summer and autumn terms. There was a major international exhibition in London. In June Joseph Jackson had gone to see it with Mary Godlee, Thomas and Isabella Pim and Jane Harrison. With Joseph and Agnes, Mary Godlee and Joseph Jackson went to see the Loan Exhibition at the South Kensington Museum of Science. The next Sunday Jane took Joseph and Agnes to the exhibition, and they went again with Jane and her husband a few days later.

In mid-September Joseph Jackson and Isabella returned to Glasgow from Upton with Joseph and 'Aggie'. Mary Godlee was astonished, presumably because Isabella's health was delicate. They reserved the 'invalid carriage' for her, and on the 17th Mary wrote to her husband: 'Mamma seemed at first rather overdone with her journey but she reports herself as better today and Aggie and she had been out for a drive while Papa and Joseph took a long walk'. Mary also reported that Joseph had gone 'every day to see poor Dr Ramsay' who was suffering from boils and an eye affliction. Shortly afterwards Ramsay's uncle, Lord Belhaven, called and asked the senior Listers to visit him at Wishaw. His call 'did Mamma good like a medicine'. The Belhavens were engaged just then, but in view of the fact that Joseph Jackson and Isabella were to leave shortly, the Belhavens insisted that they spend the day at Wishaw despite the absence of their host and hostess. All four Listers accepted the invitation and 'saw the gardens and vinaries', according to Mary Godlee,

& Mamma had the hand chair & saw the glen & the lovely views & then a lunch of roast mutton & grouse, wine, iced water & tea and coffee after it the drawing room shutters opened & they drove back to the station in her Ladyship's carriage.

Isabella and Joseph Jackson stayed until the end of September, when Arthur and Susan joined Joseph and Agnes for a two-week tour of the Highlands. The four younger Listers then travelled together to Ireland to visit the Pims.

Syme also came to Glasgow to see the launching of the *Black Prince*, the second British ironclad warship, with Agnes and Joseph. They, in turn, went to Millbank occasionally for weekends.

Lister began his lectures in November with a discourse on fees. Surgery, he said, is not a lucrative profession. 'You cannot charge for your services as a merchant does for his goods.' He objected to sending bills, and held that a fee is 'an honorarium and that it should be left to the patient's good feeling'. No criterion for a scale of charges suggested itself. 'Shall we charge for the blood which is drawn, or for the pain which we cause?' He thought the number of visits no better as a standard because the more successful the operation, the fewer the visits required. The principal reward for a surgeon, Lister maintained now, as he had when he entered the profession, was the feeling that 'he had performed an act of beneficence'. The austerity of this message may have been bolstered by his own comfortable circumstances, but it was not without influence amongst his less fortunate colleagues.

Whether because of these opening words or because of his inadequacies as a lecturer the size of the class fell. Only about a hundred students registered. However, he had taken on new duties as the secretary to the medical faculty. He wrote letters, 4 or 5 at once that are compulsory', he told his father, '& of late especially I have been occupied with about the hardest work that falls to my lot, the examining of candidates for degrees'. With the hospital and 'pretty frequent calls from private practice', he had little time for leisure.

His research continued too. In mid-March Lister dissected a knee joint. He prepared drawings with notes that defined the functions of the ligaments in accordance with their structural characteristics, a kind of descriptive analysis called morphology. He wrote, for example, 'Rotation outward is limited by the posterior crucial ligament the external rotation is checked by the internal crucial'. Anatomical study of this precision often related directly to a forthcoming operation.

He had also returned to experiments on coagulation, and he struggled to find time to prepare the Croonian lecture on the subject which he had been asked to give before the Royal Society. The research on wild rabbits, a calf, a large dead cow and an ox was conducted in his home in the customary way, with the assistance of Marcus Beck and Mrs Lister.

Despite the amount of work he had to do, he wrote to his father, 'I believe Ramsay is correct in thinking that I never was so well at the end of a previous winter session as I am now. I am in fact in thorough vigorous health. Neither lectures nor operations have cost me nearly as much anxiety as previously'.

Two weeks later Arthur wrote to Joseph:

I did not mean to suggest that the yachting trip should be dropped in the least from what I said about Iceland only that as I had heard a poor opinion of the place it was a question whether there might not be a better object for the excursion. Since then I have heard of Iceland being very interesting . . . I hope thee will be able to get away, if not I shall not care to go but if we both could go it wd be very fine—

Lister understood the value of a holiday at the end of a busy academic year, but there is no evidence whether this voyage ever took place.

He read the paper 'On the Coagulation of the Blood' on June 11, 1863. It contained little that was new although he referred to his recent experiments. He began with a summary of the problem in lay language for those Fellows who were not medical men. After describing the different theories of coagulation and demonstrating the inadequacies of each one, he showed how living tissue contains some special property which maintains the blood in a liquid state. The lecture concluded on a note first sounded in the paper on spontaneous gangrene: the manner in which healthy tissue prevents clotting was, he thought, a mystery that might remain forever unsolved.

112

His winter course, the lectures in systematic surgery, began as usual in November, meeting for an hour each day, five days a week. For the first time there is a reasonably complete record of the lectures taken down by one of the students. No significant change in the structure of the course had taken place in the nine years since Lister had begun his extra-mural lectures at Edinburgh.

His most original work during 1863 and the beginning of 1864 was in the operating theatre. 'Thy account of the last wrist excision is very interesting', wrote Joseph Jackson on March 12, 1864. 'Agnes tells me an Edinburgh surgeon has been before thee in describing his performance of it and without mention of thee—An inadvertance I hope, which thy paper will correct'. However, this paper on the operation to remove the diseased bones of the wrist, usually a product of tuberculosis, did not appear until March 1865, a year later. By that time Joseph Jackson had urged publication in at least half a dozen letters, but Lister was not to be hurried. When at last the paper appeared, he was able to present fifteen case histories. He summarized his results as four assured cures, six attained cures, two good hope for cures, one unsatisfactory 'but not hopeless' and two deaths 'of causes independent of the operation'. That is, the patients did not die of the immediate effects of the operation but later, one of pyaemia, a form of blood poisoning. A death rate of 13% was considered to be excellent, and the operation established Lister as an innovator in surgery. Happily, it is now seldom needed.

Mrs Lister had had an opportunity for talks with Joseph Jackson at Upton during March because she had gone there alone to help with the care of Lister's mother. Isabella was very ill, this time with erysipelas, an infectious disease with skin eruptions. Although Mary Godlee and Jane Harrison lived nearby, they had families of their own. Arthur had been ill himself and was recuperating near Cliveden. It was suspected that he had tuberculosis. Their father wrote to Joseph that a new partnership arrangement in the wine business was pending after which Arthur 'can either remain at Leytonstone giving occasional attention to business or leave for some other locality, as may seem best'. Arthur wished to make a partial break from the business not only because of his health but also because he had become increasingly interested in field botany. In any case there was something of a family crisis in March 1864, and Agnes brought some comfort to Isabella whose health improved temporarily. In his wife's absence Joseph was entertained, as Arthur put it, by 'grand folks' named Houldsworth.

Agnes also gave Joseph Jackson to understand that relations between Joseph and the Glasgow Infirmary Managers had not improved. Thus it was not surprising that he should have tried to leave Glasgow. James Miller, Professor of Systematic Surgery at Edinburgh University, died in June 1864. The Chair, which was worth £700 to £800 a year, held the highest status amongst the medical professorships in Scotland. With Syme's support Lister decided to apply for it. Godlee said that Lister believed his ultimate objective—to return to London—would be facilitated by the Edinburgh position. When he wrote to his father before applying for his Regius Professorship, he said that Glasgow might be a stepping stone back to Edinburgh. Though there were friends and family in the Scottish capital, his situation at the Glasgow Infirmary was probably the makeweight in his decision to apply. His tenure was still limited to ten years, but by 1871 he would be only forty-four. There would then be nowhere in Glasgow for him to go for hospital practice. In two years, furthermore, he would have to face another election. His hospital routine was onerous, beginning at 8.30 am, and left him too little time for research. Against the decision were the friendships built up in Glasgow, and his reluctance to move house a second time in four years, not arguments of sufficient weight to deter him.

By the end of June he was convinced that the appointment was his. On July 1 Joseph Jackson wrote: 'I am glad that increase of usefulness, which I think of with pleasure as a strong motive in thee, is in thy opinion likely to be the result & that this will be combined with more leisure for pursuing investigations that are on thy mind'. 'We shall like to know something about when your removal is likely to be.' On June 30 Lister received the customary testimonial from Syme's friend Dr Robert Christison, and during the first week of July letters came from James Paget, George Buchanan, Lister's colleague at University College Hospital who was now in Glasgow, Dr Allen Thomson and Sir David Brewster, a member of the Curatorial Court, the Edinburgh University body responsible for the appointment. Brewster told both Christison and Lord Brougham, one of the founders and now President of University College, that he favoured Lister. On July 6 Arthur wrote: 'though there is competition for the office I suppose there is no real question who is to be appointed'. On the 9th Joseph Jackson added: 'I have inferred from our first information (that the Edinb. professorship was offered to thee), that though there is still to be an election, with two other candidates, thy appointment is hardly doubtful'. But there were indeed two other candidates. Patrick Heron Watson, Lister's former assistant and the man whom he had twice beaten in the elections to the assistant surgeoncy at Edinburgh Royal Infirmary, was Professor Miller's son-in-law. James Spence had seniority within the Edinburgh faculty and a large support. On August 5 Lord Brougham added his own testimonial to Lister's candidacy. The date, a month after the bulk of the testimonial letters, suggests that the assurance heretofore felt by Lister and his friends had begun to dissipate. A few days later Spence was elected.

The depths of Lister's disappointment may be imagined. He may have been misled by Mr Syme's certainty of his own influence, but Lister must also have let his own desires dominate his ability to count heads. It is the first clear evidence that his weakness as a politician, exemplified by his role in the student medical society at University College, arose from the confusion between conviction and common sense that he seemed to experience. It rarely afflicted him in the operating theatre and perhaps only slightly more often in the laboratory, but in a social setting, he tended toward solipsism. Now that the election was over Syme somehow reasoned *post hoc propter hoc* that Lister was better off at Glasgow, and he urged him to publish his wrist excision cases as quickly as possible. As late as October 15 Joseph Jackson wrote that it was 'very gratifying to learn thy complete reconcilement to remaining at Glasgow'.

Before the results had been announced, however, Joseph was called to Upton. His mother had become much worse again, and on September 3 she died.

Two weeks after Isabella's death Joseph and Arthur went to Hastings where they were joined the next day by Agnes and Joseph Jackson 'after arranging many things', Mary Godlee wrote to her son. 'They lodged that night at the Queens Hotel'. Susan Lister with one of her children joined them there. Mary continued: 'I expect that Grandpa & and his sons left the rest of the party yesterday for their little excursion into Dorsetshire and it was Grandpa's wish to go to Meeting tomorrow at Sherborne where he used to go as a schoolboy and to visit Compton where he was at School'. Joseph Jackson sought some solace on a journey with his sons to places he had known before his marriage.

To fill his loneliness communication with his children became of paramount importance. 'The thought that thou wilt allow me to look for letters from thee weekly, & the letters when they come, are alike gratifying to thy poor father', he wrote to Joseph. In mid-October he noted that Joseph and Agnes would be 'setting off about this time' on a holiday with Thomas and Isabella Pim to Loch Lomond.

On November 30, 1864, Joseph Jackson referred to the '1st application of thy simple & perfectly effective instrument for the ear'. This was a small curved device to remove foreign bodies from deep within the canal leading to the ear drum. Lister found it especially useful with children who had lodged a pea or a pebble in their ears. Joseph Jackson added, '& for the sake of the public the description of it ought not I think to be long delayed— —I am glad the paper on the wrist joint is proceeding— —'Lister never did write a paper on his ear hook.

The winter lecture course had begun on November 1. The notes made during the preceding academic year with those taken by another student during the year 1864–1865, summarize Lister's view of surgery, and especially of inflammation, in the very months when, for him, they began to change.

The course fell into two Divisions, 'Affections common to all organs & Tissues', and 'Affections of Physiological Systems'. He began with the blood: corpuscles, coagulation, the blood vessels and the circulation. The nervous system followed. Lister stated his belief

that there are different sets of nerves for different sensations, thus, we know that there are special sensory nerves, those for example of hearing and there is reason to believe that in the cochlea, the different chords transmit different sound. Take also the sensory nerves of taste, there is one set for sweet tastes and another set for bitter.

These prescient suppositions have been demonstrated, but Lister unjustifiably extended them by analogy to include a special set of nerves which helped to explain inflammation and its consequences, suppuration or mortification—that is, 'rotting' of the flesh—and ulceration. 'If a noxious agent acts on any portion of tissue in such a degree as not to produce death, but prostration of vital power, inflammation is the necessary consequence', he said in introducing the subject. In other words, any injury that falls short of total destruction, such as a cut or bruise, will produce some or all of the familiar symptoms: redness, swelling, heat and pain. These symptoms reflect the occurrence of 'inflammatory congestion' which begins with the sticking together of red blood cells and may be demonstrated by the behaviour of pigment cells in the frog's web. However, the coagulation that follows upon the clumping of red blood cells is caused by the formation of fibrin, probably from 'two substances, one in the red corpuscles, and the other in the liquor sanguinis', or serum. The blood itself, Lister held, is not affected by the noxious agent, but by the tissue which the agent has paralyzed. He then went on to consider the two types of inflammation. Direct inflammation is due to the direct action of a noxious agent. So far, his description of events roughly parallels the course demonstrated by modern research although it omits much important detail. What is more, this description required little change after the 'discovery' of germs which could be seen as yet another noxious agent. The inadequacies of Lister's frame of reference only becomes apparent with the second type, indirect inflammation or inflammation 'by sympathy'.

Lister began with examples. Inflammation of the lung might occur when the chest was cooled by a draught, though the lungs themselves were protected from the cold by the chest and back. Inflammation of the kidneys following the use of an instrument to permit passage of a kidney stone could produce fatal uraemic poisoning. He knew nothing yet about the bacteria of tuberculosis or the microbes that cover a bougie, though his awakening was merely weeks away. He believed with the rest of the medical world that such inflammation occurred when the nervous system became involved. It is analogous to a reflex action, a term which had been recently introduced by Dr Marshall Hall, and reflected 'excited nervous action'. Shock, similarly, is a 'Reflex Paralysis'.

Indirect inflammation spreads 'by continuity of tissue', as in the mucus membranes inflamed by a cold, or it may metastasize through the agency of the nervous system as in the case of an inflamed testicle brought on by gonorrhea when there is no discharge. Lister said that there is 'no other connection that we conceive of'.

He went on to examine varieties of inflammation: acute, chronic, latent or acute without pain, diffuse or displaying a tendency to spread, and specific. In specific inflammation a special circulatory system might be involved, as in gout, or there might be 'specific poisons' as in gonorrhea and syphilis. Lister did not explore the nature of the specific poisons.

He then considered the symptomatic changes caused by inflammation. Of the fever he pointed out that it was not to 'be confused with fever produced by a poison in the system, such as scarlet fever'. He had distinguished between the two causes— —inflammation and 'a poison in the system'— —of a single symptom, fever, but again he did not speculate on the nature of the poison. Although medicine consisted largely of the treatment of symptoms, doctors were aware of instances such as this which suggested that their treatments should be tailored to underlying causes.

The succeeding lectures were devoted to the treatment dictated by Lister's description and analysis. Any direct cause of inflammation had to be removed. Raising a limb, for example, might permit the blood to flow more easily. Tension should be reduced. This might be accomplished by drainage as in the case of an abscess although the risk of greater inflammation and suppuration was then very high. Tension might also be reduced by inducing the arteries to contract. This was the purpose of blood-letting, the only objection to which, Lister said, was that it weakened the patient. All of the other counter-irritants sanctioned by tradition were also believed to reduce tension in the inflamed parts.

Perhaps the most remarkable aspect of these lectures is the manner in which they provide a systematic and consistent explanation which is almost wholly wrong. Much of the detail was correctly observed. The error lay in the central thesis that inflammation is a unitary 'disease'. Common sense demanded the interpretation. There it was. Look at it. Look at the patient with the swollen leg, or that one dying of uraemic poisoning. Inflammation has its own symptons, its causal relationships and of course, its therapy.

The elaborate theoretical structure built up to explain inflammation is scarcely unique in the history of science. Ptolemy's geocentric theory of the universe perpetuated an analogous mistake: an obvious observation, common sense, dictated that the sun and the stars revolved around the earth. The Ptolemaic system evolved to explain the causal relationships produced by this completely erroneous observation. It had the same kind of consistency, the same astonishingly inventive system, as the nineteenth-century theory of inflammation. Not until Copernicus, Giordano Bruno, Galileo and a host of lesser scientists had proven the nonsensical heliocentric theory by their observations, not until they had shown how it more easily explained

117

discrepancies left by the Ptolemaic system, did heliocentricity supplant the 'obvious'. These dinosaur-like theories deserve our awe and admiration: they were monumental creations. Defenders of the old theories often look foolish, if not stupid, viewed from the vantage point of knowledge that was still in the future when they spoke, but it is scarcely to be wondered at that honest men found geocentricity or the inflammatory hypothesis worthy of defence long after the new truth had been born. Nevertheless, the few great men opposed the merely honest when they recognized the light of the new truth as a rainbow bridge across the unsolved problems of the old.

Division I of Lister's systematic lectures at Glasgow University in 1864–1865 concluded with morbid conditions and growths. Division II dealt with afflictions of the heart and blood vessels, lymphatic system, bones, joints, muscles, nerves, including the brain and cord, and the 'segmental system' or gut. The course was in every respect traditional, describing the symptoms of 'affections' and the best surgical methods for their alleviation. Lister made little or no attempt to group the symptoms into disease states: aneurism or abscess could be dealt with surgically, but they often recurred because the underlying cause—tuberculosis, syphilis, gonorrhea, some other infection or dietary deficiency—was unrecognized or unknown. If Lister's course content differed at all from that of his contemporaries, it was in the emphasis that he placed on inflammation as a result of his research.

Joseph and Agnes spent Christmas 1864 at Upton with Joseph Jackson. For Joseph, 1865 began with a severe cold that brought an admonition from Syme against returning too early. Later in January, however, Lister watched Syme perform an unusual operation: the removal of a man's tongue. By suitable manipulation of his larynx, it was possible for the patient to speak.

Joseph Jackson acknowledged Joseph's 'increasing number of fees'. A month later he wrote: 'Thy practice seems still growing—and, as to this, my only fear is lest thou wouldst have too great weight on thee'. Lister was the first doctor in Glasgow to limit his practice entirely to surgery. He had evidently begun well as early as 1861, thanks in part to Ramsay's connections, and he actively continued with his private practice during the development of the antiseptic system. Not only did these patients require his time, but they also imposed a drain on his hospitality. In March 1868 Mrs Lister wrote to Mary Godlee: 'The aneurism patient got up last Saturday, and on Sunday walked about in her room—quite well'. Before the days of private beds, private hospitals or nursing homes, private operations had to be performed either in the patient's home or in the doctor's. If surgery was done in the surgeon's house, as appears to have been the case with the aneurism patient to whom Mrs Lister referred, the patient no doubt paid for the privilege and for the requisite nursing, but Mrs Lister and the regular servants could not have escaped the extra responsibility entirely.

The continuation of Lister's private practice added to an already secure financial base. In the middle of 1864 Joseph Jackson described in detail transactions that he had recently completed following the business difficulties of a company in which he had invested:

I told thee I was about to sell out the £2400 new 3%s of thine in my name on which there will probably be a loss. This was done on the 24th of last month and they realized even less than I expected—viz at $88\frac{1}{2}$ & deductg commission to Fox & Taylor £3—£2121—the loss being £79—but I have received of Overend & Co Int. on thy £1200 (recd 4m. 21) & on £100 of the previous balce in my hands (= £1300) from 4m. 16 to 6 m. 23. £6.5/- reducing the loss to £72.15/- & making the present balance in my hands

$$\left.\begin{array}{l} £2304.11.-- \\ +1200 \end{array}\right\} \text{ less } £72.15/- = £3431.16/-$$

Now I have applied £3400 of this as part of a sum I have lent to thy bror in law S. Harrison (on the security of the writings of an estate he has bought) at 5 pCent interest from 6 mo. 23 & thou mayst consider therefore that I hold it of thee at the same.

Lister was no more naive about money than his father, and there are other examples of their mutual concern for the proper management of their property in which Arthur also figures. Property was a kind of stewardship like the knowledge possessed by the surgeon.

Lister could on occasion temper duty with wit. The winter of 1864–1865 had been unusually cold in Glasgow. During January the students engaged in snowball warfare which degenerated into rioting when the police entered the College without orders. Lister blamed the police and defended the students. Joseph Jackson wrote with great solemnity on February 3 that their 'behaviour in the snowball rioting, as the paper represented it, had lowered their estimation—& I fear even thy class were not all guiltless Agnes wrote so gently about it'.

Joseph replied: 'They are certainly on the whole extremely well conducted, & in diligence & good behaviour will bear comparison with the best London students, indeed are far superior to the sample I saw at University College which was above an average specimen I believe'.

His father acknowledged his 'explanation of the snowballing & thy vindication of Scottish schools & students'. The matter of snowballs remained an issue between students and authority, however. In December 1866 the Academic Senate found it necessary to legislate fines except that: 'This Regulation is not to apply to students throwing snow at each other in any part of the College Green in which there is no danger of the Snowballs passing beyond the Rails or doing damage'. Lister attended the Senate meeting, but members' votes were not recorded.

In March 1865 Lister along with many other Glasgow medical men became deeply involved emotionally in a nasty murder case. Edward William Pritchard, a Glasgow doctor, was accused of poisoning his wife and mother-in-law while administering what the victims believed were medicines. Pritchard had long been a thorn in the flesh of the Glasgow medical profession, probably because of behaviour—he had had sexual affairs with his patients—that had provided motive for the murders, and they were horrified by this proof that they had been right. The breaking of his oath and his dreadful abuse of the trust placed in him as a physician seemed to place them all beneath a cloud. Pritchard was found guilty. 'No doubt within three weeks he will be hung', Lister wrote, 'yet the miserable man still protests his innocence! "May God have mercy on his soul" is what we may all desire'. Joseph Jackson acknowledged 'the main subject' of Joseph's letter 'which I had anxiously watched, knowing its deep interest to thee'. Pritchard was hanged 'in the presence of a vast multitude. Than this no criminal that ever suffered in the same place was so universally execrated', reported a review of events in the city. It was the last public execution to be held in Glasgow.

7

THE
ANTISEPTIC
PRINCIPLE

SOMETIME AFTER LISTER had begun his 1864 systematic lectures, he walked home across the cold, dirty city one dark afternoon with his colleague Thomas Anderson, Professor of Chemistry. They discussed putrefaction, what it is and what causes it, and Anderson suggested that Lister should read certain papers on fermentation by the French chemist Louis Pasteur. In particular Anderson recommended, 'Mémoires sur les corpuscles organisés qui existent dans l'atmosphère, Examen de la doctrine des générations spontanées,' which had been published by two scientific journals, *Annales des Sciences Naturelles* in 1861 and *Annales de Chimie et de Physique* in January 1862. The second paper mentioned by Anderson, 'Examen du rôle attribué au gaz oxygène atmosphérique dans la destruction des matières animales et végétales aprés la mort. Recherches sur la putréfaction', had appeared in the *Comptes Rendus Hebdomadaire* of the Académie des Sciences for June 29, 1863. Lister obtained the papers immediately.

Like all surgeons he saw suppurating wounds and putrefying flesh carry off patients whom he had sweated over and fought to return to useful life. One of his first Edinburgh students, Sir John Batty Tuke, recalled in a letter to Lister many years later an incident that had occurred about 1854:

. . . when extending to your dictation, Mr Syme's lectures one night late, you somewhat suddenly said, 'let us go and look at that popliteal case'. You took down the dressing, and found the wound healed, except where the ligature was. You said, 'the main object of my life is to find how to procure this result in all wounds—But why is it not healed around the ligature?' Boylike I said 'the irritation of the silk'. 'No you replied not of, but *in* or *on*'.

During his work on blood coagulation Lister first saw suppuration or the formation of pus in the tissue he had under his microscope, and he had begun experiments directed at the suppurative process itself. For three days, in November 1859, with Mrs Lister's assistance, he examined pus corpuscles from the eye of a rabbit as well as blood in its heart and arteries. Two years later he made notes and drawings of 'suppuration' in the white of an egg used

121

to cover a healthy sore as protection. Because pus consists of white blood cells called leucocytes as well as dead cells from the wounded tissue, the pus in the albumen must have come from the sore. In August 1863 Lister had performed his wrist operation on Neil Campbell, a twenty-year-old labourer. Campbell returned in January 1864 with his wrist again carious. Lister repeated the operation removing more bone. This time Campbell died of pyaemia. The notes of the case conclude:

11 P.M Query. How does the poisonous matter get from the wound into the veins? Is it that the clot in the orifices of the cut veins suppurates, or is poisonous matter absorbed by minute veins & or carried into the venous trunks?

At the same time Lister was watching formation of 'pus corpuscles' in the jugular vein of a large pony. These observations were repeated on a horse when he went to Upton during his mother's last illness in August.

Lister thought that these disparate experiments had been important in the development of his ideas and took them with him, along with several later ones, when he retired to Walmer in Kent toward the end of his life. He was planning to fit them together into a note for his *Collected Papers* to elucidate the state of his mind when he read Pasteur's papers.

The suppurative and putrefactive conditions which killed so many post-operative patients had come to be known as 'hospital diseases' because they happened so frequently in hospitals. Hospital gangrene was the most feared. It was the most frequently disastrous, almost invariably requiring amputation and often ending fatally despite this extreme remedy. Years later Lister recalled that an epidemic of gangrene occurred during his house surgeoncy under Erichsen. He had had to scrape the brown sloughs from the infected legs and pour on pernitrate of mercury. When the treatment worked, the healing sore would be left clean, and when amputation had successfully removed the gangrenous tissue, the stump too would heal cleanly.

I was greatly struck with the clear evidence which these cases seemed to afford that the disease was of the nature of a purely local poison. In the hope of discovering its nature I examined microscopically the slough from one of the sores, and I made a sketch of some bodies of pretty uniform size which I imagined might be the *materies morbi* in the shape of some kind of fungus. Thus as regards that form of hospital disease, the idea that it was probably of parasitic nature was at that early period already present in my mind.

Hospital gangrene was probably gas gangrene caused by soil-borne bacteria, which helps to explain why the disease most frequently occurred in leg wounds. Today it is treated with penicillin, and because the bacteria are anaerobic, or oxygen-hating, high pressure oxygen. Amputation may still be required to save life.

Septicaemia is a general infection of the blood stream often called blood poisoning. Puerperal or childbed fever is septicaemia. Another putrefactive disease, cellulitis, affects the soft tissues and produces grey sloughs but little pus. Both are streptococcal infections that can usually be treated with antibiotics. They were often confused with the most frequent hospital diseases, erysipelas and pyaemia.

Erysipelas, like the other forms of blood poisoning, could of course occur outside of hospitals and without previous surgery. Isabella Lister had suffered from it, though she had probably died from a heart disease. An acute and diffusing inflammation of the skin, erysipelas was known in the middle ages as St Anthony's Fire. It frequently spreads to subcutaneous tissue where suppuration takes place. Lister liked to point out to his students that it 'spread like fairy rings' with the redness dying out behind as the inflammation advanced. Like gangrene it occurred in epidemic waves which might cause the authorities to close the disease-ridden wards. A streptococcal infection, it too responds well to penicillin.

Pyaemia was fatal more often than erysipelas. The name reflects the belief that it appeared when pus passed into the blood. Although this is a misunderstanding, abscesses did appear in different parts of the body and lead to death, usually by peritonitis. It can be cured today because antibiotics prevent the growth of staphylococcal bacteria, but in 1862 pyaemia was responsible for 2% of all hospital deaths and perhaps 10% of deaths following amputations.

Pyaemia was the most frequently encountered of the hospital diseases. Their impact varied from hospital to hospital, and in an age when statistics were little used and poorly understood, observers differed as to their significance. Florence Nightingale claimed that 90.84% of patients in twenty-four London hospitals died during 1861, but she had misunderstood the figures from the official study she had used. Another report in the same year, 1863, showed that about 9% of the patients in eighteen metropolitan hospitals died of *all* causes. The mortality rate was lower in the provinces. In the Royal Infirmaries of Edinburgh and Glasgow the overall death rate fluctuated between 5% and 11%. The mortality in surgical wards was generally lower than that in medical wards! In the Glasgow Infirmary in 1862 the overall death rate was 10.3% with 16.7% mortality in the fever wards and 8.7% in others. Most of the surgical deaths appear to have occurred after accidents, an important fact in light of the prevailing belief that the hospital diseases were caused by bad air.

These infections had been given the collective name hospitalism, by Sir James Y Simpson, the discoverer of chloroform anaesthesia. Simpson had collected figures from a survey of medical practitioners by means of a questionnaire restricted to the subject of amputations. Of 2089 amputations in hospital practice, according to Simpson's respondents, 855, or nearly 40% died! On the other hand, of 2098 amputations performed outside of hospitals, 226 or 10% died. Simpson concluded: 'A man laid on the operating table in one of our surgical hospitals is exposed to more chances of death than was the English soldier on the field of Waterloo'. His pamphlet was influential because it underlined a problem that everyone—administrators, doctors *and* patients—recognized.

In British hospitals the death rate following amputation fluctuated between 25% and 50%. Erichsen considered 25% mortality 'satisfactory', according to Godlee. The average at Edinburgh Infirmary was about 43% and at Glasgow, 39.1%, in 1865. In a major Philadelphia hospital between 1831 and 1860, fatalities after amputations averaged 24.3%. At Massachusetts General Hospital in Boston they averaged 26%. The Paris hospitals were said to average 60%, and the death rate in the German hospitals was probably about the same as in the British institutions. The death rate following amputation was so high because the operation was often not undertaken until infection had made itself manifest.

Surgical deaths were proportionately lower than medical fatalities, in part because relatively few operations were performed. Yet hospitalism had scarcely been noticed until anaesthesia had freed the surgeon's hand for the performance of longer and more complicated operations. At Guy's Hospital, London, between 1827 and 1842 there were 153 fatalities following major operations and severe injuries. The risk was such that only the strongest underwent surgery, and then only if there was no alternative therapy. For example, amputations were relatively frequent, about a fifth of all operations, because the risk to the patient of 'conservative surgery' such as Lister's excision of the wrist was thought to be much greater. In 1863, 117 English and Welsh hospitals reported a surgical death rate of 8.43%. If operations on the eye were excluded, mortality rose to 12.51%. Of 1371 major operations such as removal of diseased ovaries, moreover, 210 patients or 15.3% died. The principal cause of death was sepsis, or hospital disease.

Why did these people die? The upsurge in statistics of hospital disease came with the opening of new hospitals and of new wards in the old to accommodate the increased urban populations. The question, what happened inside the body, which Lister examined, took on a new social dimension. Epidemiology grew up simultaneously with the new science of bacteriology because urban crowding and the importance of a healthy work force increased the need to identify a disease-entity with a discrete cause, rather than a group of untreatable symptoms. The hospitals themselves were thought somehow to cause the hospital diseases. So serious had the epidemics become that boards of governors and medical staff took the decision to demolish their buildings in an attempt to halt the infections. Sir James Simpson advocated formation of villages of small iron huts, each large enough to accommodate one or two patients, which could be disassembled and re-erected periodically.

Two factors were then thought to be related to hospitalism, bad air and dirt.

The notion that tainted air had something to do with the spread of hospital diseases grew up in the crowded wards of European city hospitals during the eighteenth century, but the idea of miasmas was much older. During the plague in seventeenth-century London sulphur was burnt in the streets to purify the air, either on the theory that so evil a smell must do some good or because of its demonstrable value as a cathartic. But the sulphur apart, 'miasma' was an attempt to explain the obvious relationship between overcrowding and disease.

Yet many practitioners did not accept that miasmas exist. The great John Hunter had pointed out that if a broken rib punctures a lung so that air escaped into the chest cavity, no suppuration occurred. The lungs and bronchi filter bacteria-bearing dust from inspired air. But if the rib broke through the skin, pus inevitably formed. Pasteur and Lister believed that the air was the major source of infection although the French chemist was among the first to realize that most airborne germs are benign. Lister accepted Hunter's observations as conclusive evidence against the theory of miasmas. He also recognized that wounds healed satisfactorily in the same wards where pyaemia had struck, and conversely that hospital disease sometimes occurred in a private home. His mind was prepared to accept that it was not the air but possibly something in the air. Nevertheless in 1862 James Paget told the British Medical Association that outbreaks of pyaemia could best be combated if patients were kept in a current of wind.

Dirt, the lack of proper plumbing and sanitary facilities and total ignorance of the simplest rules of hygiene, were a far more real enemy than bad air. The story is told of Astley Cooper that he cut a wen from George IV's scalp. The next day he noticed that the King treated him most uncivilly. Cooper asked his nephew, who was the King's physician, if there was something the matter. The nephew replied that had he been in Cooper's position, 'I should have put on a white cravat and a clean shirt, or at least have washed my hands before I waited on his Majesty'. Cooper looked at his blood-spattered shirt and hands and said: 'God bless me! so I ought, but I was not aware of it—and the King, sir, is so very particular'. Robert Liston was said to have cut a piece of wood from the operating table to plug a blood vessel he had severed. 'When a dresser or a house-surgeon entered upon his term of office,' wrote Lister's nephew, himself a surgeon,

he hunted up an old coat, in the lapel of which he probably carried a wisp of ordinary whipcord for tying arteries. This garment did duty for six months or a year ... There was no such time limit, however, for the surgeons themselves. Their operating coats lasted from year to year, and eventually acquired an incrustation of filth of which the owners appeared unconscious, or even proud ...

As to sanitation Lister complained that in Glasgow the toilets opened directly off the wards, but this was customary. Florence Nightingale wrote in 1854:

The nurses did not as a general rule wash patients, they could *never* wash their feet—and it was with difficulty and only in great haste that they could have a drop of water, just to *dab* their hands and face. The beds on which the patients lay were dirty. It was common practice to put a new patient into the same sheets used by the last occupant of the bed, and mattresses were generally flocksodden and seldom if ever cleaned.

Nor was it simply slovenliness that produced these conditions. What was the point, it might have been asked, of washing bedclothes if drainage from the next patient's wounds would dirty them again? Far better, surely, to save the clean linen for the patient who was mending well. Hector C Cameron, Lister's house surgeon in the early days of antiseptic treatment, wrote: 'When almost every wound was foul with suppuration, it seemed natural . . . to postpone the cleansing of hands and instruments, until the progress of dressings and probings had been finished'.

The overcrowding that was associated with hospitalism certainly exacerbated filth. Slowly, reform spread. If hospitals could not easily be pulled down and rebuilt to assure better ventilation, they could be cleaned up. Improvements slowed the advance of hospitalism, but it remained to come to grips with the most important source of infection, the staff.

In 1843 the American physician, Oliver Wendell Holmes, advised in *The New England Quarterly Journal of Medicine and Surgery* that physicians should wash their hands in calcium chloride after attending women with puerperal fever. The most important attack on this disease, however, was the work of an Hungarian doctor named Ignatz Semmelweis, who held a junior staff position in the lying-in wards of one of the largest hospitals in the world, the Allgemeines Krankenhaus in Vienna. About 1848 while Lister was suffering depression and seven years before Pasteur's first paper on fermentation, Semmelweis supposed that puerperal fever was caused by decomposing organic matter, whether from a dead body or from a living person with a disease which produced decomposition. It was common knowledge that fatalities were much higher in the lying-in ward attended by students and male doctors than in the ward supervised almost exclusively by female nursing staff. Patients, not all of them pregnant, pleaded to be admitted to the latter, and some cases literally ran away from the more dangerous ward. It occurred to Semmelweis that the students came directly to the ward from the dissecting rooms, and this observation led to the hypothesis of infection. He insisted that everyone who examined patients should first wash their hands in chlorinated lime, an unpleasant procedure in itself. The incidence of puerperal fever fell dramatically, but given the general level of hygiene, it is not surprising that cases continued to appear. Semmelweis's superior, Klein, could see no sense in the hand washing precautions. He argued that he and his students suffered no ill effects from the dissection table, and no one understood that the vaginal lining conducted bacteria into the womb. But there was room for doubt that decomposing matter could itself carry infection. Unlike Lister, Semmelweis had no other mechanism to suggest. Like Lister, however, he had a 'rooted objection to writing', as he put it, and he left it to his students and a few supporters to spread his doctrine. In part because of the opposition of Klein and in part because the police suspected that, as an Hungarian, Semmelweis had supported the 1848 uprising against the Austro-Hungarian monarchy, Semmelweis failed to win promotion in 1850. He returned to his native Budapest. A decade passed before he did at last write a book, but it was little more than an immoderate attack on his opponents. Disappointment and frustration appear to have aggravated a tendency to mental unbalance, and in 1865 he was committed to an asylum near Vienna. There he died a few weeks later, ironically, of septicaemia.

One of his supporters had been Rokitansky, then Professor of Anatomy, who had entertained the Listers during their wedding trip. But such is the harshness of history that Rokitansky did not mention Semmelweis to Lister. During 1877 Lister was elected to honorary membership in the Budapest medical society. In September 1883 he and Lady Lister visited the city, and a large party was given for him by the medical profession. At the dinner the president was Dr Lajos Markusovzky, a professor at the University, who had favourably reviewed Semmelweis's book in 1860. Yet neither he nor any other person present mentioned the name of Semmelweis. It was some years later that Lister attended a meeting in London called to establish a British committee of the newly-organized International Semmelweis Committee in Budapest. Among those present was an Hungarian doctor practising in London, Theodore Duka, who had in the interval been the first to call Lister's attention to the work of his unsung predecessor. Perhaps inevitably, the growth of Hungarian nationalism combined with the victory of the germ theory of disease to produce an assertion by an Hungarian doctor in 1904 that Lister had said: 'Without Semmelweis my labour would have been in vain. Modern surgery owes most to the great son of Hungary'. Two years later Lister wrote: 'When in 1865 I first applied the antiseptic principle to wounds, I had not heard the name of Semmelweis and knew nothing of his work'. The rehabilitation of Semmelweis continued, and on the occasion of Lister's fiftieth anniversary as a Fellow of the Royal Society in 1910, the Budapest medical profession congratulated him with a curious acknowledgement:

We are moved not only by respect, but also gratitude to England's scientific world, for in our memory is still fresh the recognition given to our famous Semmelweis at the suggestion of Sir Andrew Clark and Sir Spencer Wells.

The personal tragedy of Semmelweis could not delay the progress of an idea that was ripe. If cleanliness could reduce the incidence of hospital diseases, it was logical to improve personal hygiene as well. The attack developed simultaneously on two fronts, the nurses and the doctors and surgeons. In

1840 Elizabeth Fry had founded the English Protestant Sisters of Charity as a nursing order. Despite the early elimination of the word Protestant, the religious ethos by itself could not combat the prevailing image of Sairey Gamp. The wards were filthy places 'in which most of the patients were visibly ill, with flushed faces, parched lips, delirium, severe pain, etc.,' wrote one of Lister's house surgeons, 'and many of them were evidently on the verge of death: the wards were pervaded with a peculiar mawkish odour which was very trying to newcomers'. In such conditions the sight of a drunken nurse was scarcely surprising. In the workhouses any nursing was done by inmates. In the voluntary hospitals, although patients might not be wholly dependent on charity, and the nurses were paid, unlike the surgical staff, they were almost totally lacking in status. Only the occasional blunt and forthright trooper stayed on and became a matron by seniority. Mrs Porter, who has accused Dr Beddoe of risking Lister's life on the Salisbury Crags, continued as head nurse after Lister's return to Edinburgh, in 1869, and did not retire until after his departure for London, in 1877. R J Godlee, who knew Mrs Porter during his student days when he worked with his uncle in Edinburgh, referred to her condescendingly as 'an important and efficient personage'. As late as 1870 Lister was asked to reprimand one of Mrs Porter's nurses who had slept off drink in a hospital bed. He asked the woman if she had no sense of responsibility to her patients. 'Oh, I nae minds o' them', she is reported to have answered. Nurses were employed as servants, not as medical attendants, and as servants they carried out their duties.

It was not until the Nightingale reforms began to take effect that the matron became a housekeeper, while the management of the nursing staff was assigned to a superintendent of nurses. The Nightingale Training School was opened at St Thomas's Hospital on June 24, 1860. At the time Lister returned to Edinburgh, nurses' training had been established in the Royal Infirmary. From 1873 the Nurses' Register indicates that these professionals were assigned to his wards as well as to the rest of the hospital.

The personal hygiene of doctors and students also improved slowly. Mr Syme satisfied himself that his insistence on better hygiene during operations and the dressing of wounds had made a slight reduction in the incidence of gangrene. Cleanliness meant little more than sweeping the floor and opening the window in the operating theatre. Syme also wiped his hands on a clean towel before beginning. Surgeons like Thomas Spencer Wells of Samaritan Hospital, London, Robert Lawson Tait of Birmingham and Lister himself were members, in the mid-'sixties, of what has been called the 'cleanliness and cold water' school. They drew an analogy between the tarnishing of silver in the sulphurous air of large cities and the infections caused by bad air. If a silver spoon is washed in cold water, the formation of a sulphide coat is delayed. Therefore, it made sense to boil water and cool it in order to wash the wound site as well as the instruments, and to irrigate and dress the wound. If the

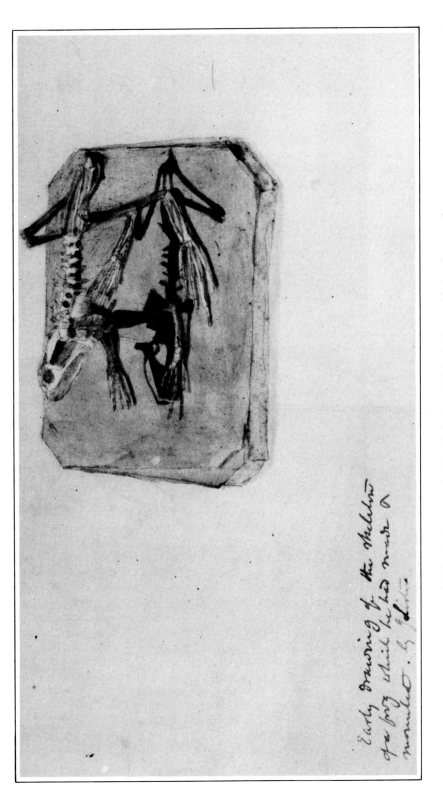

Early drawing of the skeleton of a frog which he had made & mounted. By Lister

5. *Lister's drawing of a frog skeleton which he had assembled and mounted. He was 14. (See page 30.)*

6. "The Chief" and
his associates in
Edinburgh, 1854.
(See page 62.)

Jn̅o Beddoe   John Kirk   George Hogarth Pringle   Patrick Heron Watson
Lister   David Christison   Alexander Struthers

surgeon washed his hands, it made sense also to wash the patient, at least in the vicinity of the injury or incision.

Thus, the question of how to dress a wound, an issue made more controversial by the threat of suppurative disease, became part of the problem of hygiene. The surgeon makes an incision which he drew together at the end of the operation by means of sutures. If the wound is clean and there is no bacterial infection, the incision will heal by 'first intention', that is, without inflammation, and the stitches are either clipped out or allowed to be absorbed. This sight, so common since about 1940, was always the surgical ideal, but it was rarely seen. Similarly, abrasions, or large raw surfaces, usually heal today under scabs consisting of formed elements of the blood combined with lymph and various proteins (and possibly under skin grafts too). But as late as 1924, R J Godlee wrote of this form of healing that it was common in animals but rare in man. Finally, both incised and abraded wounds can heal by the gradual filling in of the wound cavity with granular tissue, a mixture of lymph and connective-tissue cells called granulations. Such healing by 'second intention' was invariably accompanied by inflammation and suppuration. On the third or fourth day after the accident or operation redness and pus would appear in the wound accompanied by fever. Much attention was given to the free drainage of suppurating wounds. If it had been sutured, loose stitching permitted fluids to flow away, and ligatures around blood vessels within the wound were left with long ends extending beyond the lowest part of the wound surface on the not unreasonable assumption that gravity plus capillary action would promote drainage. So they did until inflammatory reactions or pus blocked the escape of fluids. Free removal of fluids served to reduce tension within a cavity, but it could not prevent the formation of more pus. Meanwhile the patient was kept on a light diet, 'ostensibly because a full diet was supposed to encourage inflammation', wrote Godlee, 'but really because the experience of ages had shown that the inevitable fever took away the appetite'. If all went well, granulation proceeded, the wound became less inflamed and painful suppuration gradually diminished and finally stopped. The process might require months, and the scars were often disabling as well as disfiguring.

So common was suppuration that many physicians considered that it must be part of the normal course of healing. It was not just an attempt to put a pleasant face on disaster, therefore, that led the great Graeco-Roman physician, Galen, to refer to 'laudable pus'. Paré, inventor of the ligature, recommended medicines that 'increaseth the matter and native heat and turneth the matter cast out of the vessels into pus and sauces', but the Swiss physician, Paracelsus, opposed the notion. It had begun to die out during the eighteenth century, and on the whole Lister was not encouraged by the appearance of pus in a wound. Nevertheless his house surgeon, Hector Cameron, wrote on September 21, 1866, in a ward journal of the Glasgow

Royal Infirmary: 'A quantity of laudable pus came away from the opening in the axilla tho' patient felt little or no pain in that region, but the stump for a short time last night'. As late as 1879, William Savory, a prominent London surgeon who opposed Lister in several matters, said in a speech to the British Medical Association:

I am neither ashamed nor afraid to see well formed pus covering the surface of granulations . . . I am accustomed to watch it carefully; for I think, in the change of character of this secretion, we have often the first signal for good or for evil, and, as a rule, the condition is satisfactory under a layer of laudable pus . . .

Dressing protect the wound from physical damage, absorb discharges so as to keep the bedclothes and the patient dry and they might control, if not prevent, suppuration. On the other hand if the air itself or something in the air caused suppuration, then it was desirable to keep air away from the wound. They were sealed with collodion, an early plastic that could be applied as a syrup at room temperature. Other sealers included goldbeater's skin, caoutchouc or raw rubber, or adhesive plaster, a technique once preferred by Syme. However, Syme later abandoned the attempt to keep air away from the wound. He left it open for a few hours after which it was closed so as to assure free drainage, and where possible, pressure was applied against the inner part of the wound rather than the outer edges. He applied a dressing consisting of a poultice of bread or linseed oil, or clean dry clothes. This so-called dry dressing was confortable and permitted discharges, but the poultices were ideal bacterial breeding grounds. Liston and many others preferred a wet dressing which meant that the lint or cloth were first soaked in water. The water was thought to exclude the air. Lister had used both dry and wet dressings, varying them according to circumstances.

When either kind of dressing was changed, it was customary to wash the wound with a solution that was believed to be antiseptic; that is, it seemed to prevent sepsis. Ignorance of the cause of sepsis meant that the definition of antisepsis was shaky and subjective. In any case antiseptics were used, as Hector Cameron wrote, 'to control and diminish suppuration after it had occurred'. The most popular was probably Condy's fluid (sodium and potassium permanganate). Archibald Malloch, a Canadian who served as Lister's dresser during the important year 1865, wrote, 'I have held the limb in one hand, and the flaps, from which all the stitches had been cut out, in the other, while Mr Lister poured kettle after kettleful of hot diluted Condy's fluid between the flaps to cleanse them; the stumps being finally covered with a linseed poultice'. Sulphite of potash or of sodium were used not only externally on the wound, but internally as an 'anti-putrescent', according to a theory advanced by Professor Polli of Milan. Polli had tested the chemicals by injecting them into pyaemic dogs, but in man they were swallowed! By 1864, Lister later said, the theory had been shown to be incorrect. He continued to use sulphite of potash externally, and he also tried copper sulphate during 1866, after he had begun the regular use of carbolic acid. The previous year he used nitric acid to control suppuration after a wrist operation. In a similar case in March 1865 he used carbolic acid for the first time to control hospital gangrene. He continued to use nitric acid, often at full strength, as a last ditch attempt to stop gangrene.

LeGros Clark, senior surgeon at St Thomas's, used lint soaked in 'spirits of wine'. Quinine; benzoin, a constituent of the ancient remedy known as Friar's Balsam; alcohol, the basis of all tinctures but used frequently abroad as an antiseptic; sodium and calcium chloride, the former having been used by Semmelweis; and iodine which had been discovered by both Humphry Davy and the French chemist, Gay-Lussac, in 1811—all had been tried. Nothing could consistently stop suppuration once it had become established.

At Glasgow according to a later house surgeon, Lister 'carried out an extensive experiment in his wards with ordinary cleanliness, but without success'. He insisted on handwashing by nurses as well as doctors between each patient. Yet as late as 1871, according to J R Leeson, students and professors at St Thomas's went from the dissecting and post mortem rooms directly to midwifery cases. Even Lister much reduced his emphasis on hygiene after his return to Edinburgh. Trained men will not change their procedures without good cause, and the underlying confusion behind the diverse methods directed toward the patient's quick recovery reflected the ignorance of cause. Time and again the confusion is evident. *The Lancet* ran a leader in August 1867, *after* it had published Lister's paper on the antiseptic system: 'It was a great part of the care of the old practitioners to avert' inflammation 'and . . . to treat it. We are not so fearful of it now. Blood-poisoning is to surgeons of the present day as great a source of dread as inflammation was to their predecessors, and is a far larger and more real evil.' Inflammation is a concomitant of suppuration, a symptom of blood poisoning. The leader writer correctly identified the 'real evil', but at the cost of confusing a disease with a symptom. No dressing or antiseptic could be expected to prevent suppuration before the distinction between symptom and disease slowly dawned, because there was no rationale behind their use. Even effective antiseptics such as nitric acid were diluted to the point where they were no more than superficially effective in order to prevent damage to the wound surface. Lister never solved the problems of wound damage because he used much stronger solutions, but at least he knew why he did it.

Meanwhile, as Lister's first biographer observed in 1913:

Large hospitals were being abandoned and hut hospitals substituted. Lister's work . . . came in the nick of time. It saved not only patients but hospitals. It prevented . . . an entire reversion of the method of dealing surgically with the poor.

Antiseptic surgery emerged when Lister realized that the analogy between suppuration and fermentation which Pasteur had drawn could be applied in practice.

In 1855 Pasteur published his first paper on fermentation, a study of the formation of lactic acid in the souring of milk. He had observed, in the souring milk, budding organisms, which he guessed might be the active causes of the fermentation. 'If anyone should say that my conclusions go beyond the established facts, I would agree,' he wrote, 'in the sense that I have taken my stand unreservedly in an order of ideas which, strictly speaking, cannot be irrefutably demonstrated.' He showed that alcoholic fermentation such as that occurring during wine production was also associated with tiny self-replicating things which would not, however, sour milk. Nor would the organism associated with lactic acid formation produce alcohol. In other words there seemed to be some specificity in the little globules that Pasteur described. The paper on lactic fermentation had concluded that the fermentative agent was a living organism carried in the air. Without them, or objects like them, he supposed that neither the lactic nor the alcoholic fermentation could occur.

The notion that sub-microscopic organisms caused fermentation, and indeed putrefaction, had not originated with Pasteur. Both a German physiologist, Theodor Schwann, and a French physiologist and engineer, Charles Cagniard de la Tour, had shown that yeast is a living organism, and that it caused the conversion of sugar to alcohol and carbonic acid. Another German physiologist, Jacob Henle, who had been Schwann's student, published a germ theory in 1840, but without experimental support.

It had been argued in reply that yeast was not required in sugar fermentations producing lactic or butyric acid, nor had it been possible to see yeast organisms in putrefying meat. Pasteur's research suggested the reason: that other organisms than yeast were responsible for these changes. But the German chemist, Justus von Leibig, taught that yeast acted as a chemical catalyst; it assisted the fermentative process but was not itself changed by it. Von Leibig maintained that both fermentation and putrefaction were forms of slow combustion in oxygen, obtained either from the substance undergoing change or from water. 'The yeast of beer, and in general all animal and plant substances undergoing putrefaction, impart to other substances the state of decomposition in which they find themselves,' he wrote. 'The movement which is imparted to their own elements, as the result of the disturbance of the equilibrium, is communicated equally to the elements of the substances which come in contact with them.' Von Leibig also believed that life arose spontaneously from the chemicals in ferments rather than the reverse. He was immensely influential. It had been von Leibig's theories that Lister heard when he learned chemistry from Professor Graham at University College. Pasteur's assertions that the organisms he had observed somehow caused fermentation, therefore, stood in opposition to the outstanding contemporary authority on chemistry.

About 1860 the argument between Pasteur and the followers of von Leibig reduced itself to a question of primacy: biological or chemical. Did life originate only from pre-existing life, or was it generated spontaneously in a broth of suitable chemicals? Pasteur did not assert that the organisms he had seen caused fermentation. Because he had seen what he took to be budding from these organisms, he supposed that it was the buds or 'germs' which caused chemical change. His opponents were in general prepared to accept that organisms in the ferments were the concomitants of the process: that is, they came into existence in the course of it and may have been in some way necessary to fermentation. Von Leibig, for example, had believed that yeast is a catalyst. In fact the yeast *is* changed in the process of fermentation: it converts the sugar in malt to alcohol by a process akin to digestion and grows and reproduces itself using the sugar as a nutrient in much the same manner as do human cells. Pasteur guessed correctly, but he could not explain how yeast or bacteria acted to produce the chemical changes. Although the evidence on yeast accumulated very rapidly, data on the bacterial toxins that cause suppuration and disease have become available only since the development of antibiotics. Without knowledge of how germs worked Pasteur had to find indirect evidence to support his theory.

He set himself to prove that without germs, fermentation is impossible. By boiling covered preparations he could prevent chemical changes from taking place in them, but his opponents argued, quite correctly in many cases, that chemical change required atmospheric oxygen which boiling drove off. Therefore Pasteur performed two series of experiments. In the first he boiled fermentable substances in flasks with necks bent in such a way as to admit air but exclude dust and other particles. The flasks remained free of fermentative changes, and of organisms. In the second series he took flasks into the countryside and high up into the mountains of the Alpes Maritimes. It was generally agreed that mountain air contained less dust than city air. Pasteur reasoned that fermentative organisms were less likely to occur in such air. Again his hypothesis was borne out by the results of his ingenious experiment.

At about this time Pasteur studied another form of fermentation, the turning of butter, in which the rancid taste and odour is produced by butyric acid. He noticed that this change seemed to happen most quickly in airless places, and he made another inspired guess: the germs of the butyric acid fermentation must grow in the absence of oxygen. They are anaerobic. The prior growth of other organisms in the butter, Pasteur thought, used up available oxygen thus protecting the butyric acid germs and facilitating their growth.

It was a fortunate observation because it enabled Pasteur to go one step further. According to a modern biographer, 'he also became convinced that similar phenomena occur during putrefaction, and that the evil-smelling decomposition . . . is the result cf the anaerobic life of specialized germs that attack proteins under the protection of aerobic forms capable of removing the oxygen from the environment'. The conclusion is an oversimplification: the bacteria that cause the more common forms of blood poisoning are aerobic, but Pasteur had drawn the first clear analogy between fermentation and putrefaction. In 1863 he told Napoleon III that it had been his ambition to understand 'the cause of putridity and contagious disease'. But Pasteur was a chemist. He had no medical training. Two more decades would pass before his work had any connection with mammals or men. His interests in the early 1860s were confined to the diseases of plants and the germs that caused them.

Pasteur's papers, which Lister read early in 1865, summarized the flask experiments and viewed his observations on butyric acid as well as the lactic and alcoholic fermentations. Lister was by no means the only medical man to have read them. In an address to the British Medical Association in 1864, Spencer Wells, the advocate of cold water for cleanliness, reviewed Pasteur's work and its relevance for surgery. He proposed that micro-organisms in the air caused the hospital diseases, but he made no attempt to follow his own logic to its conclusion and to apply it practically. Lister, who seems not to have read Wells's published paper, perceived that Pasteur's work could be applied to surgery, but he took one more giant step: he began the formulation of methods for doing so. 'All efforts to combat decomposition of the blood in open wounds were in vain until Pasteur's researches opened a new way, by combating the molecules,' he wrote in 1902. He would not only clean the wound with an antiseptic, but prevent germs from subsequently falling upon it as though it were already protected by new skin. Two practical questions of the most profound importance remained for Lister to answer, on the basis of his knowledge, experience and moral commitment as a surgeon: which antiseptic was he to use, and which cases was he to select for his experiments?

Although he intended now to apply an antiseptic in a different manner and for a different purpose, the familiar substances such as Condy's fluid and sulphite of potash were tragically linked with failure. Though carbolic acid, or phenol, was often used on the continent, as Lister was to learn to his cost, it was not familiar in British surgery.

Phenol is a coal-tar derivative. Discovered in 1834 it was first used in the raw state, as creosote, to preserve railway ties and ships' timbers. In Britain, Belgium and Holland it had been used against parasites during outbreaks of cholera and cattle plague and to reduce the odours of decomposition in sewage. Various phenol-based powders had been patented, but Lister heard or read about its application to the treatment of sewage in Carlisle, and obtained a sample of the crude acid, German creosote as it was called, from Professor Anderson. It may also have been Anderson who directed Lister to F Crace Calvert, Professor of Chemistry in the Royal Institution of

Manchester, who had begun the small-scale manufacture of carbolic acid. Calvert had been educated in Paris. In 1859 he wrote a report on the use of coal tar in medicine which had been read to the Académie des Sciences by the chemist, Chevreul. Calvert pointed out that eight years before, in Manchester, mild carbolic acid had been injected into corpses which were thereby preserved up to a month. After returning from Paris and establishing his own factory, Calvert supplied the acid to Manchester surgeons for trial. In 1862 Edward Lund wrote a report on its use in wounds, and the following year a paper by Calvert 'On the Therapeutic Properties of Carbolic Acid' appeared in *The Lancet*. Lister's announcement of the antiseptic method in 1867, with its unintentional emphasis on the central role of carbolic acid, undoubtedly helped Calvert's business. Lister himself wrote in a footnote to the published version of his address to the surgical section of the British Medical Association in 1867, 'the public are much indebted to Mr Crace Calvert, of Manchester, for his successful efforts to prepare carbolic acid in a pure form at a moderate price'. The next year Calvert opened the Tower Chemical Works in Bradford.

It was logical that Lister should have tried carbolic acid in an excision of the wrist, the operation with which he had had remarkable success. On this occasion in March 1865 he failed. He had not yet worked out methods of using the antiseptic both to clean the wound and to bar it against the later entry of germs.

On March 21 he used carbolic acid again to treat Neil Kelly, aged twenty-two, who had suffered a compound fracture of the leg. This too was unsuccessful. Suppuration occurred. Between four and five months were to pass before he made a third attempt. It would be interesting to know his state of mind after two failures, but the record is blank. Godlee, who was sixteen at the time and already planning a medical career, must have remembered the period. Yet unaccountably he confused the facts. He wrote that because of 'an unusual dearth of such accidents', Lister had to wait almost a year for a second compound fracture case. Not only did he more than double the time that elapsed between the first two compound fracture cases, but he ignored the factors that led Lister to test his new method on these injuries. No correspondence remains to clarify these questions, and the 1865 journals for Lister's wards are lost. In his first full-length paper on the antiseptic method Lister said that the case of Neil Kelly 'proved unsuccessful, in consequence, as I now believe, of improper management'. Much the same was true of the wrist case. It seems that he had made up his mind in March 1865 to use carbolic acid as the antiseptic for his experiments, but that he had as yet no clear-cut experimental design. He had not then decided to restrict his trials to accident cases admitted with compound fractures.

There are two kinds of fracture. A simple fracture requires only that the bone be set and the limb splinted. Then, as now, it normally healed without incident. A compound fracture is one in which the broken bone tears through the tissue surrounding it and punctures the skin. It makes a nasty wound which often leads to considerable loss of blood and shock. The victim is almost invariably thrown to the ground by the accident so that the wound is not only jagged but dirty. Hours are liable to have passed before admission to hospital. The wound will probably be inflamed by the time a doctor sees it, and suppuration is all but inevitable. Until the discovery of sulpha drugs in the 1930s, the most common treatment, because it was the safest from the patient's standpoint, was amputation. Lister's objective, to prevent suppuration and save the limb, could therefore be attempted with a hedge against disaster. If the treatment failed, there should still be time to save the patient's life with the sacrifice of a limb which would have been lost in any event. Ethically as well as medically, the experimental model was ideal. Lister seems to have followed this line of reasoning, but another year passed before he looked upon the compound fracture cases as an experimental series.

On August 12, 1865, an eleven-year-old boy named James Greenlees was admitted to the Infirmary with a 'compound fracture of the left leg, caused by the wheel of an empty cart passing over the limb a little below its middle'. The boy was given chloroform and the wound washed out as thoroughly as possible with a solution of carbolic acid in linseed oil. Only a pure phenol will dissolve in water, and Lister was still using a product that was crude and oily. He dressed the wound with a mixture of putty and carbolic acid. The putty was intended to hold the carbolic acid so that it would not be washed out of the dressing by discharges of blood and lymph. The carbolic putty was applied widely over the skin around the wound further to reduce the chance that germs would gain access to it, and covered by a sheet of tin foil to reduce the evaporation of carbolic acid from the putty. The leg was then splinted and bandages held both splint and dressing in place. After four days the dressing was removed. There was much soreness but no rancid smell or other sign of putrefaction. Normally hospital diseases showed themselves within seventy-two to ninety-six hours. Lister dressed the leg again in a similar manner and left it for five days, during which the boy's temperature remained near normal and his appetite, satisfactory. When the second dressing was removed, the skin around the wound had been burnt by the carbolic acid. A dressing of gauze soaked in a solution of carbolic acid in olive oil was applied and left for a further four days. The wound had begun to heal, meanwhile, and Lister judged that the danger of suppuration had greatly diminished, if it had not passed. He applied a water dressing to the excoriated skin. Six weeks and two days after his accident, James Greenlees was discharged with two whole legs.

While he was still in hospital, on September 11, 'Patrick F—a healthy labourer, aged 32', was admitted, with a compound fracture of the thigh with a small external wound. His progress under similar treatment seemed to be satisfactory, and on September 22 Mr and Mrs Lister went to Upton for a short holiday, leaving the house surgeon, Dr Macfee, in charge. Unfortunately, gangrene developed in the leg and it had to be amputated.

In the paper announcing the new techniques Lister wrote that neither of these first two cases had external punctures large enough really to test the efficacy of carbolic acid. Despite the amputation he considered them both to have had satisfactory outcomes. Now, however, he had to wait eight months before a compound fracture case was admitted to his wards.

The summer of 1865 was unusually warm and pleasant. The Listers took several excursions into the country around Glasgow, but he did not wish to be away from the Greenlees boy just yet. Of course he also treated other patients antiseptically, where it seemed appropriate. In August he dressed two ulcers, or open sores, with carbolic acid in oil using oiled paper strengthened with spirit varnish to cover one and gutta percha beneath a water dressing over the second. 'On the whole the dressing had not agreed well with the sores', he noted, 'and it was changed for ordinary water dressing covered with cotton.'

On the same day, August 28, he examined 'pus corpuscles' from the discharges from the Greenlees boy's wound, using 'a little dry carmine powder' to make them easier to see. While he and Mrs Lister were at Upton in September and after their return to Glasgow, they conducted a series of experiments on horse's blood outside the body, mixing egg albumen with pus cells obtained from 'India rubber tubes with horse's blood'. Though they were presumably on holiday, Mrs Lister's notes show that they worked long hours on consecutive days from September 19 to October 4. Mrs Lister also drew some of the sketches.

They did not go to Upton for Christmas, but spent the holiday with the Symes at Millbank. Without a compound fracture case Lister evidently decided to try antiseptic treatment of an ulcer again. In an incomplete manuscript which he may have begun for publication, he described one case with drawings of the wound. 'John L Austin, aged eighteen, a fine healthy young American was shipwrecked last Christmas and cast upon the coast of the Island of Iona' in the Hebrides. He was wounded on the leg but not admitted to hospital until January 29, 1866, by which time the sore had grown by ulceration. Lister washed it with a solution of one part carbolic acid in twenty parts of oil and dressed it with lint dipped in the same solution and covered with plaster of Paris. The sore seemed to be clean, but again there was a 'puriform discharge', that is, one like pus. He supposed 'that new pus cells are formed by the escape of the nuclei from the cells and the development of these nuclei into pus cells'. He may have been observing leucocytes, a kind of white blood cell which is part of the natural defence system, but the observation of their origin is incorrect. In any case he cultured the cells in egg white in a hot box at 100 degrees and may have seen white cell division through his microscope. Austin's ulcer responded no better to carbolic acid than had the cases in the previous August. Although it did not suppurate, it also did not heal, a side effect of the strong carbolic acid solution that Lister used and of the maintenance of wetness beneath the relatively air-tight seal. The notes on the case end on February 15, and the outcome is unknown. But he was gaining experience.

On March 27, according to Lister's own notes, he performed an operation to remove diseased bones from the wrist of a nineteen-year-old girl, Janet Forgie. Again he used antiseptic techniques, and this time he was successful. The girl was discharged cured, which usually meant only that the patient retained a moderately useful hand while the disease was temporarily arrested. This case was never published.

A third compound fracture case was finally admitted to Lister's male accident ward on May 19, 1866, immediately after he returned from a short holiday in the Highlands. John Hainy, a twenty-one-year-old moulder, had had his leg broken when a 12-hundredweight iron box containing a sand mold for the casting of an iron pipe fell from a height of about four feet 'with its full force upon his left leg which was placed obliquely under it as he stood steadying it'. The external wound measured $1\frac{1}{2}$ by $\frac{3}{4}$ inch. Lister saw Hainy three and a half hours after the accident, relatively quickly, and immediately cleaned and dressed the wound antiseptically and splinted the leg. It healed well, and Lister saw for the first time how a bloody crust over the wound formed by the bacteria-free scab was gradually 'converted into living tissue' despite the carbolic acid continually applied to it. Lister was of course consumed with interest in the transition from coagulated blood to granulation tissue under antiseptic conditions. He was observing something entirely new: germ free healing devised by the surgeon.

Unfortunately, early in July, Hainy developed bed sores which became gangrenous. The ward journal entry for July 15 reads: 'NB The patient next this one and the second from him again are both afflicted with pyaemia from amputated limbs. The bed of this patient is ordered to be changed to the other end of the ward.' It was an anxious time. In addition to carbolic acid the sores were washed with nitric acid and then dressed with water poultices. Hainy was given opium to reduce the pain. Finally on August 7 he was released, cured. On December 18 Lister wrote in his journal, 'He has called today to shew himself walking on a well shaped strong leg'. The chances are that Hainy showed himself before Lister's class as an exhibit.

It was an important victory. On May 27 he had described the case to his father: 'I tried the application of carbolic acid to the wound, to prevent decomposition of the blood, & so avoid the fearful mischief of suppuration throughout the limb. Well, it is now 8 days since the accident, & the patient has been going on exactly as if there were no external wound, that is as if the fracture were a simple one.' Two days later Joseph Jackson replied that certain 'arrangements with the dressers' about which Joseph had also written 'gives I hope a better chance of thy more important cases being given to the public'. It was the first of another long series of anxious enquiries about publication. He referred to a case in which Lister had used hydrochloric acid successfully as an antiseptic which 'ought not (I should think) for the sake of humanity to remain unpublished'. He asked about the thicker tin foil Lister was now using to cover the dressing and then gave the reason for his anxiety: 'I infer from the invitation sent thee by the Council of the British Medical Association that thy investigation of the subject is no secret'. He concluded, however, that Joseph 'was quite right to decline the proposal'. The address to the BMA was merely postponed for a year.

Lister contemplated publishing the Hainy case. He went to Edinburgh in mid-June 'to consult with Mr Syme as to the best medium of publication,' according to Godlee. But other cases 'followed in quick succession, each suggesting modifications in treatment or supplying new pathological facts'. It was, therefore, later in 1866 on the strength of the Hainy case and successes following it that he decided to treat the compound fracture cases as an experimental series for publication to the exclusion of other types of surgery.

Lister reported to his father 'another case of compound fracture under my care just now, with a very extensive wound'. On June 8, James Wylie, aged ten, was admitted. He 'was engaged in a turner's factory worked by steam power . . . when his right arm was drawn in between a strap & a shaft turn'd by it'. It took two minutes to stop the machinery. Two hours later Lister poured carbolic acid solution into the lower arm wound, which was so large that he made no attempt to close it, simply applying the dressing under the new tin foil. He later discovered that the upper arm had been broken too and set and splinted that bone. After seven weeks the wound had healed. Though the bone fragment had not knitted completely and seemed unlikely to do so, the boy was discharged 'with a very useful hand'.

Whether with Syme's advice or not, Lister now conceived of the developing series as the basis of a book. As late as January 1867 Joseph Jackson wrote about the fifth case, that of Charles Finlay:

Thy account of little Charley's cure & of thy book's progress is most interesting. I had thought that considering the important case of abscess that had been successfully treated the paper had seemed to dwell rather exclusively on compound fracture—& feel glad thou art able to extend thy subject satisfactorily. My only fear being lest the publication should be retarded.

Charles Finlay was only seven and 'a fine, intelligent boy'. He 'was knocked down at 8 p.m. on the 23rd of June, '66, by an omnibus crowded with passengers inside & out, & one if not both wheels passed over his right leg'. Lister saw him three hours later, and by that time the boy was in severe shock due to haemorrhage. He was given chloroform, and Lister poured undiluted carbolic acid into the huge wound, squeezing it repeatedly 'to induce the liquid to insinuate itself into all its interstices'. Having tried to set the bone fragments, he applied carbolic acid lint beneath tin foil. For thirty-six hours the little boy was delirious, but on the morning of the third day following his admission, he was 'again intelligent', and his pulse rate had dropped toward normal. It was then that a small subsidiary wound 'dressed separately without carbolic acid' became infected. Nevertheless the main wound, the fracture itself, remained clean. Lister noted for the first time that the bone fragments themselves were providing centres for the formation of living bone tissue as the dead bone was resorbed and replaced. The process was analogous to the replacement of scab by living tissue which he had observed in the Hainy case. Charles Finlay suffered several more infections which Lister believed were hospital gangrene, but the main wound finally healed on January 9, 1867. His leg had drawn up in the course of healing due to the scar tissue, and he was kept in hospital another two months while it was slowly straightened by means of splints and traction apparatus. Both Wylie and Finlay survived, despite severe injuries, in part at least because they were so young.

While Lister was treating them, he tried for the second time to leave Glasgow. The Chair of Systematic Surgery at University College, London, fell vacant. It would be pleasant to return to his family and his Alma Mater. A surgeoncy at the Hospital went with the Professorship, adding to its attraction. In late July Lister applied. On July 27 he wrote to Lord Brougham, the President of both the College and the Hospital, asking for his support. To accompany the application, furthermore, he had had printed a 'Notice of a New Method of treating Compound Fractures':

The disastrous effect of compound fractures, as compared with the freedom from all danger in simple fractures, evidently depends essentially upon the fact that in the former the blood effused around the fragments, being in communication with the external air through a wound, undergoes decomposition, and, becoming an acrid irritant, produces more or less extensive death of tissue and suppuration, whereas in the latter the blood, retaining its natural bland character, is converted into tissue or got rid of by absorption. With regard to the mode in which the atmosphere produces decomposition of the blood, we now know, thanks to the beautiful researches of Pasteur, that the active agents are not the gaseous elements of the air, but minute living organisms suspended in it, which, by developing in a decomposable substance, determine a change in its chemical arrangement analogous to the fermentation of sugar under the influence of the yeast-plant. Hence it occurred to me that if in a compound fracture, before decomposition of the blood has set in, a material were applied to the wound which, though it might allow the gases of the atmosphere to penetrate it, would destroy its living germs, all evil consequences might be averted. For this purpose I selected carbolic acid, having heard of its remarkable efficacy in disinfecting sewage, and about a year and a half ago, a case of compound fracture of the leg presenting itself, with a wound too large to afford hope of union by the first intention, I applied to it lint dipped in the acid, and found my anticipations fully realized; the case progressing exactly like a simple fracture, as regards absence of suppuration and of constitutional disturbance, and rapidity of osseous union of the fragments. I have since subjected to the same treatment 5 other cases, some of them as bad as any surgeon would think of saving, and the result has been better than I at first ventured to hope. The carbolic acid forms with the effused blood a dense crust which, if touched daily with the acid to ensure freedom from decomposition, may remain for weeks without a drop of pus forming beneath it, thus affording abundant time for absorption and organization of the effused blood.

The 'Notice' was published in a biannual survey of advances in medicine and physiology that appeared early in 1867, and it was the first announcement of the antiseptic method.

Lister lost the election by one vote. The Council appointed the assistant surgeon at University College Hospital, John Marshall. It appears that Sharpey voted for Marshall, probably on the grounds that he had served an apprenticeship at the Hospital lasting eighteen years.

The vote was taken on August 4. Two days later Joseph wrote to his father: 'The disappointment was at first extremely severe: More so than I had expected'. After a bad night, however, he had managed to go to the Infirmary in a frame of mind sufficiently cheerful at first to mislead his house surgeon, Hector Cameron, as to the outcome. 'And I am sure the canvass is in no way to be regretted on my account. Any effect it has had can only have been to bring me more into notice. And if another opening should occur in London, I have at least declared my willingness to go there, & perhaps paved the way for going.' On the same day Joseph Jackson had sent his 'condolence' to his son. He said that his 'expectations had never been very sanguine', but he too was disappointed. As in the case of the unsuccessful Edinburgh application two years before Syme chose to see in the decision a thinly-disguised blessing. 'In the end you may not improbably have reason to feel grateful for not being allowed to quit your present position. It is a great field, much greater for hospital practice than you could possibly have had in London'. Though he accurately compared the number of patients Lister had in the Glasgow Royal Infirmary to the much smaller number he would have had at University College Hospital, Mr Syme's judgement was conditioned by his own unhappy experience in London. He wrote that: 'In order to maintain a good metropolitan place it is necessary to do a great deal of dirty work . . . It was such considerations that led me to return from London, & they should, I think, reconcile you to not going there'.

Lister's friend and colleague Allen Thomson, the Glasgow Professor of Anatomy, helped to ease his disappointment. In mid-August he wrote from Greenock, 'I hope that Mrs Lister and you will come down and spend the end of a week or whatever more time you can spare with us'. By August 23, however, the Listers were in Torquay with Joseph Jackson, Mary Godlee, Arthur and their families. Mary wrote to her husband: 'Joseph & Aggie enjoyed last evening but poor dear J. had a bad night and does not mean to go to any more dinner parties. He is still in bed at 10:30' and Dr Ramsay had called to see the patient. When he had recovered, according to one of Arthur's sons, Uncle Joseph used the remainder of his holiday to introduce Arthur to 'the study of Systematic Botany'.

On September 25 a fifteen-year-old millworker, Georgina Robb, was admitted to Lister's female ward with a large wound on the back of her hand. Lister treated her antiseptically, and she was discharged on October 4.

Three weeks later the sixth compound fracture case was admitted. John Campbell, a fifty-seven-year-old labourer in a stone quarry, suffered a compound fracture of the thigh and a broken collar bone when a large rock fell on him. There was a six-hour delay in getting him to hospital and much bleeding. Nevertheless the first three weeks went well. Then infection set in. In the paper describing these cases Lister wrote: 'Would that I had at that time known the mode of proceeding' which he had learned from the antiseptic treatment of abscesses, begun at this time, the importance of protecting any incision that allowed the evacuation of fluid against the entrance of germs with the air that would flow in to replace the fluid. Surgeon and patient battled on until February 1867 when Campbell suffered a haemorrhage due to a hole in an artery caused by a bone fragment! He died having refused a blood transfusion which, before an understanding of blood types, might have killed him anyway, and more painfully. It was the only death in the experimental series of eleven cases.

Four days after the admission of John Campbell, a deaf-and-dumb labourer named William Chambers suffered a compound fracture of his leg when an omnibus ran over him. Chambers was admitted under the care of Lister's colleague Dr Ebenezer Watson, who asked Lister to assist. Chambers thus became part of the published series. He was discharged, cured, after eight weeks.

Chambers was counted as Case 9. Cases 7 and 8 had also been patients of a colleague, Dr James Morton. Mary Morrison, the only woman in the series, was sixty-two. She had been admitted on August 13 with a compound fracture of the forearm caused by a fall. Samuel Boyle, aged thirteen, had had both legs fractured, the left one being compound, when he was struck by the ball on the governor of a steam engine he was tending, and hurled against an iron pillar. Lister was away, but Morton's house surgeon, A T Thomson, probably assisted by Hector Cameron, had treated both cases antiseptically. Mary Morrison was discharged in mid-September, and young Boyle soon after Lister returned to Glasgow from Torquay. Despite these successes Morton later expressed doubt as to the value of Lister's methods.

According to the ward journals, the first antiseptic operation to open an abscess appears to have been the case of Mary Phillips, a twelve-year-old millworker admitted on November 7, 1866. She recovered satisfactorily and was discharged on December 12. Many years later Lister wrote that the first such case was that of a 'woman above middle age' who had an abscess on the back that had been left alone, as was then the custom. The danger of infection after an incision was too great. But this time, as sometimes happened, the abscess grew until only the skin remained. Lister said that he had faced a choice between an operation using antiseptic precautions and the accidental bursting of the abscess. He operated successfully. This may have been a private case, but he dated it early in 1867.

Abscesses most frequently arose from a tuberculous infection, and they usually recurred, unless the underlying condition was removed surgically, as could occasionally be done by the excision of tuberculous bones. The nature of infection was in any case not yet understood, and there was no way for the doctor to connect bone disease with the familiar and deadly lung disease commonly called phthisis. An abscess is a symptom like inflammation, but it too was treated as though it was a discrete disease. It was desirable to reduce the tension by removing the pus in the cavity. Lister did this under a protective veil of carbolic acid. He tried both to prevent the backflow of germs from the purulent discharge and their entry with the air that replaced the discharge. Like a compound fracture an abscess seemed to offer an ideal experimental trial, both medically and ethically, except that the causative infection remained. Immediate results were spectacular, however. The abscess ceased to produce pus almost as soon as it was lanced, and inasmuch as the carbolic acid covered a relatively small area of healthy skin around a clean incision, it usually healed quickly. On February 24, 1867, Lister wrote to his father: 'The course run by cases of abscess treated in this way is so *beautifully* in harmony with the theory of the whole subject of suppuration, and besides the treatment is now rendered so simple and easy for *any* one to put in practice, that it really charms me'.

Like the decision to restrict his trial series to compound fractures, its extension to include abscess was pragmatic. It was really an editorial decision to include the abscess cases with the fracture cases both because Lister thought they were instructive, and because they had been successful. He undertook these operations because he was compelled to do something for certain patients whose lives were, in his opinion, at risk. He was a clinician first and became an experimental scientist and a teacher only after he had done what he thought was necessary for his patients. Perhaps more important, their needs tended to distract his attention from the elaboration of a coherent experimental design. To what degree he exploited this clinical bias to avoid commitment to a general statement of his objectives, not even he could have said.

While the abscess cases dramatically supported the value of Lister's procedures, he persevered with the more difficult compound fracture cases. Case 10, Thomas McBride, 'labourer, who gave his age as 52', had been admitted on January 2, 1867, as the patient of Lister's friend George Buchanan. A luggage wagon had caused a compound fracture of his leg, but under Lister's care it healed in about six weeks.

The Listers remained in Scotland over Christmas 1866. Joseph had not been well. On December 18 his father wrote to commiserate with 'thy long continued suffering from cold . . . I do hope thy health is re-established'. Lister was almost forty. A photographic portrait made by an Edinburgh photographer shows him seated in a partially-upholstered arm chair, a book held unattended in his left hand. His expression is serious, even dour, with deep furrows running down from the corners of his mouth. The prominent nose is accentuated by the lines above it in the high forehead and by the deep-set eyes, dark shadows beneath them. His brown hair is cut long and full at the back, and shows traces of grey. He could have been fifty as easily as forty, but perhaps he had been unwell when the picture was taken.

He had continued his lectures, of course, as well as his broader re-sponsibilities as a member of the Academic Senate. In December he was appointed to a Senate committee to review the certificates and degrees in science awarded by the University. He had upwards of fifty patients in his wards, quite apart from his special antiseptic cases, and a private practice the size of which is unrecorded.

The most onerous task that he faced in the early months of 1867, however, was the preparation of the paper, as it had again become, to describe his compound fracture cases. On February 24 he told his father that he 'almost longed to be writing' the section on abscesses which 'promises to be at least as satisfactory as Part I, and very likely as long'. In the event the section occupied only the last of the five instalments in which the paper appeared.

On April 4, after publication had begun, an eleventh compound fracture case was admitted to Lister's ward. John Duncan, aged fifty-five, 'calico printer of intemperate habits', had jumped from a window into the street fifteen feet below, breaking both bones in his lower right leg. The case was particularly interesting, Lister wrote, because the 'pumping action of the fragments of the broken bones' had spread air through the tissues, but the germs, he believed, had been caught up by blood coagulated near the wound, thus helping to control infection. There is a rough truth in the observation inasmuch as bacteria caught in the clot might be dealt with by white blood cells and other natural defences, but it is more interesting as evidence of Lister's commitment to the view that nature must be encouraged to effect a cure even in the presence of germs. He told his class: 'it is never Man that heals a disease, it is always Nature: all that man can do is to remove obstacles.' Though he was still a patient when the article appeared, Duncan progressed well and was discharged cured.

'On a New Method of treating Compound Fracture, Abscess, etc., with Observations on the Conditions of Suppuration' was published by *The Lancet* beginning on March 16 with further sections in the issues for March 23 and 30, April 27 and July 27. The use of the word 'conditions' in the title had given rise to some uneasiness on Lister's part, and he had discussed with his father in several letters the advisability of using the word 'causes' instead. That he decided on the former may have been due to the fact that Joseph Jackson concurred with him in preferring it, but it also suggests how wary he was of committing himself totally to Pasteur's germ theory. On April 12 Joseph Jackson wrote of the first instalment, 'it reads to me very satisfactory (—supposing Pasteur's observations to be reliable), & the great success of thy practice based on them tells much in their favour—'. But Lister was a surgeon, not a theorist.

Of the eleven compound fracture cases one lost his leg and one died, though because of secondary haemorrhage rather than infection. Judged from the standpoint of contemporary medical practice, the amputation was not a failure, and the death represented a 9% mortality. Judged from the standpoint of Lister's objective—to cure the compound fracture as though it had been a simple fracture—his failure rate was 18%, probably below the average for this injury. William Watson Cheyne, his house surgeon in Edinburgh and London, pointed out that five of the eleven cases remained entirely free of suppuration and one more showed only slight transient evidence of infection. 'I have no hesitation in saying that up to that time Lister had never seen five cases out of eleven running an aseptic course, indeed I doubt if he had ever seen one.' Unfortunately, despite his justifiable satisfaction with these results, Lister did not yet recognize that asepsis, not antisepsis, was his central contribution. The difference may seem trivial, but it was not. Antisepsis means against putrefaction and calls attention to the means, carbolic acid. Asepsis means without putrefaction and calls attention to the end that Lister tried to obtain.

At the beginning of the paper he set forth a clear statement of the germ theory as it then stood:

... the germs of various low forms of life, long since revealed by the microscope, and regarded as merely accidental concomitants of putrescence, but now shown by Pasteur to be its essential cause, resolving the complex organic compounds into substances of simpler chemical constitution ...

It was necessary, therefore, 'to dress the wound with some material capable of killing these septic germs, provided that any substance can be found reliable for this purpose, yet not too potent as a caustic'.

As might be expected the bulk of the paper was devoted to a detailed review of the cases themselves, the nature of the accidents, the patients' general health and condition on admission and the minutiae of dressings. Like most of the articles published by *The Lancet* this one was intended to instruct rather than to make a theoretical statement. The doctor who wrote the article was saying to the doctors who read it: 'I do it this way, and suggest you might wish to try the same procedure because it seems to work'. The didactic note is most apparent at the beginning of the section devoted to abscesses:

In compound fracture there is an irregular wound, which has probably been exposed to the air for hours before it is seen by the surgeon, and may therefore contain in its interstices the atmospheric germs which are the causes of decomposition, and these must be destroyed by the energetic application of the antiseptic agent. In an unopened abscess, on the other hand, as a general rule, no septic organisms are present, so that it is not necessary to introduce the carbolic acid into the interstices. Hence the essential object is to guard against the introduction of living particles from without, at the same time that a free exit is afforded for the constant discharge of the contents.

Lister was wrong when he said that 'no septic organisms are present' in the abscess, but they were the agents, not of the hospital diseases, but of tuberculosis or of some other underlying disease, and antiseptics could not have reached them effectively anyway. From the standpoint of suppuration Lister's statement is correct, but the focus of his attention is the 'antiseptic agent', carbolic acid. The 'atmospheric germs' are of course the object of attack, but his purpose—maintenance of an aseptic wound—remains implicit. Indeed, only in the penultimate paragraph of the final instalment of the paper, on July 27, 1867, did Lister make a statement which separated the means from the end; it too is less explicit than might have been expected:

... it is impossible to judge whether or not the sinus has closed, except by examining it from time to time with a probe, which should be dipped in the antiseptic oil, and passed between folds of the antiseptic rag. This may seem a refinement, but if we could see with the naked eye a few only of the septic organisms that people every cubic inch of the atmosphere of a hospital ward, we should rather wonder that the antiseptic treatment is ever successful than omit any precautions in conducting it.

He had in fact more exactly reported his purpose in the paragraph written to accompany the application for the University College Chair a year before.

To what extent was this peculiar reticence scientific, and what part was sheer stylistic ham-handedness? Lister understood perfectly that he intended to prevent putrefaction. He evidently assumed that his readers, having also been thwarted and baffled by it, were bound to see this. The opposition took him by surprise, but it seems to have been not only predictable but even desirable in order to obtain adequate information.

He had not even explained in the first paper why he had selected carbolic acid in preference to another antiseptic, and it was certainly possible to interpret what he wrote to mean that if enough carbolic acid was swilled about, success must follow. Not until April 3, 1869—two years later—did he finally publish the statement that should have introduced the first paper:

In using the expression 'dressed antiseptically', I do not mean merely 'dressed with an antiseptic', but 'dressed so as to ensure absence of putrefaction'.

Even this appeared in a footnote!

Yet Lister was not intellectually vague or uncertain. The case approach lends itself to reportorial accuracy and meets the most rigid standards of conservative medical reporting. Lister was a surgeon, not an inventor. He reported a 'new method of treating' some of the oldest problems facing his professional colleagues, not a revolutionary way to reduce surgical risks. Naturally, he expressed himself in the language of his day.

But he used it badly. 'Lister, all his life, hardly ever succeeded in writing a good letter,' wrote Hector Cameron, one of his most devoted friends. He lacked the stylistic brilliance his father could bring to ordinary events. There was a flattening of effect in Lister's writing that made it hard for him to elevate one item above another. He did possess a sense of metaphor which is the more noticeable for its rarity. In the 'Early Stages of Inflammation' he wrote that the appearance of white corpuscles was 'something like a few flies playing about in a room', and in the same paper he said that fibrin leads to clotting 'as a thread induces the crystallization of sugar-candy'. 'The cotton', he wrote years later, 'greedily imbibes the liquid'. 'As vegetation is most abundant near a dung-hill, so the action' of nerves on blood vessels 'is increased by the freer flow of blood,' he told his students in 1864. On the other hand the metaphorical impact of a cliché is not enhanced by prolixity. About the antiseptic properties of corrosive sublimate he wrote: 'we were dealing with an edged tool, which, while it might do admirable work, was very apt to cut our fingers'.

Lister's plain-Jane approach to language revealed the man. Sir Charles Sherrington, the neurophysiologist who knew and admired him, attributed Lister's 'sobriety of expression' and his 'selfrestrained statements' to his Quaker origins. 'It is therefore significant when . . . the young author allows himself an expansive adjective' such as 'grand' or 'beautiful'. One of Lister's nieces wrote: 'My uncle's love of good English made him playfully critical of us if we used careless or slang expressions'.

Accents in language, like passion, mirror the heat and cold of experience. Lister's strongest expression, wrote John Stewart, one of his house surgeons in London, was: 'it's an infamous shame!' He never swore, and when a student tried his patience, his customary expression was the lifted eyebrow of Christian resignation. Yet he fought hard against misunderstanding and bitterly resented opposition. 'It seems to be a difficult thing for me to write the English language so as to make my meaning intelligible,' he said with irony during a lecture in 1875. His opponents could have taken the statement at face value, though they did not. They argued the case against the 'new method' on what they took to be its merits.

Before controversy could begin—indeed, before publication of the final instalment in *The Lancet*—Lister faced a personal test of the hardest sort for his antiseptic method. His sister, Isabella Pim, had a growth on a breast that was diagnosed as malignant. During July she went to London and to Edinburgh, where first James Paget and then Syme advised against operation, believing that the disease had advanced too far. She went to Glasgow, to her brother.

In common with most surgeons Lister had wide experience with tumours, both benign and malignant. Amongst his clinical notes are several referring to the removal of growths, frequently with sketches. His systematic lectures included accounts of 'Simple or Non-Malignant Growths' classified by the tissue in which they were found and of 'Malignant Growths or Cancers': Hard (for example, breast cancer), Soft (brain cancers) and Epithelial (or skin cancers). Perhaps the most recent clinical note, dated May 19, 1864, described a mammary tumour that Lister had removed, with a large watercolour of the diseased breast.

The decision to perform the operation on Isabella could not have been easy, especially against the advice of Paget and Syme. Hector Cameron believed it was the first performance of a radical mastectomy, that is, removal of the breast and of the glands in the neighbouring armpit to which the disease had spread. Lister said that he could see 'no insuperable anatomical difficulty', and 'rehearsed the procedure on the dead body'. At the last minute he went to Edinburgh to discuss the matter with Mr Syme, and on June 16 he wrote to Joseph Jackson: 'I suppose before this reaches thee the operation on darling B. will be over. It was evidently undesirable to delay a day longer than was necessary as soon as it was determined that it was to be: so last evening I finally made arrangements for the nurse for her, & we intend that the operation shall be at half past one o'clock tomorrow.' Mr Syme had said: ' "no one can say that the operation does not afford a chance" & also alluded to the carbolic acid treatment of wounds (which he has been trying with much satisfaction) as depriving the operation of danger. I felt his true kindness & manifest, though little expressed, sympathy, very much, & left Edinburgh much relieved. Not that I do not feel the prospect of operating on my sweet sister in this way very much: but that the degree of really legitimate hope that has opened up to us has greater influence. It is very satisfactory to me that B. seems to have thorough confidence in me. She distinctly says she would much rather have me to perform the operation than anyone else. And considering what the operation is to be I would rather not let anyone else do it.' The operation was performed in his house. The next day he told his father, 'I may say the operation was done at least as well as if she had not been my sister. But I do not wish to do such a thing again.' 'Those of us who assisted him saw how much it cost him to undertake so bold a procedure for the first time on one so dear to him,' Cameron wrote.

The recovery went smoothly. There was no suppuration. On July 26 Arthur replied to a letter from Joseph written after the operation: '. . . how delightful it is to hear this account of her—that danger is past as far as the operation is concerned . . . Papa has a very interesting letter from Ramsay in wh. he tells of the two other cases & how well they have done . . . it is indeed glorious to think of this success. There are two who are saved from what, I suppose, would have been certain death this time last year.' Arthur expressed a feeling of awe and relief that spread amongst the lay public as people slowly became aware of what Lister had accomplished. Those who experienced the power of the sulpha drugs to cure pneumonia when they were first introduced in the 1930s can appreciate what Arthur Lister meant.

Sadly, Isabella Pim's cancer had spread beyond any power to extirpate it. She died three years later, but they were three years she might not otherwise have had.

While Isabella was still at Woodside Place, Lister voted in favour of a motion before the Academic Senate which laid down procedures for tightening the pre-medical qualifications required for admission to the Glasgow medical courses. As medical standards rose, it was an issue that frequently exercised the Senate and the governing bodies of other British universities. To Lister the quality and techniques of medical education were a persistent, often controversial theme. English medical education, unlike that on the continent and in Scotland, favoured clinical experience to the virtual exclusion of a background in science. Lister had been differently trained at University College, and he began now to perceive that his unusual educational experience had made possible his understanding of Pasteur's relevance to surgery. The advice that he gave his cousin, Marcus Beck, in 1860, had outlined a preparatory course like the one Lister himself had followed. In a long letter dated October 2, 1867, he gave the same advice to his brother-in-law, Rickman Godlee, for Rickman's second son, Rickman John, Lister's future biographer. He described the sound academic course that he had followed with its sensible emphasis on chemistry as well as botany, physiology and anatomy. He was no innovator, as he indicated by his later stand on examination procedures and the even more fraught issue of the admission of women to medical education, but he was among the first to recognize the importance to a doctor of a good scientific background.

On August 9, 1867, Lister appeared before the meeting of the British Medical Association in Dublin to read the paper he had been asked to give the year before. Because of Isabella he decided to go at the last minute, thus exacerbating his usual difficulty. The talk was ready only at the last minute. The title was significant, however: 'On the Antiseptic Principle in the Practice of Surgery'. Although no comment on the first paper had yet been published (the last instalment had appeared two weeks earlier), it must have aroused discussion at the meeting. Lister took the first step toward generalizing his method by converting it into a principle. Unfortunately, he now confirmed it as the 'antiseptic' principle, thus leaving the focus on carbolic acid. The 'first object', he said, was 'destruction of any septic germs which may have been introduced into the wound' with full strength carbolic acid. 'The next object . . . is to guard effectually against the spreading of decomposition into the wound along the stream of blood and serum which ooze out during the first few days'. He now recommended the use of a putty of carbonate of lime with carbolic acid in linseed oil to cover the lint because it was less caustic. He reported no new cases in this brief review, but he thought it necessary to counsel 'perseverance with the antiseptic application, in spite of the appearance of suppuration, so long as other symptoms are favourable'. In order to give a wholly justified emphasis to the results he had obtained, Lister added toward the end of the paper:

... the two large wards in which most of my cases of accident and of operation are treated were amongst the unhealthiest in the whole surgical division of the Glasgow Royal Infirmary, in consequence, apparently, of those wards being unfavourably placed with reference to the supply of fresh air ... during the last nine months not a single instance of pyaemia, hospital gangrene, or erysipelas has occurred in them.

It was his first formulation of a theme which eventually provoked an angry reply from the Glasgow hospital authorities with whom he had never really been at peace.

Joseph and Agnes visited Isabella and her family after the BMA meeting and then went to Upton. Hector Cameron kept Lister informed as to the progress of patients who were undergoing antiseptic treatment. In September the Listers travelled to Wales for an extended holiday with Joseph Jackson, who wrote to Rickman Godlee on the 14th:

All of us except the little ones—i.e. Joseph & Agnes, Arthur & Susan, Bella, Joe & I returned last night from a three day excursion among the Welsh mountains—our conveyance an open two horse break—Our first night was at Capel Curig by the way of Llamorst & the Conway valley ... the next day we took the pass of Llanberis & lodged at the Victoria Hotel after visiting the fine fall which the showery weather gave us to see to the greatest advantage—& through our journey the magnificence of the clouds with the sunshine & shadows well repaid the inconvenience of the occasional rain— Yesterday we made part of the ascent of Snowdon, the rest leaving the track to mount to a high point commanding a glorious view of Llanberis pass & lakes etc & I contented myself with another, rather lower but I think as beautiful—In the afternoon we drove to Carnarvon & Bangor & then took the train home ...
Joseph has obtained an extension of his furlough & I expect we shall not return till the early part of the week after next ...

While Lister was enjoying the Welsh mountains with his family, the first winds of controversy began to blow. In fact the earliest comments on his five-part article had been by defenders. On July 6 in a paper 'On the Treatment of Incised Wounds with a View to Union by the First Intention', James Syme wrote that Lister's method made it unnecessary to keep the wound open for drainage. Syme reported seven successful cases involving both compound fractures and surgery. No less important was a leader in *The Lancet* after Lister's paper to the BMA:

If Professor Lister's conclusions with regard to the power of carbolic acid in compound fractures should be confirmed ... it will be difficult to overrate the importance of what we may really call his discovery. For although he bases his surgical use of carbolic acid upon the researches of M Pasteur, the application of these researches to the case of compound fractures, opened abscesses, and other recent wounds, is all his own. The need for determining the value of carbolic acid, and the best forms and mode of using it, is most urgent.

Lister's ambiguity had done the damage. The first storm centred on carbolic acid.

Sampson Gamgee, his friend from University College, was writing a series of articles on surgery in Paris for *The Lancet*. Though he made no reference to Lister, Gamgee noted that a mild carbolic acid solution had been used as an 'antiseptic lotion' by Maisonneuve, chief surgeon of the Hotel Dieu, for the past six years. Neither the method nor the purpose was Lister's, but the antiseptic was the same.

On September 21 a letter signed 'Chirurgicus' appeared in the *Edinburgh Daily Review* under the heading, 'Carbolic Acid in Surgery'. Referring to an article 'on the use of carbolic acid in surgical practice' reprinted by the newspaper, the writer feared it was 'calculated to bring down on us some discredit—particularly among our French and German neighbours—in as far as it attributes the first surgical employment of carbolic acid to Professor Lister . . . who has only used it a few months, whilst it has been employed for years past by some Continental surgeons, in the same cases and complications as those for which Mr Lister has availed himself of its services.' The writer called attention to 'various essays' on the subject, in particular one 'by Dr Lemaire of Páris . . . the second edition of which was published in 1865'. Lemaire had called attention to the power of carbolic acid to destroy germs 'and shows its utility in arresting suppuration in surgery, and, as a dressing to compound fractures and wounds'.

'Chirurgicus' was James Y Simpson, the discoverer of chloroform anaesthesia, who merely followed current custom by using a pen name to sign a personal attack. He circularized the medical profession of Edinburgh with the letter and never denied its authorship. Simpson chose Lister's weakest point for his attack, but he almost certainly had a secondary motive. In 1859 he had invented a technique to halt bleeding during surgery by means of metal needles which tightly fastened the cut ends of large blood vessels to the underside of the skin or muscular tissue. He called the technique acupressure. According to his biographer Simpson was jealous 'of everything that seemed fitted to set aside what he held to be useful . . . Nothing, he thought, should be tolerated whose tendency was to continue the use of the ligature in amputations, after the superiority of acupressure had, as he believed, been established'. Yet acupressure had been accepted only at the Infirmary at Aberdeen where Simpson was now a professor. It had been rejected in London by Erichsen at University College and Fergusson of King's College, and by Syme who was in a negative way the most important of all to Simpson.

Syme and Simpson had been colleagues at the University of Edinburgh. Simpson, the son of a baker, had been elected as Professor of Midwifery in 1840. Syme had backed Simpson's opponent for the position and had then joined in a movement by 'certain prominent members of the medical faculty' to abolish the Chair of General Pathology to which Simpson aspired. The Midwifery Professor was not a doctor and had not the status of his qualified medical colleagues. When Simpson proposed to collect surgical statistics, which he eventually published in the pamphlet on *Hospitalism*, Syme and others accused him of interference. The feud thus begun was temporarily suspended when Syme removed an abscess from Simpson's armpit because 'Mrs Simpson and others expressed a strong desire for Mr Syme', according to Simpson's biographer. But acupressure restored the contention. It reached a peak in 1865 when, in the theatrical manner of the medical dispute, Syme appeared before his class with a pamphlet by Simpson which he symbolically ripped in two. It was a childish act, and it may in some measure have reflected Syme's envy because Simpson had been made a baronet.

Simpson and Syme were members of a generation that had only native skill and intelligence with which to defend empirical practices lacking any real scientific foundation. Lister was a shining representative of a new generation not only because he was younger but because technology and the genius of men like himself had begun to make rational medicine possible. Simpson undoubtedly wrote to the Edinburgh newspaper because he believed that Lister was unsound, like Lister's patron, and should be brought down.

Their first difference had arisen in 1859, the year in which Simpson had introduced acupressure. At about the same time Lister had recommended the use of silver-wire sutures in preference to 'iron wire introduced by Mr Simpson'. In January 1865, furthermore, Simpson had sent Lister his pamphlet on acupressure with a covering letter criticizing the 'strange and inexplicable' surgical practice of 'sedulously and systematically implanting by the ligature . . . dead and decomposing arterial tissue in every large wound, and yet' surgeons 'wish these wounds to heal by the first intention'. Lister's reply is lost, but in 1867, the lecture notes taken by one of his students said: 'Mr Lister believes from experience that acupressure has not been proved to be trustworthy, and considers it never will. If acupressure fails in this it fails altogether.' And of course by that time antiseptic treatment had reduced if not yet eliminated the danger of septic ligatures.

The Lancet noticed the 'Chirurgicus' letter the week after its publication and concluded its editorial comment by observing: 'To Professor Lister is due the credit of having made the agent extensively known in this country.' On October 5 Lister replied that he had never seen Lemaire's book, 'which will hardly seem surprising, since it does not appear to have attracted the attention of our profession, or produced in the country where it was published, any practical effects'. Visitors to Glasgow had not questioned the originality of his system, he wrote, 'the novelty, I may remark, being, not the surgical use of carbolic acid (which I never claimed), but the methods of its employment with the view of protecting the reparatory processes from disturbances by external agency'. He ended the letter: 'Trusting that such unworthy cavils will not impede the adoption of a useful procedure, I am, Sir, Yours etc'. It was an unwise descent to the verbal fisticuffs of custom.

Two weeks later Lister had at last read Lemaire's book. Neither the Glasgow University Library nor the Faculty of Physicians and Surgeons had a copy so he had gone to Edinburgh, according to Cameron, 'where he found what he was in search of—I think in the Library of the University of Edinburgh. Very probably it had just been put there by Simpson, or obtained on his recommendation'. The book had first appeared in 1863 with the title, *De l'Acide Phénique, de Son action sur les Vegetaux, les Animaux, les Ferments, les Venins, les Miasmes; et de ses Applications à l'Industrie, à l'Hygiene, aux Sciences Anatomiques, et à la Thérapeutique*. Its 750 pages obviously covered every conceivable use for carbolic acid, including a great many that are dubious at best, of which the treatment of infection was the last. In his enthusiasm Lemaire seriously damaged his case. For example, among the diseases which Lemaire believed carbolic acid could be taken internally to cure were angina, croup, whooping cough, dysentery and cholera. Even Simpson recognized that Lemaire had gone too far. Although Lemaire recognized the relevance of Pasteur's discoveries to medicine, as had Spencer Wells in the following year, he did not suggest the use of antiseptics to create asepsis.

After reading the book Lister wrote a second letter to *The Lancet*: 'I selected carbolic acid as the most powerful of known antiseptics', he said. Nowhere does he give his authority for such a statement. The first research notes on his own experiments on the effectiveness of carbolic acid solutions are dated November 30, six weeks later. Nor had there been articles in the British medical press on the use of this or any other antiseptics in wounds between 1859 and 1865.

In France, however, a Dr Déclat had published a second review of the French literature on antiseptics in 1865. This book too was unknown to Lister. Until much later in his career he paid relatively little attention to the literature of his profession. He was evidently too busy with his own work to consult the works of others, with the important exception of Pasteur.

To his second letter, which appeared on October 19, Lister appended an unsolicited response to his earlier communication in *The Lancet* from Dr Philip Hair of Carlisle. Hair had studied at Paris during the previous winter and wrote: 'I think it my duty to say that, during my stay of six months, I never saw anything approaching to your treatment of wounds, etc., with carbolic acid'.

Two weeks later an extended reply, this time signed by Simpson, appeared in *The Lancet*. Although he did not publicly accept responsibility for the views of 'Chirurgicus', Simpson began with a sarcastic reference to the phrase, 'unworthy cavils': Lister 'appears to speak of such simple truths' as those advanced by his *nom de plume*. He mentioned the books by Lemaire and Déclat, and argued that Lister was preceded in the use of carbolic acid in compound fractures by two French surgeons in 1860, in abscesses by Lemaire and Maisonneuve, and in wounds by two French and one German surgeon in 1859. Three years earlier, furthermore, Professor Spence had used carbolic acid at Edinburgh Infirmary as a wash over amputations, but Spence had since abandoned the practice. After pointing with more cogency to Lister's ignorance of the literature on carbolic acid, Simpson concluded: 'One great and most laudable object which Professor Lister has in view in using carbolic acid as a local dressing to wounds is to close these wounds entirely by the first intention and without suppuration. . . . But these paramount objects have been obtained in the hospital of Aberdeen by the use of acupressure'. Thus Simpson revealed the point of his attack at the same time that he made it clear he had understood Lister's principle. Yet he does not appear to have perceived the difference between the use of a carbolic wash and Lister's protective methods.

Lister replied on November 2:

The elaborate communication of Sir James Simpson . . . may seem to require some reply. But as I have already endeavoured to place the matter in its true light without doing injustice to anyone, I must forbear from any comment on his allegations. In the forthcoming numbers of your journal, I have arranged to publish . . . a series of papers fully explanatory of the subject in question, and your readers will then be able to judge for themselves . . .

The reply was sensibly restrained. Lister's real feelings may be judged from two sentences in a long letter of self-justification written to his father on October 13: 'It is long since I gave up any idea of having any work I might do measured according to its deserts, whatever they might be: and I have always felt that for the editors of these medical journals to take no notice at all of any articles I might write was the best that could happen; so that the good, if there was any, in my work might quietly produce its effect in improving the knowledge and treatment of disease. "Fame is no plant that grows on mortal soil" is a passage thee quoted to me in a letter many years ago'. The note of Christian martyrdom mixed with a touch of paranoia is unmistakable. Godlee claimed that Simpson 'entered into such contests *con amore*; to Lister they were repugnant and distressing in the highest degree'. Perhaps so, but it was Simpson who let the matter drop, with Lister's reply of November 2, and it was Lister who had published the expression, 'unworthy cavil'. There is no denying that he had been unfairly criticized, but not by the editor of *The Lancet*. There is no denying, furthermore, that Simpson had a personal axe to grind, but Lister had laid himself open to misunderstanding both by his stylistic vagary and by his surprising failure to do his homework. Yet if there was right on Simpson's side of the dispute, there was truth on Lister's, the truth of discovery.

Again Lister delayed the promised articles. Arthur wrote that he supposed it could not 'be helped & I should hope it is all for the best that it is as it is, unless as Papa thinks, people will have made up their minds & will <u>disregard</u> all further accounts of the treatment, the iron will have got cold & no amount of hammering will tell then.' In the next paragraph Arthur suggests that Joseph had realized the need for an unambiguous statement. He said that they 'earnestly long to see "the rule of thumb" given to the world, but I suppose thy engagements make this very difficult, indeed impossible—' The article, 'Illustrations of the Antiseptic Treatment in Surgery. No. 1', appeared in *The Lancet* on November 30. It was little more than an introduction to what was planned as a series of case histories. The short paper nevertheless made two innovations:

Admitting . . . the truth of the germ theory, and proceeding in accordance with it, we must . . . destroy in the first instance once and for all any septic organisms which may exist within the part concerned; and after this has been done, our efforts must be directed to the prevention of the entrance of others into it. And provided that these indications are *really* fulfilled, the less the antiseptic agent comes in contact with the living tissue the better . . .

The paragraph, like the remainder of the article, refers to an 'antiseptic agent', not to carbolic acid. Its point, furthermore, is that antiseptics, if they are effective, will damage human tissue as well as the germs against which they are directed. Not only was the natural healing power of the body interfered with, but the danger of infection could actually be increased, because the antiseptic perpetuated and exacerbated the open wound.

The problem grew in importance as Lister tried one antiseptic after another. None are sufficiently selective. Those which do less damage also give less certainty of protection. His first experiments on carbolic acid at the end of November were directed at this problem. The notes, in Mrs Lister's meticulous hand and his scrawl, reveal that eighteen bits of meat removed from the neck of a freshly-slaughtered ox were moistened with water and with carbolic acid in five solutions ranging from one part carbolic to 100 parts water to one in a 1000. Each bit was wrapped in gutta percha which had been washed in the same solutions as the meat, tied with silver wire and stored at 70 degrees Fahrenheit. When the packets were opened, they were all seen and smelled to have putrefied but in varying degrees. In other words the solutions had not been strong enough. As to the series of 'Illustrations', it did not progress beyond No. 1.

The essential conservatism of the antiseptic system was effectively stated in the lectures on inflammation, putrefaction and suppuration which Lister gave his students in the autumn of 1867. On inflammation he covered essentially the same data that had first appeared in the papers of 1858. He had not yet found a role for germs, but:

Putrefaction is a variety of fermentation. Putrefaction is brought about by the agencies of minute animalculae. The motes of the sunbeam are course compared with the germs of these Fungi. They were supposed to be concomitants of putrefaction but these are the Causes.

As to suppuration, pus formation, it is either inflammatory or it is due to 'Chemical Stimulation', of which there are two kinds: the chemicals resulting from decomposition and from tissue breakdown caused by the use of antiseptics. Decomposition is presumably an aspect of putrefaction, and therefore caused by the action of germs, but Lister seems not to have made this point explicit. It is significant that neither gangrene nor hospital gangrene, though they were treated as distinct diseases, are directly associated with germs. Gangrene was said to be caused by inflammation and hospital gangrene, by suppuration.

About antiseptics Lister said: 'Carbolic acid seems to be an effective germ poisoner and has the great advantage of being an anaesthetic'. He referred to the temporary local anaesthesia that is a concomitant of the burning sensation accompanying its application. Chloride of zinc and sulphurous acid are even more painful.

Of the germs themselves Lister said cautiously: 'They are not supposed to be there by spontaneous growth or generation'. He showed his class an experiment to demonstrate that the air carries organisms which heat can kill. It was suggested by one that Pasteur had performed. Lister poured fresh urine into four glass flasks. The necks of three had then been heated and drawn out into very thin tubes which were twisted so as to leave a passage for air but not one that dust could negotiate. The neck of the fourth had been drawn out and cut off short in the original vertical direction. The flasks had been boiled so that steam from the urine came out, leaving a partial vacuum in them which the air had filled as soon as boiling stopped. The urine in the flasks with twisted necks remained clear and unclouded, whereas in the flask with its neck open vertically so that dust could enter a mould grew. According to Lister, and to Pasteur, these results showed that it was not the air but something in the air that caused putrefaction. That something was an organized germ, out of which grew the microscopic organisms seen to be moving about and multiplying in putrefying and fermenting matter. But the flasks could not prove this theory. It was also reasonable, on the basis of the flask experiment, to argue that a chemical or chemicals in the air, given a suitable medium, could become organized spontaneously into living germs. That Lister recognized this additional possibility, his cautious statement indicated. He believed incorrectly that putrefaction was caused by the invasion of healthy tissue by *airborne* substances, but he correctly identified the cause as 'germs'. The flasks enabled him to show his students why he used antiseptics.

Despite his problems in writing and speaking Lister had become a missionary. Cameron pointed out that Lister's addition to his application for the post at University College of the paragraph describing antiseptic treatment 'shows that from the first he foresaw its supreme importance'. He had not considered that the arduous operation for excision of the wrist joint was suitable because, though it was original, it was merely another aspect of the surgeon's craft.

Once he had read the papers by Pasteur and understood the connection between putrefaction and germs, he applied surgical experience to the exclusion of these organisms from wounds. He believed that his method was important because it enabled him to save lives and limbs more effectively than others could do. He did not apprehend that his laborious dressings involved a revolution in the whole conception of disease. How could he? Some scientists make discoveries by sheer slog, as Ehrlich did when he made his way through more than six hundred compounds of mercury to Salvarsan. Others achieve intuitive breakthroughs, as Newton is said to have done when the apple fell on his head. Lister followed a middle path, perhaps the one most often trod : he had an insight, but it meant nothing until the clinical details could be worked into a practical surgical routine.

8

BACTERIOLOGY

THE EARLIEST DISCIPLES were Lister's house surgeons, men like Hector Cameron from Glasgow and the Canadian, Archibald Malloch, who held the office between 1865 and 1867. His students would eventually carry the doctrine into every British hospital and a large number abroad.

Other than Syme the first of his peers to use Lister's methods, even before he had followers in England, seem to have been from the United States. According to Malloch, Dr George Derby of Boston treated one patient antiseptically in 1867. In April 1868 Lister wrote to his father about the surgeon 'from the Southern States of N. America, a very gentlemanly man, who declared himself a complete convert to the system,' after a short visit to Glasgow. A New York doctor also visited Glasgow during the early days, and many others came to observe Lister's practice later, but he seems never to have trained a surgeon who then worked in the United States. Malloch believed that he had begun the consistent application of antiseptic methods in North America after he returned to practise in Hamilton, Ontario. In February 1869 Malloch first opened an abscess antiseptically, and with complete success.

The most informed and widespread early acceptance of 'Listerism' was in Germany. Dr Carl Thiersch of Leipzig read Lister's papers in *The Lancet* and almost immediately tried the system on sixteen patients, with good results. Thiersch sent his house surgeon, Herman Georg Joseph, to Glasgow to observe Lister's work. Before the end of 1867 Joseph published a pamphlet on antisepsis in Leipzig. 'I have to thank thee for the pamphlets from India and Leipzig', Joseph Jackson wrote on February 28, 1868. He noted that the 'young German doctor' is 'evidently thy disciple'. At about this time the Surgical Clinic in Breslau adopted the antiseptic system, and German acceptance became almost universal in the next five years.

The French were less enthusiastic, but one French surgeon, Dr Just Lucas-Championnière, came to Glasgow during 1868 and was impressed by Lister's procedures. The *Australian Medical Journal* carried a report of cases successfully treated antiseptically early in 1868. In March a surgeon from St Petersburg visited Glasgow and left full of praise. Lister's methods were the subject for discussion at the June meeting of the Medical Society of Vienna, and on July 11 according to Lister's ward journal, Professor Saxtorph of the Frederik's Hospital, Copenhagen, observed an operation in Glasgow. He introduced antiseptic surgery in Denmark, and wrote to Lister that 'not a single case of pyaemia has occurred since I came home'.

Lister said, in May 1868, that the system gained acceptance abroad so quickly because Europeans had used carbolic acid as an antiseptic dressing and could see beyond it to the originality of his methods, whereas to most British surgeons the antiseptic itself was new. Godlee believed that the relative speed with which German doctors adopted the treatment reflected their medical education, which required a grounding in the arts and sciences before the surgical student went on to medical school. Cameron had an even simpler explanation: 'The English surgeons, who accounted for his great vogue in Germany by the complacent comment that the Germans, unlike the English, were a dirty people and needed disinfectants, had a certain amount of truth in their contention'. Under Lister's influence both Godlee and Cameron felt it necessary to explain what was to them his struggle for recognition, in England, if not in Scotland. No doubt there was opposition in Britain. Indeed, its strength demonstrated the intellectual richness of British medicine rather than its poverty.

But there was one group of Britons who never for a moment doubted. They were the patients whom Lister and his students treated. On March 4, 1868, Agnes Lister wrote to her sister-in-law, Mary Godlee:

A late house surgeon of Joseph's, now in practice in Glasgow ... told Joseph yesterday of a case he had treated—a terrible severe burn received by a poor boy in a foundry. We saw Dr Watson (the doctor) the day that it had taken place, and he did not think that the boy _could_ recover ... but by the help of carbolic acid he _is_ recovering and the case has excited great interest in several foundaries and deputations of their workmen have been to see the boy dressed and it is very probable that the boy's masters will appoint Dr Watson surgeon to their works which will give him a salary of £300 a year.

Another house surgeon wrote many years later: 'if recognition on the part of his colleagues was slow in coming, patients who had had experience under both systems, the old and the new, were quick to perceive the difference'. One old man readmitted to an Edinburgh ward two years after Lister had returned there from Glasgow, said: 'Man, but ye hae made a grand improvement since I was here afore'. The sickly sweet stink of decay, the shouts of delirium and the cries of pain had gone.

This awareness on the parts of the sick, the poor and the illiterate of what Lister did for them was the granite base not only for his personal fame, but also for the great work that still lay ahead. Lister it was who made germs real, almost visible, to the entire world. In order to prove that they were neither hypothetical nor spontaneous creations, he became something entirely new, a bacteriologist. A handful of his contemporaries performed experiments of greater originality and advanced the understanding of microbes more significantly, but having committed his life to the conquest of these organisms, Lister succeeded in reducing pain and delaying death. Pasteur deserves the credit which Lister always gave him for the germ theory of disease, but Lister dramatized germs by defeating them.

The flasks containing boiled urine that he had shown to his class in November 1867 were the first in a series of bacteriological experiments that occupied Lister during the rest of his life. The flasks themselves became one of his most precious teaching tools. He and Mrs Lister carried them on their knees in the railway carriage when they returned to live in Edinburgh. When they carried them to London in 1877, the urine in the three flasks with the twisted necks still retained its unclouded clarity.

At first he undertook bacteriological research in order to adapt facets of his craft to the antiseptic method. The antiseptics themselves never satisfied him, nor did the dressings. The first compound fracture cases had been dressed with a carbolized putty, and toward the end of his career he was using a carbolic acid gauze covered with gutta percha which he had manufactured himself. From the first, instruments, sutures, ligatures and the surgeon's hands had been soaked in a strong carbolic acid solution. In December 1867, however, he began a continuing series of experiments to find a better antiseptic ligature.

There is no 'perfect' ligature because a foreign body always initiates some inflammatory and immunological reactions. At the least a ligature should tie the blood vessel without danger of secondary haemorrhage, with as little irritation as possible and without infection. Lister decided to soak the familiar silk thread in a carbolic solution. It had been customary to leave the ends of ligatures long so that they provided a track for drainage, and so that they could be extracted to reduce irritation. Lister reasoned that if he could eliminate infection, there should be less need for drainage and the ligature might be absorbed in a manner analogous to the absorption of bone fragments he had observed in compound fractures. To test the theory he tied a major artery in the neck of a horse with carbolized silk using suitable antiseptic precautions. The horse died unexpectedly some six weeks later of normal old age. Cameron, who had assisted in the original operation on the animal, reported the death to Lister, who was in bed with a cold. At Lister's request Cameron returned to the Veterinary College, dissected out the left side of the horse's neck and returned with it to Woodside Place. It was now 11.00 p.m., but Lister got out of bed and worked until 2.00 a.m. to isolate the ligated site. As he had predicted although the silk remained, it had been completely covered over by new tissue.

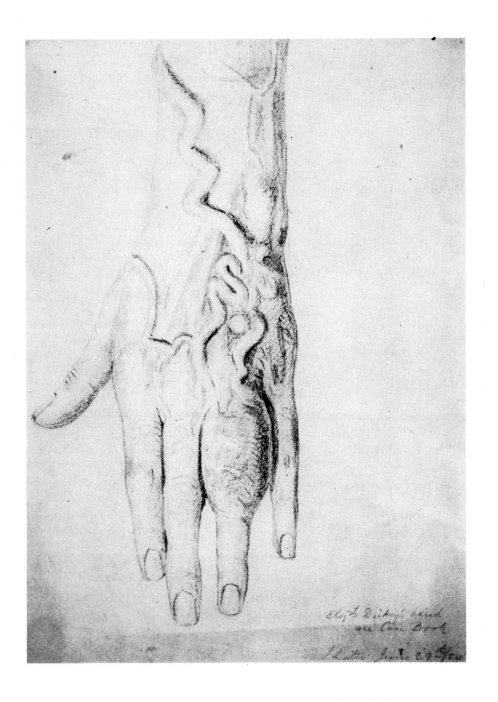

7. "*Elizth Dickey's hand see Case Book J. Lister June 29th/54*".

8. Joseph and Agnes Lister, a previously-unpublished wedding photograph. April 1856.

His cold had been sufficiently severe to keep Lister in bed for most of January. Nevertheless by February 2, 1868, he was able to adapt his horse experiment to a human patient. The severest test of a ligature is its use to close an artery because of the pressure with which blood is forced through these vessels. A private patient came to him with an aneurism, a swelling in an artery caused by a thinning of the arterial wall which can burst, leading to rapid death. Lister had 'for the first time in my life in the living subject' tied an artery in the leg of 'a respectable woman'. The patient recovered without complication, but about ten months later she died when another aneurism ruptured. Lister performed a post mortem examination which showed that much of the silk ligature had been absorbed. That which remained, however, was found within a tiny pocket of pus-like liquid. Though it was probably a deposit that had been larger but had shrunk as the ligature disappeared, Lister feared that it revealed the beginning of an abscess. He began to experiment with catgut, like silk a familiar substance for ligatures but less satisfactory because it was more unwieldy.

In the letter of February 2 to his father Lister reported three other major operations and several minor ones. A month later he wrote to Joseph Jackson: 'I have enough for three people's energies to occupy me . . . Preparation for the Lancet would do for one individual; practice hospital and private, would be amply sufficient for a second; and College duties . . . would do well for a third person'. Nevertheless he and Mrs Lister managed short Scottish holidays, first in Moffat just before the ligature of the artery, and at Dunkhill with the Symes, toward the end of March.

On April 17 before a meeting of the Royal Medico-Chirurgical Society of Glasgow in Faculty Hall, 'Mr Lister gave a lengthened exposition of the atmospheric germ theory, and illustrated it by the exhibition of M Pasteur's experiment with flasks containing urine'. He began by listing three prerequisites for success with antiseptic surgery: first, the surgeon must be so convinced of the benefits to be gained from the system that he would devote to it 'the same kind of thought and pain as he now . . . bestows upon the planning and execution of an operation'. Second, the efforts should be founded 'on sound principles', or in other words, on a belief in the germ theory. Third, he should have a 'thoroughly trustworthy practical means at his disposal', that is, a dependable antiseptic. The object of antisepsis, he said, was 'not the avoidance of suppuration, but the prevention of putrefaction in the wound'. Lister had observed correctly that suppuration, pus formation, could be caused by mechanical irritation such as pressure as well as by irritation caused by germs, but he could not yet distinguish clearly between the two.

He was still using carbolic acid in putty as the external dressing, and he told his medical audience that failures occur when the overlap is not large enough to prevent germs in the discharge that escapes under the dressing from re-entering the wound along the avenue provided by the discharge. He had also continued experiments with improved dressings, having tried and discarded a complex combination of paraffin, wax, olive oil and carbolic acid in an attempt to reduce the weight of the putty dressing. He was now able to tell the Medico-Chirurgical Society about a mixture of shellac and carbolic acid which he hoped would make both a lighter and a firmer dressing. Other than these details the two-hour talk contained nothing new. To Lister the whole content of any contribution he had made consisted of such details. He appears not to have used the 'lac plaster' in the hospital until July 1868. Only then was he satisfied that he had brought it to a trustworthy condition. The discussion that followed his paper was restricted to the 'cause of putrefaction in wounds'.

Four days after the talk he wrote to his father: 'I also took my stand distinctly as to my part in the antiseptic system'. On the whole he had been very well received. He explained that the long talk 'must be put into shape for printing and I intend to send it like the Dublin one to both the Lancet and the British Medical Journal . . . It will take a deal of polishing, and I mean to have some woodcuts, and also to have separate copies printed for private distribution. I fancy both thee and Arthur will express approval of the amount of publication, if not of the quality of the material.'

The plan for dual publication ran into difficulties and produced a minor quarrel with *The Lancet* that presaged more serious differences between Lister and the magazine. On May 2 it published a letter by one of Lister's former Glasgow students, James Coats, who was now Pathologist to the Royal Infirmary. He reported a compound fracture of the ankle that he had treated antiseptically with complete success. The next week another of Lister's Glasgow students reported three compound fracture cases in *The Lancet*. The journal had by no means taken a position on Lister's system; it was, indeed, far too early to do so. On June 20, however, Lister wrote to Dr Glover, one of the magazine's sub-editors, who became a good friend:

I am very sorry if I have occasioned you groundless annoyance by my letter. I do not think, however, that the term 'magnanimity' is quite applicable to the case. For I made no public charge, but merely expressed confidentially to yourself what my impressions were. Now however, I gladly accept your assurance that I was mistaken. But you must excuse me for not being able to comprehend why I should be treated differently from Dr Wilson Fox, or from the way in which I was myself treated, as regards simultaneous publication in the Lancet & the British Medical Journal.

However, I would cheerfully act upon Dr Wakley's suggestion, if it were possible.

He explained that unfortunately he had not the time to shorten or revise the paper. 'All therefore that I can do is to repeat my offer of the address for your pages, with the request that its insertion may be granted me as a personal favour.' *The Lancet* did not publish the address, for what seem to have been sensible editorial reasons: it was very long and the *British Medical Journal*, *The Lancet*'s most important competitor, published it in four instalments. Dr

Wakley may also have thought that it added little that was new to the discussion of antiseptic surgery. As in the Simpson controversy, however, Lister's extreme sensitivity to any suggestion of opposition reflected not only a determination to bring his treatment to the attention of his colleagues, which was wholly admirable, but also a paranoid twist which may have stemmed from the illness that had shaken him twenty years before.

Meanwhile medical visitors came to watch Lister's work. Joseph Bell of Edinburgh, formerly his student, was now a surgeon. According to Godlee, his 'attainments were somewhat overshadowed by qualities which are said to have suggested . . . Sherlock Holmes to Conan Doyle' when he was a medical student in Edinburgh in the early 1870s. William MacCormac, later President of the Royal College of Surgeons, travelled up from London. He became one of Lister's staunchest defenders. Also from London came Lister's cousin, Marcus Beck, now on the staff at University College Hospital and eager to see what new wonders Joseph had worked.

'You will be in time for a fortnightly course of lectures I am going to give on operative surgery, beginning next Tuesday,' Lister wrote on June 18, 1868. The course was 'to make up for what I was obliged to omit last session', probably because of his severe winter cold. Beck came and observed not only Lister's antiseptic practice but also his missionary eagerness. In mid-July Beck wrote to his sister that he had gone to dinner at Woodside Place along with Cameron and Archibald Malloch:

. . . the dinner was for the purpose of propagating the gospel of carbolic acid to a benighted navy surgeon who had introduced himself to Joseph at the hospital a day or two ago—but at the last minute Joseph got a note to say he was ill and could not come. So we had a quick dinner by ourselves—

Favourable reports also continued to appear in *The Lancet*. Dr John Rose, from the Kidderminster Infirmary, wrote that he had successfully used the antiseptic method for the treatment of a compound fracture of the leg. One of Lister's students, Dr J R Wylie, wrote from Alexandria that he had cured two cases of abscess. Of greater interest was a letter from Dr Pearson Cresswell, Chief Surgeon to the Dowlais Iron Works in Merthyr Tydfil, published on July 25:

The use of carbolic acid in the treatment of wounds and compound fractures has created quite a revolution in the surgical practice at the Dowlais Iron Works; for during the last 12 months I have used it extensively . . . in every instance with marked success.

The works employed 8500 people. Dr Cresswell went on to cite the case of a man who had been shot in the upper leg during practice at a rifle range. He had sustained a compound fracture, and the wound had healed without complications. Cresswell's practice is another striking example of successes that were easily recognizable to a large population of the working people whose limbs and lives were most at risk.

In his wards Lister supervised every facet of the treatment. Malloch recalled: 'Mr Lister frequently spent two hours in the wards dressing his most important cases'. The ward visits began at 8 am:

He taught . . . that there was a right way and a wrong way of doing everything, from the dressing of a case and bandaging it to the proper insertion, finally, of the pin to fix the bandage; and that the least complaint of pain or uneasiness demanded immediate attention.

It was a pleasure to see the smile on each countenance when Mr Lister entered the ward . . .

When his lectures ended in August he and Mrs Lister went to Ventnor for a holiday. Early September was very warm. On the 10th he wrote a long letter to Malloch reviewing the reports of patients which he had received the day before from the house surgeon, and describing his attempts to improve the shellac dressing.

Since I have been here I have tried whether the same object (preventing adhesion of the lac) might not be got more satisfactorily by applying some kind of powder to the surface of the lac, so as to give it a bloom (as it were) that would keep it from sticking.

He enclosed a specimen of the material that he had used his holiday to produce.

Early in September *The Lancet* observed editorially: 'Mr Lister's treatment does not find much favour in London. Are the conditions of suppuration different here from those in Glasgow or Dowlais? Or is it that the antiseptic treatment is not tried with that care without which Mr Lister has always pointed out it does not succeed?' The journal began a series of brief reports from London hospitals on the antiseptic method. 'Carbolic acid, sometimes in exact accordance with Professor Lister's method . . . and sometimes with modifications at the fancy of the surgeon, has now been pretty extensively tried in the various hospitals.' The first summary from St George's indicated how little the details of Lister's practice had in fact been understood by *The Lancet* or by the surgeons whose fancy deviated from his. In twenty-six lacerations and cuts on which carbolic dressings had been used 'according to Mr Lister's directions', seven clean cuts but no lacerations had healed by first intention. Two of four compound fractures suffered by *out-patients* had healed satisfactorily. Two weeks later Middlesex Hospital reported that Mr Nunn used carbolic acid as a disinfectant but 'the surgeons insist on the most careful and continued application both by dressing and syringing'. The Middlesex, furthermore, had anticipated one of Lister's most controversial innovations, the use of a fine spray of carbolic acid solution to purify the atmosphere.

At Bart's, Lister's friend, James Paget, had used carbolic acid in a few cases where 'it had been useless, but this may possibly have been, Mr Paget thinks, from some error in the mode of application'. At Guy's Mr Bryant thought carbolic acid worked, but Mr Birkett had had little experience of it.

In a laudatory paragraph at the end of the year *The Lancet* summarized the reports and letters that it had published:

Professor Lister has good reason to be satisfied with the testimony that comes from almost all quarters of the truth of his teaching as to the contribution of carbolic acid over the process of suppuration and putrefaction in wounds, and, through these, over one of the most deadly states which patients get into under the actual treatment of our best hospitals, and over some of the hitherto most incurable diseases of the bone.

Indeed favourable testimony did continue. The Prince of Wales General Hospital, then the Evangelical Deaconnesses' Institution, Tottenham, was said to have been the first London hospital to introduce the full antiseptic system. Berkeley Hill of University College Hospital had been amongst those who went to Glasgow to see for themselves. On January 16 *The Lancet* survey reported on progress at UCH. The Hospital had neither pyaemia nor erysipelas in cases where antiseptic treatment had been used, but the danger of carbolic acid poisoning appeared to be great. The Professor of Surgery, John Marshall, no longer attempted to apply the system because 'green urine and other toxic symptoms' had appeared after large amounts of carbolic acid were used during a breast removal. Others at UCH were divided on the value of the system.

Lister was alive to the danger of carbolic acid poisoning. He had told the Medico-Chirurgical Society that when he used the substance full strength to clean wounds, some patients had vomited persistently. He had not generalized, but in his usual way left the warning implicit in the clinical example. Other surgeons were less careful with the dilution or the amounts they used.

In *The Lancet*, surgeons at London and Westminster Hospitals reported favourably on carbolic acid. John Ross, the Kidderminster surgeon, had successfully tried it in fractures, burns, gunshot and other wounds. The German Hospital, Dalston, where the surgeon was a German, introduced Lister's methods. From Liverpool, E R Bickersteth, surgeon to the Royal Infirmary, wrote two articles praising both the antiseptic method and the catgut ligature.

On the other hand Bickersteth's articles sandwiched one by James Spence, the Edinburgh Professor of Surgery, which described a disastrous failure with the catgut ligature. That was in early June 1869. The year had begun with negative reports on antiseptic surgery from Charing Cross and the Great Northern Hospitals, London. Lister's former chief at University College Hospital, Erichsen, had failed with a serious fracture of the upper leg, though this case was not published. In February and March *The Lancet* printed two lectures on the 'Treatment of Fractures' by James Paget. He repeated that 'carbolic acid was applied, if not with all the skill that Professor Lister would employ, yet with more than is ever likely to be generally used in the treatment of fractures; and yet it certainly did no good'. To this Lister felt compelled to reply, though had the attack 'proceeded from anyone less deservedly eminent than Mr Paget', he said, he would not have bothered. He pointed out that Paget's practice departed in several important respects from that which he advised. Many years later Sir Henry Butlin, who had been Paget's house surgeon, told Cameron: 'our technique was so indifferently applied that the dressing was constantly slipping down and the bed was bathed in pus until the usual shiver occurred and the patient went the way of all flesh'.

Joseph Jackson read the medical press and was fully aware of the mounting controversy. Of Bickersteth's article he wrote: 'Surely the light that spreads so in other directions will come to shine in this wilderness of London too'. In fact approval outside of London was by no means universal, nor had Lister been everywhere rejected in the metropolis. In so far as London opposed him at this time, however, *The Lancet* was itself unwittingly at fault.

By asking hospitals about their use of carbolic acid, the magazine had put the wrong question. With the best of intentions it had perpetuated the very issue that Simpson had raised a year before, and that Lister had devoted so much energy to combating. As Lister now, at last, appreciated all too clearly, faith in the germ theory was imperative if the use of carbolic acid or any other antiseptic was to serve any coherent purpose. Without the conviction that germs are a real and present danger, the antiseptic treatment appeared to many surgeons, even those as painstaking as Paget and Spence, to be absurdly complicated and unnecessarily repetitive. Spence's failure with catgut exemplified this aspect of the opposition.

Catgut requires careful preparation if it is to be supple enough to use but not so slippery that it does not hold a knot. With his usual care Lister decided to test a commercial product. He and Mrs Lister went to Upton for Christmas, the last they were ever to spend there. They returned to Glasgow before the New Year, but a part of this unusually short visit was used to begin an experiment with catgut ligatures. The major artery in the neck of a calf was tied. The family museum on the first floor served as a laboratory, and the operation was performed under chloroform. 'I have a vivid recollection of the operation, the first at which I assisted him,' wrote Godlee; 'the shaving and the purification of the part, the meticulous attention to every antiseptic detail, the dressing formed of a towel soaked in carbolized oil; and my grandfather's alabaster Buddha on the mantelpiece contemplating with inscrutable gaze the services of beast to man.' After a month the relevant parts were dissected out according to Lister's instructions and sent to him. 'The meat of the Calf was divided among the 4 men much I believe to their satisfaction', wrote Joseph Jackson of the employees who had helped with the work. Lister found that the catgut had been replaced by new tissue and thus confirmed its value as a ligature. However, later experiments showed that it was absorbed too rapidly, placing the patient in danger of secondary haemorrhage. Amidst his clinical work, his lectures and his bacterial experiments, Lister devoted hours to the improvement of catgut until he was too old to proceed further with it.

On April 3, 1869, 'Observations on Ligature of Arteries on the Antiseptic System' reported the calf experiment in *The Lancet*. The magazine commented that the catgut ligature promised to be 'far more than a mere contribution to practical surgery. It enlarges our ideas of life' by showing the absorption of dead organic substance in the living body. Of the successes *The Lancet* continued: 'But it will be objected they cannot be obtained by other surgeons. Be it so . . . they are obtained by Mr Lister, and . . . he attributes them to a refined and scrupulous carrying out of the antiseptic principle'. Lister could hardly have put the point better.

In the early months of 1869 a profound change in his circumstances had begun to take shape. In February Jemima Syme died. Joseph Jackson wrote to Joseph: 'I have truly felt for thy estimable father-in-law under his bereavement and the desolation he must feel in his home—May it not lay on you a duty of frequently visiting him'. Then, in April, Syme suffered a severe stroke.

Agnes shared the nursing duties with her younger sister, Lucy. Now in her late twenties and a beautiful girl, Lucy was still unmarried. She suffered severely from some mysterious and persistent nervous affliction. In 1868 Marcus Beck told his mother: 'Miss Syme is still here and has been rather unwell with the tic for the last few days but is better now'. Joseph Jackson thought she might derive a positive advantage from the responsibility of caring for her father. Nevertheless, both Joseph and Agnes were frequently at Millbank, and when Lister had to return to Glasgow in June, Joseph Jackson wondered whether Agnes had been able to come with him.

Syme was almost seventy. His illness forced him to resign the chair of Clinical Surgery, and his personal choice of a successor fell naturally on Lister, who applied at once. In a letter to Dr Dyce Duckworth, the founder of an eminent medical family, Lister said that other candidates were collecting signatures in support of their applications. 'I confess they seem to me extremely undignified. . . . I intend to content myself with a very few testimonials, believing that the authorities concerned will be more influenced by the quality than by the quantity.' And he did, selecting only six: James Paget, John Erichsen and William Sharpey from London, E R Bickersteth from Liverpool, Edward Lund, surgeon to the Manchester Royal Infirmary and the Reverend Thomas Barclay, Principal of the University of Edinburgh. Lister was elected on August 17. It was an auspicious return under sad circumstances, but *The Lancet* expressed satisfaction: 'We have throughout strongly supported the candidature of Mr Lister . . . Even if the hopes which have been raised in connection with his antiseptic labours have to be qualified, he is well calculated to raise the scientific character of surgery'.

Lister attended the Glasgow Academic Senate for the last time on April 27. Although the lectures had ended, his responsibilities at the Infirmary continued with 'various cases of a disturbing kind', as he wrote on June 6 in response to a request for an article. His private practice required him to make 'several calls to the country', and his obligations had been temporarily complicated by Spence's failure with the catgut ligature. In May he made a hurried trip to London, in part to see Joseph Jackson whose health was declining, and possibly also on business with *The Lancet*. He and Mrs Lister now went every Sunday to Millbank. In late August they took Syme to Mull for a holiday.

The thirty-seventh annual meeting of the British Medical Association assembled in Leeds at the beginning of August. The surgical section was addressed by Mr Nunneley of the Leeds hospital. Nunneley stated that he did not accept the germ theory of disease. For three years, furthermore, he had treated his patients without carbolic acid while his colleagues who had used the antiseptic obtained no better results. Now, said Nunneley, his colleagues were abandoning carbolic acid. *The Lancet* commented editorially that 'the success of the treatment would depend entirely upon the precise observation of many precautions' and wondered whether failures were not due to remissness in this respect. On the other hand the editor observed that 'any new kind of treatment was frequently attended by improved results, for no other reason than that the patients subjected to it were watched and tended with special care and assiduity'. *The Lancet* recommended that the British Medical Association appoint a committee on antiseptic treatment.

Writing from Glasgow on August 24, Lister asked *The Lancet* to publish a letter he had received from T Pridgin Teale, a colleague of Nunneley's at Leeds, who had not abandoned antisepsis. Teale, like *The Lancet*, ascribed failure 'to imperfection in carrying out your rules'.

Thereupon Lister's Glasgow colleague, James Morton, wrote to *The Lancet* supporting Nunneley. 'Those who mount a hobby generally allow it to carry them too far,' he said. It was the first statement of an important theme in the attack on Lister, though it became more exactly focused on the germ theory as time passed. He was being accused of the very thing that had aroused his suspicions of Simpson: overstating his claims to his own ends.

Lister replied sharply that Morton 'has never had the curiosity to enter my wards', and that he had used carbolic acid as a 'remedy', taking Morton's word, 'without reference to antiseptic principles'. To which Morton replied in turn that he had 'often' been in Lister's wards, and: 'That in the trial . . . I caused to be made . . . the cases were dressed by pupils of Mr Lister'. With Morton's second letter *The Lancet* published one from D Campbell Black, another Glasgow physician, who believed that 'the bulk of the profession in Glasgow' supported Nunneley and Morton with regard to 'the latest toy of medical science so-called' which he named 'the carbolic mania'.

This brief storm reflects the controversy at its lowest, most poorly-informed level. For example, Morton had asked 'pupils' of Lister to dress his patients. Any surgeon who would thus shrug off responsibility is hardly to be taken seriously. Two of Morton's cases, furthermore, had figured amongst Lister's original compound fracture series, both of them successfully. Both Morton and Black had cited the work of Dr Thomas Keith at the Edinburgh Royal Infirmary as evidence for their case against Lister. Keith had had great success with ovariotomy, removal of the ovaries, then considered to be a dangerous operation because it broke the general rule against opening the abdomen.

Keith and Spencer Wells, the London surgeon who used cold water for cleanliness, had had some 30% mortality in their earlier cases, but had gradually improved this dismal record. In September 1869 Keith wrote to *The Lancet* that he had performed ninety-two ovariotomies since 1862, and that he had 'more or less perfectly, used some antiseptic dressing'. On all other wounds he used 'Mr Lister's method', but neither he nor Wells found that it bettered their record with ovariotomies. Keith irrigated the wound with distilled water during the operation and disturbed the tissue as little as possible, thus, in practice, reducing the risk of infection. Lister regretted that Keith would not adopt the antiseptic treatment completely, but he was forced to consider whether it was something Keith and Wells did, or whether ovariotomy was itself for some reason an exceptional operation. He concluded that both factors operated to improve their record. In August 1871 he told the annual BMA meeting that there might be four reasons. The first was Keith's general cleanliness. He even boiled his sponges. The remaining three had to do with the structure of the abdomen itself. Lister guessed that the membranes lining the abdominal cavity might have some special defensive quality, as they do, but he did not greatly increase the frequency with which he performed abdominal surgery himself.

Keith became Lister's friend and defender. The attempt by Morton and Black to use him against Lister failed because they did not understand the principles underlying the work of either man.

While this unenlightened argument was occupying space in *The Lancet*, Lister wrote to his father on September 12, 1869, that he and Mrs Lister had entertained Dr Sharpey and Dr and Mrs Allen Thomson at lunch at Woodside Place. It was to be his last letter to Joseph Jackson.

On October 19 Arthur wrote, 'we were all much interested with Aggy's graphic description of your last hours at Glasgow'. They had moved that week to a furnished house at 17 Abercromby Place, Edinburgh, where they lived for several months before they moved into their own house at 9 Charlotte Square. The house had belonged to Syme before he bought Millbank. It cost Lister a 'Most enormous sum', but he was a relatively rich man, in addition to which the income from class fees received by the Professor of Clinical Surgery at Edinburgh was reported to be £1200 to £1500 per year. In any case Lister thought that the fashionable situation would be an advantage to his practice. His neighbours included Patrick Heron Watson at

169

number 18 and J Matthews Duncan at number 30. It was also a short walk to Princes Street Gardens, then kept locked at night, and Lister proposed to obtain a key so that he could walk there before breakfast 'to meditate'.

Most of Arthur's letter of October 19 described Joseph Jackson's increasing weakness. He was now eighty-two. On the whole he had enjoyed the kind of rude good health that seems to have characterized the Lister inheritance. He had been on holiday with Joseph on the Dorset coast some twenty years before when he suddenly suffered the excruciating pain of kidney stones. Joseph applied hot compresses until it was possible to get his father into a horse cart that carried him the six miles to the railway station. The jolting of the cart on the rough track caused the stones to descend into the bladder, and Joseph Jackson was able to pass them before the train arrived. During 1866 he had had a cough so bad that Joseph thought it might have been whooping cough, and later the same year a bad knee had made him lame for a time. One of his last letters to Joseph contained a complaint about a 'skin affection of my ankle'. His clear copperplate handwriting had become more and more spidery. He died at Upton on October 24, only five days after Arthur's warning letter. Joseph and his other surviving children were in the house.

The bulk of the property was divided amongst them. Many of the books went to Joseph, and the portrait of Joseph Jackson by Delafour went to Mary Godlee. They agreed to the sale of Upton which was completed in January 1870.

After it was over and he had returned to Edinburgh from his last visit to the house where he had been born, Joseph wrote to Rickman Godlee: 'I dreamt two nights ago that I came down in the morning and was met by Papa, firm and erect and bright and beautiful as of old. He shook me warmly by the hand and kissed me as he used to do when I was a little boy. I asked him if he had slept well after his long journey. He said No, but that he was quite well, whereat I rejoiced. He had in his hand a little book which I understood contained notes of his journey! I woke and thought how interesting it would be to read notes of that journey!' It was Joseph instead who wrote the 'notes of his journey', first in the form of an obituary for the *Monthly Microscopical Journal* and later as an entry for the *Dictionary of National Biography*.

There had been a special relationship between Joseph Jackson and his second son. The father perceived the sensitivity, the uncertainty, even the confusion that persisted in Joseph's make-up. Joseph in turn responded with all the warmth that he barred from other relationships. He loved Arthur and his sisters and Agnes but in ways that had their boundaries; there were no boundaries around his love for Joseph Jackson. The long letters Joseph wrote contain not only information, but confession, and the repeated cry for love to which his father responded. Joseph knew how much his mind and his career owed to the man who had decried his religious enthusiasm. Joseph Jackson

170

stood for probity, scientific as well as personal, objectivity mixed with sympathy, and an embracing awareness of Joseph's need for informed understanding: 'And however slowly and imperfectly the improvements suggested by thee may be adopted', he wrote to his son on June 6, 1869, 'and however thy claims may be slighted or disputed, it is a great thing to have been permitted to be the means of introducing so great a blessing as the antiseptic treatment to thy fellow mortals, and thou hast abundant cause to persevere'.

A fortnight after his father's death Lister delivered his Introductory Lecture to the Edinburgh students. His opening remarks paid homage to Syme, who was present:

> . . . we may all rejoice that our master is still among us, to cheer us by his presence and aid us by his counsel; and it is a source of great satisfaction to myself that, as I have the privilege of free access to his inexhaustible store of wisdom and experience, he will, in some sense, through me be still your teacher.

He went on to define his subject, clinical surgery, as 'surgery at the bed-side; surgery illustrated by cases in hospital, as distinguished from surgery taught systematically in the class-room'. For a proper understanding the student 'must not only see the diseases and watch their treatment by others, but handle them and be personally concerned in their management'. It was essential to avail oneself of the opportunities afforded by the hospital offices— dresser, clerk and house surgeon—to obtain direct experience before assuming the responsibilities of practice, Lister said. He often repeated the advice. Like his own research it reflected his faith in observation and manipulation as the only source of truth, in the wards as in the laboratory. The attitude, so familiar today, was far more common in France and Germany than it was in Britain. In this lecture Lister's précis of scientific method served to introduce the flasks, brought so carefully from Glasgow, which in his view illustrated the validity of the germ theory. To the printed version of the lecture he added a footnote, however: 'Such experiments are peculiarly likely to fail in the hands of those who perform them with the object of confuting the germ theory. In fact, a belief in the theory is almost essential in order that the experimenter may be sufficiently keenly alive to the subtle sources of failure.' This is a remarkably advanced statement of the effect of the experimenter on the experiment, confirmed many hundreds of times, but of course it cuts both ways. The conviction that germs exist might cause them to appear on microscope slides: 'Seek, and ye shall find'.

Immediately after the lecture Lister returned to Glasgow to pack up his museum, the exhibits and preparations that illustrated his lectures. He told Arthur that 'it felt more melancholy than I had expected, to think that I no longer had anything to do with the place where I had worked for the last nine years'. In the same letter he reported his 'first foreign honour! viz. a diploma making me foreign associate of the Society of Medicine of Norway'.

In December Lister wrote a paper for *The Lancet,* 'On the Effects of the Antiseptic System of Treatment upon the Salubrity of a Surgical Hospital'. He had made his great contribution in a setting and amongst people with whom he had little sympathy, and who had paid him in the same coin. The paper was his first attempt to summarize his Glasgow experience, and it reveals all too clearly his well-founded conviction that he had a case to make. Early in the article he repeated the essential definition of the antiseptic system:

... by which I mean, not the mere use of an antiseptic, however potent, but *such management of the case as shall effectually prevent the occurrence of putrefaction in the part concerned.*

First, however, he had pointed out that: 'A few inches below the surface of the ground, on a level with the floor of the two lowest male accident wards, with only the basement area, four feet wide, intervening, was found the uppermost tier of a multitude of coffins, which had been placed there at the time of the cholera epidemic of 1849, the corpses having undergone so little change ... that the clothes they had on ... were plainly discernable'. The hospital managers, 'having discovered this monstrous evil' which could not be removed, spread carbolic acid, quicklime and an additional layer of soil over the necropolis, 'and further, a high wall at right angles with the end of the building, and reaching up to the level of the first floor, so as necessarily to confine the bad air most prejudicially, was pulled down'. As though the cholera victims were not enough to endanger the living, moreover, 'one end of the building is coterminous with the old Cathedral churchyard, which is of large size and much used, and in which the system of "pit burial" of paupers has hitherto prevailed'.

Whether one accepted the germ theory or not, and in 1870 most of the managers of the Glasgow Royal Infirmary certainly did not, such conditions would be considered only a degree worse than piling the corpses in the wards themselves. The shock value of Lister's description was great because not even he realized that the bacteria responsible for putrefaction are not, in the main, airborne.

All the more impressive, therefore, were his results. Between 1864 and 1866 he had performed thirty-five amputations of which sixteen died. Then between 1867 and 1869 he had performed forty with only six deaths. Of thirty-two cases of compound fracture, not including those that had required amputations, *none* had contracted pyaemia. In Lister's wards there had been two deaths from pyaemia between 1867 and 1869, one from erysipelas, and in 1869, one case of hospital gangrene. In 1867 the other ground-floor male accident ward, where antiseptic precautions were not in force, was closed due to an outbreak of hospital diseases. Yet it was separated from Lister's 'merely by a passage twelve feet broad'. His wards, furthermore, had 'remained during the three years without the annual cleaning . . . On my asking the superintendent the reason for the omission, he replied that, as those wards had continued healthy, and there was nothing dirty in their appearance, it had seemed unnecessary to disturb them.' Whatever may have been the response of his medical colleagues to these claims, Lister had argued them well, within the context of current knowledge, avoiding the highly controversial germ theory.

Perhaps it was only to be expected that, when he wrote about his Glasgow experience, he should have wished to settle old scores with the Infirmary managers. Unfortunately, he lacked the self-discipline or the perspicacity to suppress the urge, and his father, who had criticized his lack of moderation, was dead. Apparently Mrs Lister, although her secretarial role gave her the opportunity to influence his writing, either would not or could not do so. In the early 1860s, he wrote: 'I was engaged in a perpetual contest with the managing body, who, anxious to provide hospital accommodation for the increasing population of Glasgow . . . were disposed to introduce additional beds' into the wards. 'It is, I believe, fairly attributable to the firmness of my resistance in the matter that, though my patients suffered from the evils' of hospital diseases 'in a way that was sickening and often heartrending, so as to make me sometimes feel it is a questionable privilege to be connected with the institution, yet none of my wards ever assumed the frightful condition which sometimes showed itself in other parts of the building, making it necessary to shut them up entirely for a time.' Hector Cameron referred to Lister's 'guilelessness' in making both these charges and comparisons which were invidious to the efforts of his colleagues. The word arrogance might also apply.

The managers were quickly off the mark with a letter from Henry Lamond, Secretary to the Directors, published by *The Lancet* on January 29, 1870. Lamond wrote: 'his remarks, so far as they relate to the alleged unhealthiness and condition of this hospital . . . are unfair and not supported by facts'. He cited statistics to show that the death rate for amputees and general surgical cases was lower year by year than in other hospitals listed by Sir James Simpson in his pamphlet on *Hospitalism*. As to the 'contest' which Lister had mentioned over the number of beds in his wards, Lamond pointed out that the number of surgical patients in the hospital had been kept constant at 144. Neither of these points directly refutes Lister's claims, but the Secretary went on: 'The only "contest" which the managers ever had with Professor Lister' had to do with the length of stay of his patients which averaged 180 days. Because of the irritating effect of strong antiseptics such as carbolic acid, Listerian patients probably developed subsidiary sores more often than others and the extended period of treatment that this required became a frequent complaint of the Edinburgh Royal Infirmary managers too. Lamond continued that Lister's wards had had the same cleaning as others and pointed out that pit burials had not begun until 1869. He concluded with the claim that 'the improved health and satisfactory condition of the hospital . . . is mainly attributable to the better ventilation, the improved dietary, and the excellent nursing to which the Directors have given so much attention of late years'. The claim was undoubtedly true, and it was in general no less true of the other large hospitals to which Lamond had compared his own.

Lister replied point by point in a letter to *The Lancet* which was also published by the *Glasgow Daily Herald* on February 5, along with a covering letter from Lister. He admitted that his choice of the word 'contest' was 'unfortunate', and backtracked in tone if not in matters of content. And he managed to conclude more positively:

There is one point with regard to the figures given in the letter which is extremely satisfactory to myself, viz, that they serve to contradict, on competent authority, an anonymous statement which was made some time ago in one of the medical journals . . . implying that the use of antiseptic measures in the Glasgow Infirmary had led to an increased mortality. The statement . . . I could hardly have contradicted, although it was entirely the reverse of the truth as regarded my own department, without appearing to cast a slur upon the practice of my colleagues. But I rejoice to find that taking the results of the practice of all the four surgeons of the hospital, the death rate during the three years of the antiseptic period has been less by fully one-fifth than during the five previous years.

Nevertheless, damage had been done, thanks, once again, largely to Lister's apparent inability to express himself clearly. Having at last perceived the central point of his own treatment—exclusion of putrefaction from the wound—he now began the long battle to justify it by unnecessarily offending the authorities who would have been only too pleased, had he but met them part way, to support his claims because they reflected credit on the Glasgow Royal Infirmary.

As though some evil fate had now established dominion over him, moreover, one of Lister's first Edinburgh cases involved him in serious embarrassment. A Dr James Cullen of Airdrie had sent his patient, Joseph M Dyer, to the Infirmary with a compound fracture. Dyer had been treated antiseptically by Lister, but after four days the leg had become infected. Lister recommended immediate amputation. The patient asked that he be allowed to consult Lister's colleague, Patrick Heron Watson, but had been told that Watson was not available. He had then asked to discuss the amputation with his wife. She happened to be in the hospital at the time. The amputation was carried out, but Dyer died.

Dr Cullen wrote angrily to the Infirmary manager on 26th November, 1869. He had seen his patient soon after the operation and had thought him quite well. He had also seen the amputated limb and neither saw nor smelled any putrefaction. And why, he wished to know, had the leg been amputated above the knee when the fracture had been below it. The managers sent Cullen's letter to Lister.

On December 1 Lister replied. Putrefaction had set in, he wrote, because of the pumping of air into the fracture wound before Dyer's admission. To consult Watson would have required a day, and Lister had felt that immediate amputation was essential. Both Dyer and his wife had agreed. He had amputated above the knee because of the danger that putrefaction had spread into the joint. The operation went well, but the next day Dyer 'had decided delirium tremens, and though the stump seemed doing well, he finally sank exhausted'.

The minutes of the meeting that received Lister's letter note, 'Managers think Mr Lister's explanation as to the treatment satisfactory', but they resolved to require consultation in major amputations if requested by the patient or his friends, except on emergency admissions.

Dr Cullen replied at the end of December with a bitter attack on Lister. A month later the managers appointed a Committee to consider what was to be said to Cullen, or to Lister. They wrote to Cullen asking that he withdraw his letter because it was too strong, implying that they would then investigate further. Another month passed and on February 26 Cullen did withdraw the letter 'in order that there may be no obstacle to prevent a thorough investigation into the whole circumstance of the case'. The managers returned Cullen's December letter on March 7, but the minutes reveal no further reference to the issue.

The actions taken by the managers make it quite clear that they supported Lister throughout. Yet that any question should have been raised about his ethical and professional judgement must have deeply upset him. Whether the incident coloured his relationship with the managers, it is impossible to say. Neither his nephew nor Cameron mentions the incident, and he may have told no one about it. Though there was never the antipathy that had existed in Glasgow, conflicts between Lister and the Infirmary managers were to arise.

If the year 1870 began inauspiciously for him at the Royal Infirmary, he was able to make some minor improvements in details of the antiseptic method during the next few weeks. On January 27 he wrote the pristine entry in the first of four 300 page, folio-sized Common-place Books which contain the notes of the great bulk of his laboratory work for thirty years. Many of the entries are in Mrs Lister's handwriting, but this first one was in Lister's. It concerned a new shellac preparation. However, the series of experiments beginning on February 5 that inaugurated the Common-place Books dealt with the preparation of catgut, variations in the amount of time it was to be soaked first in water, then in carbolic acid solution, and then dried. It was the same subject on which the research notes were to end in 1899.

On February 14 Lister delivered a lecture at the Infirmary 'On a Case of Compound Dislocation of the Ankle with other Injuries; illustrating the Antiseptic System of Treatment', which *The Lancet* published. It was a case history and begins with the details of treatment. Lister recognized that, essential though it was to exclude germs, the injured tissues must be given a chance to recover. Once antiseptic has been properly applied, 'ALL THEY NEED IS TO BE LET ALONE. Nature will take care of them.' He was reported to have said on another occasion: 'There is no such thing as a "healing" ointment'. To reduce the contact between antiseptic and skin, therefore, a protective layer was required beneath the dressing. Itself non-antiseptic—though it would have been made aseptic by being treated with an antiseptic—the protective would be non-caustic: 'we have not yet got a perfect protective', he admitted, but as with ligatures and the dressings themselves, Lister was to spend hours seeking a formula that would improve it.

The dextrine shellac preparation described in the first Common-place Book entry was intended as a protective. Before it he had tried block tin (too rigid), tin foil (too easily torn), and cotton coated with caoutchouc on one side and further treated to make it pliable and water repellent (but carbolic acid passed through it). The best protective he could find was a modification of the dextrine shellac which emerged from his laboratory after a series of experiments between July 5 and October 25, 1871. It consisted of a piece of oiled silk varnished on both sides with copal, a resin. He was still using this 'copal'd oiled-silk' a decade later.

On June 26, 1870, Syme suffered a second stroke and died. His funeral was four days later. He left the bulk of his estate to his son James, but Agnes and Lucy each received £5000. Lister was given several items from Syme's consulting rooms: a skeleton, certain anatomical preparations and a portrait engraving of John Hunter by Sharp which thereafter hung in Lister's study. The Hunter portrait symbolized the relationship between Syme and Lister. Sharpey, Graham and Lindley of University College were names 'frequently on his lips', according to Cameron: they gave Lister an analytical under-standing of physiology, chemistry and botany, respectively. Hunter, on the other hand, provided an 'inexhaustible treasury of original observation and profound reflection', Lister wrote in 1858. Syme too acknowledged his debt to Hunter, as should any surgeon, and in so doing laid the foundation for his influence on Lister. In contrast to the personality of Lister's father Syme's dour remoteness gave a kind of cachet to Lister's cool, introspective submersion of his emotions. Dr John Brown wrote of Syme: 'It has been happily said of him, that he never wastes a word, or a drop of ink, or a drop of blood'. His advice and strength were as necessary to Lister professionally as his father's had been privately.

On June 28 *The Scotsman* carried an obituary of Syme the authorship of which was attributed to Lister, nor did he ever deny it. It ended with an acknowledgement of 'a most warm heart, a true love for his fellow-creatures, and a general appreciation of sterling merit in whatsoever form it might present itself. Mr Syme, in short, besides being a surgical genius of the highest order, was a perfect gentleman, and a good as well as a great man.'

By a quirk of fate Syme had outlived his former colleague and enemy, Simpson, by some fifty days. Thus within two months Edinburgh lost two of its most illustrious medical men.

In July the Listers moved into their house on Charlotte Square. Lister's study which is the only room that has been described, was probably at the back of the house overlooking the garden. The walls between the large windows were lined with glass-fronted mahogany bookcases. Lister used a writing table on which were a Powell and Lealand microscope and often a rack of test tubes plugged with white cotton wool. Other than the Hunter engraving the only work of art known to have been in the study was an etching by Francis Seymour Haden. Haden was founder-President of the Royal Society of Painter-Engravers and Etchers, but he had also been trained as a surgeon and was a Fellow of the Royal College of Surgeons and an acquaintance of Syme's.

The domestic arrangements at Charlotte Square included a butler, cook, junior staff and a coachman who drove the two carriages, one of them an open landau. In 1875 Mrs Lister wrote to Jane Harrison asking for advice on the best carriage-maker in London so that they could 'take steps toward procuring a new carriage'. The household seems to have been rich without opulence and comfortable within the limits fixed by Victorian technology. One imagines that it was a practical rather than a beautiful home, but housekeeping was complicated by a continuous research program going on beneath its roof. On the other hand there were no children and relatively few visitors.

Lister's entertainment was primarily formal and professional. It was a formal era, and the distance between professor and student was maintained as rigidly as any class distinction. Lister more than others held people at arm's length. He always addressed his father-in-law as Mr Syme, and, on the other side, Cameron's letters forty years later saluted his old friend with the words: 'My dear professor'. The natural gravity of Lister's demeanour was heightened by his fame, and his awareness that he had a great discovery to defend on behalf of mankind. His students almost walked in awe of him. Nevertheless, there were chores that they performed, perhaps in return for some remission of their fees. In 1873, Francis M Caird helped his professor by enlarging camera lucida drawings to serve as illustrations for a lecture. Caird's enlargements had to be drawn on scrolls of paper spread out on the carpet in Lister's study. Lister helped on his hands and knees. About midnight, Caird wrote many years later, Mrs Lister brought in sherry and biscuits.

Lister's reputation had, in the meantime, reached the highest circles. On July 2, 1870, Sir William Jenner, President of the Royal College of Physicians and Physician in Ordinary to the Queen, wrote to Victoria: 'Under all the conditions I am sure Your Majesty will do well as Your Majesty says to appoint an Edinburgh Surgeon—There is a surgeon of the highest reputation in Edinburgh who succeeded Mr Syme in his professorship (Mr Lister formerly at Glasgow)'. The Queen accepted the suggestion and appointed Lister Surgeon in Ordinary in Scotland. In practice the title meant that Lister was on call whenever the Queen was at Balmoral, Victoria's favourite residence after the death of Prince Albert.

Lister was first called upon in October. Princess Louise, the youngest daughter, had been ill for some weeks, probably with an abscess on a leg. On October 29 the Queen noted in her Journal: 'As Louise does not get better, Dr Fore would like to have another opinion & Professor Lister, from Edinburgh is going to be sent for'. On the following day she wrote: 'After luncheon Profr Lister arrived & Dr Fore brought him to me: I then went with them to Louise, & she was carefully examined. He said perfect rest was necessary but that there was no inflammation.—Took a short drive with Beatrice, but it came on to rain.—Saw Dr Fore when I came in, & he told me Profr Lister had prescribed various things, & had said that with complete rest, even if the leg & [illegible] get better, Louise would not be able to be moved before a fortnight.' The Queen recorded another visit on November 8, and on the 15th she wrote: 'Profr Lister came again, reported decided improvement & saw no objection to Louise being moved on the 24th entirely carried & lying on an invalid couch'. Inasmuch as the patient was married the next year, Lister's treatment seems to have served well, though of course, in the event, he did nothing.

Late in 1870 when his success with the Princess must have been known to his associates, he dressed a patient whose breast had been removed, and showed two or three of his assistants a clean primary union. One of them recalled that Lister said: 'What would they say of antiseptic surgery if this patient had been a Princess of the realm?' The utmost secrecy then surrounded the treatment of royalty, and private achievement did not ease his sensitivity to criticism.

On July 22, 1870, he had finished writing a short account of his record during the first nine months in Edinburgh, 'Further Evidence regarding the Salubrity of a Surgical Hospital'. Early in the article he quoted a letter that he had recently received from Saxtorph in Copenhagen, who insisted upon the 'greatest precautions in every dressing till the wound is either healed or filled with granulations . . . It certainly takes much longer time, and demands much greater precautions, than any other dressing; but the reward is certain.' Lister repeated that a belief in the germ theory was essential; otherwise 'trivial' mistakes were too easily made. But in his fifty beds, there had been no pyaemia, no hospital gangrene and only two cases of 'superficial erysipelas' which Lister attributed to cold.

Despite the early fiasco it was an excellent beginning in Edinburgh. Nor was he fighting alone. Earlier in July E R Bickersteth of Liverpool reported two more successful cases. In *The Lancet* for July 22 a letter from G A Turner, another of Lister's students, reported the use of antiseptic methods in his own practice—in Samoa. A *Lancet* leader in September once again said that failures 'are due to neglect in carrying out certain minute precautions which the plan requires'. In November and December GPs from Barnsley, a coal-mining town, and a rural practice in Nottinghamshire, respectively, praised antiseptic surgery and emphasized the importance of attention to details.

During 1869 and 1870 *The Lancet* published a large number of letters and articles devoted to Listerism, a majority of which were favourable. Though the London surgical establishment, the chief surgeons in the larger hospitals, did not in the main accept antisepsis, Lister was nevertheless asked to preside over the surgical section of the British Medical Association meeting at Newcastle-on-Tyne in August 1870. A year later he delivered the major address in surgery at the Plymouth conference, and in 1875, in Edinburgh, he again presided over the surgical section. He was in no sense being forbidden a platform by his colleagues. Far fewer items devoted to antiseptic treatment appeared in *The Lancet* during 1871 and one only in 1872. Lister and his closest friends interpreted the relative silence as neglect. But the profession seemed to be leaving it up to them to prove their case.

The opposition that did exist had begun to focus on the central dogma of antisepsis, the germ theory. Cameron said that Lister devoted his Introductory Lecture at Edinburgh to the germ theory in part at least because his colleague, Dr J Hughes Bennett, the Professor of Physiology, refused to have anything to do with it. Bennett, who did use the microscope himself, was said to have asked: 'Where are the germs? show them to us and we will believe. Has anybody seen these germs?' This argument was not new. Where indeed were they, and were they really necessary as an explanation in any case? In September 1867 Dr J R Wolfe had written to *The Lancet* praising Lister's series of compound fracture cases, but questioning 'the panspermatism hypothesis' of M Pasteur. 'I am rather inclined to attribute the action of carbolic acid entirely to its antiseptic properties—that is, of preserving organizable material from passing into a putrescent condition' due to the action of 'the contaminated air'. In March 1868, William Adams, the orthopaedic surgeon who had doubted the value of Syme's operation, advanced the same opinion in a talk to the Medical Society of London: 'The practical question is whether antiseptics are to be employed upon the "germ theory" of M Pasteur, and applied at caustic strength . . . or whether they are to be used simply as antiseptics in a mild and unirritating form'. At the end of January, 1870, Lister's Glasgow antagonist, James Morton, returned to the attack. He defined 'Lister's method' accurately enough as the acceptance of Pasteur's theory, the assumption that airborne germs are injurous and that wounds must be disinfected because air cannot be excluded from them. But

Pasteur's theory was not relevant, Morton said. Nor had it been demonstrated that airborne germs are injurious, and, in any event, was it likely that Nature would act like 'some murderous hag'? Bad air was caused by overcrowding.

Morton's commonsensical argument against the germ theory and its ramifications had a specious validity. Pasteur, Lister and others who had begun to accept the notion of germs, stressed their minuteness as the explanation for their invisibility and the ease with which they could be carried on air currents. Insects or fungi might cause hair and skin diseases, everyone agreed, but how could a thing as small as a germ damage a man? Even through a microscope these tiny objects looked alike. How then was it possible that they caused diseases as different as cholera, gangrene and typhoid fever? *The Lancet* underlined the commonsense question in a leader dated September 17, 1870:

Professor Lister says that only faith in the germ theory will procure a thorough trial of the practice. Whatever becomes of the germ theory, the results obtained by Lister, Saxtorph, and others are new facts in surgery, or rather physiology, and must have a scientific definition.

These germs looked to some people suspiciously like an attempt to revive the eighteenth-century vitalist dogma. The vitalists held that life could not exist without a 'vital force', a romantic, somewhat mystical phrase which meant that it took more than mere mechanism to explain life. In October, 1870, a Dr Angus Mackintosh wrote to *The Lancet* neither supporting nor attacking Listerism but certain that carbolic acid had been efficacious in his practice:

Query.—Has the carbolic acid brought about this desired effect by first destroying the putrefactive organisms of the atmosphere which are supposed to favour if not to create pus, and hence the cure; or has it diminished the quantity of pus by giving increased tone of vitality to the parts through its stimulating and chemical effects, and thus preventing the tendency in the parts to disorganization and putrefaction?

Macintosh seemed to put germs on one side and the vital force on the other. In his own work on inflammation Lister had accepted that some vital force in the blood vessels kept the blood liquid. Yet the most important figures of early nineteenth-century physiology, men like the chemist, von Leibig, and the great Virchow who had proposed that all living matter is organized in cells, denied the existence of a vital force that distinguished living matter from the non-living variety. Their strongest evidence was the synthesis of urea, a molecule found in life, out of nitrogen, oxygen, hydrogen and carbon in the laboratory. If there was no vital force, germs might be merely the appearance of organized life formed out of the chemicals in a broth, or in the air. Thus the powerful scientific voices who introduced the modern view that life is explicable by the laws of physics and chemistry also provided what looked like a firm foundation for abiogenesis: spontaneous generation. Defenders of the germ theory, on the other hand, by opposing abiogenesis seemed to defend vitalism.

The facts aside, there is nothing inherently any more absurd in the notion of continuous creation of life than in the perfectly respectable cosmological equivalent, the continuous creation theory of the universe. If new stars and new planets are in process of formation then why should this not be true of organisms, especially if the same physio-chemical laws apply to both? The theory that life can arise only from life, for it is only a theory, is now accepted because no one has yet reported an exception. In 1870 important orders of microscopic magnitude were still invisible. Even the strongest light microscope cannot reveal virus particles, for example, whereas an electron microscope makes it possible to see an insulin molecule.

In addition to the commonsense arguments against the germ theory and the alternative theories of chemical infection by miasmas or other substances, a third possible answer existed in 1870. Perhaps some diseases *are* caused by germs, but they need not have been transmitted through the air. The harmful germs could have originated by spontaneous generation in the wound itself, or even in the air for that matter. John Hughes Bennett, who asked to be shown Lister's germs, argued accordingly. In 1869 the *British Medical Journal* commented:

There is such a mass of positive and presumptive evidence in favour of the possibility of a new evolution of life taking place now in our own day, as to fully entitle us to believe that such a thing may be—nay, that it probably does take place. The mass of evidence is so overwhelming, that even Professor Owen ... has lately ... bodly announced his assent to the doctrine.

The zoologist, Richard Owen, had written testimonials for Lister and had been his father's friend. Thomas Huxley, Darwin's staunchest defender, had matriculated in the University of London two years before Lister and had worked with Owen on the morphological typing of animals. In 1870 he supported the theory of abiogenesis.

Its most original and forceful British proponent was Henry Charlton Bastian, at this time Professor of Pathological Anatomy and Assistant Physician at University College Hospital, London. Bastian published a book in 1872 called *The Beginning of Life: Being Some Account of the Nature, Modes of Origin and Transformation of Lower Organisms*. He filled 1115 pages with accounts of experiments and the arguments that he believed they supported. For example, he heated urine to 110 degrees Centigrade, 10 degrees above the boiling point of water. He neutralized its acidity with sterile potash, but the urine nevertheless became clouded showing that it was infected by organisms. Thus he seemed to demonstrate that chemicals in the urine had given rise *de novo* to the organisms. Later research and improved technology suggest two possible sources of error in Bastian's experimental design. He used distilled water in which to dissolve his potash, but there are always some bacteria in distilled water. Also urine contains the spores of dormant bacteria which can be destroyed with steam pressure at 120 degrees Centigrade but not with dry heat as high as 160 degrees Centigrade. At the time, however, Bastian's work greatly strengthened the argument for abiogenesis and indirectly cast doubt on Lister's ability to exclude germs by his antiseptic method.

Pasteur and his associates took Bastian's work seriously, as did the physicist, John Tyndall, Huxley's friend and contemporary. During the sixties Tyndall had done research on radiant heat. He had observed that a light beam became invisible when it passed through moteless air and proposed the use of a light beam to detect germs in the air. Tyndall visited Lister's Edinburgh wards about 1870 to watch his techniques and continued his own experiments on the behaviour of putrefactive organisms and the sterilization of ligatures with heat. His experiments were published in 1876 and 1877 and firmly supported the germ theory.

Lister's conviction that germs originated only from pre-existing organisms led to his experiment with the flasks of urine before he left Glasgow, but during the early months in Edinburgh he did nothing more to test the theory. He was at this time concerned primarily with the improvement of ligatures and the dressings that were so essential to the success of the antiseptic method. During the summer of 1870 war imposed a major trial of his practice. On July 15 the French government declared war on Prussia. An Anglo-American ambulance team under the joint command of Lister's friend, William MacCormac, and an American surgeon, Marian Sims, tried unsuccessfully to use the prescribed rules. The Germans, although sympathetic, had not begun to use Lister's techniques in the army, and the French were not sympathetic. Bottles of carbolic acid were sent to the French field stations and returned unopened. Lucas-Championnière, the French surgeon who had visited Lister in Glasgow, was ordered not to use antiseptic techniques. The short war proved to be anything but an auspicious laboratory for Lister.

Marcus Beck had gone with MacCormac as part of the ambulance team. He wrote to his mother about conditions in the hospital at Sedan:

I have seen what surgery after a great battle is & I must say it is not pleasant—The nursing arrangements are necessarily very inefficient & antiseptic surgery being unknown the amount of discharge from the wounds is awful. The bullets shatter the bones in a frightful way & as all the cases I saw were those in which an attempt had been made to save the limb, the amount of pus from each case was tremendous. The smell was kept down as much as possible . . . & on the whole the hospital was not unhealthy.

The battle of Sedan had ended with a disastrous French defeat leading to the flight of Emperor Louis Napoleon on September 4. On the 3rd the *British Medical Journal* published Lister's proposals for simplifying his rules for battle conditions, 'A Method of Antiseptic Treatment applicable to Wounded Soldiers in the present War'. He wrote nothing further on the military uses of antiseptics, although on February 15, 1884, he addressed the Woolwich Medical Society. According to a report of the talk in *The Lancet* Lister showed how it was possible 'to simplify the method', and he recommended corrosive sublimate as the most suitable antiseptic.

Meanwhile, the Russo-Turkish War of 1877–1878 afforded a second field test, less severe than the first and according to Godlee, with better results. The Russian surgeon, Karl Reyher, had studied with Lister in Edinburgh. He treated field injuries with rigid antiseptic principles and obtained results comparable to those in civil practice. The Berlin surgeon, von Bergmann, who had accepted Listerism, also served in the army.

The British colonial wars further tested the doctrine. T B Moriarity, a military surgeon, reported two successful cases during the Afghan War of 1878. Another military surgeon, Edgar M Crookshank, who had been Lister's house surgeon, reported in 1882 widespread use of antiseptic methods during the Egyptian campaign. But the first important test for antisepsis by the British forces came in the Boer War. Lord Wolseley, the Commander in Chief, had bluntly remarked that, 'Medical advice is a very good thing—when it is asked for'. Nevertheless, every soldier received a first aid packet containing an antiseptic dressing of gauze and mackintoshed jaconet with pins and one-in-a-thousand solution of corrosive sublimate. Base hospitals were equipped 'with all the requisites for antiseptic surgery,' Godlee wrote. He said that the success rate had been high, though he attributed it to the short battles, low *British* casualties and the 'dry fresh air of the open Veldt'. By 1899 several of Lister's former students were teaching or in practice where they could influence military medicine, Godlee amongst them, and it is not surprising that antiseptic techniques were used or that relatively fewer deaths from infection occurred. On the other hand, according to contemporary reports typhoid and dysentery took more lives than the Boers.

In 1870 the techniques demanded by Lister to protect the patient and maintain an aseptic wound were too time-consuming and cumbersome for field conditions. His early attempt to simplify them tended merely to make' harassed military surgeons more slipshod. The trouble was not so much the need for an improvement in general hygiene; neither the knowledge nor the clinical experience existed to distinguish essential antiseptic measures from those that were unimportant or even useless. From Lister's standpoint every step meant another weapon in the struggle to defeat the enemies that were the more insidious because of their size.

At about the same time that he wrote the abortive article aimed at simplifying his method, Lister began a clinical experiment that was to last, against mounting evidence that it was useless, for almost fifteen years. If germs floated in the air, the armament arrayed against them would be immeasurably strengthened by killing them in the air before they could approach the wound. He had boiled flasks of urine to kill bacteria and prevented their re-entry with aseptic cotton wool plugs or twisted necks, but these techniques were scarcely applicable to an operating theatre or a ward. Lister determined to use carbolic acid to purify the air and adapted for the purpose the Richardson spray, in effect a large scent bottle. Thomas Nunn first used his own modification of the spray at the Middlesex Hospital two years before. According to Abraham Wallace who became Lister's dresser in 1871, Lister was already using 'a syringe to sprinkle a solution of carbolic acid over wounds, when changing the dressings'. Wallace and another student were discussing the possibility of using a 'fine cloud of carbolated solution . . . instead of the syringe' when Lister's assistant surgeon, Dr John Chiene, overheard them. Chiene mentioned the idea to Lister who adopted the Richardson hand spray the 'next day'. Lister publicly described his use of the spray for the first time in a paper dated December 31, 1870.

The spray was one of those 'details' that became part of the Lister legend, like carbolic acid itself. Lister's hands had always come away white after an operation from the effect of the carbolic acid solution. Now the surgeon and his assistants as well as the patient were enveloped in a cloud of yellowish mist, and the pungent carbolic odour diffused even more widely. One of the first British women to study medicine wrote:

I was to know . . . the 'Lister Spray,' very well indeed. Unforgettable, the operating theatre of the great hospital on the Thames Embankment, looking across to the Houses of Parliament. Unforgettable the scene—often, even in the daytime, by gaslight; the 'Case' for operation, the small group about the table . . . the raised tiers of students, the tense silence, the faint odour of the carbolized steam, the sense of security in the little hissing whisper of the Lister Spray—the 'unconscious caretaker,' Lister himself has called it. It was always there, always whispering . . .

Lister sought constantly to improve the apparatus, of course at his own expense. For example, on June 9, 1873, in the Common-place Book, Mrs Lister described a new machine, 'Dr Siegle's Patent Spray Producer', and Lister drew it. In its final form the spray apparatus, a large copper atomizer worked by a foot treadle, with the solution in a container beneath the atomizer, sat on a tripod about three feet high. A foot-long handle on the atomizer could be used to direct the spray as required. The whole apparatus weighed about ten pounds and was carried into the theatre by a clerk or one of the dressers who operated it throughout the operation. One of the house surgeons gave a somewhat less reverent description:

The Professor had entered the theatre in his usual thoughtful and solemn manner, followed by the clerk who was carrying the spray. Chatter immediately ceased and dead silence ensued, when suddenly from the top of the theatre, in sonorous and clerical tones, a voice was heard: 'Let us s-pray!' . . . we were too staggered even to smile. Slowly Lister raised his eyes to the speaker with sad and pitying glance without uttering a word! . . . the most oppresive silence followed . . . A year later the man died of general paralysis; we knew nothing then of spirochetes and it was playfully suggested Jove had smitten him for the sacrilege!

The spray typified not only the lengths to which Lister was prepared to go in order to assure an aseptic wound, but also the importance of his belief that airborne germs were either wholly or partly the cause of infection.

Unpleasant though the spray was, Lister retained his confidence in the awkward machine. In a major demonstration at Charity Hospital, New York, during his American tour in 1876, a breeze through an open window in the amphitheatre pushed the spray cloud to one side. Lister 'at once called attention to this as an important point to be observed. The window must be shut otherwise the spray would be diverted from the wound'. In February, 1878 he acknowledged a letter from Dr Albert Wilson of Leytonstone in which Wilson had described using the spray to prevent germs from entering milk during the milking process. Wilson's experiment, Mrs Lister wrote at her husband's dictation, 'is all the more interesting as confirming the trustworthiness of the spray'. But of course bacteria that sour milk *are* frequently airborne. In 1880 experiments by Dr Chiene seemed to confirm that the spray excluded germs from the wound. The next year the International Medical Congress met in London. A Professor Bruns of Tübingen read a paper in which he asserted that the spray was useless and called for a return to irrigation of the wound with carbolic acid solution. He called the paper *'Fort mit dem Spray'*. In the course of a longer address Lister replied that carbolic acid solution caused too much irritation. He too was willing to say *'Fort mit dem Spray'*, however, if 'it should indeed be proved that all idea of atmospheric contamination . . . may be thrown to the wind'. But he added, 'the spray is, beyond all question, the least important of our antiseptic means'.

Soon afterward Dr Robert Koch published his own experiments with antiseptics. He had found that bacterial spores could not be killed by any known antiseptic, but the results for naked airborne organisms were less clear. More and more experimental work using better techniques began to show that the spray was probably ineffectual, but still Lister refused to abandon it entirely. According to William Watson Cheyne, he hesitated in part because:

surgeons had not yet become very expert with their antiseptic methods . . . so that many loopholes were left for the entrance of sepsis, and it was quite likely that the spray, by keeping the hands and instruments and towels and the wound itself constantly bedewed by a thin film of carbolic acid, might just save the situation . . .

The spray, Lister wrote, in a letter published by *The Lancet* in 1883, 'is a very mild form of antiseptic irrigation, and tends to keep the *entourage* of the wound, including the surgeon's hands and instruments, pure'. An entry in the King's College Hospital ward journal dated July 30, 1883, reads: 'Dr[essing]. no spray. W[oun]d not touched, but only surrounding parts washed.' The abscess eventually healed. In December Lister performed a chest operation under the spray, but a few months later it was not used until he began to close the incision.

Finally, in 1887 he abandoned it entirely. To the International Medical Congress in Berlin in 1890 he said:

As regards the spray, I feel ashamed that I should have ever recommended it for the purpose of destroying the microbes of the air. If we watch the formation of the spray and observe how its narrow initial cone expands as it advances, with fresh portions of air continually drawn into the vortex, we see that many of the microbes . . . cannot possibly have been deprived of their vitality.

It was Lister's characteristic admission of error, whether it had been by omission or comission—a compound of honesty and dignity with just a pinch of sanctimony. He had not yet accepted the central point that the principle causative agents of wound infection are in the main not airborne, but abandon the spray he did, to the great relief of his assistants. Being dramatic and obvious, it had become so much a part of Listerism in the public mind that in a review of the century's achievements, published in 1898, Alfred Russell Wallace referred to 'a copious spray of carbolic acid' as though it were still canonical.

The essential elements of the antiseptic system were all in place by the end of 1870. Its solid foundation was the germ theory. The object was to use an antiseptic to exclude germs from wounds until they healed. Antiseptics strong enough to destroy germs also destroy flesh, which both lengthens the recovery period and, by enlarging the wound, exacerbates the risk of infection. Therefore, the secondary objective of Lister's method was to reduce the irritant effect of the antiseptic. The surgeon had three means with which to achieve this end: he could use the spray to reduce the need for direct antiseptic irrigation of the wound; he could use improved dressings which retained their antiseptic quality so that dressings had to be changed less frequently; and he could protect the tissue against the antiseptic with an aseptic covering between wound and dressing. The details changed, but the outlines remained essentially the same.

In the paper that first added the spray to the armamentarium, 'On a Case illustrating the present Aspect of the Antiseptic Treatment in Surgery', published in the *British Medical Journal* on January 14, 1871, Lister recommended oakum as a protective in preference to the lac plaster. He had used oakum on the case reported, a refracture of improperly knit arm bones, and he provided the formula for its preparation. The Common-place Book shows that his experiments with the 'Oakum Principle' to find the right formula went on from December 12, 1870, the date of the operation, to January 17, three days after publication of the paper. Lister subsequently returned to the shellac protective.

These shifts in direction on minor matters annoyed his contemporaries and gave them another reason to criticize the antiseptic system. He never seemed to realize that the convolutions of his own experiments, which he reported as a matter of duty to the profession, confused those who were not party to them.

Had he written a book, he would have been forced to assign priorities, and that is, of course, precisely the reason why he did not write one. He had thought about it in 1867, but decided instead to settle for *The Lancet* paper. Now he made a second attempt. Seven pages of manuscript in his wife's legible hand are headed: 'Selected Lectures on Clinical Surgery, by Joseph Lister F.R.S. Professor of Clinical Surgery in the University of Edinburgh. I. On Granulations. In the course of a lecture on the 9th Jan 1871 the following remarks were made'. The idea of collecting his lectures may also have occurred to Cheyne when he was Lister's student two years later. He wrote careful notes on the course and gave them two titles. The second, 'Lectures on Clinical Surgery by Joseph Lister F.R.S. etc', suggests they were intended for publication. Both attempts were abortive.

Lister's reluctance to publish these lectures was wholly admirable. He knew best how incomplete his work was. Better to publish case histories embodying the results of current research than to attempt generalizations which he himself would not trust. It was a line his father would have approved.

He continued to conduct research for immediate classroom use as well as for the clinic. During May and June 1871 a series of drawings and notes devoted to the subject of nervous growth in granulating tissue contains the remark: 'The above inference . . . mentioned to the class yesterday J. L.'.

The sense of immediacy this technique imparted to his lectures produced striking results. The University of Edinburgh Medical Faculty had 560 students in 1870, about the same number as it had had a decade before. Soon after his return Lister's class numbered almost 200. By the time he left Edinburgh for London in 1877, he lectured regularly to some 350 students, again a new record for a surgical class. By the end of the decade the Medical Faculty had almost three times the number of students as in 1870. Lister's influence and reputation contributed materially to this growth. It was made possible physically by the opening in 1877 of the new Royal Infirmary in Lauriston Place.

There was seldom anything cut-and-dried about the content of his lectures. 'Why is this?' he frequently asked his class, and often replied, 'We do not know'. He told each year's class that 'John Hunter was a man who never let a fact escape him; though it opposed his own idea'. In 1864 he added: 'you should never let theories stand in the way of making your own observation'.

Most medical men subscribed to this sentiment, but to Lister it was more than a sentiment. One of his house surgeons recalled how he made a surgical disaster the subject for a lecture: he had performed a relatively new operation for removal of a bad goitre, an enlargement of the thyroid gland caused by disease. The patient died of haemorrhage. Lister was naturally distressed: he told his class 'that had he ligatured the thyroid arteries before he removed the gland, a life might have been saved'. In March, 1873 the *Edinburgh Medical Journal* published a case history by Lister which reported the death of a patient that he believed he could have prevented: 'I now regret deeply that I did not leave word with my House-Surgeon that if symptoms of failure of the vital powers should supervene, transfusion should be at once resorted to, for I heard on the following day that he sank three hours after the conclusion of the operation'. Such unusual openness endeared Lister to students too often afflicted by a sense that their professors considered God to be a mere assistant. Professor Lister was human, however formal and withdrawn his behaviour in face-to-face situations.

At about the time of the case report in the *Edinburgh Medical Journal*, he later wrote, he was demonstrating the effect of position on blood flow in a limb:

by raising one of my hands to the utmost while the other was kept dependent, in order to exhibit the contrast between them in redness, when a sensation of chilliness . . . in the hand that was raised made me feel, and at once express, the conviction that something more was occurring than would be explained by the mere mechanical effect of the position of the part upon the blood in the vessels, and that the diminution of pressure upon their walls . . . must operate as a stimulant to the vaso-motor nervous apparatus of the limb, so as to induce reflex contraction of the arteries.

The picture summoned up of the tall, blue-frock-coated, rather solemn gentleman standing on the amphitheatre platform, one arm raised while he speaks, effectively balances the customary image of eminent Victorians.

Between fifty and sixty cases were demonstrated to the class during the winter session at two lectures each week. 'Around the walls of the theatre, chairs were set for his assistants and for the distinguished strangers', wrote Cameron's son. The students sat in the permanent, tiered seating between them and the platform, which had a window behind it. Lister entered the theatre with his house surgeon, the instrument clerk carrying a cloth-covered tray, the clerk with the spray and the chloroform clerk. He began his lecture, wrote J R Leeson, 'seated . . . on the old worn horsehair-covered chair', using the blackboard for diagrams. Upon Lister's signal four dressers in blue-checked overalls brought in the patient who walked if possible or was otherwise carried in a long wicker basket. There were no nurses and no scrubbing up procedures. In front of Lister 'stood the operating table, a plain kitchen table devoid of all accessories, upon an old wooden floor frayed with wear and stained with years of blood, upon which was sprinkled a few

188

handfuls of sawdust'. Gloves and masks were twenty years in the future. Lister discussed the case in terms that became more technical as the patient was anaesthetized and continued to lecture as he operated. He sweated profusely and required one of his assistants to mop his forehead frequently. 'His tone was easy and conversational, something he could never achieve when he came to write a letter', wrote young Cameron.

Simple arithmetic shows that Listerian students quickly outnumbered non-Listerians at Edinburgh. In order to obtain the coveted appointments as one of his hospital assistants, it was customary for the student to call on Lister at his home. The student asked to have his name added to the list of applicants to await a vacancy. Lister made the appointments on his own judgement of merit based principally on the three written examinations given during each course. He also awarded a prize, silver catheters in a wooden case, after the final examination of the session.

The number of Lister's students grew and eminent visitors came from every continent to Edinburgh, but there remained half the race whom Lister excluded from his lectures and his wards except as patients. As far as the records show, no woman ever attended his classes. The wife of a colleague at King's College, London, actually came to the Hospital one day to hear Lister lecture. The house surgeon recalled: 'When he came I told him this lady was waiting and she wanted to hear the lecture. He showed by his usual manner his annoyance', that is, he lifted his eyebrows and sighed deeply.

He went to the anteroom of the amphitheatre and took the lady's hands between both his and said: I am very, very sorry, but I have never given lectures to a lot of doctors with a lady present at the same time. I hope you will forgive me, but you will understand.

Pressure for the admission of women to medical schools was probably given its greatest boost by the founding of the Nightingale Schools of Nursing. They removed any doubt that educated women of the 'better' classes could stand up to blood, dirt, smells and the basic facts of the body. At first Nightingale herself had little sympathy with the idea that women should become doctors; she believed that they were better suited to be nurses and midwives. Nevertheless, she became a member of the National Society for Women's Suffrage, and in 1877 supported admission of women to the University of London medical school. In 1869 the University of Edinburgh had become the first in Britain to admit women, but the medical faculty had made difficulties, and the managers of the Royal Infirmary refused to have anything to do with female trainees, except as nurses.

Nothing more happened until April 10, 1871, when a Committee of the managers recommended admission of women for clinical instruction. The whole Board voted an amendment which effectively delayed implementation of the Committee report. In the autumn of 1872 faced with mounting pressure from the University and in particular from Dr Sophie Jex-Blake, one of the first women doctors in Britain who now practised in Edinburgh, the managers asked the entire medical faculty to give their opinions on two questions: did they 'consider it practicable to admit female students to the Hospital on exactly the same terms and at the same hours as the male students', and could they 'suggest any scheme to enable female students to obtain a qualifying course of instruction at the Infirmary'. With two exceptions the faculty replies favoured admission of women on equal terms with men. The exceptions were Lister and J Hughes Bennett, his antagonist on the subject of germs.

To the first question Lister replied:

The reasons which are generally held to make it inexpedient for ladies to attend lectures on medical subjects along with male students in the College class-rooms apply with tenfold force against such mixed attendance in the wards of an hospital, where the treatment of the living human body takes the place of theoretical discussion and inanimate illustration, and the students instead of being placed under the eye of the teacher are necessarily crowded together and withdrawn more or less from his control.

The second question had been designed to elicit any new ideas for alternatives to full equality of status. After pointing out that any attempt to give women separate-but-equal status would place intolerable burdens on the faculty, Lister continued:

There are some other difficulties attendant on this question to which, as my opinion has been asked, I feel it needful to allude. One is that if ladies are admitted as students they must also be allowed to hold hospital offices, without which no studentship can be regarded as complete, while at the same time without female junior officials, the avoidance of mixed attendance would be an impossibility. Thus we should have not only female Dressers and Clerks, but female House-Surgeons and House Physicians, on whom would devolve the charge of the patients in the absence of their superior officers. And it must be a matter of serious consideration to the Managers whether they would be prepared to entrust to young ladies duties which often tax to the utmost the energies of men.

... the fact of these young people residing under the same roof with the corresponding officers of the other sex, and being thrown into intimate association with them for consultation and aid in professional emergencies, would, I fear, lead in the long run to great inconvenience and scandal.

This very long letter was, as usual, in the handwriting of Mrs Lister though the irony must certainly have escaped them both.

On December 30, 1872, the Managers voted to admit women under severe restrictions. The Royal College of Physicians and Surgeons of Edinburgh admitted women in 1886, and three years later the Universities (Scotland) Act removed all remaining disabilities affecting women in Scottish medical schools.

When Lister gave the managers his views, his only experience with women in medicine had been the nurses of the old school, tough, usually illiterate and always from the servant class, but that is the most that can be said in his defence. He never changed his mind.

His opinions were consistent with his background, and his shyness may have exacerbated his reluctance to cope with women in education. He may also have been afraid of women. In 1864 he told his Glasgow class that like young children, 'the female sex also is more excitable, and so you will think less of a quick pulse in a young lady than in a staid adult man'. He did not like excitability and unpredictability. His wife was cool and rational, 'like a staid adult man'.

He was of course unfailingly polite to women. Dr Mary Scharlieb, a London practitioner, recalled that she had heard Lister lecture at the Royal Free Hospital when she had been a student there. 'When the lecture was finished I went up to ask him a question of Antiseptics as applied to Midwifery, he gave me a very courteous reception.' His courtesy mirrored the Victorian view that women require protection against ugliness and pain in exchange for their willing submission.

In 1897 he wrote to Lord George Hamilton, the Secretary of State for India, opposing a proposal that female hospital atendants be employed in military hospitals under direction of medical officers for the examination and treatment of prostitutes. In the first place the guidance of qualified doctors must be indirect in the circumstances, and the use of unqualified people could not be justified. Even if the women were fully trained, however, the Army Sanitary Commission was proposing an innovation which 'would not be thought of for any Lock Hospital . . . under military management in this country'. He agreed that 'medical women have been very useful' in India 'although the necessity for them is perhaps not so great as is generally assumed to be the case!' He had learned from an Indian Medical Officer, he said, that even high caste women accept male doctors, and he argued that to be concerned about the alleged preferences of prostitutes was 'false sentiment'. Lord Lansdowne, Secretary of State for War to whom Lister had sent a copy of the letter, replied that, 'It may be necessary for reasons of policy, to try something of the sort on a small scale experimentally'.

In April, 1871 Lister was elected to Honorary Membership in the Royal Medical Society of Edinburgh. This local recognition signalled a widening acceptance of his medical opinions, at least in Scotland. His first opportunity to talk to the whole profession came when he was asked to give the Address in Surgery to the British Medical Association on August 10. This speech was a formal presentation before the whole meeting, unlike the brief paper he had read to the Surgical Section in Dublin three years before.

The meeting was in Plymouth. He left his patients in the care of his assistant, Dr Chiene. As usual he had not begun to write the speech by the time he and Mrs Lister left Edinburgh by the night train on August 2. They travelled through London, with time only to transfer from King's Cross to Paddington, intending to go directly to Plymouth. On the journey west they shared a compartment with 'a Cornish gentleman' who persuaded them 'to try our luck' at Looe, he wrote to Arthur. They left the train at Menheniot and 'enquired if any conveyance went to Looe and found that an omnibus meets that one train of all trains in the day'. The hotel recommended by Murray's 'Devon and Cornwall' was full, but they found satisfactory 'lodgings over the provision shop'. They stayed at Looe until the 9th.

The Address is frankly propagandist. 'The fact that my name is associated with this topic tended to make me shrink from' speaking about it to the BMA,

but, on the other hand, I could not but feel that this very circumstance has led in all probability to my standing before you to-day, so that you might naturally expect to hear something from me on the subject, while it is at the same time my sincere conviction that I could not turn the present occasion to better account than by exciting in you a keener interest in the antiseptic system than it has yet elicited, and by placing you more in a position to diffuse its benefits among mankind.

He recognized two factors 'which have hitherto interfered with the general acceptance of this mode of treatment'. The 'most prejudicial' was doubt about the germ theory. Less important was the apparent complexity of the system because experience dispelled that problem. He went on to describe the flask experiment and concluded his discussion of the germ theory with an important concession. There was no need to argue the proposition of spontaneous generation, he said; the essential point was to accept that dust is a source of infection whether the source is already living or not. No doubt he made the concession to meet the allegation, said to have been current at the meeting, that 'Professor Lister's solutions became weaker and weaker, while his faith appears to grow more and more'. But the risk that accompanies an alteration in theory unsupported by experimental evidence is that it may merely confuse the opposition. If spontaneous generation is not a central issue, they might argue, infections could just as well arise from chemicals in the wound rather than from dust in the air. Then of what use is Lister's insistence upon the exclusion of germs, or of dust? Two years before, he had sought to moderate contention by avoiding any reference to the germ theory. Not only was there now no new evidence, but the debate itself had evolved since then. This was the last pronouncement Lister was to make on the germ theory for almost two years. It was time that he did more research of his own.

In the rest of the Address he described details such as the spray and the protective. The latter, for example, was now a mixture of shellac with unvulcanized rubber. He reviewed the types of cases in which he had used the antiseptic method: abscesses, the ligature of arteries to control aneurisms,

9. *Lister in his late 30's, about 1865. When this picture was taken, he was at Glasgow, probably in the midst of the series of compound fracture cases with which he introduced antiseptic surgery.*

On a new method of treating Compound Fracture, Abscess, &c., with observations on the Conditions of Suppuration. By Joseph Lister Esq., F.R.S., Professor of Surgery in the University of Glasgow. Part I On Compound Fracture.

The frequency of disastrous consequences on Compound Fractures contrasted with the complete immunity from danger to life or limb in Simple Fracture is one of the most striking as well as melancholy facts in surgical practice.

If we enquire how it is that an external wound communicating with the seat of fracture leads to such grave results, we cannot but conclude that it is by inducing through the atmosphere access of the blood which is effused in greater or less amount around the fragments & among the interstices of the tissues, decomposition through the influence of the atmosphere losing its natural bland character & assuming the properties of an acrid irritant, occasions both local & general disturbance.

We know that blood kept exposed to the air at the temperature of the body in a vessel of glass or other material chemically inert soon decomposes, & there is no reason to suppose that the living tissues surrounding a mass of extravasated blood could preserve it from being affected in a similar manner by the atmosphere. On the contrary it may be ascertained as a matter of observation that in a compound fracture twenty four hours after the accident the coloured serum which oozes from the wound is already distinctly tainted with the odour of decomposition, & during the next two or three days, before suppuration has set in the smell of the effused fluids becomes more & more offensive.

10. First page of first draft of the articles describing antiseptic surgery, 1867, published by The Lancet. The handwriting is Mrs Lister's with corrections by both Mr and Mrs Lister. Note in the second line of the title that the word 'Causes' has been crossed out and 'Conditions' written above it. (See pages 144–145.)

hernias, refractures of badly set bones, the opening of the knee and wrist joints and the treatment of ulcers. Finally, he told his professional audience there had been no pyaemia, gangrene or erysipelas in the Edinburgh Royal Infirmary in the two years since he had returned there.

From Plymouth Mr and Mrs Lister returned to London where they spent several days with Arthur and his family at Leytonstone. Arthur and Joseph had agreed to buy a holiday house at Lyme Regis. It was called High Cliff because of its situation and had a beautiful view toward Portland Bill. For thirty years 'the joyous family gatherings at Lyme were an essential part of Lister's life', wrote Godlee: There the childless couple watched their nieces and nephews grow up. After Agnes Lister's death, Joseph sold his share in High Cliff to Arthur.

Joseph and Agnes went to Manchester and thence to Ambleside at the end of August. On September 3 he received a telegram from Dr Marshall, the Queen's physician at Balmoral. A large abscess had developed in Her Majesty's left armpit, a painful complaint that was even more annoying because it was so undignified. Victoria was in any case not well. Lister arrived on the afternoon of the 4th. Victoria noted:

Sir William Jenner explained everything about my arm to him, but he naturally said he could do nothing or give any opinion till he had made an examination. I had to wait nearly half an hour before Mr Lister and Dr Marshall appeared! In a few minutes he had ascertained all & went out again with the others. Sir William Jenner returned saying Dr Lister thought the swelling ought to be cut; he could wait twenty-four hours, but it would be better not. I felt dreadfully nervous, as I bear pain so badly. I shall be given chloroform, but not very much, as I am so far from well otherwise, so I begged the part might be frozen, which was agreed. Sir William Jenner gave me some whiffs of chloroform whilst Mr Lister froze the place, Dr Marshall holding my arm. The abscess, which was six inches in diameter, was very quickly cut and I hardly felt anything excepting the last touch, when I was given a little more chloroform. In an instant there was relief. I was then tightly bandaged, and rested on my bed. Quite late saw Beatrice and Alfie for a moment, after Mr Lister had been in to see me. Felt very shaken and exhausted.

The next day she wrote in her Journal:

Had a cup of coffee before the terrible long dressing of the wound took place. Dr Marshall assisted Mr Lister, whose great invention a carbolic spray to destroy all organic germs, was used before the bandages were removed, and during the dressing . . .

According to Godlee, the use of the spray was not entirely without incident. Marshall accidentally directed it full into the Queen's face. When she complained, he replied 'that he was only the man who worked the bellows'.

During one early visit Lister was disturbed to find that the abscess was reforming as fluid collected again in the former cavity. He could see that the wound was not draining properly, in part because of the tight bandages, and it occurred to him to try drainage tubes. He manufactured them on the spot by cutting sections from one of the rubber connections between the spray atomizer and the container of carbolic acid solution. He was then able to freeze the incision and to slide the tubes into place without opening it. Lister was not then aware that the French surgeon, Chassaignac, had introduced drainage tubes in 1859. It was another brilliant example of his originality in solving a clinical problem, and it typified his technical inventive skill. Lister did not report the incident until 1908.

Properly drained, the incision healed rapidly, and Lister was able to leave Balmoral within a week. The Queen recorded the event on September 11: 'Thankful and happy to be relieved of my bandages', though now she was suffering 'from a violent attack of rheumatism'. Godlee said that she described 'the whole performance as "a most disagreeable duty most pleasantly performed"'. Naturally, some folklore has precipitated around the event. One of Lister's house surgeons reported that:

After one visit he had driven away from the Castle to the railway station at Ballater. Arrived there he suddenly remembered that he had forgotten *the* safety pin! Instead of thinking first of his own amour propre and leaving the event to chance, he drove back the eight miles to Balmoral and there faced the embarrassing duty of displaying his own oversight and asking Her Majesty to undress so that he might secure his handiwork by the one, single, forgotten safety pin!

Another quoted Lister as having once said: 'Gentlemen, I am the only man who has ever stuck a knife into the Queen!' When Victoria died in 1901, Lister presented the address of sympathy and homage from the Royal Medical and Chirurgical Society of London. In it he wrote: 'I believe that I happen to be the only person who ever exercised upon her sacred body the divine art of surgery. The occasion was a most critical and anxious one, but, while she treated me with queenly dignity, nothing could exceed her kindness.'

The Queen was the most eminent patient in Lister's expanding private practice. Although his Royal patients paid him only in prestige, one of his London house surgeons reported that the team of horses that pulled Lister's carriage had been a gift from the Queen. And the knowledge that he was one of the Royal surgeons carried great weight.

Flora Masson, the student who later described the spray in operation at St Thomas's, brought Lister a patient, one evening, at his home. In 1871 she was in her early 'teens. Her father, a professor in the arts faculty at Edinburgh University, probably knew Lister, but the Masson family doctor was Thomas Keith. Flora's parents were out, however, when a maid came to the young lady saying she had swallowed a pin, 'a bent pin, and that it was sticking in her throat, not very far down'. There was a Scottish nanny, but the young mistress put herself in charge. Somehow she knew that Keith was not available so that having ordered a cab and got into it with the maid, she directed the driver 'to Professor Lister's house'. 'We were shown into the dining room, and immediately, while we were still standing, the great surgeon came in. He stood, silently benign, looking at us, while I made my little explanatory appeal.'

I remember the kind, grave face looking down at me as he listened; and without a word he led the way into his consulting room. I remember the look of the chair, a glorified dentist's chair, in which he placed the trembling girl. I remember standing by— indeed, she had taken a firm grip of me—and watching the surgeon's hands, their leisurely, gentle manipulation of the long, shining instruments; they seemed to grow longer and longer, as the search for that pin proceeded.

Then, at last, he desisted. 'I do not think,' he said slowly, looking at the girl in the chair, 'there is any pin there. I think, if there had been, I should have found it.'

Just now, in November 1871, there was another death in the family. Rickman Godlee was sixty-seven years old, a successful lawyer and an active Quaker. From the time of Joseph's illness Godlee had been as close to him as any of his Lister brothers and sisters. Both Joseph and Agnes wrote to Mary Godlee on November 14. Agnes had been a member of the family for fifteen years, but even given the nature of her relationship to the Godlees, the contrast between her letter and her husband's is striking. She wrote:

My dearest Mary,
What can words of mine be to thee at this time! Yet I must write to try to tell thee of my sorrow for thee and thy children in your great grief, and my sorrow <u>with</u> you in feeling the blank made in the family circle by the removal of one for whom our regard was very warm, and whose interest in all that concerned us was always so ready and so great . . . .

And Joseph's letter:

My darling Mary,
To be silent would be unbrotherly. But how can I write without adding to the sorrow that overwhelms thee!
   To tell thee how I loved and honoured Rickman, or to say that thee have my deep sympathy, is surely needless. Nor does it seem needful to express my full assurance that with him all is well!
   If my engagements will permit, I hope to be with you on the solemn occasion that must follow.
   I will not write more, darling, except a message of tender love to you all . . .

Descendants of their nieces and nephews say that Agnes Lister lacked warmth, and suggest that she was not popular in the family. Perhaps her failure to have children confirmed the efficiency and detachment of her life.

Lister could not go to London for Rickman Godlee's funeral, he wrote to Mary the next day, because of his commitments to patients and to his students at the beginning of a new session. On the following day he began the monumental series of bacteriological experiments that were to occupy him for ten years. The immediate spur was a report by Dr John Burdon-Sanderson, the physiologist and medical officer to the Privy Council, on experiments seeming to show that although the air carries fungi, it does not carry bacteria, that bacteria are conveyed by water and that they are killed by dry heat at 100 degrees Fahrenheit. Lister's first series of experiments continued until January 22, 1873—more than a year- -with two breaks in the spring and summer of 1872. They were continued at Leytonstone when Joseph and Agnes went there for Christmas 1871 and at High Cliff during September 1872. Not only were they moved about the country but about the Charlotte Square house as convenience required. On August 15, 1872, Mrs Lister wrote in the Common-place Book:

The Pasteur's solution was heated up stairs in a dressing room little occupied and the rest of the experiment hitherto, including the superheating of the wine glasses had been done in the dining room as less likely to contain germs than the study. The glasses are now transferred (after filling) to the mantel-piece in the study . . .

The word bacteriology did not exist in 1871, nor indeed was the word bacteria commonly heard. Lister's last paper to appear for eighteen months, 'On Antiseptic Dressing under some Circumstances of Difficulty, including Amputation at the Hip-Joint', was read to the Medico-Chirurgical Society of Edinburgh on June 6, 1871. In it Lister referred to 'ferments'.

As in the case of clinical equipment, antiseptics and dressing, Lister and his contemporary experimenters had to invent their techniques as well as their language. On January 17, 1872, for example, he devised a means for obtaining filtered water in a tube of glass that had been capped and heated. The tests began at 6.28 p.m. and ran until 11.30, beginning again at 0.15 a.m. on the 18th and continuing until Lister was satisfied that 'bacteria' could make 'their way through a partition which opposed partial obstruction to albumen'. In February 1873 he invented what he called a 'glass garden', a thick plate glass with wells ground into it suitable for culturing organisms. Each well could be covered with a slip and the whole 'garden' examined seriatim under a microscope by moving only one piece of glass. Although Lister also used glasses and test tubes for the purpose, it was this device which made possible his most remarkable technical achievement, the serial dilution of cultures to a point where he could specify with a statistical certainty how many bacteria a given culture contained. In 1875 he sketched and described a hot box for sterilization which he continued to improve until the end of that year.

In addition to the equipment that emerged from Lister's laboratory, he developed culture media suitable for bacterial growth. The first had been urine, and he began again with this easily obtainable material. The following note appears in the Common-place Book in Mrs Lister's handwriting, although he was no doubt the source: 'About 6.20 p.m. some twelve ounces of urine were passed (after antiseptic precaution with one to forty lotion applied to the glans) through a glass tube'. He also used acetic acid, alcohol, albumen, bread, gelatine, artificial milk (a mixture of milk, sugar and water), cucumber and turnip infusion (sliced cucumber or turnip, respectively, simmered for seven hours), boiled and unboiled milk and Pasteur's solution, consisting of lump sugar, tartrate of ammonia, salts of wood ashes and tap water. All of these media were being used by others working in the field at the time.

With Mrs Lister in almost constant attendance and assisted by almost anyone else who happened to be in the house, including the servants, he worked with single-minded intensity. Lectures had to be given and patients cared for, but otherwise his life for the next decade focused through a microscope. He began work at 7.00 and occasionally at 4.30 in the morning. At Leytonstone, on Boxing Day, 1871, Arthur Lister noted the time of an observation as 0.30 a.m. On occasion entries would be made in the Common-place Books at intervals of from five to fifteen seconds for periods of an hour or more. Lister often remained at his microscope from early evening, immediately after dinner, until well past midnight, his wife with him to note down his observations. No one who has not peered through a microscope for three or four hours under electric light, let alone gas light, can imagine how tiring such work can be.

In 1871 not more than a handful of men in France and Germany, and only two or three in Britain, even attempted to pursue germs with anything approaching the thoroughness with which Lister worked. In all the world he was the only surgeon, if not the only medical man, to turn to bacteriology.

9

RETURN
TO LONDON

PASTEUR VISITED LONDON during 1871. Among other scientists whom he met was John Tyndall, the physicist, who had recently visited Lister's wards. Tyndall told Pasteur about Lister's achievements. It was the first time Lister's name had come to Pasteur's attention.

Pasteur was still concerned to prove once and for all that spontaneous generation could not take place. His activities had been much circumscribed, however, by a stroke in October 1868. He was recovering very slowly, though he never fully regained his health. His research inevitably suffered, but in 1870 he had isolated the cause of a disease of silkworms that had severely damaged the French silk industry.

Perhaps the most important bacteriological work, in 1871, was being done by a Breslau doctor, Ferdinand Cohn. In a book published the following year, Cohn presented evidence that bacteria exhibit a constancy in form which could be used to classify them into genera and species. The diphtheria bacillus was identified in 1871, the first bacteria to be associated with a specific disease, though years passed before it was proved to be the cause. In his book, Cohn described the class of Schizomycetes which included fungi as well as some bacteria. So broad a classification proved very little, but Cohn held the view that each of the fermentations Pasteur had identified, for example, was produced by an unique bacterium which reproduced true.

The alternative possibility, that some, if not all, bacteria are either different stages in development or different forms produced by environmental changes, is called pleomorphism. It is wrong, but it reflected the primitive state of the science. Relatively few organisms had been observed. Without staining, which Koch introduced a decade later, morphological or formal structural differences were extremely hard to see. Many fungi, for example, bud into spores which bear a strong resemblance to several cocci. Bacterial spores are often round, though the non-vegetative bacteria may be shaped quite differently. Thus Lister began by believing that all germs were related to each other and to fungi and yeast-like organisms. He did not read Cohn's book until the spring of 1874.

Almost the first organism he identified was a penicillium mould. He had undertaken the experiment to ascertain 'whether the growth of fungi renders the liquid a less favourable nidus for bacteria'. Whether or not they had a relationship, fungi and bacteria were different enough, Lister thought, to make it possible that they could not grow in the same culture. Fungi were of course very large by comparison with bacteria, but they might still be different stages in development of a single organism. Thus in February 1872 Mrs Lister wrote in the Common-place Book: 'That these bacteria are derived from the yeast cannot be doubted . . . These bacteria are seen also in the form of long chains, a further indication of their analogy with ordinary bacteria'. In the previous December Lister had described a 'pseudo-bacteria' which he later named 'Granuligera'. A few days after identifying the pseudo-bacteria, he observed that 'fluid in which bacteria develop so luxuriantly' seemed to poison a torula, a kind of fungus, but urine—the medium—could not possibly poison the torula, which grows in diabetic urine, 'unless indeed the peculiar richness of this specimen of urine renders it exceptional. It seems more probable that the urine is deficient in some material *torulae cerevisiae* requires'. These uncertainties about the culture media were multiplied by the variety of organisms that could be seen in them. On February 27, 1872, Lister observed: 'I can hardly doubt that this specimen is indeed a beautiful example of what I have before described as vibrionellae when in motion and claviculariae when motionless . . . and it is a comfort to feel the matter is so far simplified.' There was great excitement in these discoveries despite the hard work and confusion: 'How very wonderful this fact is! We seem to have the case of "Dematium" very closely paralleled', he wrote in the Common-place Book at 11:7 a.m. on March 10, 1872. Dematium was the name assigned to an organism that had seemed to pass through several forms. A note in August referring to 'mycelium of Leytonstone' seen during the Christmas visit, declared that it could not have been an illusion, beside which Lister wrote months later: '!!! but it was'.

When Joseph and Agnes left Edinburgh on September 14, they took with them his glass containers, his microscope and the Common-place Book. He recorded their arrival in Leytonstone the next day, and the subsequent journey:

Arthur & Susan, Agnes & I went off on the 16th on a delightful ramble on our way to this place (Lyme), going that afternoon, to Oxford, next even. the 17th to Stratford on Avon, on the 18th to Malvern, on the 19th to Hereford, on the 20th to Ross on the 21st to Tintern by boat down the Wye, & after spending Sunday the 22nd at Tintern, came here on the 23rd visiting the Wynd cliff on our way to Chepstow & thence taking steamer down the Wye across the Severn & up the Avon to Bristol, whence by rail to Chard and by carriages to this place, for our first carriage met with a serious collision & damage near Axminster. At Stratford on Avon I examined P₅0bA . . .

being one of the glasses containing a culture. At Tintern he examined another of his glasses and drew one of the organisms in it.

Mr and Mrs Lister returned to Edinburgh on October 29 in time for his winter lectures. Immediately before Christmas they went to Leytonstone, where the observations continued. On January 1, 1873, Agnes and Joseph both wrote in the Common-place Book:

Yesterday ... Having washed the udder & hypogastrium of a cow of Smith Harrison's with 1 to 20 watery solution of carbolic acid and injected a few drops of the solution into the main duct of each teat, grasping the upper part to prevent it from going in too far a milkman with sleeves tacked up & arms washed with the solution milked the cow into vessels arranged for the purpose ...

They returned to Edinburgh the next day with the milk in its aseptic test tubes. They were accompanied by young Rickman John Godlee who was now a medical student at University College Hospital. He remained with his aunt and uncle until February 17, frequently assisting with experiments and relieving his aunt of some of her secretarial duties. Godlee returned again two years later to act as his uncle's laboratory assistant for a fortnight.

On April 7, 1873, Lister read a paper before the Royal Society of Edinburgh, presenting results from his first year and a half of bacteriological research. A student who was present recalled many years later that one of the demonstrations required the tasting of milk that had been boiled and kept covered in sterile wine glasses. Lister sipped the contents of one glass and passed it to a faculty colleague, a physics professor, 'who agreed as to its quality. How many more of the venerable fellows tasted it I have forgotten'. Lister described 'Granuligeria', and said that 'bacteria of similar morphological characters may differ entirely as regards the fermentative changes to which they give rise'. Yet he continued to assert that despite their different actions, 'some of them at least' originate from fungi. He added that this conclusion, based on investigations using the 'glass garden', was 'entirely opposite to the preconceived notion with which I entered upon this inquiry'. In other words he had abandoned his first guess—which had been correct— that fungi and bacteria were different genera, and now believed— incorrectly—that they might be the same. The paper also contained a description of an organism grown in Pasteur's solution which had caused a transformation in urine. Lister said: 'we have here another example of fermentative change of putrefactive character induced in urine by other agency than bacteria'. He had evidently assumed that the organism, which he called 'Oidium', was of some non-bacterial species.

Nature, the new scientific journal then in its fifth year, abstracted the paper and commented favourably on it. Lister had not finished his research, however. Immediately after the Royal Society address he and Mrs Lister went to Lyme Regis. Back in Edinburgh at the end of April he renewed his experiments.

At the same time he continued to look for improvements in clinical details of the antiseptic method. On May 24 he noted that egg shells had been coated with carbolic acid to determine its value as a preservative. On August 28 Mrs Lister wrote in the Common-place Book: 'This morning one of these eggs was boiled for breakfast, rather slightly boiled and I ate it.' It is not clear that she was taking dictation.

Meanwhile there were private patients. On July 16 Lister was called to Aberdeen to operate. After surgery he visited a patient near Elton. Mrs Lister described the next day in a letter to Mary Godlee:

He returned to Aberdeen on Wednesday evening & started at 9 on Thursday morning & was here at 2.45. We dined at a rather reasonable hour last evening, & just before dinner an instrument maker came to show Joseph how he had progressed, or rather to tell him what difficulties he had encountered, in making a new spray producer. And then a new message came asking Joseph to go to an operation abt $1\frac{1}{2}$ miles off—and from that he did not get home till midnight.

A few months later she described an ordinary day in Edinburgh:

First directly after breakfast to an instrument maker's about a spray producer—work here between 10 & 11—& at 11 an operation in private which occupied him till nearly 12 Then to the hospital—an operation there...Home about $\frac{1}{4}$ past 3—Lunch & patients & off to a meeting of the Medical Faculty at the college before 4—Home abt. 5.45 having seen some patients on the way back from the College. Tea & an interview with another spray producer individual. Out again, with Dr Bishop, to see some one near—& now out again.

It was then $\frac{1}{2}$ past 7'. Dr Bishop was one of his assistants.

During August 1873, in the midst of these diverse activities, Lister made an important observation. He identified *Bacterium lactis* which is responsible for the lactic fermentation, one of several possible fermentations of milk. Pasteur had described the organism and its effect without naming it.

Late in August the Listers went to Moffat so that he could begin work on a new paper to describe the lactic acid experiments. He wrote to Arthur:

And most charming this place now is, so different from its appearance as *we* knew it. Now the little gardens are full of bright flowers, the trees in full unimpaired summer foliage, the cornfields golden with the late harvest, the lower hills emerald green, and the higher ones purple with heather blossom. I have to-day been (with Aggie) meditating on the Gallows' Hill where *fungi* are evidently in profusion.

Toward the end of September they were all together again at High Cliff. Meanwhile on August 23 *The Lancet* entered its first dissent:

We are not going to enter upon a discussion of the 'germ theory'...The disciples of Mr Lister are somewhat difficult to convince, because they have the convenient saving clause, that if the treatment fails some error must have been committed. The modern school cannot believe apparently in healthy suppuration, and speaks of 'putridity' where the ancients would have seen nothing but *'pus laudabile.'* Mr Wood, on the other hand, favours Mr Lund's motto, 'Keep the wound clean'; and this is, we believe, the great secret of Mr Lister's success.

The comment was prescient. Not only does it raise the question of validation which is so hard for any scientist to answer, but it suggests at the end what was later shown to be the truth.

How could the value of antiseptic surgery be demonstrated if the disciples replied every time there was a failure:

I am at a loss to account for the many failures those who try the system meet with, unless it be the want of faith in the 'germ theory' of putrefaction. If this is believed in, the system becomes easy, and the minutiae which seem to trouble some so much are mere matters of intuition.

So wrote J K Thornton, a former Lister house surgeon, in September 1873 in answer to a description of failures in Lister's ward that *The Lancet* had published.

The Lancet's leader signified a change of tack. In 1870 and again the next year the editor had taken the line used by Thornton. The 1871 leader had also carried remarks from three metropolitan hospitals, St George's, the Middlesex and London, all overwhelmingly favourable to Lister. They were followed by praise from St Mary's, London, the Birmingham General Hospital and St Bartholomew's, Chatham. *The Lancet* published additional testimonials such as a somewhat measured comment from the Bristol Royal Infirmary in 1874, but the suggestion that it was losing patience with the antiseptic surgeons, if not the system, shook Lister. It underlined the importance of his bacteriological research.

In October his second paper on bacteria appeared, published, in fact, before the April address to the Royal Society of Edinburgh. 'I have ventured to give this little organism the name Bacterium lactis,' he wrote; 'for . . . no doubt there are different kinds of bacteria.' This is the first clear indication that Lister recognized a morphologically-distinct bacterial species. Yet the matter was by no means resolved. Earlier in the same paper he wrote: 'we shall . . . see reason to believe that one and the same bacterium may differ at different times in its fermentative effects on one and the same organic solution'. It is, of course, true that in different conditions, chemical or atmospheric, a bacterial species may grow rapidly or vegetate, but this does not appear to have been what Lister meant. He noted in November that 'granular bodies' growing in Pasteur's solution 'are derived from the torula', a fungus. Early the next year a note in the Common-place Book referred to 'different species, some long and delicate, straight or curved; some short and highly refracting', but he was not yet convinced that each form lived a distinctive life: 'large numbers of bacteria' varying in structure, he noted four days later, 'yet I suspect of one species only, possibly bacterium lactis'.

On February 10, 1874, he was in London to perform a dissection and give a lecture at the Seamen's Hospital, Greenwich. On the same day he wrote to Pasteur for the first time. Lister wrote in French. He enclosed a copy of the paper published the previous October describing *B. lactis*. He thanked Pasteur sincerely 'for having, through your brilliant research, demonstrated the truth of the germ theory of putrefaction and for having thus given me the only principle which could assure the success of the antiseptic system'. He invited Pasteur to come to Edinburgh and concluded with suitable expressions of respect.

Pasteur, who wrote only in French, replied a fortnight later. He thanked Lister for the paper and said that he knew of Lister's work, though not enough about it. He was also impressed by Lister's bacteriological research, 'and it is an enigma to me that you can devote yourself to researches which demand so much care, time and incessant painstaking, at the same time that you devote yourself to the profession of surgery and to that of chief surgeon to a great hospital'. He asked Lister to send him a detailed account of the antiseptic system for communication to the Académie des Sciences, and for copies of his 'principal scientific works' which Pasteur wished to read. He then turned to the pleomorphism in Lister's paper. With apologies he gave an analogy of Lister's work from his own research on the organisms that cause vinegar and various other fermentations, respectively. 'Suppose that I was absolutely ignorant of the nature of what I was sowing, as you are of yours; should I not be justified in saying that the Myc. vini changes into the Myc. aceti and vice versa? And yet it does nothing of the sort. Your method of culture is remarkable for its exactitude . . . but I venture to tell you that I could wish it were more rigorous still.'

Lister welcomed this precise, informed criticism within the context of the principle he sought to defend. The correspondence was the beginning of a close professional friendship. Lister repeated and extended the experiments during March and April 1874. He also read some of the current material published by others, perhaps the most important being the book by Ferdinand Cohn. Lister's notes also show that he had been interested by research on the development of bacteria reported in *Nature* by Dr Leonard Sedgwick. He slowly abandoned pleomorphism as his own research revealed more evidence for the unique properties of the different organisms he observed.

In June a German article on the antiseptic method questioned its efficacy against certain forms of bacteria. Lister wrote his objections in the Commonplace Book. Commentaries on antisepsis were becoming increasingly frequent. As early as October 1871 *The Lancet* had reviewed a book called *The Antiseptic Treatment: a Treatise on Carbolic Acid and Its Compounds* by Arthur Ernest Sansom MD. Two years later James Cuming MD published *An Inquiry into the Theory and Practice of Antiseptic Surgery. The Lancet* called it: 'A sensible and well-written little book'. The first important textbook on the antiseptic system was written by Lucas-Championnière in 1876.

Other writers were doing what Lister would not do. He had instead undertaken to demonstrate the correctness of the germ theory upon which his practice was based. It was a two-pronged theory holding that living organisms originate only from other living organisms and that noxious bacteria are transmitted in the air. Bastian had suggested in 1873 that there are three classes of fermentable fluids: those altered by living germs, by living germs and dead organic matter, and by spontaneous generation from combinations of chemicals. As long as the third alternative could be seriously advanced, the foundation for Lister's work was insecure. In practice that theoretical insecurity spelled danger to his patients.

The role of airborne bacteria was secondary from the standpoint of the bacteriologists, but to Lister it was at least as significant as the question of biogenesis. Like Pasteur, Lister had been able to demonstrate that the germs which cause milk to sour and urine to become cloudy are airborne. But what about the bacteria that infect wounds? He accepted that they are distinct species. Are they also airborne? In fact Lister's research did not answer these questions, and although he had guessed right about biogenesis, he was wrong in his belief that putrefactive organisms are airborne. His bacteriological research gave him breathing space. He was able to say to his opponents: I am learning more and more about these germs, and everything I learn tends to support the theory. They could answer only with scepticism, a healthy state of mind but a poor weapon. Because the editor believed it was necessary to get on with the business of medicine, *The Lancet* tried to separate the antiseptic system from the germ theory: 'The germ theory may be perfectly well founded; but nine surgeons out of 10 do not care much whether it is or not, so long as they cure their cases and reduce their mortality to the lowest possible degree.' Lister knew better and recognized the vital factor: unless you believed in germs, you tended to skimp the details. If you skimped, the system failed. No one yet knew that the system failed not just because of carelessness, but also because these minute organisms could escape the most rigid antiseptic precautions, whether they were airborne or not.

Lister finally broke with his old friend, Sampson Gamgee, over these issues. Gamgee had a successful surgical practice in Birmingham. Late in 1873 he came to Edinburgh to visit Lister's wards, and in January 1874 he published an article reviewing six of the cases he had observed and praising Lister's work. In his comments on the cases, however, Gamgee said that there had been changes in Lister's methods but not in his theories. Only the methods, he believed, were important, and they should be subjected to 'thorough scientific examination'. Lister objected in *The Lancet* to Gamgee's derogation of the germ theory. Gamgee replied that he had submitted the proofs of his article to Lister for comment. Lister had returned the first batch of proofs with notes, but across the second he had written: 'Nothing to suggest as to matters of fact. In great haste.—J.L.'. Gamgee implied that Lister had carelessly overlooked that of which he now complained. Lister replied that Gamgee had 'distinctly stipulated . . . that my corrections were to refer merely to statements of fact . . . it would obviously have been unsuitable for me to have interfered with Mr Gamgee's comments; while it is equally clear that I was entitled to utter a public protest against them.' Lister was right, as Gamgee's letter makes perfectly clear, but a public quarrel is seldom resolved. In 1878 Gamgee published a book *On the Treatment of Wounds*. On October 30 Lister addressed the opening session of the Midland Medical Society in Birmingham. He described two classes of surgical problems illustrated by spinal abscess and compound fracture of the leg, respectively. In his experience, he said, both could now be cured because of antisepsis. Because he was in Birmingham, he referred to Gamgee's book, admitting that it was *possible* that the compound fracture case would have recovered without antiseptic treatment. Though he made no attempt to patch up the quarrel, he did try to speak fairly.

His own conviction that the antiseptic system worked freed his hand to try new surgical techniques. Early in 1873 he published a brief case history describing the method he had adopted to control an arterial rupture that had occurred accidentally as he was attempting to reduce a dislocation of the shoulder. Four more clinical articles appeared during the year. Lister was always a conservative surgeon in the best sense. He would not operate if any other treatment could be made to work, and when he did operate, he cut as little as possible. It was a difficult decision, for example, in the operation for breast cancer that he had perfected, whether to remove the glands in the arm pit as well as those in the breast. The procedure is normally followed today for breast cancer, but Lister had no way to determine whether the tumour was benign or malignant. His options were limited because he had fewer means for diagnosis.

Conservatism did not keep him from attempting operations that had been considered unjustified if not impossible before antisepsis. Cheyne's notes of Lister's clinical lectures for 1872–1873 reveal a number of new procedures and new operations. He reintroduced a form of lithotomy, removal of kidney stones, which had been abandoned because, though the route was shorter, it meant cutting into the forbidden abdominal cavity. He improved the operation for varicose veins and practised it more often. He performed several operations to correct bone deformities which were frequently encountered because inadequate diet led either to rickets or to tuberculosis. One of the most common was *genu Vulgum* or knock knees. The operation to correct the condition had first been performed by Dr William Macewen of the Glasgow Royal Infirmary, but according to Macewen, Lister did the second in 1875 or 1876. He also began to open the elbow and knee joints to make repairs on the common injuries sustained by these parts, previously interdicted like the abdomen. As early as January 1867 Lister's Glasgow ward journal contained a description of the restoration of the left eyebrow of a badly-burned seaman. Two years later he operated on a ten-year-old girl to repair her harelip, a procedure that he subsequently used often.

Plastic surgery also became possible to repair scars. In 1875 he described the method of skin grafting used to reduce the scarring after mastectomy. Bits of skin one-sixth of an inch square from the inner side of the upper arm provided twelve grafts that were dotted on the wound surface. A year later he noted in the Common-place Book a 'new mode of procedure' suggested by a Glasgow doctor which involved the use of some fatty tissue as well as skin for the graft. A surgical textbook published one hundred years later says that the healing of large wounds is slow, 'and bacterial contamination is inevitable, so in modern practice open wounds should always be covered by skin grafts'. In this procedure too Lister was not just an innovator but a clinician whose experience has made possible modern surgery.

His button remover and aortic tourniquet were useful mechanical additions to the art. About 1873 he introduced the button suture 'to take the place of the tips of two fingers of the two hands in giving support to the deeper parts of the wound.' The suture consisted of oval pieces of lead on either side of the wound connected to and holding silver-wire sutures running through the wound. He modified the device nine years later to make it suitable 'in approximating gaping wounds', especially after breast removal. The oval pieces of lead became 'broad pieces of thin leaden plate, perforated in the centre' to take the silver wire.

His principal surgical practice continued to be his patients at the Edinburgh Royal Infirmary, not only because of their number but also because the hospital practice offered far more variety than private practice. Syme had had seventy beds, but Lister had only fifty-four in the same wards, a measure of the attempt by the hospital authorities to reduce crowding and improve hygiene. Nevertheless Lister often had as many as seventy patients, using one bed for two or three children and pallets on the floor for adults. This was evidently his own doing, however, and against the policy of the hospital. On March 13, 1876, the managers wrote to Lister asking that he restrict the number of his patients to the 'number of beds allotted to you'.

One of the explanations of overcrowding in his wards arose out of the antiseptic system itself. Antiseptics gave Lister an opportunity to save a limb, but if the conservative treatment failed, he usually had time to amputate. Similarly, he could open an abscess safely. While the incision healed a new one might appear and that too could be drained. Without being able to treat the underlying cause, Lister could control the symptoms while the patient remained in hospital.

As early as June 28, 1871, the managers wrote to Lister about the requisite renewal of passes for patients who stayed over a hundred days. In October 1872 one of his colleagues reporting to the managers on the number of patients 'above 40 days in Professor Lister's Wards called attention to the expense of the Antiseptic treatment'. The managers appointed a committee of three to look into the matter. Two weeks later the committee reported that it was unable to reach a decision because records were inadequate and asked 'the new Statistician of the Infirmary' to assemble the necessary data. In December, and again in January 1873, the managers reappointed the committee which finally reported in June: Statistics 'show that during the last twelve months the duration of residence in Hospital, has been very much alike with both methods, and that the results are such as to induce your Committee to recommend, that no interference be taken on the part of the Managers on account of the expense of the treatment'. There were further complaints, and in response to Lister's request for a hearing, the managers asked him to 'have the goodness to meet them in the Board room on the 15th December'. He seems to have satisfied the managers because nothing more on the subject is to be found in the minutes of Board meetings until March 1875. On the 24th the Clerk asked Lister to comment on four patients whose combined residences added up to almost six years. Three days later Lister replied.

John Wright, who had been in hospital 389 days, had a diseased foot which Lister had at first treated conservatively in an attempt to save the foot. The operation appeared to have been successful, but then it had become necessary to amputate. He would soon be discharged.

William E Henley, the poet, had been in hospital 565 days. Although Henley was barely twenty-four, he had already lost one leg below the knee to tuberculosis, and had been recommended to Lister 'by a Lady in the South of England . . . of very considerable influence in London Society, and she has sent a pecuniary donation to the Infirmary'. A letter from Agnes Lister to Mary Godlee written on July 18, 1873—roughly 565 days before Lister's letter to the managers—almost certainly identifies the influential person as Lady Churchill, whom he had met at Balmoral. 'What would the London surgeons say if they read' her letter to Lister? Agnes asked Mary. Lady Churchill had offered to pay Henley's hospital expenses, but Lister had replied that 'no expense would be incurred'. Sadly, it had been necessary to amputate the other leg, but Lister apparently slowed the disease process. Henley died in 1903. He had expressed his gratitude in a poem entitled 'The Chief', first published in the *Cornhill Magazine* for May 1875 and subsequently in a volume called *In Hospital: Rhymes and Rhythms*.

> His brow spreads large and placid, and his eye
> Is deep and bright, with steady looks that still.
> Soft lines of tranquil thought his face fulfill—

His face at once benign and proud and shy.
If envy scout, if ignorance deny,
His faultless patience, his unyielding will,
Beautiful gentleness, and splendid skill,
Innumerable gratitudes reply.
His wise, rare smile is sweet with certainties,
And seems in all his patients to compel
Such love and faith as failure cannot quell.
We hold him for another Herakles,
Battling with custom, prejudice, disease,
As once the son of Zeus with Death and Hell.

Henley too was about to leave the hospital, Lister wrote to the managers, for the seaside.

His third long-stay patient, Annie McCanna, had been resident 567 days. A lumbar abscess had been treated satisfactorily, but a second abscess had then appeared, followed by a third and a fourth. The longest resident, however, was Jane Maid. She had been admitted 696 days before because of 'chronic suppuration of the sheaths' surrounding a major tendon in her leg. This healed, but abscesses appeared because of the 'weakness of her Constitution'. She could not go home because she lived in Arbroath. The poor woman was probably riddled with tuberculosis, and one can sympathize both with Lister and with the hospital managers, who were not operating a home for the incurably ill.

Lister's letter then went over to the attack. Karl Reyher, the Russian surgeon who was to adapt antiseptic techniques to field conditions during the Russo-Turkish war, had acted as Lister's assistant and attended his winter lectures during the 1873–1874 session. He had asked permission to compare Lister's practice with that of his predecessor, and had found an improvement. Syme's mortality rate for 120 amputations performed between 1865 and 1868 had been 23.3% whereas Lister's during the period 1870–1873 had been 17%. The figure reveals an astonishingly high failure rate in Lister's wards, but it was not this point that concerned him in his letter to the managers. Reyher had also shown that 'although the antiseptic treatment had led to the retention in hospitals of some patients for a very much longer time than was formerly the case (this being commonly caused by persons being kept alive who without antiseptic treatment would have died) yet on the other hand this mode of treatment cures other patients much more quickly . . . and that to so great an extent that the latter effect more than counterbalances the former'. The managers accepted Lister's explanations.

The issue came up again in November, and again a committee was appointed by the managers to consult with Lister. One of its number on this occasion was Syme's old friend, Sir Robert Christison, but the minutes contain no further reference to the committee's deliberations.

When Lister left Edinburgh two years later, he moved six patients into a private nursing home at his own expense, and had one young woman brought to London to King's College Hospital. The long-stay phenomenon continued there, but the King's College Hospital managers seem to have accepted the situation, just as had their counterparts in Edinburgh. The patients did eventually walk out.

In August 1875 Lister addressed the surgical section of the British Medical Association meeting in Edinburgh, 'On the Effect of the Antiseptic Treatment upon the General Salubrity of Surgical Hospitals'. He repeated the argument that what was lost on the long-stay swings was regained on the short-stay roundabouts. For three years, he said, his wards had not received a general cleaning, with one exception when a case of sore throat had made it desirable to purify the ward, because moving the patients put them at greater risk than the danger of infection. His wards had remained almost entirely free of hospital disease, though in 1873 there was an epidemic of erysipelas in Edinburgh as well as a severe outbreak of smallpox. Tetanus too had begun to disappear. Lister said years later that he thought the last case in Edinburgh had occurred in 1870. According to Godlee, he suggested the bacterial origin of the disease 'as early as 1872'. In the address to the BMA he denied that he worked 'under superior hygienic conditions'.

... my patients have the dirtiest wounds and sores in the world. I often keep on the dressings for a week at a time, during which the discharges accumulate and undergo chemical alteration . . . and, when the wounds are exposed after such an interval, the altered blood with its various shades of colour conveys often both to the eye and to the nose an idea of anything rather than cleanliness. Aesthetically they are dirty, though surgically clean.

He often repeated this contrast between surgical purity and aesthetic impurity, attributing it to Mr Syme. Blood and pus in one to forty carbolic acid solution were surgically pure, however unpleasant they looked. The contrast seems to have aroused no especial notice at the time, but it set the stage for a remarkable paradox: by recognizing the threat of germs, Lister made mere cleanliness seem irrelevant.

The paradox explains the outraged observation made on November 2, 1871, by Dr Michael Beverley, Consultant Surgeon to the Norfolk and Norwich Hospital, who began his visit to Lister's wards on that day:

Remarks. Although great care is evidently taken to carry out the antiseptic treatment so far as dressings etc are concerned—there is a great want of general cleanliness in the wards—the bed-clothes & patients linen are needlessly stained with blood and discharge—The Nursing appears to be of the very worst kinds.

In the long-term Listerism rationalized and hastened the improvement of hospital hygiene, but the surprising fact is that in these early days 'The Chief' allowed his confidence in carbolic acid to sweep his wards for him. Although Lister gave Beverley express permission 'to allude to anything you saw here in your paper', Beverley never published his opinion of Lister's ward hygiene.

In 1883 St Clair Thomson, then Lister's house surgeon, said that Lister wore 'an old blue frock-coat for operations, which he had previously worn in the dissecting room. It was stiff and glazed with blood'. Ten years later *The Lancet* ran two leaders on 'Antisepticism and Edinburgh Surgery' which cited a letter from a New York doctor criticizing the 'want of care in excluding sepsis on the part of the surgeon, the nurses or the assistants'. The editor quoted a Glasgow surgeon who had said: 'For clean, aseptic surgery go to Hamburg or Glasgow; for dirty surgery go to Edinburgh'. Lister had been gone from the city for sixteen years, but in this respect too his influence seems to have remained.

In practice, soaking instruments, dressings, wounds, the surgeon's hands and the air itself in carbolic acid solution had an effect analogous to that produced by the hygiene of Thomas Keith and Spencer Wells. Conversely, cleanliness could also work wonders, but Lister had tried mere cleanliness in his wards prior to 1865 with the usual sad failures. The antiseptic system offered better results. Curiously, the germ theory notwithstanding, Lister seemed not to realize at first that cleanliness *plus* antisepsis might further reduce his risks and even shorten the length of time that some of his patients had to stay in hospital. The gears in the machinery of medical progress seemed to slip. It took the virtual abandonment of antiseptic methods and their replacement by aseptic surgery during the last fifteen years of the century to restore hospital hygiene to the conditions that had applied generally in the 1860s.

Lister was scarcely aware of this unexpected blemish on his reputation. Even his opponents, who had perforce to give greater emphasis to hospital hygiene, never publicly attacked him for the conditions that Beverley described. By the time he came to London in 1877, moreover, Lister seems to have adopted more modern practices. In part the change may have been due to a higher standard of nursing though the nurses at King's College Hospital caused difficulties of their own.

In the Edinburgh Royal Infirmary any lack of hygiene was compensated for by Lister's care and perseverance. His ward visits in the early 70s followed a pattern described by John Rudd Leeson, one of his house surgeons during the period. He customarily arrived at noon, in the landau drawn by a pair of horses. Sprays had been got ready in advance. As many as thirty students often awaited him, along with frequent foreign visitors. He 'tripped up the stairs, often taking two at a time,' and went first to the house surgeon's private room on the first floor. Newly-arrived visitors introduced themselves there. As the rounds began, 'He spoke little, and that chiefly in short sentences to the foreigners.' Lister often described his actions in their language to ensure that he was being understood. He had learned French at school, and he had a copy of a *New Method of Learning Italian* inscribed 'J & A Lister June 1856', the date of their wedding tour. According to one of his Edinburgh assistants Lister learned German at this time because he had so many German visitors. At the end of his active career in 1893 he is said to have conducted an abdominal operation while speaking in German because there were three German and two French professors in his audience.

No nurses attended him during his ward rounds, and little teaching took place. According to Sir James Russell, 75% of his teaching was devoted to dressing and the remainder to 'Text-book Surgery'. The hospital assistants were expected to attend the ward rounds as a matter of course, but the bedside could accommodate only a handful of observers.

If any discharge was evident through a dressing, two basins of 1 to 40 carbolic acid solution, one for the instruments and the other for hands, were brought up by a clerk. The dramatic dumb show that followed was described with impeccable British assurance by Cheyne:

... the dresser on duty got on his knees at the side of the bed, and as soon as the bandages had been cut he started his hand spray. Lister then lifted off the outer dressing, which was solemnly handed round to each distinguished foreigner to smell. Having satisfied themselves that there was no putrefaction, the deeper piece of gauze which was generally placed over the region of the wound was passed round to show that there was no pus, and then in cases where it had not been possible to bring the edges of the wound completely together... came the *piece de resistance*. In such cases Lister usually covered the wound with a... 'protective', and when this was exposed he would take a pair of forceps and peel off the protective, exposing the wound with the adherent organizing blood clot lying in the spaces where the edges had not come together ... with not a sign of inflammation or suppuration in the wound. As a rule this was followed by a gasp of surprise by the distinguished foreigners, and then a violent conversation ... accompanied by equally violent gesticulation, so that one became alarmed lest the peace of nations was ... endangered.

Lister removed any drainage tubes from the wound, washed them in carbolic acid solution and cut them shorter or replaced them with smaller ones if necessary. Dressings were always soaked off, never pulled away dry, so as to protect newly-formed skin. He would not leave the bedside, wrote Leeson, 'until the patient admitted that he was comfortable'. The average rounds took about ninety minutes.

Lister's Sunday visits were a more leisurely version of the daily rounds. He and Mrs Lister went to church at Trinity, the Scottish Episcopal church in Princes Street Gardens, a short walk from Charlotte Square. After lunch at about 2.00, Lister climbed the steep hill to the Infirmary, about a mile from his house. On Sunday he tried to see every patient and to make time for the discussion of minor operations and day-to-day treatment that had been carried out by his staff. He customarily went first to the Reserve ward for men, the largest, thence to the other men's ward, followed by the women's, where there were usually also several children, ranging in age from a few weeks to six or seven. Older boys had beds in the men's wards. Henley, a 'tall, gaunt, russet-bearded figure', had been put into a small room at the back of the hospital off one of the wards. According to John Stewart, who went to London with Lister and became his house surgeon there, late in 1873 three small boys shared the other bed in the same room. Thomas Miller, Willie Shotts and Roden Shields all had tuberculosis of the bones, like Henley. Shields was seven and came from Glasgow. After Lister died, Shields wrote to the *Westminster Gazette*:

My mother, who had travelled from Glasgow to visit me, was battling along Princes-street one day against wind and rain on her way to the infirmary. Lister happened to be passing in his carriage, and recognized her. He instantly stopped, picked up the poor, bedraggled woman in the most fashionable thoroughfare in Scotland and conveyed her to their common destination.

The Sunday visits took upwards of four hours and were, Stewart wrote, 'Among the happiest recollections of those Edinburgh days.'

In his letter to the managers reviewing the cases of Henley and the other three long-stay patients, Lister also asked permission to take a leave of absence for eight weeks so that he could visit continental hospitals. Dr Chiene would be responsible for his wards. The projected tour could only improve the reputation of the Infirmary, and the managers unhesitatingly agreed.

Although Mrs Lister was worried about the health of her sister, Lucy, who now lived with the Listers, she and Joseph left early in May 1875. At Cannes they met Arthur and Susan and their two eldest daughters. The party travelled by private carriage along the Corniche to Genoa and via Spezzia and Pisa to Naples 'where Lister, full of his classical memories, made the orthodox undignified entry into the Sibyl's Cave' on hands and knees, wrote Godlee. From Sorrento the brothers went on an expedition to Capri. On the way back a storm drove them into Naples. They sent a telegram to Agnes and Susan, who had been told that in such weather the boat would not leave Capri. The party stayed ten days in Rome and drove through the Campagna, where a chill led to a rheumatic shoulder which Lister believed was cured 'by the cold air in the Adelsberg cave some weeks later,' according to Godlee. From Florence the party travelled to Milan, spent Whit Monday at Bellagio and went on to Venice for four days. They stayed in Trieste long enough to explore the caves and travelled to Vienna where they separated. Agnes and Joseph went on to Munich to begin the professional part of the journey.

Agnes's long letters to Susan Lister about the German tour began in Leipzig, the next stop, so nothing was recorded about their visit to Munich. Lister had gone there to see one of his earliest continental supporters, Theodore Billroth.

They arrived in Leipzig on June 7. Lister was the academic guest of

Professor Thiersch, but they stayed 'at the Hotel de Prusse . . . we wondered when it was, as Bradshaw calls it, <u>newly</u> furnished'. After an early breakfast on the 8th, Agnes wrote to Susan that evening, Lister went to the hospital before 8.00. Thiersch 'introduced him to the students, who were present in greater numbers than usual, and who rose and bowed to him, no "Hoch" being on this occasion called for by their Professor'. At noon he returned to their hotel and told Agnes that at 1.30 they were to dine with Thiersch and his wife. Mrs Thiersch was the daughter of the chemist, von Leibig, and to Agnes's relief, knew English. In addition to 'a young medical man from Kiel', the luncheon party included the four Thiersch daughters, aged '10 to 16 about' and their governess.

An elaborate meal was followed by a formal banquet at eight that night in honour of Lister. Mrs Lister was accommodated in a gallery of the banquet hall with Mrs Thiersch and the wife and two daughters of Thiersch's colleague, Professor Carus, where 'we could see and hear without being seen'. They arrived as Lister was finishing his speech in reply to the toast to his health by Thiersch. Mrs Lister's description is amusing as well as detailed:

Joseph's speech was very warmly received, & he heard afterwards that the students were very pleased by his speaking in German. About 250 people were present—about 100 Leipzig students, and about 50 from Halle. Some Professors from Halle also came, among them two Professors Volkmann, father & son—the former Professor of anatomy, 78 years of age . . .

An article by the younger Volkmann had appeared in the *Edinburgh Medical Journal* in March with an introduction by Lister, who was probably also its translator. Mrs Lister continued:

It is a very handsome room—& the effect looking down from where we were on the great number of people, & the thought of the object of it all—well it was a great thing to see . . . Soon after Joseph had spoken, four students left their supper places & sang, in parts, a German song, & then the band, in the gallery opposite to that in which we ladies were, played, while the bountiful supper proceeded a little farther. There were many speeches. (I wish I had understood them). Toasts were proposed & warmly responded to—but no 'speeches in reply' were made, except Joseph's. Professor Carus . . . proposed the University of Edinburgh—and spoke most handsomely of Joseph,—calling him 'facile princeps' there. A medical man from Dresden spoke, and one from Magdeburg, the hospital of which was the most unhealthy in Germany, and now, through antiseptic treatment, it is healthy. Everybody was most cordial—& Joseph was in many toasts, either by himself, or in connection with antiseptic principles, or united with Profs. Thiersch & Volkmann—& how the glasses clinked—& how the 'Hochs' . . . resounded—strengthened by the roll of a drum & the blowing of several trumpets! The students sang, very nicely—John Anderson my Jo, in German; & two songs written by students for the occasion . . .

The Lancet's correspondent reported that one of the songs was called '*Carbolsaüre Tingel-Tangel*', or roughly, 'The Carbolic Acid Rag'. Agnes went on:

A copy was given to each individual, and it was a sight to see all, except Joseph, & perhaps a very few others, singing together. The ladies were not forgotten—but they tried to get quite out of sight when their health was proposed under the title of 'strangers in the gallery'. Late in the evening a kind young man... I think by Prof. Thiersch's desire, brought some cake & a bottle of champagne to our gallery—very welcome refreshment. I went back to the hotel with Mrs Thiersch . . . at abt 11.15 . . . Joseph got to our hotel about the same time I did.

The next morning:

Joseph & the King of Saxony attended Prof. Thiersch's clinical lecture! ... This is the first time the present King has visited Leipzig & people seemed inclined to think that his going to the University etc was merely with a view to his own popularity... Joseph was at the hospital before 8.30 a.m., the hour at which the lecture begins, & at which the King was to arrive... When his Majesty arrived he was first conducted by Prof. T. to one of the wards ... & then brought to the Operating theatre. There Prof. T. presented Joseph to him, mentioning his having introduced antiseptic treatment—the King shook hands with him, & they sat down near each other. An operation was performed for the King's instruction—the removal of very large growths, called loose cartilages, from the interior of a knee joint. Prof. T. explained that without antiseptic means the operation could not have been undertaken... The King enquired of Joseph the nature of the loose cartilage, & in order to reply Joseph moved to a chair next but one to the King—a Minister being between them. The King bore the operation quite well—it was thought that some of his attendants did not like it much.

From Leipzig, where Lister also performed an operation at Thiersch's invitation, the couple went by train to Halle and were met by Professor Volkmann, the surgeon, a Professor Schmidt from Leipzig and 'a young Privat Docent [University lecturer] from Leipzig, one of the editors of the "*Centralblatt*", a weekly medical paper' for which he had translated Lister's current *Lancet* articles on improvements in the antiseptic method. Seven instalments appeared from March 13 to June 5, 1875, describing new dressings and operative techniques, but the series remained unfinished.

Volkmann took Lister home to have breakfast, but because Mrs Volkmann had just had a baby, Mrs Lister remained at their hotel. Lister attended Volkmann's clinical class during the morning. He and Mrs Lister were driven through the city to Volkmann's house where their gastronomic tour continued at 4.00 pm:

The dinner was very elaborate—well cooked & well served; soup, which was accompanied with grated cheese, & with boiled rice & stewed prunes—Then came roast beef, with vegetables—then fish—then two dishes of vegetables, peas, & French beans, & as accompaniment to them various small dishes to choose portions from—herring—salted salmon, ham & something else—Then lobster & salad sauce—then roast roe & salad—Stilton cheese & ice—ladies and gentlemen went upstairs at the same time—& the gentlemen smoked in the 'saloon', a larger drawing room. We stayed till nearly 7—

The next morning they went on to Berlin. From their hotel room they could see the Unter den Linden, and on the first day, 'took holiday—(that is to say Joseph did)', to do some sightseeing. Mrs Lister thought that the bas reliefs on the newly-constructed victory column represented 'the horrors of war, but I suppose the Prussians think of the splendour of the victories'. They walked to the Tiergarten where Joseph recognized a hoopoe bird. The business side of the visit occupied a day during which Lister visited the two important Berlin hospitals. They dined with Professor Bardeleben of the Charité hospital that evening, and at 10 pm, left for Magdeburg. There Lister called on a surgeon whom he had met both at Leipzig and at Halle, but the man was absent and his assistants showed Joseph around their hospital, until recently 'the most unhealthy in Germany'. That same night, June 15, they went on to Bonn. In the morning Lister called on Professor Busch at the hospital, where he saw also 'Dr Madelung, the assistant—a very nice young man, who was in Edinburgh last summer'. Mrs Lister 'walked a little about Bonn, and went to the post office.'

At Bonn, Lister's professional itinerary ended. They boarded a river steamer for Mayence and then went by train to Heidelberg. From there they returned to London via Brussels, Calais and Dover. On the train journey between London and Edinburgh Lister relaxed by reading Tennyson's play *Queen Mary*.

The tour had been a triumph. In the small hospital at Bonn Professor Busch took Lister to meet his students, 'and said to them . . . that few have the happiness of discovering means of such benefit to humanity as the antiseptic treatment.' Soon after his return to Edinburgh the Medical Societies of Munich and Leipzig elected Lister to honorary memberships. On August 1, 1875, George Friederick Stromeyer, surgeon, of Hannover, published a celebratory poem in both German and English:

> Mankind looks gratefully now on thee
> For what thou didst in surgery
> And Death must often go amiss,
> By smelling antiseptic bliss.
>
> By Volkmann's skill and industry
> Famous Thou art in Germany!
> Who could a better Prophet be,
> Than Richard Hotspur was to Thee?

In the German version Hotspur was replaced by Volkmann. Of course Lister had selected the hospitals he had visited, and not only had he been able to determine that his techniques were being used successfully, but also correctly. The excitement and enthusiasm that had greeted him were reported in *The Lancet* and must have enhanced his standing at home.

But the tour publicity did not prevent a new attack based on a new theme, statistics. Lister's Edinburgh colleague, James Spence, had questioned the value of Lister's catgut ligature in 1869. In August 1875 he used the platform afforded by the BMA meeting in Edinburgh to call for statistical evidence that the antiseptic method had any real superiority over other methods. In three years he had done sixty-three amputations with only three deaths and twenty-three joint excisions with two deaths. He washed wounds with tepid water, occasionally applied iodine and used a dry dressing unencumbered by carbolic acid.

There was a noticeable silence from the Listerians. Godlee pointed out at the time that Lister undertook operations considered too risky by those who did not adopt his system.

Meanwhile on October 16 *The Lancet* said: 'Mr Lister and his disciples are themselves to blame for much of the obscurity that overshadows' the question of the value of antiseptic surgery 'inasmuch as they have never yet openly and fairly met the challenges that have been thrown out to them to produce the statistical results of their practice'. These 'challenges' had not appeared in *The Lancet*, wherever they had appeared, but the leader served to launch a discussion of the antiseptic method at the Clinical Society of London. The first session was devoted to two clinical reports. Dr Callender of St Bartholomew's, who believed in the practice of 'cleanliness alone' like Spence, reported on the inadequacy of salicylic acid as an antiseptic, a point with which Lister later agreed. The second clinical paper described antiseptic treatment of a fractured knee cap.

The next week *The Lancet* continued its editorial discussion, calling attention to the general improvement in hospital cleanliness that had followed publication of Sir James Simpson's pamphlet on *Hospitalism*. The leader continued: 'it is more than probable that much of the credit due to increasing care and cleanliness has been accorded to the antiseptic plan of dressing wounds'. Although the periodical seemed unaware of the actual state of Lister's wards, this bitter attack on a matter about which Lister had spoken in his own address to the BMA on the improvement of conditions in the Edinburgh Infirmary has broadly-speaking stood the test of time.

The Clinical Society discussion went on for another week too. Mr Pick, the surgeon who had treated the fractured knee cap, enthusiastically defended antiseptic surgery. Mr Maunder, though he was not antipathetic, had obtained good results with other systems. He thought Pick's care and attention had been very important. Mr Holmes supported antiseptic surgery but could not accept the germ theory. Mr De Morgan considered antiseptic surgery 'of great use'. Mr Barwell wished to separate Lister's methods from antiseptics themselves. He considered many of the methods 'repulsive', but looked upon antiseptics as valuable. Mr Christopher Heath praised Lister's system. Though he recognized the importance of the details, he rejected the spray. Mr Thomas Smith said one must either accept it all or reject it all. He for one accepted it. Mr Barwell returned to say that he wished only to simplify the system. Mr Croft concluded the session, noting that improvements in the wards brought about by antiseptic treatment had helped to prevent suppuration in non-surgical cases.

A month later the Clinical Society concluded its discussion of the subject. Marcus Beck, Lister's cousin, said that in 1868 Lister prevented 'decomposition' in only about 30% of his cases. His success rate had greatly increased as his methods had improved. Mr Holmes, who accepted the antiseptic method but not germs, summarized the discussion: 'the remarks of surgeons present indicated a great uniformity of opinion that the care in dressing, the cleanliness, avoidance of the introduction of foreign bodies, especially those of a putrefactive nature, constituted the great advantage of antiseptic surgery.'

With its report of the final debate on November 20, 1875, *The Lancet* commented editorially: 'We sympathize with those advocates of Lister's methods who would have wished to discuss the general question' of the value of antiseptic surgery. They may 'say that, whilst refusing to allow the value of the free use of carbolic acid', the doubters 'place unlimited faith in a minute quantity of it'.

. . . few of the speakers either place faith in Lister's theory or carry out his practice in full . . . some have tried it, but they gave it up for weariness of the details, or dislike of the mechanical procedures needed, and especially the disagreeableness of the spray . . . while others have resented the insistence on a theory which they could not accept on the evidence given, and without which the practice seems tediously minute and even repulsive.

Lister's advocates could still bring forward a series of cases demonstrating good results, *The Lancet* concluded: 'But with the present state of feeling on the subject, we question whether they would gain much by doing so'.

The editorial represented a nadir in Lister's influence. It all but wrote off the antiseptic system, a far more radical conclusion than the inconclusive Clinical Society debate justified. Nevertheless the very indecisiveness of that discussion supplied reason enough for the leader. All of Lister's decisions from this time forward were conditioned by this virtual dismissal. It became imperative, if the antiseptic system was to achieve acceptance, that he demonstrate by word and deed the truth of his assertions directly to the London medical establishment. Senior London physicians and surgeons numbered about 2% of the profession, but they dominated it because they held a disproportionate number of offices in the Royal Colleges and leadership positions on the General Medical Council, and they came into social contact with Members of Parliament and Government Ministers. Cases, even statistics, had become less important than personal contact.

Whatever the opposition to his teachings, Lister was already recognized in the medical profession as an innovator. Such was his local standing that he was asked by the University of Edinburgh to address its graduation ceremony on August 1, 1876. He held one of the most important surgical professorships in the world, and he had of course received Royal recognition which counted for a great deal in Victoria's Britain. He was also acknowledged to be an educator of competent surgeons. In June 1874 a Birmingham surgeon, Oliver Pemberton, wrote to Lister: 'We have a vacancy at our Hospital for House Surgeon—have you a _Man?_' Beyond the expanding circle of his patients he had no standing with the public as yet, but he returned from Europe in 1875 to find that with many of his colleagues he had been caught up in an issue of major public interest, the antivivisection campaign.

On June 15 the Queen's private secretary, Sir Henry Ponsonby, wrote to Lister and to a number of his professional colleagues on the Queen's behalf. She wished them to speak out against the practice of experimentation on living animals prior to the hearings of the Royal Commission that had been appointed by the Home Secretary on May 24. Lister's reply was a 1000-word defence of vivisection: 'I should deeply regret that I cannot see my way to complying with this request,' he began, 'were I not persuaded that my doing so would not promote the real good of the community'. He could not even accept that operations should always be performed under anaesthesia. His use of animals, he pointed out, had more long-range benefits than the castration used to fatten bullocks for food. Animal food was not even essential for man, though it was universal, and its use was sanctioned by Scripture. As to the suffering endured by animals, 'all physiological experiment teaches us that the sensibilities of an animal are less acute the lower it is in the scale of creation'. Perhaps he was aware that 'physiological experience' taught no such thing because he sought an explanation in the 'absence of the faculty of reflection ... and the comparable instinctive character of their mental operations'. But then he came to the most important vivisectionist argument: 'An act is cruel or otherwise, not according to the pain which it involves, but according to the mind and object of the actor'. Research on animals had the overriding purpose of serving human life and reducing human suffering and was therefore totally validated.

Lister often anaesthetized the animals on which he experimented but not invariably. One of his more dubious experiments was recorded in the Common-place Book by Mrs Lister on August 10, 1872. Lister injected sterilized mercury into the jugular vein of a dog, and the unsterilized metal into another. The dogs were killed with potassium cyanide and their viscera examined. The results are unrecorded. Although he did the actual injections under chloroform, no consideration appears to have been given to the sensations of the animals while the mercury formed thromboses in their blood vessels. In 1878 he reported an incident that had taken place in a Glasgow slaughter-house in 1861. He had been observing the effect of chloroform on the larynx of a sheep.

I had just got so far with my observations when the inspector of the slaughter house walked up and told me he would not allow such brutality ... and forthwith ordered me off the premises. Thus, I had a taste of what has been since alas! experienced so largely by our profession, viz, how ignorant prejudice with good intentions may obstruct legitimate scientific inquiry.

Lister's opinions were shared with the overwhelming majority of his professional colleagues. During the 1860s the medical press had distinguished between vivisection for research, which it approved of, and animal experiments only for instruction, but it had consistently opposed legal restrictions.

The first regulatory legislation had been introduced in 1822. It outlawed cruelty to the larger domestic animals, horses and cows, but not dogs or cats. Two years later the Society for Prevention of Cruelty to Animals was organized. It became the Royal Society in 1857, and in 1862 set itself against all *painful* vivisection. On the 50th Anniversary of the Society Queen Victoria sent a congratulatory message in which she aligned herself with its drive for partial prohibition and regulation of animal experiments. This was the position that she wished Lister and his professional colleagues to support.

On the other hand the RSPCA position was far too conservative for the strong radical antivivisectionist current that had evolved in response to the publicity given several unusual cases of experimental cruelty by newspapers which recognized that a substantial public responded to such stories. In particular, at the Norwich meeting of the British Medical Association in 1874, a French physiologist, Eugène Magnan, injected absinthe into dogs to show the effects of alcohol on the circulation. There were protests at the meeting, and the RSPCA brought a prosecution under the 1822 act against Magnan and three Norwich doctors who had arranged the demonstration. The RSPCA lost the case, but even the medical press was divided by it. As a direct result of the case, however, a remarkable Anglo-Irish spinster named Frances Power Cobbe organized a memorial calling on the RSPCA to introduce regulatory legislation. The memorial, presented in January 1875, was signed by the Archbishops of York and Westminster, the Lord Chief Justice, Tennyson, Browning and Carlyle, but Darwin was amongst those who refused. Because the RSPCA havered, Cobbe got her own bill introduced in May. Meanwhile a second bill suggested to Thomas Huxley by Darwin received the support of J Burdon Sanderson, Sir John Simon, medical officer of the Local Government Board, Michael Forster, Professor of Physiology at Cambridge and James Paget. *The Lancet* and *The Medical Times and Gazette* preferred the second bill, though there was no principled difference between them, but the *British Medical Journal* staunchly opposed both. Confronted with two private bills the Government took the time-honoured course of appointing a Royal Commission. Hearings began on July 5, 1875, and continued until December 15. The Commission heard fifty-three witnesses and received some written evidence. Lister appeared on November 1, and read a statement. He said that 'my first experiments were performed with the object of preparing myself for teaching, while I was not a person of recognized scientific attainments'. Thomas Huxley asked him about these early experiments. Lister replied that they had supplied 'a kind of pathological information, without which I believe I could not by possibility have made my way in the subject of antiseptics'. Erichsen led him through an exchange about whether experimentation on living animals had been required for his work with catgut, the point being that any such ligature 'must be tested by experiments' on animals. He repeated the opinion expressed to Ponsonby that legislation was unnecessary and undesirable. The Commission thought otherwise, however, and recommended moderate regulatory measures.

In November Frances Cobbe organized the Society for the Protection of Animals Liable to Vivisection, later known as the Victoria Street Society because of its address. The purpose of the organization was to mobilize antivivisectionist sentiment in the face of the RSPCA's vacillation. The Society's first fruit was a Government bill introduced into the House of Lords by Lord Carnarvon, Disraeli's Minister for Colonies, on May 15, 1876. It required that experiments involving living animals be licensed by the Home Office, and permitted vivisection only for the 'advancement by new discovery of knowledge which will be useful in saving or prolonging life, or alleviating human suffering'. Experiments on cats and dogs were forbidden, and experiments without anaesthesia required a special licence.

At this time Lister was appointed to the General Medical Council. He attended the May meeting, having come to London for the occasion with Mrs Lister. They stayed at the Wimpole Hotel rather than at Leytonstone, and from the hotel Mrs Lister wrote on May 24:

Joseph agreed before we left home to propose a motion against legislation with regard to vivisection. So his thoughts have been busy. He pondered during the forenoon yesterday, & then went for a little walk, & came back in time to meet Professor Turner (of Edinburgh) who fixed to come to lunch at 1.

After lunch, she continued, Lister and Turner called on Sir John Simon, also newly appointed to the General Medical Council. Lister wanted Simon to second his motion, but Simon refused for political reasons and recommended Dr George Humphry of Cambridge. That evening Joseph went without Agnes 'to dine at Hyde Park Gardens with Mr and Mrs Arthur Mills (she is Dr Ackland's sister) to meet Lord Sandon & Dr Ackland'. Acland, Professor of Medicine at Oxford, was then President of the Council. Sandon and another dinner guest, Mr Cowper Temple, were members of the Parliamentary Committee on Education. There were eighteen at dinner, including Paget and Dr Allen Thomson, Lister's old friend from Glasgow.

The next day Lister moved: 'That a Committee be appointed to consider the Bill introduced by the Earl of Carnarvon on cruelty to animals; and to report to the Council during the present session'. The Council agreed and appointed Lister Chairman of the Committee which went to work at once.

Mrs Lister continued her letter:

. . . Joseph has gone to see Mr Bright! to speak to him about vivisection. The Medical Council's Report on the subject is now completed—but only yesterday. Joseph has been complimented on his chairmanship & on his speaking.

Both Allen Thomson and George Rolleston, Professor of Physiology at Oxford, had praised him. Rolleston, however, dissented from the Council's Report which called for modification of the Bill. Lister and several other members had wished to oppose any legislation.

The Listers spent the Whitsun weekend at Dr Acland's Oxford home. Joseph wrote to Arthur: 'Dr Acland's house teems with beautiful pictures and engravings. He is a great friend of Ruskin, Millais and Richmond'. On Sunday they heard Canon Liddell preach, after which Lister and Acland walked about Oxford and attended services twice again. That evening they met Liddell, who was the father of 'none other than the original of "Alice in Wonderland"', Lister told Arthur. He was shown the manuscript of the book. His letter gives an insight that is almost unique into the dozens of such social weekends the Listers passed with friends and acquaintances during the long Victorian afternoon. This occasion was his formal début within the Establishment of British medicine. As Godlee observed, the week in the south 'was a time for making friendly acquaintance with influential men'.

Under pressure from the General Medical Council, the BMA and the medical press, the Government modified its Bill. It proposed to allow vivisection in some private laboratories, to require special licences for experiments on cats only if anaesthesia was not to be used, to forbid prosecutions unless approved by the Home Secretary and to make the Act applicable only to warm-blooded animals. Through what was probably a misunderstanding on the part of many legislators, the latter restriction was amended during the debate on the third reading so that the Act covered vertebrates, which includes frogs. It received the Royal assent on August 15, 1876, and remained in force a century later.

The kind of experiment that Lister had performed on the calf whose jugular vein he had ligatured in his father's museum with the help of Godlee and his father's gardeners was now forbidden in Britain. Not only would he have had to obtain a licence for the experiment, but his father's house would also have required a licence. Lister did not hold a licence and probably never applied for one, perhaps because he believed that it would be refused. In 1880 when he again wished to do some work on the putrefaction of blood, he went to the Ecole Vétérinaire at Toulouse to conduct his experiments.

At the end of 1881 Lister wrote to Sir William Vernon Harcourt, then the Home Secretary, in defence of the vivisectionist cause. Harcourt thanked him, saying the letter 'will be of great use to me'. Meanwhile, the Home Secretary had been forced to authorize a prosecution brought by the antivivisectionists under the Act against a London physiologist, David Ferrier, because he had done research on monkeys' brains. Ferrier was interested in the spots on the cerebral cortex of the brain that control the movement of various parts. He did not anaesthetize the animals, but no one was then aware that the brain contains no nerves sensitive to pain. In response to the prosecution, leading medical men organized the Association for the Advancement of Medicine by Research, in March 1882. Lister became a member of the first governing Council. Sir William Jenner was its chairman and other members included Sir James Paget, Michael Forster and J S Burdon-Sanderson. The Association measured its success by a reduction in the number of licences and certificates refused by the Home Secretary.

In 1886 John E Erichsen became an Inspector under the Act and held the position until 1900. Though he was one of the more moderate vivisectionists, those who were demanding total prohibition of live-animal experiments took the appointment as a challenge and increased their activity. In addition to a press that was often scandalous as well as inaccurate, various compilations of evidence of vivisectionist cruelty were published by the movement. One of these contained a chapter called 'Human Beings, Experiments upon' and quoted Lister as having told the Berlin International Medical Congress in 1890: 'It is a serious thing to experiment when the lives of our fellow creatures are concerned but I think the time has arrived when it may be safely tried'. The quotation was out of context: in the speech 'it' referred to a new dressing Lister had been developing. When he was told about the misuse of the statement, he replied: 'I have long since ceased to take any notice of the perversions of the truth which these people indulge in'. In 1898 he was asked by an American acquaintance, Dr W W Keen of Philadelphia, to comment on an attempt in the United States Congress to pass a law similar to the British Act. 'Our law on this subject should never have been passed and ought to be repealed,' he replied. 'It serves no good purpose and interferes with enquiries which are of paramount importance to mankind.' The American bill was defeated. Two years later Stephen Paget, son of the surgeon, published a book to counteract the antivivisectionist propaganda. Lister wrote an introduction to it:

The action of these well-meaning persons is based upon ignorance. They allow that man is permitted to inflict pain upon the lower animals when some substantial advantage is to be gained; but they deny that any good has ever resulted from the researches which they condemn.

It was his last pronouncement on a subject that has never lent itself to rational discussion.

After the May meeting of the General Medical Council, the Listers returned to Edinburgh. In November 1875 he had renewed his attempts to obtain a catgut ligature that was supple, long-lasting and antiseptic. Throughout the spring he tested dozens of different combinations of chemicals, temperatures and soaking times. The Common-place Book is filled with the usual detailed notes in his hand as well as Mrs Lister's, but between the dates August 4, 1876, and November 5, one word appears: 'America!'

In 1876 the United States celebrated its centennial with an array of events that included a meeting of the International Medical Congress in Philadelphia in September. Lister had been invited to act as President of the Surgical Section. He and Agnes, along with Arthur and Susan, crossed the Atlantic on the *Scythia*, one of the last Cunarders with full sail as well as steam, capable of fifteen knots. Before going to Philadelphia they went up the Hudson by boat, crossed Lake Champlain and visited Quebec, Montreal and Toronto, re-entering the United States at Niagara Falls.

The Medical Congress was a vast affair attended by 480 doctors. On the second day Lister spoke for two and a half hours on antiseptic surgery, a detailed statement intended both to introduce the treatment to the American medical profession and to provide details of the method. At the ceremonial banquet which concluded the Congress, Ulysses S Grant, President of the United States, honoured the gathering. Lister, unquestionably the most eminent foreigner present, was place on Grant's right.

Immediately following these professional endeavours the four Listers set out on a transcontinental train journey. For about three weeks they travelled through the Rockies to San Francisco and back by way of Salt Lake City to Chicago. In 1876 the American frontier still existed. On June 25, Sioux Indians, under Crazy Horse and Sitting Bull, annihilated an Army contingent under Colonel George A Custer at a bend of the Little Big Horn River in Montana Territory. San Francisco had recovered from the Gold Rush and was a thriving trade centre. Salt Lake City was a raw settlement still ruled by its great founder, the Mormon leader, Brigham Young. What the Listers made of it all cannot be said, however, for neither letters nor diaries survive.

Chicago, unburned and rough, was already a great meat-packing centre and the Great Lakes port for the crops of the rich Mississippi valley. There, according to Cameron's son, Lister met a former patient:

One of his earliest successes in Glasgow was the cure of a young girl who had been terribly injured while at work in a mill. After prolonged treatment she made a good recovery, though no longer capable of the manual work she had done before. Lister, as was his way, interested himself in her future and induced her employer to give her a trial in the department for design. She proved so efficient that when the firm sent its wares to a great exhibition in Chicago, it was in her charge that the exhibition went. In Chicago she married a young American manufacturer, who, as is the way of Americans, duly became one of the richest men in the States.

She it was who 'claimed and secured the honour of being his hostess' in Chicago.

From the middle-western metropolis the party went on to Boston, where

Lister had professional connections. They returned to New York early in October, and on the 10th Lister delivered a clinical lecture on 'The Antiseptic Method of Dressing Open Wounds' at the Charity Hospital. The response to him of the profession in the United States was at best sceptical. Lister had one follower, Malloch, in Hamilton, Ontario, and individuals in the United States practised antisepsis, but there was no general acceptance of Listerism within the American Medical Association, and excepting reports of his two speeches very little comment at the time in the medical press.

On October 12 the Listers sailed from New York on the *Bothnia*. By November 5, Joseph and Agnes had returned to Edinburgh and were engaged once again in the attempt to improve the catgut ligature. This series of tests went on almost continuously until February.

Mrs Lister was directly involved in the work on catgut, as she was in all laboratory research. At 11.45 one night, earlier in the decade, she wrote in the Common-place Book, 'On returning from dinner out I again inspected the specimen'. It is not clear whether she was taking her husband's dictation or had herself carried out the inspection. In 1877 shortly before they left Edinburgh he noted: 'At 1.30, the second milking time at the dairy in the Costerphine Road, we charged (Agnes & I) twelve little test tubes' with milk to serve as medium for bacterial cultures. A few lines further along Agnes wrote: 'Agnes lifted in succession each glass cap & I introduced the 10 minims or so into each tube'.

She was his secretary not only for professional notes and correspondence, but also on occasion for his family letters. On January 16, 1876, she began: 'My dear Arthur, While I am doctoring my spray-producer's lamp-wick *I get my faithful scribe (she would not write it herself)* to pen a few lines'. The italicized words are in Joseph's hand. They suggest a certain resistance on her part to his archness.

On January 21 Lister wrote to Arthur that he had received an invitation from Dr Murchison, President of the Pathological Society in London, to address the organization in April. It was an invitation to present the doctrine before a London audience, and he accepted. But a much more important opportunity arose which necessitated postponement of the talk.

On February 10, Sir William Fergusson died. He had been Professor of Surgery at King's College, London. His flamboyance and brilliance had assured that his popularity as a teacher matched his achievement in the operating theatre. He was one of those who practised cleanliness but had no use for antiseptic methods.

King's College was founded in 1828, two years after University College. The latter had been opened for religious dissenters who could not enter Oxford or Cambridge, and King's was established as a Church of England University in London. A week after Sir William's death the *British Medical Journal* summarized the problem King's Medical School faced: 'with the

11. "*Catgut ligature prepared by steeping for a month in watery solution of carbolic 1 to 20: removed seven days after introduction into the integument of the chest, after removal of the mamma. Cam. Lucida. 5 diamr J. Lister 30 June/69.*"

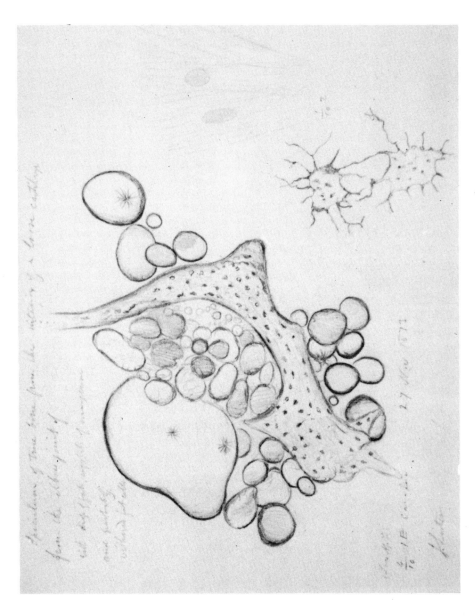

12. "Spiculum of
true bone from the
interior of a loose
cartilage from the
elbow joint of . . ."
The patient's name
is missing, but the
drawing, which also
contains fat,
crystals and
probably withered
fat cells, is signed
and dated:
'27 Nov 1873'.

severe and successful competition of the great schools and colleges of the metropolis' at Guy's, St Bartholomew's, St Thomas's, St George's, the Royal Free, the Middlesex and University College, King's must 'make some unusual efforts to give its surgical staff the brilliancy and fame which only a reputation of the foremost class can bestow'. By seniority Fergusson's successor should have been Mr John Wood, a competent but unexciting surgeon, but the *BMJ* had another suggestion: 'Mr Lister's science and practice is now the most notable circumstance in British, or indeed European, surgery and forms the theme of lecture, discussion and experiment in every great hospital and school throughout the world'.

It seems probable that the *British Medical Journal* editorial was inspired by a small group who were then a minority on the King's College Council. Either Sir William Bowman or Dr Priestley had proposed Lister to succeed Fergusson and they were joined at the outset by Dr George Johnson. Lister was sounded informally, probably by Bowman, and specified conditions that had to be met if he were to accept Fergusson's place, two of which he soon made public: he was to be allowed all necessary facilities for the practice of antiseptic surgery in his own wards, and he was to be permitted to teach clinical surgery in the operating theatre as he did in Scotland, and not just in the wards as was then the practice in London. Lister had learned clinical teaching from Mr Syme who had introduced the techniques into Minto House, his private hospital, and believed that he had been the first to use them at Edinburgh University. Lister maintained that this method of clinical teaching underlay the acceptance of antiseptic surgery in Scotland and on the continent. It permitted the student to observe the application of those details that were the quintessence of the system. Bowman and his colleagues proposed to appoint Wood to the Surgery Chair, and to accomodate more easily the conditions Lister had made, they wished to create a new Professorship of Clinical Surgery.

At the end of Lister's clinical lecture on February 22, an address on illuminated vellum signed by more than 700 Edinburgh students was presented by one of his class, Isaac Bayley Balfour. It was reported in *The Scotsman*:

We eagerly seize this occasion to acknowledge the deep debt of gratitude we owe the invaluable instruction we have derived from your clinical teaching . . . Your self-devotion to the advance of surgery, and the indomitable energy which has characterized your search after, and conquest of, the causes of those deplorable disasters once and even now so frequent a sequence to our surgical operations, have given us a mental impetus for good . . . many have gone forth, and many will still go forth, determined to carry your principles into practice and spread . . . that system of surgery of which you are the founder. (Cheers) . . . you have . . . increased the ancient prestige and glory of our medical school, and attracted to it a number of students quite unprecedented in its history. (Applause) The welfare of our school is so intimately bound up with your presence that . . . we would yet earnestly hope that . . . the day may never come when your name will cease to be associated with that of the Edinburgh Medical School. (Continuous cheers)

The Scotsman also reported Lister's spontaneous reply:

... Meeting my class quietly twice a week and endeavouring to do my humble best, I know no one more conscious, I trust, of its imperfections than myself. I have not been aware that there existed among the students of this great and glorious school—(applause)—anything like the feeling of which I have had evidence on the present occasion. As I said to you at the last lecture, there has really been no actual offer made to me by the authorities of King's College ... there exists nothing in London at the present time which I should consider good enough to call me away from this school. (Cheers) ... if I turn to London and ask how instruction in clinical surgery is conducted there, I find that ... it is, when compared with our system here, a mere sham. (Applause) Clinical medical teaching is in various London schools exceedingly well and ably conducted; but that in clinical surgery is simply neglected and slurred over in London. And ... even if ... I should have the topmost position in London in private practice, and have to teach clinical surgery as it is taught in any London school at the present time, I would certainly not go to London. (Cheers)

That night Mrs Lister wrote a letter to Arthur to her husband's dictation describing some of the colour and spirit of the occasion, unusual in its warmth and spontaneity even for those days of formal presentations and addresses:

... I am today somewhat sick at heart, having received several very strong proofs of extraordinarily kind feeling on the part of my medical brethren & others here, & having experienced at my lecture today a demonstration of enthusiastic & affectionate loyalty on the part of the students such as I daresay was never before given to a medical teacher here. The theatre was crammed, & towards the conclusion of the hour an address was read to me by one of the senior students, son of Professor Balfour ...

Toward the end of the letter Lister said: 'I learn from Dr Priestley that Sir Thomas Watson, though he foresees difficulties in carrying out my programme, does not regard it as insuperable, & that the matter is likely to be brought soon to a decision'. Watson was Chairman of the King's College Council.

After reading a full report of the presentation in *The Times* the next day, Arthur wrote to his brother: 'it looks as if there might be some noise made—I can hardly suppose the difficulty of accepting thy conditions is insurmountable at King's—they would look so very small if they withdrew the offer on the ground that the liberty allowed thee at Edinburgh was too much for London, still I can well understand the conditions may be found hard to swallow by some of the Council.' Arthur saw, however dimly, what his brother had not seen. With that extraordinary insensitivity that had characterized his paper on conditions in his wards at the Glasgow Royal Infirmary, Lister publicly attacked the practices of the very men whom he was asking to change their ways on his behalf. He made it impossible for the King's College Council to accept his demands without appearing to condone his views of London teaching, including, of course, teaching by their own faculty. Not surprising that there was indeed 'some noise made'.

On February 27 Lister wrote again to Arthur:

I have received a letter from Dr Priestley today, telling that on Friday a conference took place between the medical members of the King's College Council and members of the staff of the hospital including Mr Wood, & that Mr Wood made such strong objections to the idea of an outsider being appointed over his head, declaring that he would leave King's altogether if it occurred, that it was concluded that it would be out of the question to ask me to go there. This was the result without my conditions having been referred to, or any allusion being made to any communication having taken place with me, the report in The Times etc alone being made the basis of the discussion . . . Priestley says in a PS that since writing his letter he learns that the matter is not yet considered settled. For my part I confess I do not now desire that any further steps should be taken by them, the advantages of my position here, & the difficulties & disagreeables that I should meet with there being both more apparent than ever. Of course all this information about Wood is an entire secret.

He was annoyed not only by the hesitation at King's but by the implication in the way his friends had approached Wood that he had assumed without adequate cause the vacant chair might be his. He was piqued by the setback, but Lister knew that the game was worth the candle. He wrote on March 8 that if King's did accept his conditions, one of his objectives was 'the thorough working of the antiseptic system with a view to its diffusion in the Metropolis'. The other was 'the introduction of a more efficient method of clinical teaching than has hitherto prevailed in London'. This letter to a medical colleague in Edinburgh continued:

I should not care about the rank I held in the smallest degree, but I should consider it essential that I should be allowed to give a regular course of clinical lectures in the operating theatre twice a week, to be on the same footing as other college courses, & that I should not be required to deliver systematic lectures.
. . . as Mr Wood would rank as senior surgeon, & as there is nothing in the nature of things to make the clinical chair higher in dignity than the systematic, I do not see that Mr Wood need feel aggrieved by the proposed arrangement . . .

Two days later The Lancet took up the matter. It published letters from Thomas Bryant, chief surgeon at Guys, Walter A Leslie, retired Surgeon Major of the Madras Army now at the London Hospital, and Dr Thomas Smith, Lister's defender in the Clinical Society debate three months before. They all protested Lister's derogation of London teaching methods. In a leader The Lancet pulled out most of the stops: 'At least Mr Lister has shown that he is not proof against the seductions . . . of flattery' by his students. He

so far forgot all the rules of decency and good taste as to contemptuously decline an offer that had never been made to him . . . like a man who in the excitement of enthusiasm raves at the false creations of his heat-oppressed brain, Mr Lister . . . proceeded to stigmatize the teaching of clinical surgery in London . . . as 'a mere sham'.
. . . it is to be regretted that Mr Lister allowed himself to make such a foolish and

offensive reply to the kind and generous memorial of his well-meaning pupils. In many quarters Mr Lister has acquired the reputation of a thoughtful, painstaking surgeon, and has done some service to practical surgery by insisting on the importance of cleanliness in the treatment of wounds, although this has been done by the glorification of an idea which is neither original nor universally accepted . . .

But he has no right, the magazine concluded, 'to sit in judgement on his fellows'.

Lister's response was a long letter full of pained surprise. 'I was alluding to clinical surgery as taught in lectures, and not at all to clinical surgical instruction conducted otherwise'. He recalled 'with gratitude' his own 'bedside instruction' at University College Hospital, and went on:

I cannot but feel surprised at the misapprehension that has prevailed . . . the very point of my observations was directed against the system of the London chairs of clinical surgery not their occupants, with whom it would be as presumptious as it would be offensive for me to challenge a comparison.

At best Lister was disingenuous. At worst he was less than candid with himself, let alone his accusers. In the enthusiasm of the occasion he had allowed the overt approval of his students to elevate his preference for the Edinburgh kind of clinical teaching to a pedagogical principle. It is a common enough sin.

His difference with the London establishment was not just a matter of teaching methods, nor even what must have been to many of his colleagues his insufferable self-righteousness. As the Clinical Society debate had shown, London medical men were divided. Then, as now, *The Lancet* represented the general practitioners, the less prestigious men in the profession, while the *British Medical Journal*, the official publication of the British Medical Association, represented the organization and to a certain extent the governors of British medicine. But the distinction thus crudely drawn was exacerbated in 1877 by the revolution that was underway in medicine itself. Broadly speaking, *The Lancet* represented traditional clinical medicine whereas the *BMJ*, largely in the person of its strong editor, Dr Ernest Hart, stood for the new scientific medicine. Lister, Bowman, Burdon-Sanderson and a few others performed experiments in fields—among them bacteriology—which seemed to the traditionalists to be at best peripheral to the proper concerns of a doctor. The traditional physician, and certainly the traditional surgeon observed the symptoms, and the patient who had come for treatment, and then used what knowledge and skill they had. They did not waste time with esoteric specialties.

The experimental approach to medicine that was emerging in Britain had grown up on the continent. If it seemed strange and tendentious to British doctors, it was even less comprehensible to the lay public. The anti-vivisectionist campaign acquired power and momentum because it gave a focus to the uneasiness about medical research felt by most laymen and many doctors. What were these germs, invisible, multitudinous and deadly? Why should a man want to know what part of the brain controlled movement in the wrist, or what alcohol did in a dog's veins—both questions asked by research workers involved in notorious vivisectionist cases? Within five years, thanks to Pasteur in France, Koch in Germany and Lister in Britain, the germ theory would provide a firm foundation for scientific medicine. In the meantime it was not that London opposed Lister, but that part of English medicine could not understand him. Fortunately those who did appreciate the importance of his work refused to allow his tactlessness to blind them.

The governing Council of King's College appointed John Wood to Fergusson's chair. On March 28 Lister wrote to his Edinburgh colleague, William Turner, 'it is finally decided today that I am not going to Kings'. On the same day he thanked Hart for his help, and told him that the position had fallen through because of Lister's insistence on 'being able to transfer my Edinburgh teaching thither in its entirety'. He had not realized that his tactlessness had been more damaging than his insistence. 'I find it easy', he wrote to Hart, 'to fall back on the belief that my position here is that in which I can best serve my generation'.

There was certainly satisfaction in Edinburgh. A second memorial asking him to remain had been handed to Lister on behalf of some 230 former students on March 20. This time there had been little ceremony. The presentation had taken place in Lister's small office in the Infirmary, and there were no reporters present. On March 29, Dr John Brown expressed an astonishing prescience as well as genuine pleasure at the turn of events:

My dear OLD Agnes

Thank Josephus the victorious for his goodness in writing me, with all his work & him so fond of writing! He has done nobly &, in the true old Latin sense, virtuously & as few men in his shoes would have done. It was not small temptation that He (for of course it was the Devil) held before his eyes. The kingdom of the world & the glory of it—Kings & Queens & Lords & Ladies & £15000 a year (at least) and a Baronetcy & Westminster Abbey—by & very far by—& his own City the head & heart of the world & his own people! it was not an unsplendid bait—but as he (& as the beloved friend who is gone knew) knows, there is another & a dark side—Goodbye, my dear two—made for each other & for our good—

A somewhat less perceptive but equally joyful effusion written by one of Lister's students, John Stuart Blackie, appeared in the *Ayr Advertiser* a few days later:

> To Professor Lister
> On Learning His Determination not to Leave Edinburgh for London
> Some live to feed ambition, some for fame;
> Others for gold; and some, the noble few,
> For honest work achieved and service true,
> With wage of truth and love. This last thy claim
> And glory, Lister. When the Southrons laid
> Their golden snare for thee, and every charm

Of that gross-monstered Babylon displayed,
To lure thee from thy station for our harm,
Thou didst stand firm. For this my humble rhyme
Thee honours, and Edina gives thee place
High-perched, with the prime patterns of her race,
Scott, Chalmers, Wilson, Hamilton, and Syme,
And bids thee bloom on Scottish soil, and grow
Proudly, like stout old pines where stiff old breezes blow.

This mixture of Scottish patriotism and xenophobia, like Dr Brown's letter, misinterprets the lure of London in financial terms. Though earthly rewards were certainly not excluded from the attractions of the metropolis, they were not paramount to Lister. In any case he cannot be blamed for feeling that he belonged in Edinburgh.

His London friends had not given up, however. Because there had been no formal offer made to Lister, there had also been no formal rejection. On April 11, 1877, Dr Johnson introduced a resolution before the Board of King's College Hospital:

That this Board is of opinion that public attention having been directed to the probability of Professor Lister accepting office in our Hospital the determination of the Council not to appoint him a Professor of Clinical Surgery is likely to be very injurious to the best interests of the school.

The Board therefore respectfully but earnestly memorializes the Council to reconsider their decision in the hope that a way may be found to invite Prof. Lister to accept a Professorship of Clinical Surgery. The Board begs further to express its belief that the appointment of Professor Lister will not only increase the number of our pupils but that it would be a great benefit to the school.

Professor Wood thereupon moved an amendment: 'while much regretting the inability of Professor Lister to accept the Chair of Surgery offered to him', the Board commended the Council's decisions which had included the appointment of Professor Wood. Wood and one other member of the Board voted for the amendment, which therefore failed. Eleven voted for Johnson's motion, with two against and two abstaining.

Lister went to London himself for the May meeting of the General Medical Council. Whatever took place then was off the record, but Godlee, who was on the University College Hospital staff, wrote that: 'Negotiations were . . . renewed and carried on with great activity'. On June 6, the Hospital Board approved Lister's appointment, and on the 18th the Council of King's College formally appointed him to a new chair of Clinical Surgery. Attendance on his course was made obligatory. To provide Lister with his own wards, the Council opened one that had been closed some years before and constructed a new ward, increasing the number of beds from 172 to 205.

The Minutes of the Hospital Board now provide evidence that Lister's conditions had not been restricted to the freedom to practise surgery and teach students in the ways he believed to be best. The Board meeting of June 18 received from the Council the conditions the Council had accepted. There were thirteen. No. 1 dealt with the provision of Lister's own wards, 2 with his right to select his own assistants, 3 with his clinical lectures, 11, 12 and 13 also with the number and method of selection of his assistants. Numbers 4 to 10 set down with Lister's usual attention to detail the fees that students in the Medical and Surgical courses and in Hospital practice were to pay, and the division of these fees amongst the teaching staff and especially between the two Professors of Clinical Surgery, Wood and Lister. Lister was aware not only that the King's College Medical School was much smaller than that of Edinburgh University, but also that he might at first find it hard to attract students. He evidently had no intention of moving to London, a much more expensive place to live than Edinburgh, without an assurance that his income would bear some relationship to his expenses—Dr John Brown and other sentimentalists to the contrary notwithstanding.

Though he was casual about fees from private patients, and despite his inheritance from Joseph Jackson, Lister did not treat money lightly. Like his father he was careful about his household expenses and canny about his investments. On January 16, 1876, he wrote to Arthur acknowledging the safe receipt of 'Allegheny bonds'. The brothers still dealt in common with some financial matters. Although Lister's London butler, Henry Jones, remained in his employ to the end of Lister's life, Lister always kept the key to the wine cellar on his own person. His providence in no way contradicts his commitment to a useful life, a career of service. Even less does his concern with students' fees imply that his insistence upon the right to teach in his own way was hypocritical or devious. His expenses were large, proportionately much greater than those of latter-day professors. Not only did he maintain a household suitable to his station, but he paid for his own laboratory equipment and for his own travel. He could depend neither on foundations nor on government grants, and the College provided few perks. His inheritance was meant to provide his own estate and for his retirement. Like most of his contemporaries Lister tried to live on his income, and apart from stock dividends his income consisted of fees from students and patients.

Lister's conditions had not been easy for King's College to accept, quite apart from the new professorship and the new wards. According to the letter transmitting the conditions to the Board:

The Council are quite aware that in agreeing to . . . these conditions, they are somewhat diminishing temporarily at least the fees of the existing (College) Medical and Hospital Staff (as they propose that one half of the new fee shall fall on the members of each staff) but they trust that the unusual prosperity of the Medical School which is expected to follow on the important step taken today will soon and amply compensate for the reduction. In no other way could the Council have succeeded in securing the services of Professor Lister.

In other words the governing Council of the College was saying to the Hospital Board, this is what you wanted and now you must pay for it because we have no intention of robbing Peter—the rest of the College—to pay your Paul. Not only the College but the medical staff gave tangible evidence that even in London Lister's reputation stood second to none in Britain. His later complaints about neglect and humiliation must be seen in this light.

Lister did not forget that he had almost destroyed the opportunity to preach his gospel in the wilderness. It was part of his make up, once he had found himself in error, to admit it. On December 10 after he had been lecturing at King's for two months, he demonstrated an important new surgical technique, excision of the knee joint. The lecture was published by *The Lancet*. In it he apologized for the remarks he had made eleven months before about London teaching methods. He had not spoken for publication, and he had not known of the changes that had taken place in clinical teaching since his student days! 'The London schools are both numerous and independent and the changes to which I allude have, I understand, taken place in different degrees in different institutions'.

Cameron said that Lister had not realized that conditions in London were very different from those in Edinburgh. Whereas the large number of medical students at Edinburgh made bedside teaching impossible, 'In London there were so many teachers that each was responsible for only a few students . . . each student could find a place by the bed'. Both Lister's apology and Cameron's explanation call attention to objective factors that Lister had misjudged. Neither deals with the less tangible reasons behind the misjudgements, his reluctance to leave Edinburgh to begin the last great struggle for acceptance, and the stubborn arrogance that he adopted to mask the imponderables in London and the uncertainties they gave rise to.

He determined to begin as he had begun his lectures before, with new research. From August 3 until September 9 he and Mrs Lister carried out a series of bacteriological experiments in Edinburgh. On August 11 he noted the addition of boiling water to a number of flasks. 'The reason for this procedure was that I wished to have about as many bacteria in the boiled water as would give one on the average to every hundredth of a minim. Now I had found that there were about twenty bacteria across each field . . . so $20 \times 20 = 400$ bacteria in a field', a field being the area seen through the microscope at a given magnification. After some further calculations he continued: 'the milk requires to be diluted 500,000 times in order that every $1/100$ minim may contain one bacterium'. 'The ultimate object of the experiment is to try to isolate the bacteria' in one sample of fresh milk 'which are evidently of more kinds than one'. This is the first example of an important new technique, the serial cultivation of bacteria to obtain what he hoped would be pure strains. With a pure strain it should be possible to establish a causal relationship between any change in the medium and the bacteria. But without stains to make them more visible, the labour involved in counting alone must have been enormous.

The Listers moved to London on September 11. Until December they lived at the Wimpole Hotel, though Lister had taken the lease on 12 Park Crescent, an elegant terrace designed by the Regency architect, John Nash, at the bottom of Regent's Park. He set up his laboratory there immediately. When they arrived in London, Lister placed the serial flasks in his new laboratory and checked their contents once more. In the Common-place Book he wrote on September 12 that the boiled milk in tube fourteen was 'Still fluid (noon)'.

10

TRIUMPH AND
DOUBT

MR AND MRS LISTER left London immediately for a holiday on the Swiss lakes. Both Agnes and Joseph wrote long letters from Lugano on September 20, he to Arthur and she to Mary Godlee. He said they had gone from Cologne to Basle and thence to Chur via Zurich where they had 'visited the University' for an hour! From Chur they travelled by diligence across the San Bernadino Pass, and Joseph described the source of the Rhine, adding: 'Among the Alpine plants was a kind of elder with bright scarlet berries in perfect bundles, extremely beautiful; with the leaves like common elder & the wood with central pith like our plant . . . Thee remember the elder we found in California: this was of course quite different'. Monday they had steamed across Lago Maggiore which Lister thought very 'grand'. He said that he had decided not to curtail their short vacation by attending the Munich meeting of the International Medical Congress as he had planned to do. 'As it is, our holiday is being a pretty perfect one', and he concluded by asking Arthur to save 'this scrawl . . . as some record of our trip'.

Agnes's letter was devoted almost entirely to a climb they had made the previous day up Monte Bre across the lake from Lugano. They had begun the journey 'after seeing some exceedingly fine frescoes in a church close to this hotel (by Bernardino Luino)'. They had walked up through terraced vineyards and found themselves at lunchtime passing 'a garden in which a young woman was sitting at work in the shade.' In response to their query about a trattoria in the village, she offered them bread, cheese and wine, which they accepted gratefully along with 'clear and cold' water and grapes from the vineyard. Mrs Lister described the house, 'one of the superior class of peasant homes. Very nice it was—several rooms, and tidy furniture. The sitting room not papered, but coloured and a pattern painted on the walls, birds painted on the ceiling—the window opening as a door out to a pleasant little bit of garden (with a beautiful view of the lake).' The rest helped them to complete their climb. They intended to go on the next day to Lake Como, she told Mary, thence to Lake Garda, 'and from there must hasten homewards'.

On October 1 Lister delivered his introductory lecture at King's. John Stewart, who had come with him from Edinburgh as an assistant, wrote:

Cheyne and I called at his house early in the afternoon. We found him in his shirt sleeves, perspiring as usual, busy getting in order the exhibits for his lecture. Mrs Lister was helping, also his nephew Mr Godlee . . . who had prepared some very beautiful coloured drawings as illustrations . . . We drove from his house to the lecture hall in Somerset House. We supported the trays and glasses as carefully as possible. They had been brought successfully all the way from Edinburgh but were now in perilous passage . . .

Lister was fifty. Of medium height, he always stood erect, looking trim and elegant. The youthful features had acquired firmness and crowsfeet appeared at the outer corners of the eyes. His hair, while still mostly a luxuriant brown, had thinned on top. It was cut full at the sides and curled over his ears and neck. Grey side whiskers further softened the outlines of a comforting and sympathetic face. He looked more than ever like an assured and favoured uncle.

He called the opening address at King's, 'On the Nature of Fermentation'. It thrust directly at the devil of doubt by using the results of his recent research to describe and defend the germ theory. He began with the assertion that grapes ferment because of the yeast on their skins, one of Pasteur's great contributions. He then showed his audience a glass of sterilized Pasteur's solution and compared it to blood within the body, the putrefaction of which was analogous to fermentation. He showed bulls' blood maintained pure under aseptic conditions and held up a tube of healthy blood plugged with cotton wool through which the air could move freely, demonstrating that air is not the cause of infection. Inasmuch as he could infect it with a minute drop of putrid blood, 'putrefaction is a true fermentation' caused by bacteria. But are the germs causes or concomitants? The evidence for a chemical cause of fermentation fell, he said, because chemical reactions lacked 'the faculty of self propagation' which is essential to 'genuine fermentation'. But is it not theoretically possible for chemical reactions to become self-propagating? The answer is affirmative, but it was to demonstrate that this was not in fact what happened that he had undertaken the new research.

For convenience, he had used the lactic fermentation instead of putrefactive changes. In the lactic souring of milk each molecule of milk sugar (Lister called them 'atoms') is converted to four of lactic acid. After describing the *Bacterium lactis*, Lister showed a flask containing unfermented boiled milk and other flasks where fermentation had produced substances other than lactic acid. They must contain organisms, he said, but not the *B lactis*. Or if they had contained *B lactis*, the other organisms had successfully competed for the available sugar. In order to explore this hypothesis he had used serial dilution to obtain drops containing an average of one bacterium each. Of five glasses, each containing boiled milk inoculated with one of the drops, one curdled due to the lactic fermentation. Others did not curdle, suggesting they contained no bacteria, and that the other organisms occur less frequently than *B lactis* so that they are less likely to appear after a dilution designed to obtain one *B lactis* per drop. Using the pure lactic fermentation, he now demonstrated, by a similar serial dilution, that with a 50–50 chance of infection, half the glasses remained fresh: 'where there was curdling and souring, the *B lactis* was present; and in no instance in which there was no lactic fermentation was any bacterium of any sort to be discovered. I believe that fact demonstrates that the B lactis is the cause of this very specific lactic fermentation'.

This time his logic was flawless. Although the research technique owes much to Pasteur, Lister had provided a new dimension with serial dilution. By showing that the lactic fermentation occurred only in the presence of *B lactis*, he had proven the germ theory statistically, at least in so far as the lactic fermentation is concerned.

It was on this occasion that the *Medical Examiner* described Lister as 'the apostle of the surgery of thought' in contrast to the 'surgery of action' of which King's College was the 'stronghold'. William Watson Cheyne, who had come from Edinburgh as Lister's first King's College house surgeon, recalled that: 'The expression on the faces of the audience was . . . rather amusing; the majority of the surgeons present could not understand what the lactic fermentation of milk had to do with surgery'. As to the students, their reactions were summarized by one of them, St Clair Thomson, who became Lister's house surgeon and friend:

We showed our boredom, as was the manner of those unregenerate days, by shuffling our feet. Whenever Lister referred to a cow we tried to emit the 'Boo' of that animal; each time that he mentioned the contaminating hand of the dairy-maid we said 'tut-tut'; when five o'clock struck we reminded him audibly that it was 'tea-time' . . .

Such behaviour must have angered and wounded Lister. Even if his friends' recollections exaggerate the antagonism to him, they reflect the attitudes of those who had not awakened to the revolution in medicine.

Lister and his associates entered London with a siege mentality. John Stewart described the introductory lecture as 'a campaign in the enemy's country'. Lister brought four assistants from Edinburgh. Cheyne, the senior amongst them, had entered his chief's clinical course at the beginning of October 1872 quite accidentally, by following 'crowds of students hurrying along the lobbies on the first day of term'. He had won Lister's prize, the silver catheters, at the end of the course in competition with older men, and became a Dresser. Having qualified, Cheyne went to Vienna and Strasbourg for a year, returning, in October 1876, to the position of Lister's house surgeon. He was allowed 'to examine the wounds in his wards and go into the various bacteriological questions'. Thenceforward, Cheyne usually undertook analysis of wound discharges, especially from those that became septic, in order to determine if possible the nature of the pathogenic organism. In London he was given his own laboratory above the operating theatre.

The King's house surgeoncy had been offered to Cheyne on the spur of the moment after Lister's Sunday morning walk in Princes Street Gardens a day or two after the correspondence with his friends at King's had begun.

. . . I was sleeping quietly in the house surgeon's bedroom. I woke up to find someone shaking me, and to my astonishment. . . it was Lister. He told me about his invitation to London. He had not yet at all made up his mind . . . he had come down that morning to know whether . . . I would go with him and again act as his house surgeon for six months . . . Go with Lister to London! I could not believe my ears! Of course I would go with him to London or anywhere else.

Cheyne became surgeon to King's College Hospital and President of the Royal College of Surgeons. He was one of those few associates, like Cameron, who became something more than a professional friend for Lister. In 1902 he helped to organize a Jubilee Number of the British Medical Journal to celebrate the fiftieth anniversary of Lister's qualification as a surgeon. Lister thanked him, adding: 'Now that I am on the shelf, my professional brethren seem to grow in kindly feeling to me'. The letter ended: 'Wishing Mrs Cheyne and you and the bairns a prosperous and happy new year'.

Dr John Stewart had also qualified and was Lister's senior clerk at the time of the move to London. He became house surgeon for a term in 1878 before returning to practise in Halifax, Nova Scotia. Stewart, who never married, worshipped Lister. He remained a devoted follower and was profoundly affected when Lister died, like a son who had lost his father.

Neither W H Dobie nor James Altham had yet qualified when they left Edinburgh with Lister. Dobie served as dresser and clerk, and went on to practise at Chester, where he also did useful research on the structure of muscle fibre. Altham, who was also Lister's clerk in London, practised for several years at Penrith but died young.

'During the first winter,' Stewart recalled, 'Cheyne, Dobie, Altham and I did practically all the dressings and more Edinburgo, took turns at giving chloroform, taking charge of instruments, and seeing out patients.' Dobie and Altham shared responsibility for the male ward, Victoria ward, and Stewart was in charge of the women in Fergusson ward. No one else at the Hospital had yet been trained in antiseptic techniques. But at first the wards were not so crowded as to make unreasonable demands on them. From the bustling wards and respectfully-filled classrooms of Edinburgh the four men arrived to find empty beds and indifference. The we-and-they psychology was enhanced by other, less important criteria. St Clair Thomson recalled Stewart saying 'that the only embarrassment they felt was that they were all bearded, while their English colleagues were all shaven!' It was understandably dispiriting and led to conflict.

The most overt clash involved the nursing staff. They were Sisters of St

John, a Church of England Order which had not yet adopted the new Nightingale standards of training. Knowing nothing of Lister's method and little more of the man's reputation, they were supremely confident that their own ways were the best—just as Mrs Porter of the Edinburgh Royal Infirmary might have been had the situation been reversed. Cheyne recalled that the nurses offered the 'main opposition' and 'hampered him as much as they could'. Stewart contrasted the 'simple, kindly, common sense routine' of the Edinburgh Infirmary to 'this cold machine-like system'. He gave Godlee two examples. One was the long-stay patient whom Lister had had brought to London from Edinburgh. Lizzie Thomas had been admitted to the Royal Infirmary on August 1, 1876, with a huge abscess of the hip and spine probably caused by tuberculosis. The decision to move her to London was taken in part no doubt because she was a parlour maid from Torquay who had been in service in Edinburgh, but Lister had acted principally because he knew she still needed hospital care. She had come by train, accompanied by none other than Mrs Porter, in one of the large wicker baskets the Royal Infirmary used to move patients.

It was a cold bleak morning in the end of October. The porter helped us in with the basket and its contents, and then we had to lay it down while the porter went to notify the 'Sister in charge'. He was gone for some time, and came back, looking very much perturbed, and reported that the patient could not be admitted without proper admission papers! There we stood, very foolish-looking, all but the patient with her brown hair, blue eyes, rosy cheeks and cheerful smile . . . I ran upstairs and saw the Sister, who reproved me loftily for my irregular behaviour. It was in vain that I pled ignorance of the rules, that I asserted I had Mr Lister's permission to admit the patient, that I thought the rules might be relaxed in the case of this patient who had been travelling all night and was tired and cold. I was told she could not be admitted until the Secretary came and drew up the papers. That would be 10 am, over two hours!
I came downstairs. I was too angry to see the comic side of the affair. Vaughan the porter, an old Crimean soldier, stood dubious and perplexed. I said, 'Now Vaughan, an old soldier like you can't stand and see a pretty girl lying on this stone-cold floor, give us a hand.' He flushed, and saying 'I will sir, if it costs me my place,' took a corner of the basket, and we carried Lizzie upstairs and down the corridor to the ward, where I demanded admission for my patient. One of the Sisters placed herself in front of the closed door to bar the way. Others asked if I were not ashamed of my scandalous conduct. I said I was not, but there would be a scandal very shortly if they did not take my patient in and put her to bed, as otherwise we would take her in and put her to bed ourselves. I suppose I looked as roughly as I spoke, for resistance gave way and the poor girl was put to bed. But she was a 'speckled bird' for many a day.

Lizzie Thomas was moved just before Christmas 1877, from King's to the private nursing home Lister used, but he performed a second operation on her at King's in 1880. She was sent home in July 1880, and Lister met her in Torquay in 1897, a healthy woman of 49.

However much these conflicts owed to the over-sensitivity of Lister's assistants, the King's nurses were also at fault. One of Lister's patients, a girl from whose shoulder he removed three tumours in November 1878, was readmitted four months later with two new growths. 'As the patient resolutely refused to return to King's College Hospital for reasons connected with the nursing arrangements,' according to a note in the ward journal, 'she was sent to 15 Fitzroy Sq.', the nursing home. Even in 1883 Sir William Bowman wrote to Lister apologizing for 'the nursing' and 'the annoyance to which I know you have been so long exposed by the action of that perverse woman', the sister-in-charge. Bowman blamed the Council because it had 'not kept a sufficiently firm hold of its position within St John House'. As a result of Lister's dissatisfaction and no doubt because Nightingale-trained nurses had slowly taken over the old jobs, conflicts eased. In May 1884 a sixty-year-old man whose fractured knee cap had begun to heal satisfactorily was discharged prematurely because he had been 'abusive to the Nurses'. Lister's attitude toward the nursing staff, and perhaps the way in which nurses performed their tasks, appears to have changed in the years since the tumour patient was allowed to go to Fitzroy Square.

Both Lister and his Edinburgh assistants had been even more distressed by the small number of students and their irresponsibility. In December Lister complained publicly that there were only fifty in his class and 'not half that number had accompanied me to the ward'. Naturally he compared the paltry attendance to the 350 eager students who had crowded into the Edinburgh operating theatre twice each week. In fact King's was a much smaller school, as Lister knew perfectly well before he went there. Religious orthodoxy and the competition of other London medical schools contributed to keeping it small. About twenty-five new medical students entered each year, compared to 189 in Edinburgh. In 1877 there were only 172 men in the four-year course. Fifty was not a bad showing.

It was sometimes much worse. No more than a dozen would appear, and these included his four assistants and other faculty members. Indeed on January 4, 1878, Dobie noted in his diary: 'Lister just returned from his holiday; he was prepared to lecture, but found no audience!' On the 15th he wrote: 'Lister said he occasionally felt it was not worth the "fash" to be working as he did and with so few taking interest in his methods. Yet on second thoughts, he said that surgery was such a noble art, and the results themselves were the surgeon's reward.' During the summer session of 1878, however, he had seventy students on one day. Nevertheless he complained again that his classes were small: 'students did not find that the material I gave them seemed to be a direct preparation for the examination'. He returned to this issue in his testimony before a Royal Commission on medical education in 1889, but by that time no surgeon in London attracted more students than Lister. Presumably he knew it.

As he had done in Edinburgh, Lister gave two clinical lectures each week. A patient was brought into the theatre, wrote one of his London students, and 'surgeon and patient sat side by side in the area; the patient was encouraged to tell his or her story, the salient points of the case were indicated in as few words as possible, and the patient then retired while the history and the appropriate treatment were discussed. If the operation required were a short one, it would be performed then and there, and there was then . . . a minutely detailed demonstration of the method of dressing the case'.

The first patient so to be exhibited at King's was 'a poor Scottish travelling tutor sent to us from France', said Stewart. Although he had two large tuberculous abscesses and pulmonary tuberculosis, Stewart denigrated the demonstration as an example of the 'succession of uninteresting cases' with which the clinical lectures began. Stewart contrasted the twenty men who attended this clinic with the 400 at an Edinburgh 'introductory'. Lister opened both abscesses. When the incisions had healed, the man returned to Scotland, presumably to die of lung disease.

As Lister became more established, his colleagues as well as the Hospital authorities began to fill his wards with patients. Perhaps the most important convert to antiseptic surgery in these early days was John Wood. Wood had reported his own unsuccessful trial of Lister's methods in a talk to the British Medical Association in 1873. Lister replied briefly and moderately in a letter to *The Lancet*, pointing out that Wood had not persevered sufficiently with the technical details. An editorial in the same issue had agreed. Wood never expressed strong antipathy for antisepsis and came into personal conflict with Lister only in the sense that he refused to accept a lower status than that accorded to the new man. Lister in turn had demanded no more than equality.

Wood visited Lister's wards and was especially impressed by a satisfactory hip-joint amputation Lister performed in late October. On November 10 he invited Lister to assist him at a goitre operation. Lister's role was 'to superintend the "antiseptics" ', according to Stewart. In the language of surgical etiquette Wood had asked Lister to instruct him in antiseptic techniques, and Lister had acknowledged Wood's overall responsibility for the patient.

Cheyne thought that the King's medical faculty were not 'particularly cordial, Johnny Wood never said much but Henry Smith used to chaff his students if they said much about antiseptics'. Stewart disagreed. He recalled that part of the faculty were strongly in Lister's favour, particularly Dr Lyon Playfair, Sir George Johnson *and* Henry Smith. Smith was a surgeon, but Playfair taught midwifery and Johnson, clinical medicine. The disagreement between the recollections of Lister's two senior assistants could reflect their attitudes toward him. Stewart may have found it hard to acknowledge antipathy toward his revered chief while Cheyne's cooler view was more accurate.

Another King's physician, Dr J Burney Yeo, published with Lister a joint communication that was read to the Clinical Society in February 1878. It was an interesting case in which Lister had removed diseased vocal chords but preserved a 'deep gruff but perfectly audible voice', according to a note of the case in the ward journal. There had been some dissent following the paper, however. Felix Semon was a German who had come to England in 1878 and established himself as a throat specialist. At his retirement, in 1909, Sir Felix recalled that his first public speech in English had been delivered after Lister's paper. He had found the operative procedure objectionable, judged from the standpoint of his own specialization. He had been applauded, but perhaps more because of his youth and effrontery than for his opinion. In any case the paper, like the operation in which Lister assisted Wood, shows that he was able to engage in the more practical kinds of collaboration with his colleagues, whatever their opinions of him.

Early in 1878 the Listers began again the small dinner parties at which they had entertained important visitors in Glasgow and Edinburgh. On April 3 Stewart wrote in his diary: 'Dined at Listers. Cheyne, Mr Beck, Mr Godlee, Dr Atherton of Fredericton, New Brunswick & Dr Gordon of Halifax, Nova Scotia'. If the foreign guests did not speak English, Lister customarily asked his house surgeon to sit beside Mrs Lister so that he would be free to talk to the visitors in their own language. At another such dinner that Stewart attended, he recalled,

there was a stalwart young Dane a very Viking, but modest & bashful—when we went upstairs we had some music. The versatile Cheyne played & sang. Geo Rice—a former Edinburgh resident also played. Mrs Lister asked the Danish guest to sing. He blushingly denied the gift of song. Then the late Dr Glover (of the Lancet) gallantly volunteered a song. I think he sang that pretty Scottish song 'M Nannies awa'—a great favourite of Lister's. There was loud applause. This fired the bashful Norseman, who now volunteered a song, & he simply <u>roared</u> 'King Christian' until the furniture trembled. The contrast between the gigantic yellow bearded figure and the compact little figure of Glover made me think of a sea-eagle and a sparrow. Of course he was applauded & he immediately volunteered another!

Lister enjoyed singing himself. Though neither he nor Mrs Lister attended concerts or the theatre by choice, he was willing to entertain in his own drawing room. It is said that his favourite was a traditional Scottish song, 'Jock o'Hazeldean'.

John Dobie reported that his chief was full of fun at these dinners. Once, he told Dobie, he had been a teetotaller 'for about a week, when I was a boy at school'. 'He agreed', Dobie said, 'that wine was the milk of old age.' Letters from Arthur, who was still engaged in the wine business, are sprinkled with references to gifts for Joseph of claret, port, sherry and other wines.

When the guests were the dressers and clerks who assisted him at Hospital, however, the occasions could seem less felicitous. The Listers held these evenings once every six months for the students then in office. Leeson described one such dinner:

Unfortunately I was placed by Mrs Lister. It was very good of her to grace the gathering as she must have felt strangely out of touch with her guests.

I remember my attempts at conversation. The weather was soon exhausted, athletics had not then become a cult, for literature we had no time; the drama was unfashionable in Edinburgh, and the highest flight of the imagination could never have associated the Listers with the theatre. The only thing we had in common was the progress of antiseptics; but in those Victorian days ladies had hardly heard of surgery! . .

The dinner was perfectly correct, verging a little on the side of plainness, as became a Puritan household. There was no smoking, and the wine was partaken sparingly.

The guests departed by 10, and relieved they were to do so, according to Leeson's account. But there are two or three suspicious notes. Mrs Lister was certainly not an ordinary Victorian lady who 'had hardly heard of surgery!' She may have been hard to talk to—or she could have found Leeson a bit of a prig—but surgery and Lister's work ought to have been among the subjects on which she shone. Perhaps there was no smoking, but was the wine 'partaken sparingly' because it was in short supply, or because Lister was preoccupied, or his guests nervous? Because of his formality Lister was reputed a good host, and Mrs Lister had both the skill and the staff necessary to do the thing comfortably.

Her staff was not large. Henry Jones, the butler, had begun as a servant at Upton House. He had stayed with the family, and went to Park Crescent soon after the Listers moved there. Like everyone else in the house he assisted in Lister's experiments. For example in 1887, 'the blood (bullock's) had been procured by Jones today, receiving it from the animal's throat into a . . . bottle and whipping it with a glass stirring rod'. Another servant, Margaret Duncan, was trusted to note the conditions of bottles containing bacterial cultures in milk when the Listers went to Cornwall for their holiday in September 1878.

Park Crescent was furnished in the dark, solemn, substantial Victorian manner. There was a library of some 3000 books. In the main they were scientific and medical, but they also reflected Mrs Lister's religious interests, and there were classics, some in translation, travel books, books on Scotland and a selection from Joseph Jackson's library. There was also a large laboratory.

Now that they were in London, Lister was at last near his family. All three of his remaining siblings—Mary Godlee, Arthur Lister and Jane Harrison— lived near London. They had grown children whom the Listers enjoyed socially. Mary's second son, R J Godlee, became Lister's assistant in his private practice while continuing as Registrar of University College Hospital. Isabella Pim's daughters also made part of the family circle in London from time to time.

Very soon after his arrival in the metropolis, Thomas Huxley and John Tyndall proposed Lister for membership in the Athenaeum. He was elected under the club's Rule II which allows the General Committee to vote on 'persons of distinguished eminence', having been proposed by Sir Joseph Hooker, the Director of the Botanic Gardens at Kew. Lister served as *ex officio* member of the General Committee, the governing body of the Athenaeum, when he was President of the Royal Society at the end of the century.

At King's Dr Johnson and Sir William Bowman counted amongst his professional friends. Others in London with whom he was in 'friendly intimacy', according to Godlee, included William Jenner, James Paget and John Erichsen. One of his oldest Edinburgh friends, Dr James Matthews Duncan, the gynaecologist, came to St Bartholomew's at almost the same time as Lister went to King's. Eight years later his fellow student at University College, now Sir William Roberts, came to London from Manchester, where he had practised medicine since leaving University. Roberts and Lister still took occasional botanizing walks and did some fishing together.

Godlee called Lister a 'diligent amateur' fisherman. He had renewed his interest in the art at Moffat. After coming to London he fished at Bakewell when he went there with Mrs Lister for the waters. Like skating and bathing, also sports he had enjoyed as a boy, fishing required time, preparation and travel which were not often easily assembled. Summer and autumn holidays at Lyme Regis included swimming, but fond as he was of bathing, it too could not be done in London. Skating had been easier in Edinburgh because of the weather. He and his wife skated together for welcome relaxation during January and February.

But walking was always possible regardless of season and place. He had taken the house on Park Crescent in part because he could walk across the road into Regent's Park. If walking could be combined with field botany or in later years, bird watching, so much the better. These were among the ties that bound him to Agnes. Even before her marriage she had been an enthusiast. Their holidays invariably included walks and wild flower collecting. Cameron wrote that Lister carried a pocket lens to examine plants and flowers. According to a niece, Gulielma Lister, herself a botanist, the flowers were 'carefully pressed in paper prepared beforehand by being dipped in a weak solution of corrosive sublimate'. 'Each collection was kept by itself and the flowers retained in the order in which they had been gathered so that they formed a kind of journal which he and my aunt would often refresh themselves by examining on Sunday mornings after their return to London.'

Their interest in bird watching developed after about 1877, and both at the Botanic Gardens and at Lyme they kept records of bird sightings and of migrant birds. Many years later he saw wood pigeons eating stones on a path below his window at Wadhurst, Sussex, at 4.00 one July morning. 'I imagine that the rocks here being of a soft sandy nature, the stones derived from them very soon get worn away in the birds' gizzards and require replenishing', he wrote to Gulielma. 'I wonder what kind of appetite they feel to show them more stones are wanted.' He observed in order to relax, varying only the subject of his observation between work and rest.

After the move to London his own research had to be suspended until they were living at Park Crescent so that he could get into the laboratory regularly. There was plenty to keep him busy. Lister began private practice when he returned from the Swiss holiday. On October 20 he performed an operation in the Langham Hotel at the other end of Portland Place from Park Crescent. Private patients requiring extended care went to the nursing home, one of only two in London at the time, at 15 Fitzroy Square, also within a short walk of Park Crescent. Although the nursing home did not belong to Lister, 'his patients occupied the greater number of its rooms', according to Cameron.

His private practice was 'never really large', Godlee wrote. Patients came from all parts of the country and many from abroad, referred to Lister by some older surgeons and by general practitioners, but there were factors that militated against referrals to him. The first that Godlee listed was Lister's perpetual unpunctuality. Cheyne wrote:

I have known him to be hour or two late for a consultation . . . he would look in at his nursing home . . . and if anyone said that they did not feel quite comfortable he would take off his coat and readjust dressings or splints, quite regardless of the fact that his waiting-room was full of irate doctors and patients vowing they would never consult him again.

In Glasgow, Cameron said, he simply forgot about appointments and consultations 'being absorbed in the interest of his hospital or laboratory work'. Indeed, he could be preoccupied by explanations to visitors from which they might well find it hard to extricate themselves. Mealtimes were infinitely flexible. Mrs Lister not only became accustomed to this lack of routine, but her own stints in the laboratory suggest that she accepted it. An assistant accompanying Lister on his ward rounds might become as impatient as an empty stomach could make him without in the least disturbing the Chief. His examination of patients was always unhurried and painstaking, but that only made matters worse for the attendant physician in a private case. Joseph Jackson had recognized that Joseph's unpunctuality, like his insensitivity and his tendency to overwork, were all facets of a central disaffection. He wrote in 1864:

In thy description of increased ease in lecturing & the superior character of the students I was gratified to find too that thou hadst been able to be more regular & punctual at the Hospl. than before. I can well imagine how difficult this may be, fully occupied as thy time is, but perhaps on that very account, to keep in view a habit of punctuality is especially important—& might tend to lighten the weight of engagements that I sometimes fear will press too much upon thee . . .

In addition to unpunctuality Godlee cited as reasons for Lister's small private practice his attitudes towards fees and his interference in post-operative care. Lister preferred to leave the size of his fee to the patient, thus treating it as a tip rather than as a wage for work done. Doctors and other surgeons, many of them less financially secure than Lister, found this attitude both frustrating and insufferable.

Post-operative care was normally the responsibility of the referring doctor, but few G.P.s knew the details of antiseptic dressing. As time passed Lister left aftercare to Godlee and Cheyne and himself saw the patient only when the final dressing was removed. The responsibility remained in his hands, however, and general practitioners had to accept this unusual arrangement or refer their patients to other surgeons. Many did.

Lister's routine was similar to that of other London consulting surgeons. He performed private operations in the early mornings and held consultations at home before lunch. Hospital visits, operations and clinical lectures occupied the afternoons. After 1883 he had a surgery on Mondays, Wednesdays and Fridays at 1.30 at the Hospital. The evenings were often taken up with meetings of societies. 'On the whole', Godlee wrote, 'Lister's life was less strenuous in London than it had been in Edinburgh.' With two important exceptions—the hydraulics of blood circulation and nerve surgery—his work had become consolidating rather than innovative.

Being in London gave Lister better opportunities than he had had in Edinburgh to entertain hospital visitors. In one week in late November 1877 three important British scientists came to see his wards. On the 20th Stewart noted in his diary: 'Dr Burdon-Sanderson spent the afternoon with Mr Lister in the wards'. On the 26th John Tyndall and John Simon ' "went round" with the Chief'. Other visitors included Professor Saxtorph from Copenhagen 'as before', Marian Sims, the American surgeon who had driven the ambulance with William MacCormac in France seven years before, Professor Bottini of Pavia, a Moscow surgeon, Lucas-Championnière and various German surgeons.

On December 18 he delivered the long-postponed address before the Pathological Society. 'On the Lactic Fermentation and its Bearings on Pathology' has much the same structure as his introductory lecture at King's and was based on the same research. He also chose this opportunity to make one of those confessions of error that he considered to be so important a part of the scientist's job: the apparent development of *B lactis* from a filamentous fungus 'which I had described . . . as due to modification of the *Bacterium lactis* in urine and Pasteur's solution had been entirely deceptive, and had been occasioned by the accidental accompaniment of other species'. The long address was delivered in the old library in the Society headquarters in Berners Street near the Middlesex Hospital to a large and distinguished audience. The vote of thanks was moved by Burdon-Sanderson and seconded by none other than Bastian, the defender of spontaneous generation, who expressed his great admiration for Lister's experimental results.

Lister strengthened the germ theory, but it remained to show that what was true for milk or urine or beer applied with equal force to diseases of the body. Bacteria had certainly been found in wounds as well as in the blood of diphtheria patients, but it was still unclear whether they were causes or incidental phenomena.

In August 1877 Lister's friend, William Roberts, physician to the Manchester Royal Infirmary, spoke on the germ theory to the British Medical Association. He reviewed Lister's research along with that done by Professor Cohn of Breslau and asserted that their observations lent great weight to the germ theory. *The Lancet* praised the address but did not mention Lister. Its antipathy remained. As late as August 1879 it published an article by J R Smith, Surgeon to the Bristol Royal Infirmary, in which Smith wrote: 'The practical results of antiseptics would be no more influenced by the fall of the germ theory than the operations of chemistry from the fall of the atomic theory'. Not even defenders of spontaneous generation went that far. In Britain Lister had not only to prove the existence of germs, but also to establish a theory from which practice would grow in a medical garden that had a very acid soil indeed.

At Edinburgh the students sang:

> There's nae Germs about the Hoose
> Germs, busy Germs.

Arthur Conan Doyle, who was a medical student there from 1876 to 1880, wrote: 'Archer's one of the carbolic men. Hayes is the leader of the cleanliness-and-cold water school and they all hate each other like poison'. If it was true in Edinburgh, the capital of antisepsis, what then of London? J R Leeson had become house physician at St Thomas's Hospital. In the College House:

One day the serving man was handing me some melted butter, and was loudly and imperiously questioned as to whether the sauce contained its quantum of carbolic acid. He ... was sternly ordered away with the dangerous liquid lest the life of a 'Listerman' should be endangered!

At St Bartholomew's an unnamed surgeon was said to have called to everyone entering his operating theatre: 'shut the door *quickly* lest one of Mr Lister's microbes should come in'. It was a kind of praise. He was making headway against silence if not ignorance.

Nor was Lister without support at this time in the medical press. Dr Kenneth Macleod introduced antiseptic surgery into his Calcutta military hospital after spending part of a furlough in Lister's Edinburgh wards early in 1877. During July 1878 *The Lancet* published a series of cases that had been successfully treated antiseptically by Dr J C Ogilvie Will, Surgeon to the Aberdeen Royal Infirmary, once Sir James Simpson's preserve. Will said, 'there is something more in it than careful drainage and absolute cleanliness'.

In March 1878 Lister and his wife were able to return to the serial experiments designed to isolate and study *B lactis* and other airborne bacteria. The milk now came from Newman's dairy in Albany Street close by.

Lister had also undertaken another research project with immediate practical applications. On May 13 he went to Neath, near Swansea, to visit a private patient. At the railway station, while he was awaiting the return train for London, Lister raised his hand until it went pale, and then lowered it so that the colour became a brighter pink than normally. He proceeded to raise and lower his arms alternatively several times, to the mystification of his fellow travellers, until the train arrived.

The next day he continued similar observations in the privacy of his laboratory at Park Crescent. He was in fact preparing for a talk, later in May, to the Harveian Society in London. The Society was named for the discoverer of the circulation of the blood, William Harvey, and Lister decided to return to the tissue that had so often been the object of his experiments in pre-antiseptic days: the blood. He took as his subject blood hydraulics and began by reviewing his own experience. During 1863 and 1864 he had originated a form of 'bloodless' surgery, which had proved useful for operations on limbs. Before beginning he elevated the limb and applied a tourniquet which remained in place during the operation. In 1873 during a clinical lecture he had made observations on the movement of blood in his arms similar to those that preoccupied him in the railway station at Neath. They led to an experiment that interrupted his bacteriological research. He had obtained from the Veterinary College in Edinburgh a 'small white horse purchased for dissection'. By hanging the animal in a sling it could be turned sideways or upside down. Under chloroform he exposed a leg artery and watched as the animal's position was changed. The effect of reflex nervous action on the bore of the artery, which he had observed by raising and lowering his arms, now became more obvious. He compared this vaso-motor reflex, which seemed to bathe rapidly a deprived region, to the *besoin de respirer*. It is an interesting theoretical paper, but, again, the less sophisticated general practitioners in his audience must have found its relevance questionable.

The paper was not published until June 1879, a year later, because Lister continued his experiments. The Physiological Laboratory at King's College had the double advantage of being a permitted place for experiments on live animals under the 1876 act and large enough to cope with what Lister now planned. He designed nothing less than a primitive barograph consisting of a large role of 'cheap paper-hanger's paper' on to which the blood of an immobilized rabbit or dog was sprayed by the simple means of cutting its throat. The apparatus was described in the Common-place Book:

Mr Cheyne was to draw this paper over the table while the laboratory assistant constantly took charge of the paper at the other end of the table . . . that it might be drawn in a straight line. The edge of the paper next the rabbit was $4\frac{1}{2}$ inches from the carotid artery, and we could thus tell the distance to which the blood should be projected from the tube. The object of the experiment was to get rid of any possible fallacies from the use of instruments as measurers of blood pressure, making the blood write its own record on the paper moved along as it fell . . .

Cheyne could not walk along a straight enough line until a string had been stretched for him along the correct path into the next room. The rolls of yellowing paper, the brown spots of dried blood rising and falling along them, still exist in the Royal College of Surgeons of England, numbered and dated between July 26 and 31, 1878, an impressive record of Lister's originality and perseverance.

On June 5, soon after he read the paper to the Harveian Society, the Listers went to Paris for a month. The Universal Exhibition was in progress, and Lister had been appointed by the Prince of Wales to be President of the British Commission to the jury on Medicine, Hygiene and Public Relief. He had not been in Paris since 1855 when, as he wrote to Arthur, he 'was of course an unknown stranger'. Now the Academy of Medicine asked him to speak. He decided to repeat the talk he had just given in London. 'I have not nearly finished writing it in English; and therefore to get it ready for delivery in French by next Tuesday will be rather a serious undertaking! As a rule a certain time only is allotted for every communication; but I am to have the whole sitting at my disposal.'

His principal duty was the work of the jury, of which he became President, but of equal importance to Lister was the opportunity to meet Pasteur. After the meeting of the Academy of Medicine, he told Arthur, 'Agnes and I are to dine with Dr Gueneau de Mussy, who was physician to Louis Philippe and stayed with him in England during his exile. He thus knows English well, and he is also an intimate friend of Pasteur who will meet us at his house.' Unfortunately the meeting was not recorded, but there was naturally much for the two men to discuss. Pasteur had just begun the work that led to descriptions of *Staphylococcus (microbes en amas de graines)* and *Streptococcus pyogenes (microbes en chapelet de graines)*. He invited Lister to lunch with him on June 21, offering to postpone the time from 11.30 to noon if that would suit Lister's schedule at the Exposition.

A banquet was given in Lister's honour at which leaders of the French profession paid tribute to antiseptic surgery. He also found time to visit Parisian hospitals. In early September he returned to Paris briefly to give a demonstration.

Less dramatic work on the hydraulics of blood flow occupied most of August. On September 14 the Listers left for a month's holiday at St Ives. They walked, kept daily records of the birds they identified and collected wild flowers. 'I never saw hart's tongue fern in such wonderful beauty', he wrote to

Arthur. But Lister had gone to St Ives to work. He had at last to finish for publication the manuscript of his address 'On the Lactic Fermentation' which he had delivered before the Pathological Society ten months before. 'I must confess that for such work I have been better here than with the sweet distractions of Lyme.'

A few days before his second trip to Paris in September Lister made an interesting note in the Common-place Book:

7.30 p.m. What is the cause of the retarding influence of air upon the lactic fermentation? If oxygen is unfavourable to the bacteria, it seems hardly likely that they should consume it, & that thus it should be got rid of in the deep or closed vessels. Nor can we suppose the consumption of oxygen to be affected by concomitant organisms . . .

He wondered whether the inhibition of the growth of *B lactis* might be due to formation of carbonic acid when oxygen is readily available, but noted on the next day:

If then oxygen is unfavourable to the growth of the bacteria, we seem to have the whole matter explained without supposing that the bacteria consume the oxygen or that any considerable amount of carbonic acid is produced.

He added a footnote about this discovery to the published version of the Pathological Society address.

Pasteur had observed anaerobic or oxygen-hating bacteria in the butyric fermentation of butter, but no one understood why oxygen should inhibit organic growth. Lister returned to the subject on January 21, 1881, with a note in the Common-place Book:

Near air bubbles the isolated Bacilli were frequently seen quivering or swimming slowly, confirming the idea suggested by the serum that this form of Bacillus is aërobious to Anglicize Pasteur's word.

That there are bacteria which thrive in the absence of oxygen deep inside wounds required no alteration of Lister's basic techniques. He used antiseptics to wash out accidental wounds as well as to exclude bacteria from surgical incisions.

After he returned from Cornwall, in October 1878, having completed the manuscript of the paper 'On the Lactic Fermentation', Lister set aside bacteriology temporarily and returned to the movement of the blood. During his address to the Midlands Medical Association, in Birmingham at the end of the month, he discussed the effect of pressure on blood coagulation. New experiments on the 'Relations of the stream to the propelling Force', in November, were more directly related to the physics of blood flow, and remained unreported for four years.

An account of some of Lister's cases at King's College appeared in February 1879 in the *Medical Times and Gazette*, inveterate antagonist to *The Lancet*. After fourteen months in London both his classes and his wards had grown more populous. On April 18 he wrote to a general practitioner who had asked Lister to examine his 'little patients' that although the children needed an operation, there was no room at the Hospital for them. In June Mr and Mrs Lister went to Dublin where he gave a demonstration at the Richmond Hospital. The University of Dublin awarded him an honorary Doctor of Medicine, and he was made an Honorary Fellow of the Royal Society of Ireland. Shortly afterward the University of Glasgow gave Lister the degree of Doctor of Laws.

These mounting signs of acceptance set the stage for a vigorous new attack on Listerism by William Savory, Surgeon at St Bartholomew's. Savory delivered the address on surgery to the Cork meeting of the British Medical Association, in August 1879. He spoke on the prevention of blood poisoning. The presence of bacteria probably indicates toxic changes, he said, 'but the exact relation they hold to such changes is at present with many a vexed question, and it is not necessary now to disturb it'. Having then reiterated the familiar fact that formation of healthy new tissue to cover a wound assures that it is 'tolerably impregnable' to blood poisoning, Savory turned to the opposite condition. If poisoning did occur, he 'rejoiced in laudable pus' because it told him where the poison was and how much of it was at work. His apparently reactionary restoration of the dreadful old phrase, laudable pus, to the dignity of a professional address truly shocked the Listerians, who considered any pus at all as a crisis calling for the sternest measures. Nor did Savory disagree. Antiseptic surgery, he argued, meant clean surgery 'which means the prevention or removal or destruction of all matter which may prove poisonous . . . in this sense, I suppose all surgeons now-a-days practise antiseptic surgery'. But for Savory 'clean water, adequately used' was 'amongst the simplest, safest, best of antiseptics'. It was the argument used by Lister's friend and former Edinburgh colleague, Thomas Keith. Savory said that at Bart's deaths from pyaemia and erysipelas—blood poisoning—were about $1\frac{1}{2}\%$ and asked the Listerians to show any improvement on that figure. He concluded, however, by asserting that antiseptic methods were more useful in 'a pestilential atmosphere like pre-Lister German hospitals'.

Savory's address was a coherent and measured statement of the opposing stream in British surgery. Even the *British Medical Journal* asked: 'if it be true that the atmosphere is loaded with germs which are . . . deadly . . . how does it happen that we see wounds healing so very kindly when exposed?' The leader backed Savory's call for statistical data from Lister and his followers. It concluded by noting that both Savory and Lister had made 'successful efforts toward the attainment of the great object which all surgeons have . . . the prevention of blood-poisoning'. The editor might have added that Lister had been the first to see that the objective was attainable, and to attain it.

Neither Lister, nor any of his partisans, attempted any immediate reply, a measure perhaps of their respect for Savory and for what he had had to say. In

1886, when he was President of the Royal College of Surgeons, the Listers dined informally with him; they remained professional friends. Savory was Sir James Paget's colleague at Bart's. It was during these months in 1879 that Paget recommended Lister to do an operation on a 'young lady of good family', according to John Stewart, that required a very large wound with a concomitantly great risk of infection. Sir Prescott Hewett, then President of the Royal College of Surgeons, as well as Paget, attended the operation, in the patient's home. Happily it went well. Paget's support offset Savory's opposition, and may also have helped to determine a diplomatic silence on Lister's part.

Of even greater importance to him, perhaps, was a leader the following week in *The Lancet*. After pointing out that: 'All surgery ought to be antiseptic' in the sense that Mr Savory had used the word, the magazine went on:

Mr Lister has done an important and lasting service to the cause of humanity and surgery by his unwearied attempts to eradicate septic diseases from surgical practice, and to make operations effectual and safe. To scrutinize the accuracy of the principles that guide his practice, or to dispute the indispensable necessity of all the details thereof, is the privilege and duty of every practical surgeon. We may allow that 'antiseptic surgery' has been an important phase in the evolution of sound and scientific knowledge of the nature of septic diseases, but deny that it is the culmination.

Though Lister may have disliked the conclusion of the paragraph, he could scarcely deny its abstract truth, and its praise suggested that after two years, the editor's opposition to him had begun to moderate. Finally on August 30, 1879, the *BMJ* said: 'history will infallibly say, even if the details of Mr Lister's method are superseded, that the man who has done the most to take the "disgrace" out of surgery is Mr Lister'.

One reason for Lister's silence was that he had not attended the Cork meeting. He and Mrs Lister had sailed early in July from Newcastle to Trondheim. In Christiania they bought a Norwegian dictionary and grammar. Lister had some success at trout fishing 'near the head of the Romsdal' using an Ilkley rod and net. From Faleide on August 11 he wrote to Arthur about a day trip they had taken up the fjord. Their boatman and guide had conducted them to an upland farmhouse for a lunch of milk, served in bowls, and sour milk. 'This soured milk seems to be a very important article of diet with the Norwegians, and to a hungry and thirsty mortal is wonderfully . . . refreshing. We added to it some Peak and Frean's biscuits . . . while our boatman chewed alternately soft "flad bröd" . . . and slices of a loaf of black rye bread . . . The wild raspberries and a good draught of the fresh milk completed what proved a most sustaining meal. Having deposited a krone (1 1/9 shilling) on the table, by our guide's direction', they left. Lister supposed that his family had originated in Norway—in old Norse (and in Scottish) Lister means a salmon-spearer—and one of his less-pressing objectives during the holiday was a search for distant kin that proved fruitless.

From Christiania, on July 29, Mrs Lister wrote a letter for her husband to J W R Tilanus, Professor of Surgery at the University of Amsterdam. Lister apologized for not having replied before to Tilanus's invitation of June 15 to address the International Medical Congress which was to be held in Amsterdam that September. He accepted, and proposed to talk 'on the subject of the treatment of wounds'. A month later he wrote again to Tilanus from Christiania saying that he and Mrs Lister were coming to Amsterdam via Stockholm and Copenhagen, where he had been invited to visit Professor Saxtorph.

In the official record of the Congress, Lister's address, on September 9, was called 'Discours improvisé sur la chirurgie antiseptique'. He spoke in French, answering objections to the antiseptic system. According to the report of the meeting in the *British Medical Journal*:

Professor Lister was received by the whole Congress with an enthusiasm that knew no bounds. When he stepped forward . . . the whole assembly rose to their feet; and, with deafening and repeated rounds of cheers, waving of hats and handkerchiefs, hailed the distinguished Professor of King's College with acclimations renewed . . . time after time . . . This remarkable scene—unprecedented, we imagine, in the history of medical science—continued for some minutes until Professor Donders, the President . . . taking Professor Lister by the hand, as he stood overwhelmed by this magnificent ovation, obtained a moments silence, and addressing him said: 'Professor Lister, it is not only our admiration which we offer you; it is our gratitude, and that of the nations to which we belong.'

Amsterdam celebrated the great medical assembly with suitable entertainments in the evenings during the meetings. One theatrical evening offered living tableaux drawn from various inspirations including the engraving, famous Victorian Europe, of Ambroise Paré dressing a soldier's wounds. The artist who arranged the tableau had placed Lister in the place of Paré, and in the foreground was a vat labelled carbolic acid. According to the *BMJ*:

. . .from the whole theatre there arose such an universal acclimation . . . that it was only after Mr Lister had, under compulsion, bowed his acknowledgements from his place, and after the curtain had risen and fallen three times, that the enthusiasm had subsided.

The final evening was given over to a banquet. After dinner, wrote Godlee, 'a fanfare of trumpets was heard without, and the guests adjourned to the balcony. The students had assembled with bands and torches lighting up the narrow way bordering the canal; Donders made a graceful speech, and then there were renewed cries for Lister, who was again the subject of an enthusiastic and picturesque ovation.' Whatever the celebratory excesses of the solid Dutch, the international medical community seemed to have few remaining doubts about antiseptic surgery.

Lister returned to an expanding practice. His reputation had grown particularly from his successes with mastectomy, the various abscesses caused by tuberculous processes, and the correction of joint and bone malformations caused by tuberculosis, malnutrition and accidents. He was not a brilliant surgeon, but slow and thorough, with a kind of pachydermatous skill born of confidence in his techniques. An operation was not a soccer game to be hurried through for applause and approbation, but a cricket match in which form counted as much as style. One of his assistants recalled that Lister once removed two kidney stones in thirty-two seconds. The students applauded, but Lister turned round and admonished them: 'Gentlemen, gentlemen,' he said, 'remember where you are'. In 1857, at his surgical début, he had accepted the cheers of his students with relief and thankfulness.

Toward his patients Lister's responsibilities were straightforward. 'My dear Bo', he wrote in his own hand to 'Master Style, 15 Fitzroy Square' on March 22, 1878. 'I thank you for your kind little note. It is very nice to think that you have a straight good leg. I send you my picture, as you wish it. Yours affectionately.' A year later Sarah Pattle, aged 21, of Bury St Edmunds, was admitted to King's College Hospital with a psoas abscess. The drained abscess proceeded well enough until August. While Lister was on the continent, the dressing was continued as usual, but when he returned to London, he had the girl removed to Fitzroy Square. On February 25, 1880, she was discharged cured. That was his duty if cure was possible, and if not, he must do what he could.

Two of Lister's cases at King's in the autumn of 1879 offer insights into the treatments he attempted. In May a young man required excision of an elbow joint. Three weeks later Lister opened an abscess on his back. Both the operative wound and the abscess healed slowly, but in October the arm on which the operation had been performed developed paralysis. Lister attempted galvanism, the use of an electric shock to make the muscle contract, which was known to be useful if paralysis was due to post-operative scar tissue. In this case the man appeared at one of Lister's clinical lectures in July 1880. He had recovered some movement in the arm, but it was not normal.

The second case was that of a fifty-five-year-old woman who had a tumour removed from her back. That night she haemorrhaged. Lister was sent for, but the haemorrhage had stopped by the time he arrived from Park Crescent. Despite severe loss of blood, he 'did not think transfusion necessary'. Blood transfusion was a new technique used only in the most extreme cases. Whole blood was introduced into a vein by means of a hypodermic with all the risk that a clot might form. Nothing was known about blood types so that there was high risk of a rejection reaction which would kill the patient. But without antisepsis the procedure might have been considered unjustified whatever the patient's condition. This woman recovered and was discharged two months later. She should have blessed Lister's decision.

In addition to antiseptics he used a variety of medicines, most of them traditional remedies which occasionally helped and seldom hurt. Silver nitrate applied to a granulating sore, one which had just begun to heal, protected the new tissue and acted as an oxidizing agent that helped to kill anaerobic bacteria. Opium soothed pain, especially post-operative pain which might be made worse if the anaesthetic had left the patient nauseous. Lister said in the 1870s that he had never seen adverse effects from the opiates—opium, morphine and heroin—but others had already noted their addictive nature. Calomel was used as a purgative. Potassium nitrate, ether and potassium bitartrate reduced excess water in the tissues caused by temporary blockages due to surgical cutting of blood vessels, poor general circulation or impaired kidney function. Alcohol was a stimulant and helped to improve the patient's sense of wellbeing. Belladonna and its derivative atropine relaxed the pupil of the eye, and the Calabar bean could be used to contract it.

Lister's pharmacopeia was perhaps more restricted than it needed to have been. Before he left Edinburgh, two of his colleagues had shown that chemical manipulation of certain alkaloids, natural plant extracts such as nicotine and caffeine, could convert them into muscle-relaxing drugs. Lister was apparently unaware of their work because at King's he prescribed the Calabar bean for a patient with tetanus, a strange selection in any case. The bean produces contraction of muscles and could only exacerbate the painful and eventually fatal muscular contractions characteristic of tetanus.

In the Common-place Book he said that he was 'not chemist enough' to understand a reaction between two substances that he had observed. Though he had done well in chemistry as a student thirty years before, he had not kept up with the subject. Like bacteriology, it had grown very rapidly. Lister had not time to become a biochemist too.

Yet he did use some old drugs in new ways. In October 1879 he successfully injected atropine into a patient to ease severe muscular spasms caused by injury. Ergot was sensibly used to control bleeding, and belladonna, to soothe persistent pain, which it may have done successfully if the pain originated in abnormally-contracted muscles. At King's College Hospital, in 1885, one of his patients was given *Cannabis indica* to relieve headache. It did not work, but quinine was slightly more effective. Quinine also served as a tonic when mixed with citrate of iron. Ipecac, an emetic, was prescribed for a cough, in combination with morphine which might have been effective for the purpose. A patient with acute bronchitis was given chloroform in combination with tincture of camphor and ammonia. The patient had been admitted to King's College Hospital on July 26, 1879, and was discharged well on August 20. The medicine, in which the action of the chloroform would seem to have contradicted that of the other two ingredients, may have had little to do with his recovery.

Chloral hydrate, a sleeping medicine which Lister prescribed often, was the first of the synthetic drugs. It was introduced in 1869. Paraldehyde, another sleeping medicine, and aspirin, were, with the exception of some antiseptics, the only other synthetics introduced before the end of the century. Lister's prescriptions were no more primitive than those of the majority of his contemporaries. Until there was a better understanding of body functions, normal as well as abnormal, the use of any drug was completely empirical.

Diagnosis, too, was impaired by the confusion between symptoms and diseases. Until the end of his life Lister treated inflammation as a disease, although he had been among the first to perceive that it could be a symptom of bacterial infection. By 1879 he had begun to examine wound discharges and body fluids for bacteria, but only in doubtful cases of inflammation. The information he obtained was of little diagnostic value because his ability to recognize and distinguish amongst infectious agents was too limited. About 1885 Lister began to use urinalysis to assist diagnosis when the patient was admitted. The case notes regularly show the specific gravity of the patient's urine, whether it was acid and contained albumen or sugar. The data were not quantified, and a second analysis was rarely done. His principal diagnostic tools were time-honoured: manipulation, osculation, tapping, breathing, 'sweetness' of the breath, fever, pulse, pain, inflammation and general health. Blood tests, tissue cultures and biopsies were unknown.

If Lister never clearly distinguished between a disease and the symptoms that made diagnosis possible, it was because he was not comfortable with theoretical generalizations. He was a practical man, a practising surgeon, who experimented to a practical end. He was not really interested in theories.

But there was more to it. Disease still possessed a symbolic meaning for Lister. 'Never ask a patient if he has had syphilis,' he was said to have told his students in London. 'If you know your work, there will be no need to do so, and why add to the poor fellow's transgressions by tempting him to tell a lie; surely he has done wrong enough already.' When he confronted a case of congenital syphilis, he no doubt thought about the sins of the fathers. Yet he knew that the body was a kind of chemical factory. He thought living matter was subject to physical laws like any other material object. Nevertheless, concomitantly with his rejection of abiogenesis, Lister never completely abandoned vitalism. In 1878 he apologized to the Midland Medical Society for using the phrase 'vital energies—But certain it is that whatever be the nature of life and whatever its relation to chemistry and physics, it does exist in the tissues no less than in the entire body'. It is a confusion born of ignorance. No one knew of the elementary energy exchanges of which 'life' consists, but as long as vitalism remained, disease was a denial of vital power. In so far as vital power was associated with divine power, disease was, at least symbolically, a moral problem. Lister's personal experience of serious illness, moreover, had been inextricably locked into the fundamental issues of right and wrong. No wonder that he always remained confused and ambivalent about the conditions he had to treat, conditions such as drunkenness, clap and the pox, often seen in the dregs of society. The progress of his own bacteriological research made it possible for the first time to show that diseases had causes, but the notion that they were God's punishment could not easily be rooted out.

The relevance of general health and balanced diet to bacterial infection was just beginning to be understood. In May 1879 Lister commented on a paper Cheyne had prepared for the Pathological Society of London. He noted Cheyne's statement that malnutrition favours development of organisms, and said that Cheyne had confirmed his own opinion as well as that of Pasteur. He also recognized that a good appetite is often a sign that there is no infection, a common and generally accurate piece of folk wisdom. In 1883 Lister prescribed the following daily diet for a man of thirty-eight with severe tb: milk, beef tea or bouillon, two pounds of meat, potatoes, bread pudding and two eggs. The absence of green vegetables and fruit is striking—the date was May 26—but there is plenty of protein! The general use of cod liver oil is associated with Lister's Edinburgh colleague, J Hughes Bennett. Lister prescribed it in cases of gout, rheumatism, 'scrofula', pulmonary tuberculosis and malignant tumours, for which it was combined with potassium iodide. The vitamin D it contains may have been of some value in the treatment of tuberculosis, but the other uses of cod liver oil reflect an ignorance which is scarcely surprising in view of the fact that the first vitamin was described in the year before Lister died. He also used cod liver oil to achieve a general improvement in health, especially for children, which is the way it has been used in every generation since then. The prescription of different food substances was just as empirical as the use of drugs.

Lister's most common non-surgical remedies were those of his young manhood. According to his King's College Hospital ward journals, he last used leeches to bleed a patient on June 17, 1879, and then in combination with potassium nitrate. The twenty-two-year-old girl suffered from seriously swollen neck glands and gradually improved under the prescribed treatment. But if he abandoned bleeding in all of its manifestations, Lister frequently used irritants and vesicants. Blisters were applied in two cases of swollen knee joint admitted in January 1882. The earlier of the two, a twenty-four-year-old man, finally required a leg amputation. The second, also a young man, had his knee drained of accumulated fluid and was released cured in June. Lister continued to use blisters until the end of his career, not just to counteract pain but also to reduce enlarged glands. Actual cautery, the direct application to the afflicted part of a hot iron, was last noted in the ward journals in February 1888. Its use then for internal piles, without chloroform, was rational if painful. Other uses of counterirritants may relieve symptoms, but do not cure.

13. Lister with his assistants, nurses and patients, King's College Hospital about 1890.

14. The donkey engine used for the carbolic acid spray. Now on display in the lobby of the Royal College of Surgeons of England, London. (See pages 184–186.)

On one occasion Lister used what he called acupuncture to control intractable pain. Henry Nash, aged forty, a former sailor, in good health but for sciatica, was admitted to King's College Hospital on May 19, 1884. '10 Acupuncture needles driven in along course of nerve,' Lister's clerk noted. 'These were left in for half an hour & were then taken out: collodion painted over the punctures.' No reference was made to meridians; the needles followed the course of the sciatic nerve. On July 3 the clerk wrote: 'Blister applied along course of sciatic nerve'. Though the exotic treatment failed, the homely blister did not. Nash was discharged 'cured' eight days later.

Lister's clinical medicine displayed few surprises. He was perhaps more open to new techniques and more ready to experiment with drugs and other therapies than many of his colleagues, but in the medical as distinct from the surgical arena he made no discoveries. Perhaps it is at least as important that there is no record of any major mistake with a drug, or a diagnosis leading to unjustified surgery.

On his surgical practice his colleagues were approaching agreement. During the last two months of 1879 the Metropolitan Counties (Southern London District) Branch of the British Medical Association devoted two meetings to a debate on antiseptic surgery. They were well attended and fully reported in the medical press. John Wood, Lister's colleague at King's, chaired both sessions. Lister himself was there and concluded the first meeting with a talk. With two exceptions the speakers who preceded him were favourable, and those two acknowledged Lister's contribution to hygiene. Even Mr Spencer Wells, the advocate of clean water, now acknowledged the value of antiseptic methods. He reported no deaths in thirty-eight antiseptic operations.

Lister took this opportunity to reject the charges that Savory had made in Cork. He questioned the value of Savory's statistics; for example, Savory had grouped together the practices of four surgeons at St Bartholomew's, two of whom used the antiseptic system. He then offered his own figures: a death rate at Edinburgh of 5.1% for all major operations, as against 5.8% at Bart's. Deaths from blood-poisoning, taking Savory's figures, were 1.44% at Bart's as against .82% during Lister's years in Edinburgh. Lister's doubts about gross numbers can be justified by the fact that no two cases are quite the same, but he accepted at last the need to satisfy his critics.

The Lancet responded with a leader that further modified its anti-Lister stance. The editor said: 'it is certain that he originated the idea of preventing the occurrence of putrefaction in the discharges of wounds, and of thus saving his patients from septic toxaemia'. An acknowledgement of historical fact, if not of Lister's current value.

The second session of the London BMA debate reflected the same pro-Lister sentiment as the first. Only one speaker, Morrant Baker of London, opposed the use of antiseptics. Wood, the chairman, said that he had had good results with antiseptic techniques despite some instances of carbolic acid poisoning. Yet some of his patients recovered without antiseptics. He praised Lister's originality, hard work and surgical practice. Now at last James Paget said that he had also found antiseptic surgery valuable, especially with bone surgery, the opening of uninfected joints and of large abscesses, and in ovariotomies! Paget said that mortality in his practice both at Barts and privately had fallen, and he thought the reasons were antiseptic treatment, better nursing and sanitation, and the abandonment of leeching and bleeding. Only one of the speakers, Knowsley Thornton, had been Lister's student. Short of their worshipful silence, Lister could scarcely have wished for stronger support from the meeting.

Opposition continued, but British medical men were slowly awakening to the great power of scientific research and quantifiable results to improve the therapeutic arts. Even Lister had resisted the demands for statistical proof because he had understood the value of quantification little better than his antagonists, but their very insistence accustomed doctors to the use of objective data. Nevertheless, the quantifiability of Lister's results provided the last platform from which his opponents could speak. The next attack came from his former Edinburgh colleague, James Spence, Professor of Surgery. Spence had denied the value of antiseptic surgery when he addressed the British Medical Association in 1875, with no noticeable effect. Now he was nearing the end of a useful career during which he had practised the surgery of cleanliness. He again demanded of Lister the statistical evidence for the superiority of antiseptic surgery. The attack stung. In a letter to Dr Wilson of Leytonstone, Lister called it 'ungentlemanlike'.

In the *British Medical Journal* on February 14, 1880, Lister said that Spence's data was highly selective. He had used figures from his own practice in 1861–1862. Cheyne assembled 331 of Spence's cases for various periods between 1872 and 1878, and showed that Spence had had a mortality rate of 17.5%. According to Cheyne the gross mortality for all major operations performed by Lister from 1870 to 1877 was 5.1%. The figures for fatalities following major amputations are also favourable to Lister: 25.7% in Spence's practice against 11.2% in Lister's. These include primary amputations, however; that is, amputations after injuries. Lister considered that a more accurate assessment could be obtained if primary amputations were excluded. He then gave two figures within a few lines of each other: five deaths following sixty-four amputations, or 7.8%, and three deaths following sixty-two amputations, or 4.8%. The second figure probably excludes two patients who died within twenty-four hours of the amputations, and presumably therefore, from causes other than suppuration. Both figures are certainly better than the one Spence gave. Of twenty-six amputations at the thigh, moreover, Lister had had one death, and in that case the patient died nine weeks later—of diphtheria. Spence, on the other hand, had had two deaths in twenty-five cases of amputation at the thigh. Finally, Lister cited thirty-eight operations on the breast, twenty-four of which included removal of the axillary glands. Of the whole group, three, or 6%, died, two of the three of blood-poisoning. These two, Lister emphasized, were the only deaths from blood-poisoning during his Edinburgh years.

Spence replied to these convincing figures by accusing Lister of falsification. Lister had left several cases of uncured abscesses in the Edinburgh Royal Infirmary when he had moved to London, Spence said, and these had been omitted from his data. It was an ill-natured argument if only because none of these cases had died.

In his answer Lister made a new point: 'even a much larger unbroken series of successes . . . would only afford probability, not proof, of the value of the principle'. He continued:

It is this lack of demonstrative force in surgical statistics which has always made me regard them with little favour, and kept me from producing them until I found it repeatedly hinted . . . that my silence implied some general failure of antiseptic treatment in my hands . . .

Despite the retrograde denial intended by the final paragraph, Lister had proven himself not only a better surgeon but also a better statistician than his antagonists. For a second time his powers of generalization proved to be superlative. As in the case of his first series of compound fracture cases, he resisted theoretical statements until the exigencies of his practical situation forced his hand. Now he realized that statistics raise two problems. The first is the question of what precisely they summarize. Thus, should a death from diphtheria nine weeks after an amputation be counted amongst deaths *due to* amputation even though the death follows the operation while the patient is still in hospital? Obviously not. The second question is much harder to answer. What does a statistic prove? Supposing all amputations to have healed successfully, there is no guarantee that the next one will not be accompanied by infection and lead to death. Given even a long series of successes, there is only a probability that the next amputation will also be successful. The probability that a given event will follow other similar events is also a question of the significance of that event. The statistics of probability and significance involve complicated mathematics that had barely begun to evolve in the work of Lister's colleague in the Royal Society, Francis Galton. That Lister saw the statistical problems clearly enough to state them was a considerable achievement.

Following the London debate on antiseptic surgery even *The Lancet* noted: 'It does not seem to us by any means plain that the relative value of Lister's system . . . can be determined by the figures, but must be referred to the accumulating conviction of individual surgeons'. The last bastion of opposition had begun to crumble.

In 1879 the managers of the Glasgow Royal Infirmary conducted a comparative study of results obtained by their own Listerian and non-Listerian surgeons. They found that 'under antiseptic treatment, the mortality is a little more than one-half of those treated in the non-antiseptic manner', and the mortality in the hospital had consistently declined. Professor Macewen of Glasgow reported, in 1884, that he had performed 1800 operations to remove parts of bones or joints without one serious infection. In 1902 the *British Medical Journal* carried the information that hospital mortality after major operations had fallen from 45.13% in the eleven years after 1859 to 7.1% in the four years 1886-1890. Of 2702 cases admitted to King's College Hospital under Lister's care, furthermore, the overall mortality was 4.2%. In all operations that he performed, 2% died. Surely a remarkable triumph.

On the other hand in the years 1894 to 1896 Chelsea Hospital for Women reported 45% mortality following exploratory abdominal surgery for diagnostic purposes. In 1912 surgeons at St Bartholomew's performed 3561 operations with 6% mortality and forty-nine amputations with 14.3% mortality! By comparison in 1865, the year Lister made his preliminary announcement of the antiseptic method, there were 410 operations at Bart's with 12.7% mortality, and ninety-three amputations with 22.7% deaths. Though there had been improvement, the Bart's record for 1912 is not as good as Lister's at King's or in Edinburgh. By 1912 the use of antiseptics during surgery had been largely abandoned as autoclaves, detergents and other aseptic techniques reduced the need for them. Lister always fought this aseptic surgery because he held that it afforded inadequate protection, but there is evidence in these data that infectious accidents occur whatever the hygienic precautions.

At the end of 1879 he was re-examining two aspects of the antiseptic system. In November he introduced an improved carbolic acid gauze for his dressing. He had first used a gauze dressing instead of putty or lint in 1870. Then as in 1879 he had made the dressing himself. The new one consisted of nine layers of carbolic-acid-impregnated gauze with a thin layer of macintosh under the outermost layer to stop any discharge from the wound coming through to the air. The pad was held in place by a bandage of the same gauze. To assure that the dressing was applied right side up, with the macintosh away from the wound, it was dyed pink.

In December Lister renewed his attempts to improve catgut for ligatures. This series of experiments continued, with occasional breaks, until March 1882. Mrs Lister assisted him throughout. In February 1880 he tried a linen thread as a ligature for a superficial operation, but did not again use vegetable fibre for the purpose. He used carbolic acid exclusively to sterilize the gut until June 1884, but then began to experiment with other antiseptics as he became interested in them for dressings.

On May 3, 1880, Lister gave the prizes to the graduates of the Bristol Medical School. In his address he praised the school, which had been among the first to accept his teachings. After the ceremony he gave a demonstration of antiseptic surgery at the Bristol Royal Infirmary followed by a second on the next day at Bristol General Hospital.

In July Lister was elected to the Council of the Royal College of Surgeons. Its twenty-four members each held office for eight years, and the Council met monthly. Along with the Fellows of the Royal College of Physicians, the Council set the examinations for admission to the Medical Register, and thereby effectively dictated the content of medical education in England and Wales. His election placed Lister firmly in the political arena of British medicine where contending methods, treatments and claims for prestige and honours were politely, but none the less forcefully, fought out. Though he never shirked this role, it was not one for which he was well-equipped.

His leading opponent on the Council was William Savory. Like Spence and many others, Savory rejected antiseptic methods because he believed he could do as well without the complex dressings, the time-consuming preparations, the excoriation or frank poisoning caused by strong antiseptics, and above all, the spray. Even when these men appreciated that Lister fought for a principle, exclusion of infectious agents from the wound, even if their denigration of the germ theory had by this time been quietened if not quashed, they could not accept that a theory should dictate surgical practice. This was not sheer blindness. The habit of thought which demands a scientific reason for the use of a drug or a dressing is modern. Even in 1880 most British medical practitioners had been educated in schools that did not require a general scientific training. This was not the case in Germany where Lister had been quickly understood, and it was less true in Scotland. In England the men of Lister's generation, men now in their fifties and at the peaks of their careers, had in most cases been educated in a manner that had changed very little for 200 years. Lister's students, on the other hand, were the new generation, trained to use microscopes for diagnosis and antiseptics to kill bacteria, trained to be scientific doctors. Far from being blind, Savory and men like him sensed that they were about to be displaced from the positions of power, prestige and financial reward to which their seniority entitled them by scientifically trained interlopers. It was in this way that matters of scientific theory and medical, especially surgical practice became a political issue within the Royal Colleges.

If the 'reactionary' politics of Savory and his kind was a gut reaction, so too was Lister's 'progressive' stance. But Lister lacked the tact, the diplomatic skill and above all the interest in manipulation so essential to the successful politician. He had all the patience necessary to count the number of bacteria in a microscopic field, but it did not extend to counting heads. He would spare no effort to demonstrate a point of surgical practice, but if reasoned argument failed to persuade, he had no alternative.

In 1885 Lister was offered the opportunity to become President of the Royal College of Surgeons at the next election. The offer probably came from a group on the Council who believed that they represented a majority. Whether they did or not, Lister refused. Godlee said he did not wish to be President, that he 'considered himself unfitted for the office'. Perhaps Lister also disliked the need to campaign because, in the event, Savory, then a Vice-President, was elected. Lister was appointed to the Museum Committee, an appointment he also held on the Board of King's College Hospital. In 1886 he became a member of the Committee of Management and a Vice-President of the Royal College of Surgeons. Of the twenty-eight meetings of the Committee of Management while Lister was a member, he attended sixteen, but he also sat on several temporary building and arrangements committees. On December 7, 1887, he delivered the annual Bradshaw Lecture to the Royal College on 'The Present Position of Antiseptic Treatment in Surgery'. No record of the address exists, but, typically, it began ten minutes late.

The President of the Royal College is elected every three years by the Council. In December 1887 Lister moved a resolution before the Council which would have required that the President be elected by the Fellows of the College. There was a precedent in the Royal College of Physicians, but that College had no governing Council. The Royal College of Surgeons had then some 18,000 members, all of those who had passed the examinations set by the College. Of these members about 1300 had passed a special examination to become Fellows. It was they who elected the Council.

Lister's resolution was an important political step. Savory intended to stand for re-election in 1888. Lister may have believed that although his supporters remained a minority on the Council because of an eight-year term of office, they made up a much larger group, if not a majority, amongst the Fellows. If that were the case, extension of the Presidential franchise to the Fellows would have hastened the Listerian victory, but the incident is a little mysterious. Without a majority on the Council, it was impossible to pass the resolution. Perhaps, in his usual way, Lister simply stood on a matter of principle: the desirability of a wider franchise. In the event Erichsen and three others voted with him and thirteen voted against. Savory again became President. At the end of his term in July 1888 Lister refused re-election to the Council. It was understood that if he had accepted re-election, he would have succeeded Savory. In 1895, after Lister's retirement from practice, Sir William MacCormac, one of Lister's earliest supporters in London, became President.

Lister's election to the Council of the Royal College of Surgeons was the first of a series of acknowledgements that mark the year 1880 as a watershed in his career. In August he led a discussion of 'The Treatment of Wounds' before the surgical section of the BMA meeting at Cambridge. On the 12th, moreover, he delivered an address to the pathological section 'On the Relation of Micro-organisms to Disease'. Because he had done no new bacteriological research for two years, this paper is a review of work by others. It is a useful summary, unique in Britain at the time, of three closely-related scientific areas: the bacteriology of Robert Koch, Pasteur's early work on vaccines and the body's own defences. Lister began by calling attention to the very recent emergence of bacteria as something more than 'scientific curiosities'. 'They were causes of putrefaction, or other fermentative changes, was a thing scarcely thought of; the notion that they had special relations to disease would have been regarded as the wildest speculations.'

He then turned to 'Dr Koch, of Wollstein' whom he described as 'a hard-worked general practitioner'. Both Koch and Pasteur had been working on anthrax, principally a disease of sheep, and in 1876 Koch had not only isolated the *Bacillus anthracis* but proved that it caused the disease. This was the pristine demonstration of a bacterially-caused illness and as such, of immense theoretical importance. The next year Koch published a book defining the relation of bacteria to infectious disease that became a classic. The book described the use of aniline dyes for staining and a second important technological development, the oil-immersion microscope lens. He showed conclusively that there are several different kinds of infectious bacteria by using the bodies of living animals—mice and rabbits—as 'a pure cultivating apparatus', in Lister's phrase. Koch's book had been translated into English by Cheyne and was published in 1880.

As a practical application of Koch's work Lister proposed to illustrate with the disease known as chicken cholera. Pasteur had written to Lister on January 2, 1880, describing his attempt to develop a vaccine against the disease consisting of attenuated viruses. Lister replied, asking for a culture of the organism and for vaccinated chickens. Pasteur's cordial answer promising both was written on August 7, immediately before the BMA meeting. Lister was able to show his audience the two chickens Pasteur had sent to him.

The chicken cholera organism, Lister said, 'is a good example of a bacterium which is more destructive as a disease, but which is at the same time entirely destitute of septic properties, in the primitive sense . . . as equivalent to putrefaction'. Although he could now distinguish amongst classes and types of micro-organisms, there is still much confusion between bacteria and viruses, which are even smaller. In 1875 Lister had distinguished 'minute organisms of a fungoid bacteric nature' from viruses which were 'not proved to be organisms'. In the sense that they cannot reproduce themselves except by becoming parasitic within other organisms, viruses are not 'alive'. Both Pasteur and Lister spoke of them in their correspondence about chicken cholera when they were discussing bacteria.

Lister told the BMA that Pasteur's paper on vaccination against chicken cholera had been published very recently. He had attenuated the culture to reduce the toxicity of the organisms 'in chicken broth, to which access of air is permitted while dust is excluded'. Lister speculated on the explanations for the 'enfeeblement' that resulted. He also described experiments by Dr Burdon-Sanderson two years before culminating in the growth in mouse blood of an organism associated with a disease of cattle and explained how this work was relevant to the development of vaccines. By passaging the causative agent through mice, it had become attenuated in a manner analogous to Pasteur's chicken cholera organisms. A different kind of immunization had been obtained, Lister continued, by his friend Professor Toussaint, of Toulouse, who was in the audience. Toussaint had successfully used the blood from which bacteria had been removed as a vaccine. He had thus introduced what has come to be known as passive immunization.

Towards the end of his review Lister broadened his consideration of these successful attempts to vaccinate against disease by enquiring what mechanisms in the body responded to vaccines and gave protection:

. . . the blood and tissues of the foetus of an animal dying of anthrax contain no bacilli, while those of the mother swarm with them. Putting these two observations together we are led to the inference that while the integrity of the placental vessels prevents the bacilli from entering the foetal circulation, the foetus is so dosed with soluble products of the development of the bacilli in the maternal blood as to be rendered proof against the disease.

He had been aware for years that face wounds heal more rapidly than those at the extremities, and children faster than adults. That ovariotomies could heal aseptically when performed with due regard for ordinary cleanliness, he had correctly attributed to special qualities of the gut wall lining. It was impossible to dress wounds of the lower lip or of the urethra antiseptically, but they healed satisfactorily, he had said in 1875; 'the healthy living tissues prevent the development of septic organisms in their immediate vicinity; and this I believe to be the explanation of the possibility of primary union without antiseptic treatment'. His research had already demonstrated that organisms introduced into milk, urine or Pasteur's solution would cause putrefaction, whereas the same dilution in ox blood did not. Having made these observations, Lister could go no further, but he had been remarkably prescient.

This brilliant address reveals Lister's grasp of the new scientific medicine. Appropriately perhaps it also contained his first published use of the Centigrade thermometer, though he gave the Fahrenheit equivalent. His summary of new research revealed a major nexus. At long last the germ theory and Pasteur's work on vaccines provided an explanation for the phenomenon of artificial immunization discovered by Edward Jenner when he began to vaccinate against smallpox at the end of the eighteenth century. More than that, recent advances had made it possible to ask old questions in a new and useful way: Why had some wounds healed always by first intention? The immunizing action of attenuated bacterial or viral agents exposed the existence of a biological mechanism that they triggered. What is it? A century later immunologists know that the mechanism of biological self-defence consists of a plethora of factors, but their relationships remain unclear. Lister had prepared himself to appreciate the new data that began to accumulate rapidly.

Soon after the Cambridge meeting he visited Professor Toussaint at the Ecole Vétérinaire in Toulouse. He wished to perform additional experiments on the resistance of blood to putrefaction, and required the jugular vein of a living donkey in which to do so. He said that he went because the antivivisectionist legislation forbade him to do the research in England, but there may have been another reason why it was convenient to work in Toulouse. He had received a 6000 franc prize from the French Academy of Sciences, a one-time bequest by a M Boudet, to be given in 1880 to the man who had contributed most effectively to medicine in the field of Pasteur's work. Lister may have determined to spend the money in France because in September, when the experiments at Toulouse were completed, he and Mrs Lister took their holiday in the Pyrenees.

He returned to his routine in October, with meetings of the King's College Hospital Board, operations and clinical lectures. As the year 1880 drew to a close Lister renewed his bacteriological research. On December 2 he took pus from the psoas abscess of a hospital patient. With assistance from Arthur as well as Agnes he examined cultures of the pus for bacterial growth. Similar tests were conducted in February on fluid from a hydrocele, a testicular growth often associated with either tuberculosis or syphilis. The notes on this series of tests were written by Mrs Lister and R J Godlee. Two more brief bacteriological experiments followed between June and August 1882 and in August 1883. All were related to the effect of the body fluids, pus, hydrocele or blood serum, on the development of bacteria.

The emphasis of Lister's bacteriology had shifted. From his original concern with the existence and nature of micro-organisms, matters which Koch and his associates had advanced very rapidly, Lister turned, in these experiments, to the immunological properties of body fluids. In 1883 the Russian physiologist, Metchnikoff, published his discovery of white cells called phagocytes and described their function as scavengers in body fluids of foreign substances such as bacteria. Metchnikoff thus provided the first step toward identification of the complex immunological mechanisms.

With the discovery of phagocytes Lister saw little reason for further bacteriological research. Research for its own sake did not interest him, and as he grew older, his mind focused more on surgery. That is not to say he stopped using his microscope, but after 1883 he did so either to check the effectiveness of antiseptics or the antiseptic efficiency of dressings and ligatures, and occasionally for diagnosis.

Once again opposition flared up in a debate on antiseptic surgery before the Royal Medical and Chirurgical Society in December 1880. Two eminent gynaecologists, Dr George Bantock and Mr Lawson Tait, opposed its use, but the weight of the opinions expressed favoured Lister. He was not present. It was left to Matthews Duncan, Knowsley Thornton and his one-time antagonist, Spencer Wells, to suppress this minor revolt.

Lister's life seemed now to approximate ever more closely to the Victorian ideal of the public man. Antiseptic surgery was acknowledged by appointments both honorary and administrative. In November 1880 he was recommended by the Council of the Royal Society to receive the Royal Medal. At the annual banquet of the Society in December when he received the Medal, Lister was elected to the Council.

In the same week he was nominated for the Presidency of the Clinical Society. *The Lancet* said that the Council

contains a very fair representation of the leading surgeons and physicians of London, and even if they may prove to have been a little premature, and perhaps unmindful of the strong claims of one or two of their own numbers, it will remain that they have paid a high compliment to the author of the antiseptic system of surgery.

Election after nomination was a formality. Lister's presidential address, on January 18, 1881, described improvements of catgut.

11

THE DEATH
OF
LADY LISTER

THE AVAILABLE RECORDS make it all but impossible to see Mrs Lister as anything other than an extension of her husband. She lives through the Common-place Books, and as they are less often used, even that connection diminishes. That she had a strong personality, earlier evidence makes clear. It may have been strengthened by her need to survive in the face of Lister's single-mindedness, his casualness about such ordinary events as meals and the professional demands on his time and vitality. In any case on March 24, 1881, she wrote a letter which provides a welcome insight into her life as distinct from that of her husband.

The letter was addressed to Mrs Tilanus, wife of the professor who invited Lister to address the International Medical Congress in Amsterdam, in September 1879. Mrs Lister thanked her for a Christmas card and continued:

I have to take part in holding a Bazaar in aid of our Hospital, and . . . I wonder whether your daughters could spare time and would be so kind as to work something for me to sell at it. It is to take place early in May . . .

May I also ask you to tell me what sort of weather you generally have in Amsterdam in April? Is it a cold month? Do you think it would be a suitable time of year for my sister to go?

Lucy Syme had lived with the Listers since shortly after her father's death, but she seems to have been little involved in their lives. She seldom entered the laboratory, and she did not accompany the Listers on their holidays. A spinster, Lucy had money from her father, but she seemed utterly dependent.

Agnes was certainly the organizer. Not only had she the energy, but she showed some enterprise in writing to Amsterdam for a contribution to the Hospital Bazaar. She had had experience with this sort of thing in her church work too.

In London the Listers attended the fashionable Grosvenor Chapel in Mayfair. Mrs Lister certainly supervised work amongst the poor, and she probably organized it. In August 1899, six years after her death, Lister wrote to the Reverend Evart B Barter of the Grosvenor Chapel about a Miss Watkinson:

You are no doubt aware that she was appointed as Mission Woman by Mr Oldham about 22 years ago. At that time there was a good deal for her to do among the poor of the district, and she did it largely under the supervision of my late wife who, though well aware of Miss Watkinson's defects, had a sincere regard for her.

Lister had been contributing to Miss Watkinson's support through the Chapel and continued to take an anonymous interest in her welfare. In 1900 he wrote again to Barter saying that Miss Watkinson had told Lucy Syme that she had been given only six months notice by the Chapel to vacate rooms 'connected with the former school'. Lister asked what provision had been made for her. In his will he provided an annuity of £26 for Miss Watkinson, who then lived at Birchington-on-Sea, Kent. He also left £100 to the Reverend Oldham, and he contributed regularly to the Mission Woman Fund every year until his death. These contributions were in memory of Mrs Lister. The Mission work must have meant much to her.

Her life obviously centred around Lister, however, as his did in a domestic sense around her. In April 1881 they took a long spring holiday in Spain travelling by land through the Basque country to Oran, whence they sailed to Malaga. They inspected the Alhambra, and visited the mosque at Cordoba three times. From Seville they went to Cadiz, hoping to find a steamer directly to London. None was immediately available, but they used the visit 'to see in a church where Murillo's last picture, left unfinished because he fell from the scaffolding on which he was working at it, and broke his leg.' Lister wrote to Arthur on May 3. 'I suppose it was a compound fracture, for the limb was amputated, and he died in his native city of Seville in consequence of the injury or the operation. It seems wonderful to think that he was only thirty-three when this happened'. Lister himself was barely fifty-four when he thus subsumed art to the service of surgery. Murillo stands very nearly alone as a painter whose work inspired written comment from any Lister, but Joseph's own skilful drawings depicted principally pathology.

They returned home in mid-May. In June he performed the first of a remarkable new series of innovatory operations at King's. Emma Harris, aged sixteen, had been admitted because an accidental cut across her wrist two months before had healed with the loss of some sensation and movement in the hand which was twisted into a claw. Lister opened the wrist and found not only the main tendons but also two nerve trunks cut and shrunken. He pulled the hand down toward the arm to reduce the distance and tension, and sutured the nerve trunks as well as the tendons. He knew that tendons would grow together, but the evidence about nerves was almost non-existent. Under suitable conditions such as those which Lister created surgically, some but not all of the nerve cells in a major trunk will repair themselves. Emma Harris was discharged on August 12, 1881, with partial return of sensation and considerable improvement in the movement of her hand. She returned on January 25, 1890, possibly to act as a demonstration for a clinical lecture, and in nine years she had regained almost full use of her hand.

Following this initial success Lister performed several more nerve resections, the technical term for the operation, with varying degrees of improvement as a result. On November 2, 1886, he wrote to Cameron in reply to a query from his former assistant. Cameron had a patient who suffered from a tumour which seemed to involve the sciatic nerve. There was a chance that the growth could be removed without destroying more than a short section of the nerve. In that case, Lister advised, 'it would, I think be worthwhile to try whether regeneration of nerve fibres might be brought about by connecting the ends of the nerve by means of several very fine catgut stitches applied with a sewing needle so as to form a channel, along which nerve-tissue might develop'. He added a diagram to illustrate what he had in mind and sent along suitable catgut. The outcome is unknown, though it would have depended in good measure on the age of the patient.

Meanwhile Lister faced a more delicate operation on the nervous system. On November 19, 1882, a two-year-old girl was admitted with a fractured skull. It was a Sunday, and the house surgeon treated the child antiseptically of course. But Lister was sent for. He raised a bone fragment and snipped off a portion of the brain substance itself, applied silver sutures and dressed the wound with iodoform powder, the antiseptic currently in use. On January 21 the little patient was discharged cured!

This had been an intervention into the brain necessitated by an accident. It was a different matter to open up the skull intentionally. The first such operation was performed by Lister's nephew, R J Godlee, on November 17, 1884. Two months later to the day Lister did the second. Eli Morgan, a forty-two-year-old gardener, had been admitted on December 10 with severe disturbances of his sight and movement. He was given a thorough examination. His eyes were checked with an ophthalmoscope. His muscles were stimulated electrically to check their responsiveness. Tests were conducted on his other sensory levels. Though he was semi-comatose, Morgan could answer questions. Dr Ferrier, the physician in charge, diagnosed an abscess and possibly a tumour. At 9.00 am on January 17, 1885, Lister opened the skull 'at a spot fixed by Dr Ferrier'. He used a blunt instrument to divide the brain, inserted his fingers about $1\frac{1}{2}$ inches and burst a large abscess. The operation took an hour and forty-five minutes. Two days later the patient showed recovery of sensation and improved control over his bladder muscles. He responded to voices. On the 26th, however, he died. Post mortem examination revealed a tumour of the hind brain. Whether that or a disturbance incidental to the operation killed him, it is impossible to say. Perhaps inevitably, other questions also arise: had Lister thought of the death almost forty years before of his brother John? Had he recalled the terrible symptoms, understanding now their cause?

These remarkable operations were made possible by antisepsis. Like operations to open the knee joint and to repair a fractured patella, the bony covering of the knee, nerve and brain surgery proved that with proper precautions, any wound would heal, any tissue withstand surgical intervention. Yet Lister rarely published such cases and then only when they had been the subjects of clinical lectures. When Cheyne asked to be allowed to do for Lister's surgery what Lister had done for Syme's—to write the articles himself—Lister refused. He could not take the responsibility, he said, for the half measures of others. These new operations could only be done safely with full antiseptic precautions, he maintained. Surgeons who doubted the value of antisepsis or whose antiseptic techniques were slipshod because they doubted the germ theory might read the articles, try the operation and lose the patient to infection. Whether the argument was sound or not Lister held to it as a matter of principle. It was regrettable because it meant that as his research work tailed off, his public statements if not his clinical lectures lost the immediacy of new results that had always characterized them.

The International Medical Congress met in London in 1881. On August 5, Lister addressed the pathological section on 'the Relation of minute Organisms to Inflammation'. Pasteur and Koch were both in the audience. The talk covered much old ground, but Lister warned against exaggerating the role of bacteria in the disease process. The excellent results of antiseptic treatment 'suggest the idea that all inflammation is caused by micro-organisms . . . if that is the sole cause . . . to what purpose is it to employ counter-irritation? . . . Again, in the case of those important diseases which we term strumous . . . there is at the present time a tendency to look upon this as altogether of an infective nature. This also I believe to be an exaggerated view'. In both cases he was at least partly right. Inflammatory reactions do not necessarily symptomatize infection; they can arise from irritation or an immunological response such as the hay fever reaction to pollen. Lister still saw inflammation as a disease rather than as a process symptomatic of diseases, but he would have recognized that bacteria may vary in their effect depending on the tissue they attack and the general health of the patient.

'Strumous diseases' are the various forms of tuberculosis of the bones, blood vessels and skin. Although no one knew it, Lister saw the diverse symptoms of one disease caused by *Mycobacterium tuberculosis*. The situation was the reverse of that in inflammation which is a symptom of many diseases, but again the tissue attacked by the bacteria depended on non-bacterial factors such as inheritance and environment. In both cases the research techniques and tools were now available to reduce the need for speculation thanks in part to Lister's efforts. This address seemed to look backward for the first time.

Three days later Lister spoke to the surgical section 'On the Treatment of

Wounds'. Godlee, who was no doubt in the audience, said of this talk that it was 'one of the most important . . . he ever made'. It is an extended defence of antiseptic surgery. He recalled the research on bacteria in blood that he had done at Toulouse and described the appearance in the clots, formed after the animals were killed, of cells that had not been present before, though they resembled white cells. He ascribed to those cells the temporary resistance of the blood clots to bacterial infection, and he associated the lymph with the aseptic healing of wounds as in ovariotomies. Thus he came close to identifying the cells that Metchnikoff called phagocytes two years later. He assigned their function correctly without describing how it was performed and implied a connection with the lymphatic tissue where phagocytes do proliferate. Nevertheless the research had been done almost a year before. This talk too looked back.

His role had become that of elder statesman. Over 3000 medical men met at various London scientific institutions while the Congress was in session. It had been opened jointly by the Prince of Wales, later King Edward VII, and the German Crown Prince who became the Emperor Frederick. Sir James Paget was President. Lister had been invited to be Honorary Secretary-General but declined. Virchow, the great German cell biologist, gave one of six addresses to the plenary meetings. He spoke on advances in surgery and gave special tribute to Lister. Pasteur also delivered a general address as did Volkmann and Huxley. Pasteur had completed large scale public tests of his anthrax vaccine a few weeks before the Congress. Speaking in French, he used the occasion to describe the results, proposing to continue to use the words vaccine and vaccination in homage to 'one of the greatest men of England, your Jenner.' The words derive from the Latin *vacca*, cow, from which Edward Jenner had obtained the cowpox inoculum against smallpox. Pasteur continued: 'By your warm reception, you have revived in me the lively sentiment of satisfaction that I felt when your great surgeon, Lister, declared that my publication of 1857 on the lactic fermentation had been for him the beginning of the reflections on his precious surgical methods'. It was not precisely the paper that Lister had first read, but the spirit of the praise was what counted.

In reputation Pasteur overshadowed a large French delegation, but he was very much one with his countrymen in their detestation of the Germans, who were led by Volkmann. Koch had only begun to establish his name. Cheyne recalled that he had not heard Lister's paper on the defensive cells in blood clot because he 'had been detailed to attach myself to Koch and take him about'. Lister arranged for Koch to demonstrate his solid gel culture medium at King's College Hospital. Despite Pasteur's chauvinism, Lister succeeded in arranging a meeting between them at the demonstration, a statesmanlike act in itself. Lister wrote that he heard Pasteur say to Koch:'C'est un grand progrès, monsieur'. Koch also spoke to the pathological section of the

Congress, showing microphotographs of the effects of germs on tissues.

Professor Tilanus of Amsterdam and his wife and daughters had been invited to be the Listers' guests at Park Crescent during the Congress, and Hector Cameron also stayed in the house. He reported that his host and hostess gave two separate dinners 'on two separate evenings' for the French and the Germans. During the French evening Lister took the course, unusual for an English host, of proposing a toast to Pasteur.

In September, after the meeting, the Listers went on holiday to the Engadine and Tyrol. He devoted mornings to the preparation for publication of the two papers he had read to the Congress, but the afternoons 'have been always sacred to enjoyment', he wrote to Arthur. They did not find 'walks of full twelve miles too much for either of us'.

During the last months of 1881 he renewed research on catgut and continued this series of tests until March when they were abandoned for two years. In February 1882 he had also begun experiments to determine the effectiveness of iodoform as an antiseptic. It was introduced into clinical practice soon afterwards.

Almost from the outset Lister had been aware of the limitations of carbolic acid: its corrosiveness and the danger of poisoning after continued use. He had tested a number of possible substitutes in a search that went on until the end of his active career. Chloride of zinc, though less volatile, was even more caustic. Boracic acid had been suggested to him by a Norwegian friend, Dr Strang. Lister first tried it in 1872 on his own inflamed nail matrix. It is bland and almost without irritation, but experience soon showed that it was too weak to be safely used except for superficial sores. In August and September he tested salicylic acid, and a year later he compared its potency experimentally to that of carbolic acid and boracic acid. Lister said, in 1883, that he would not use salicylic acid for serious cases.

Charles Darwin wrote to him on October 7, 1878, suggesting benzoic acid as an antiseptic. Darwin had found that it killed a plant which boric acid had not injured. There is no other correspondence between them, and they probably never met.

During 1881 he had expressed an interest in oil of eucalyptus and also agreed to test an oxidized oil of turpentine. No more was heard of either substance. The next year according to Cheyne, he began to dip his instruments and finger tips into a solution of bichloride and biniodide of mercury, corrosive sublimate. It was far too strong to be applied to the wound, but at this time, Cheyne said, Lister had entirely stopped using antiseptics as a douche during surgery.

In 1883 Lister cited Koch's distinction between two actions of antiseptics: one killed bacteria. Such antiseptics are germicidal. The other arrested the growth of bacteria. Lister called this an inhibitory action. Today, it would be called bacteriostatic. The distinction made it possible to rationalize the use of antiseptics. Lister, for example, did use such bacteriostats as salicylic acid, but for anything more than a superficial wound his system required germicides.

He tested new antiseptics concurrently with new dressings. As late as 1888 Lister was still making all his own gauze. Five years before he had begun clinical tests with a gauze containing corrosive sublimate beneath which he used a rubber protective. It proved inadequate and was replaced in 1885 with a gauze impregnated by Sal Alembroth, the double cyanide of mercury and zinc. He tried various zinc and mercury compounds, often in combination with the new aniline dyes. Of these later preparations Lister preferred Sal Alembroth despite its caustic quality, but his attempts to improve both the antiseptic solution and the gauze continued after his retirement. In the Common-place Book there is a copy letter dated February 21, 1896, to S Maw, Son and Thompson of Aldersgate concerning preparation of a new Sal Alembroth gauze. Lister's last published communication on the gauze appeared in the *British Medical Journal* on April 6, 1907, the day after his 80th birthday!

Though his research declined precipitously after 1882, Lister was not one to accept statements about clinically-relevant techniques, no matter how authoritative, without testing them. The British Medical Association's committee appointed to examine and report on various anaesthetics had questioned the safety of chloroform. Lister's experience with the drug continued to be good, but with a revision of Holmes's *A System of Surgery* before him, he decided to undertake further tests. Thus it was late in 1882 that he and Mrs Lister breathed chloroform in order to discover an optimal air-chloroform ratio. The revised chapter repeated Lister's preference for chloroform and reported his new research. His chapter on amputation required less extensive revision.

A distant echo of opposition to antisepsis appeared in *The Lancet* early in July 1882, roundly condemned by the correspondent who reported it. At the third annual meeting of the American Surgical Association in June, the anti-Listerians were in the majority. Some publicly rejected the germ theory, and *The Lancet* observed that it was 'too late in the day' for that. Others judged that the statistical battle between Listerians and anti-Listerians had been drawn, and therefore rejected the antiseptic system. Although Lister had American proponents, their influence was limited as much by the geography of the country as by its educational diversity. Each state had its own licensing body, and they set standards that varied widely. Lister himself never trained a doctor who practised in the United States.

On July 7 King's College Hospital was 'closed for several weeks . . . in order to have the drains renovated', Lister wrote to a general practitioner who wanted him to open an abscess for a patient. 'Could you not manage yourself to give him' antiseptic treatment, he asked. The Hospital reopened in the autumn, and Lister conducted his clinical lectures as usual. One of them dealt with a gunshot wound and was published by the *Medical Times and Gazette* on December 2. At the same time *The Lancet* carried a brief communication 'On the Application of a Knowledge of Hydrostatics to Practical Medicine'. Lister reported the use of elevation and a tourniquet in a recent operation.

This subject also provided the substance of a talk on 'The Relation of Physics to Medicine' which he delivered on October 11 to the student Medical Society of University College. It was the only time after he left University College that he attended a meeting of the Society over which he had once presided. Indeed according to a history of the College it was the 'only occasion on which Lister is known to have returned to his old Medical School', though he had been elected a Fellow of the College in 1861. After his retirement Lister expressed an interest in becoming a member of the Academic Senate of the newly-reorganized University of London, but he never did so.

On Boxing Day 1882 he wrote in the Common-place Book, 'I now prepare to go to Barcelona for 10 days.' It is the only reference to a holiday during that year though the Listers may have gone to Lyme Regis in September. At Easter 1883 they went to Swanage for the first time and found the town so attractive and congenial that they returned often for a spring holiday thereafter. Mornings were as usual devoted to writing and afternoons to walks, bird watching and flower collecting.

Toward the end of 1882 Lister had begun once more to consider the role of air dust as an infective agent. On November 30 he noted in the Common-place Book that he had dressed a mastectomy using boiling water, a boiled protective and cotton wool containing salicylic acid but no other antiseptic. Clinical notes on Hospital patients were usually entered in the ward journals, but Lister was conducting an experiment on this patient. On December 20 he washed away the discharge with unboiled tap water and placed a new dressing over the wound. Two days later he examined the discharge microscopically and found neither bacilli nor microcci though he did see granules, possibly spores, that he could not identify. The wound continued to heal satisfactorily. The case seemed to lend weight to the cold-water-and-cleanliness school, and it had been conducted in the context of a new decision on the spray. But Lister knew that under proper care wounds could heal kindly without antiseptics. He believed nevertheless that the risk was much greater, and in the spirit that one swallow does not make a summer, he continued the use of the spray.

The test with this particular case was made because a new kind of aseptic surgery was beginning to emerge, though it had not yet been given a name. Cameron recalled that Lister introduced the word, aseptic, 'to indicate the condition of a wound from which Sepsis is absent'. The idea of asepsis grew logically out of the non-Listerian operations of men like Spencer Wells and Thomas Keith. In August 1880 the *British Medical Journal* wrote editorially that not all 'the improvements of surgery had been improvements in antiseptics'. Cleanliness, wound drainage, even the more judicious selection of cases for operation so that the patients were in better general health could all be labelled 'antiseptic means'. The leader stretched the meaning of the phrase, but it made a point: 'it was only of late years that surgeons had aimed at being aseptic instead of antiseptic, to the total exclusion of septic agencies, which differed *toto coelo* from antiseptic treatment'. In other words the surgeon's intention to exclude bacteria could be effected by antiseptic means or by heat and cleanliness.

The distinction that emerged between antiseptic and aseptic surgery is one of means, not ends. The older Listerians, and especially Lister himself, fought against aseptic surgery on the grounds that it abandoned one whole line of defence, which in fact it did. The change could be justified only because the technology of hygiene was improving. The conflict was largely a matter of words, however, and ironically it need never have occurred at all if Lister had not chosen to focus attention on the antiseptic means rather than the aseptic end fifteen years before.

Lister made further experiments to reduce his own dependence on antiseptics. On November 6, 1883, he removed a tumour from the shoulder of a sixty-four-year-old woman, a private patient: 'I did it so as to ensure ... aseptic purity without contact of any antiseptic material with the wound. For this purpose the sponges, purified as usual by being kept in 1 to 20 carbolic solution, had the carbolic acid removed by washing in water that had been boiled, and other things were similarly treated.' Dressings consisted of salicylic cotton wool covered with gauze washed in boiling water. Recovery proceeded well.

Toward the end of November he performed three private operations without the spray. All were mastectomies. The first and second progressed well. The third patient contracted erysipelas, but energetic antiseptic measures halted the disease. She was out of danger by Christmas. Accidents such as this convinced Lister that antiseptic precautions simply could not be abandoned.

On the other hand new technical innovations made asepsis without antiseptics more feasible. Surgical rubber gloves were patented in 1878, though they were first introduced in an operating room by William S Halstead at Johns Hopkins Hospital, Baltimore, in 1890. In 1881 and 1882 Koch, with his assistant, Dr Wolfhügel, began to use steam sterilization for their laboratory equipment. During 1883 a German surgeon, G Neuber, tried to make the environment surrounding the operation completely germ free. He was probably the first surgeon to boil his operating gowns, but

Neuber also continued to use the spray until 1892, five years after Lister had given it up. Antiseptics themselves were applied to the instruments and the surroundings, but not to the wound. Slowly it became necessary to answer a new question: how did the risk from antiseptics, the delays in healing and the possibility of poisoning, compare to the risk from using all aseptic means *except* antiseptics?

Lister always maintained that the risk without antiseptics was greater than the risk with them. In 1884 a German surgeon was convicted of malpractice because he had not used antiseptic methods and his patient had died. *The Lancet*, like the German medical press, opposed the verdict because it was a totally unjustified interference by a court with the surgeon's professional decision. Lister no doubt sympathized with the verdict, but he must also have approved the editorial sentiments of the medical press. As he hesitantly reduced his own dependence on caustics and finally abandoned the spray, his concern grew that antiseptic means were being neglected unwisely.

In September 1883 before his clinical tests of aseptic methods, Mr and Mrs Lister visited Budapest in response to an invitation from the medical faculty at the University. On the 29th a banquet at the Hotel of the English Queen was followed by a torchlight procession through the town. Dr Lajos Markusovzky, who had reviewed Semmelweis's book in 1860, presided at the banquet, which was reported by *The Lancet*.

On October 23 Lister addressed the Medical Society of London 'On the Treatment of Fracture of the Patella'. He reviewed cases in which he had secured the knee cap by silver-wire sutures. All of them had required the opening of healthy knee joints with the risk of infection, but thanks to antiseptic methods, all had been successful. Lister concluded: 'Gentlemen, I thank you most heartily for your cheers; for there was a time when such remarks might have met with a different reaction'. It was true of course, but how oddly querulous and oversensitive it must have sounded.

St Clair Thomson, his house surgeon in 1883, recalled:

. . . I was standing beside him on the steps of the Hospital . . . soon after the attack made upon him for daring to open a healthy knee joint. He began by quietly remarking that the day must surely come when the profession would accept the principles of his methods . . . 'if the profession does not recognize them, the public will learn of them and the law will insist on them'. Then he placed his hand on my shoulder and added pathetically: 'Thomson, I do not expect to see that day, but you may'.

No matter that he was universally honoured and that his name had achieved world-wide fame, the breath of self-doubt persisted. It was rarely expressed so openly, and his smooth avuncular features revealed little sign of inner distress. Lister seemed to know that his plaintive sighs were unjustified, but he could not help himself.

Less than five weeks after the address to the Medical Society he received a letter from Gladstone, the Prime Minister, offering him a knighthood. On

December 5, he accepted. It had naturally been in the air for some time. Just before he received Gladstone's letter, Lister had accidentally met Sir Henry Acland, the Oxford friend with whom he and Mrs Lister had spent a weekend after his appointment to the General Medical Council. Acland had 'urged strongly the absolute wrong this not being offered to you' before, but had wondered whether Lister 'had not refused'. Lister assumed that Acland had had an immediate influence on the decision to honour him now and wrote to thank him. On December 9 Acland replied: 'No—It was a coincidence . . . It was strange my meeting you, for I was going to write to you at once—having to write to Mr Gladstone on another matter, and meaning . . . to *beg* him to do this—I will tell you more another day—but I had nothing *now* to do with this great pleasure to us all'. Acland concluded: 'Pray do not go on calling me Dr'. Perhaps the delay to which Acland referred reflected the last lingering opposition from Savory and the anti-Lister majority within the Council of the Royal College of Surgeons, but they were no longer enough to deter the Government and the Crown. In a sense Lister's recent prediction to Thomson had been rapidly fulfilled, excepting that he *had* seen 'that day'.

In the King's College Hospital ward journals from this time onwards, his clinical clerks referred to him as Sir Joseph Lister, Sir Joseph and later, when perhaps he examined the journals less frequently, as Sir J Lister. It is of course customary for everyone but close friends to use the title, but its regular appearance in what are otherwise often very abbreviated notes suggests that the clerks had been instructed by the house surgeons in the etiquette that Lister expected. The title was the visible symbol of his acceptance, as a grateful State meant it to be.

In 1884 while Lister was still a member of the Council of the Royal College of Surgeons, that College, with the Royal College of Physicians, established a Conjoint Board to coordinate their examinations of medical and surgical applicants for admission to the Medical Register. The Board itself consisted of administrators and specialists who were under the control of a Committee of Management appointed by the two Colleges. Lister became a member of the Committee in 1886. He was thus publicly involved in a debate over who should examine students which had aroused him privately for years. He had always preferred the Edinburgh system in which the student was examined by his own teachers to the London system under which examiners were strangers to the students.

Lister's friend and teacher, William Sharpey, had written to *The Lancet* in 1864 approving 'the plan of substituting class examinations for final examinations of degrees and licenses in the Scotch schools'. Lister wrote to Sharpey on March 27 praising the letter. The proposal would mean an end to cramming, he said, and the students would be freed 'to work at each subject earnestly while they engage in it'. His criticism of London clinical teaching in 1877 had extended to the system of examination. There is no doubt that

Lister and his close associates believed the early struggle to obtain students at King's was entirely due to the examination system: the students knew they would later be examined by non-Listerian surgeons.

The examination issue was complicated and confused by a move in England and Ireland to establish a single examination for the entire Kingdom. Lister disapproved the so-called 'one board' system, in part at least, because it made the examiners even more remote from the student. The proposal was also opposed in Scotland where it was less necessary because Scottish medical students usually attended the universities from which they were graduated. This was not possible in London where the medical schools were, in all but two cases, King's and University College, attached to the hospitals, which could not grant degrees. The London examination system had grown up because the Royal Colleges were in a position to supervise all of the medical schools. In London, furthermore, the degree of Doctor of Medicine could be granted only by the University of London, which imposed what Godlee called an 'extraordinarily rigid, indeed almost prohibitive, test'. In the eyes of the public most London doctors with diplomas from the Royal Colleges stood at a disadvantage with respect to the Scottish doctors and those from other English universities which granted MDs with less severity.

In 1880, before Lister became a member of the Council of the Royal College of Surgeons, an attempt had been made to establish a new degree-granting University in London. Such an institution would have administered its own examinations, but it could not exist without the support of the two Royal Colleges. The attempt to establish the Conjoint Board had failed in that year and again in 1881, but when it succeeded in 1884, the idea of a new University could be revived.

The alternative was to allow the two Royal Colleges to grant degrees in both Medicine and Surgery. In November 1885 a joint Committee recommended this course. The council of the Royal College of Surgeons then defeated a motion to establish a new medical University for London, whereupon Lister moved that the recommendation of the joint Committee be approved. Sir Spencer Wells seconded and the motion was carried. Lister was appointed to the Committee which the Council now set up to work out the technical details with the Physicians.

In 1886 the Society of Apothecaries asked to join the Royal Colleges in granting degrees. The joint Committee rejected the request, although the General Medical Council favoured it. In March 1887 the Council of the Royal College of Surgeons approved a motion introduced by Lister rejecting the Apothecaries. In the event the Apothecaries lost nothing because the Royal Colleges have never granted degrees.

Lister continued to argue for the Scottish system of examination by the student's classroom teachers. On the Committee of Management his principal opponent was William Savory. Their disputes often delayed the adjournment of Committee meetings and led to the imposition of a 10.30 adjournment rule. Most opinion in London and a growing body in Scotland supported Savory. As medical education increased in complexity, Lister's preference became frankly reactionary. No single instructor, indeed no single faculty, could adequately represent the growing number of relevant disciplines—as Lister should have been among the first to recognize. As competition increased, furthermore, the students themselves took more seriously questions of personal bias.

In 1889 a Royal Commission was established to recommend on the persisting question of a degree-granting medical University in London. Lister told the Commission that although he had favoured the Royal Colleges as degree-granting bodies, he had changed his mind. 'It seems to me that it would be a degradation of the degree to give it on the minimum possible of professional qualification.' But he still opposed the system of examination. Students must know that the matter put before them by their professors would also be acceptable to their examiners, he told the Commissioners with some bitterness. He described the 'humiliating experience' of his early neglect at King's.

The tendency as regards the student . . . if he feels that he is to be examined by somebody who is not his teacher, is to distract his attention from the teacher, and to make him rather try to find out where he can get what are called 'tips' with regard to what is likely to be asked at the examination boards.

Quite apart from the fact that his classes were as large as any at King's by this time, Lister overlooked the counter argument: that if all professors were equally remote from examinations, the students would find no advantage in selecting one as against another. On the other hand his complaint about 'tips' applied with increasing frequency as students depended more on crammers who could teach what the examiners wanted. On July 2, 1892, he told yet another Royal Commission on medical education that 'students made a very great mistake in going to them rather than to those who are more experienced'. Just though the argument is, the return to more personal teaching which alone could root out the crammers became less feasible because of the emergence of scientific medicine for which Lister himself was so largely responsible.

Lister's position on examinations was political and personal though he never recognized it as such. The King's College students stayed away at first because the weight of surgical opinion, even at King's, was against antiseptic methods. When this balance changed, Lister had also changed. His tetchiness had probably arisen out of the self-doubt that lay at the very core of his being, but it must have been severely inflamed by the experiences that he described with such emotion to the Royal Commission of 1889.

Like his belief that he was never really understood, the closely-related opinion that students ought to be examined by their own teachers became an *idée fixe*. In 1897 he told the students and faculty of Queens College, Belfast, that a good medical education required three elements: practical experience with the microscope, animal experiment and examinations by the classroom teachers. The English examination system had slowly invaded Scotland, and on May 11, 1901, Lister spoke against the trend to the Edinburgh University Club. Almost four years later he wrote to his old friend, Sir William Turner, now the Principal of Edinburgh University:

Among the improvements in the examinations which you say are likely to be made, one no doubt will be to insist that at an oral examination the two examiners always sit at the same table. To have them at different tables in the same room, even if they always confer before *rejecting* a candidate, gives no security against a (theoretical) disposition of a professor to deal too leniently with those who have been his students.

In this as in all other aspects of his life, Lister bothered about the trivia. He was alive to the danger of bias in the classroom teacher.

Despite the educational changes there, his sympathies remained in Edinburgh. He had decided to leave various mementoes and awards to the University, he wrote to Sir William Turner on July 27, 1907, because: 'My sympathies have never been with a merely examining body like the College of Surgeons, but with a teaching University, & above all with that of Edinburgh'. No doubt memories of his wife and of Syme influenced the decision, but the examination system was of a piece with them.

Lister's practice and his administrative responsibilities now largely filled his life. On November 20, 1885, he wrote to Dr Wilson of Leytonstone, 'I wish I had more beds at my disposal; but I am most seriously crippled in this respect'. He had had to turn down a patient of Wilson's but suggested he might do as well at home. Whatever the state of his classroom, the beds in Lister's wards at King's were seldom empty.

During 1884 he had also found time to read two papers. The first, a talk to the Woolwich Military Medical Society on February 15 on the application of antiseptic surgery to field conditions, required little preparation. The second summarized new research. On October 20 he addressed the Medical Society 'On Corrosive Sublimate as a Surgical Dressing'. Except for the lost Bradshaw Lecture to the Royal College of Surgeons, he neither spoke outside his classroom nor published again until 1889.

In April 1886 the Listers abandoned Swanage for a holiday in Jamaica. Arthur, his son Arthur Hugh, who was already practising medicine in Aberdeen, and his daughter Gulielma made up the party. Near Kingston they stayed with Dr Mandeville, the resident British physician. 'I often imagine myself looking down from your lofty position, toward Crocodile pond & Black River & the sea', Lister wrote to him, in January 1887.

Apart from such imaginings these holidays to foreign places made no visible impact on him. Like his wife, Lister found them relaxing because he was away from the pressure of work and routine. Even when they met natives, as their letters from Switzerland and Norway indicate they did, the exchange was picturesque, of passing interest because it was different, but had no lasting effect. They brought back few artefacts other than wild flowers. They travelled either because Lister's professional commitments required it or for the purest kind of recreation.

Shortly before Lister went to Jamaica, the Government appointed him to a Commission to consider what action, if any, the British medical profession wished to take in connection with Pasteur's most recent and best publicized discovery: a rabies vaccine. Sir James Paget was President of the Commission, and other members included Richard Quain, Professor of Surgery at University College Hospital, and John Burdon-Sanderson.

Pasteur had begun his search for a vaccine against rabies, or hydrophobia, in 1880 but the fowl cholera and anthrax research had taken precedence. Two years passed before he was able to devote himself for the first time to a disease of humans. Then in July 1885 an Alsatian boy named Joseph Meister, who had been bitten by a mad dog, was brought to Pasteur's laboratory. With understandable reluctance Pasteur gave the boy the long and painful course of untested inoculations. Meister contracted only a mild form of the disease and recovered.

In England alone an average of forty-five deaths from rabies occurred each year between 1875 and 1885. The disease was much more widespread on the continent. The news of Joseph Meister, spread by telegraph, caused tremendous international excitement. Because the disease was so familiar and so terrible, Pasteur's vaccine was perhaps the first example of medical intervention to affect masses of people. It spread his personal fame beyond professional science, amongst doctors as well as laymen. The rabies vaccine became the keystone of the arch that supported the germ theory. In Britain Lister had done more than any other man to build that arch. The sheer dramatic impact of the rabies vaccine, therefore, lifted the implicit debate between the non-scientific medical *ancien régime* and the Listerians on to a public stage. Whatever Lister's inadequacies as a propagandist, he possessed the one weapon that mattered with people—success, the banishment of fear from surgery. The fact that he was a remote and awesome figure, unlike the eloquent and volatile Pasteur, may actually have enhanced his prestige. Not only did the British expect their public figures to be solid like the Queen herself, but also the public sensed the profound sympathy and real commitment to them that Lister's patients experienced in the touch of his hands, the soft smile, the slightly hesitant speech and the gentle eyes. It was to be expected that he would soon become at least the titular leader of the movement to establish a British institute to make and administer rabies vaccine.

Pasteur realized quickly that he could not cope alone with the flood of applications for treatment, many of them as pitiful as they were hopeless, from all of Europe and north America. Before the end of 1885 he had organized a Service that was incorporated as the Institut Pasteur in November 1888. The delay occurred because there were failures with the vaccine. Some deaths were attributed to it. Meanwhile between 1885 and 1889 some 200 Britons were sent to Paris to receive the new treatment. By 1888 seven rabies institutes had been established in Russia, five in Italy, and one each in Vienna, Constantinople, Barcelona, Bucharest, Rio de Janeiro, Havana and Buenos Aires, and committees existed in Chicago and on the island of Malta.

The Commission established in 1886 carried out its own tests of Pasteur's vaccine and reported favourably next June. Immediately the House of Lords appointed a select committee which recommended in August that all dogs should be muzzled, stray dogs destroyed, imported dogs quarantined and the Pasteur system applied in England if it was proven to be effective. Ten years passed before these proposals were given effect in law, but by 1902 rabies had effectively disappeared in Britain.

Further steps to establish a rabies institute languished until July 1889 when the Lord Mayor of London presided over a meeting in the Mansion House organized by Paget and other members of the 1886 Commission. Lister was one of the principal speakers. The meeting called for muzzling and quarantine legislation and established a committee to raise a fund for the purpose of making a contribution to the Institut Pasteur and providing money to pay the expenses of British patients who went there. On November 6 the committee sent £2000 to the Institut Pasteur, but instead of disbanding itself, those who attended considered the desirability of establishing a British equivalent. A second meeting at the Mansion House on December 5 led to the establishment of an Executive Committee for a British Institute of Preventive Medicine. This Committee was larger than the Commission of 1886 and included laymen such as John Sidney Turner, a dog breeder who was said to have suggested the idea of the British Institute. Sir Spencer Wells, Sir James Paget, Thomas Huxley and William Watson Cheyne were also members. Sir Joseph Lister was its Chairman.

News of the proposed Institute aroused the antivivisectionists who assumed, quite rightly, that it would conduct live-animal experiments. Had the Committee proceeded with greater speed, it might have achieved its objective before the opposition gained coherence, but about eighteen months passed while a scheme was drawn up. At last, early in 1891, Lister wrote on behalf of the Committee to the President of the Board of Trade, Sir Michael Hicks-Beach, requesting incorporation. He pointed out that unlike the institutes in other countries, the proposed British body would require no Government funds but would be self-supporting! Under pressure from the antivivisectionists Hicks-Beach refused. On May 26, 1891, Lister wrote to the Royal Society and the Royal Colleges asking that they send representatives for a deputation to Hicks-Beach on June 5 to seek a reversal of his decision. The deputation, including the Duke of Westminster, the Earl of Derby, Huxley, Tyndall, Everett Millais, the naturalist, and R B Haldane, MP, pointed out that the Committee had asked only for incorporation. It had not applied for a licence to experiment on live animals because that could be granted only by the Home Office. The deputation achieved its end, and the licence of incorporation for the British Institute of Preventive Medicine was granted on August 1.

Lister became the first Chairman. The objectives of the Institute were to study and improve the prevention and cure of infectious diseases in men and animals, to instruct Medical Officers of Health, medical practitioners, veterinarians and students, to prepare and supply drugs and to treat patients. Rabies was not specifically mentioned, and the Institute never treated patients with the disease. They continued to go to Paris. A year went by while sufficient funds were raised and suitable quarters found. At last in 1893 the British Institute was amalgamated with the College of State Medicine which conducted the post-graduate education of Medical Officers of Health. The facilities of the College, on Great Russell Street, in many respects inadequate for the Institute, had the great merit of possessing a licence from the Home Office. Dr Armand Ruffer, a protégé of Pasteur, then became Director. He held the position until 1898.

The first major task confronting the Institute was the manufacture of diphtheria antitoxin, introduced clinically in 1893. Lister wrote a letter to *The Times* appealing for contributions to a special fund to support the antitoxin programme. The Institute bought a farm at Sudbury for the purpose, but the first British antitoxin was developed by Ruffer, working with a young physiologist, Charles S Sherrington, who was then Superintendent of The Brown Animal Sanatory Institution in Battersea. The vaccine was tested for the first time to save the life of Sherrington's nephew. When the child was out of danger, Sherrington wrote, 'I returned to London, and sought out Ruffer. His reaction was that we must tell Lister about it. The great surgeon . . . had visitors, some Continental surgeons, to dinner. "You must tell my guests about it," he said, and insisted—so we told them in the drawing room, at Park Crescent.'

The Duke of Westminster gave the Institute a tract of land on the Chelsea Embankment where it began the construction of its own building. Although the antivivisectionists opposed the granting of a licence, the new building was formally opened in May 1897.

Meanwhile on December 9, 1896, Lister had chaired a meeting in the Board Room of St George's Hospital, where Edward Jenner had been a student, called to agree on a suitable commemoration of the centenary of Jenner's discovery of smallpox vaccination in 1797. The meeting approved a suggestion that the memorial bearing Jenner's name should be established in connection with the British Institute and formed a committee to organize a public meeting which would determine upon a suitable memorial and raise money for it. The meeting of medical men in March 1897 held in the Theatre of the University of London was chaired by the Duke of Westminster. It approved the proposal originated by the meeting at St George's and established a continuations committee chaired by Lister. The committee hoped to raise £100,000 but received only £5770 of which £5000 came from Lord Ivreagh, £600 from the Duke of Westminster and £100 from Lister. The name of the Institute was nevertheless changed to the Jenner Institute of Preventive Medicine.

Lister sat on the Governing Board of the Jenner Institute as the representative of the Royal Society. Between 1898 and 1904 when he resigned because of his health, he served as Chairman. He never actually did research there himself, but the Director, Dr Ruffer, performed tests on the germicidal properties of carbolic acid in oil to which Lister referred in a speech at Glasgow University in 1894. In 1900 he received a letter from his friend, Dr Wilson, describing an unfortunate episode suffered by one of his patients after vaccination. On November 2 Lister replied: 'The Jenner Institute has nothing whatever to do with the vaccine lymph . . . the entire responsibility for the preparation of the lymph rests with the LGB.' Some of the rooms in the new building were occupied by the Local Government Board. Among the Board's duties was administration of the smallpox vaccination programme. Vaccination had been compulsory in England since 1853, though a conscience clause in the act allowed parents to refuse to allow the vaccination of their children. The Local Government Board, Lister told Dr Wilson, had sent 'a public vaccinator for Marylebone, who vaccinated my household a few days ago.' He also recommended that the skin be wiped with carbolic acid before and after the injection.

Soon after the Jenner Institute was so named, the Directors learned of the existence of a registered company in Battersea with the name, Jenner Institute for Calf Lymph. They had no alternative but to change the name a second time. In 1903 'much against Lister's inclination', wrote Godlee, it became the Lister Institute of Preventive Medicine. A Jenner Scholarship was established with the money contributed for a Jenner Memorial.

Lister became the President of the Lister Institute in 1904 and held the title until 1911. Day-to-day operations rested with the Director. Before Lister died, the organization was doing research in bacteriology, biochemistry, proto-zoology, experimental pathology, entomology and statistics. It eventually produced vaccines against smallpox, typhoid fever, cholera and plague, operated three farms and participated in a number of public health functions such as the analysis of milk for the London County Council. (Having jealously guarded its independence, the Lister Institute was caught up by the contraction of financial resources in post-imperial Britain. In 1975 although one laboratory at Elstree was being retained, the Chelsea head-quarters were advertised for sale.)

Soon after he returned from Jamaica in 1886, Lister went to Glasgow to consult with Hector Cameron about a patient of Cameron's. The visit was recalled by Cameron's son, then a boy of eight. The visitor was to be a house guest, and his importance was impressed on the child 'by the magnitude of the preparations . . . Not only were new chintz covers bought to drape the hideous outlines of mid-Victorian sofas and easy chairs but, an unheard of event, my aunt, who after my mother's death lived with us . . . added to her wardrobe a black velvet gown of immense size and dignity.' Young Cameron described his impressions of the great man:

When I was admitted to the drawing room Lister was standing with his back to the fire, tea cup in hand. As I remember him he was nearly always standing. Others sat while he talked, Lister stood. If for a few minutes he was seated, some new turn in the conversation seemed inevitably to force him to his feet. Not that he was restless or that he conveyed to others any feeling of disquiet by doing so . . . He stood because he was absorbed in the interest of what he was saying or of what was being said to him. He was in many ways shy and reserved. When agitated or embarrassed, his repressed emotional state showed clearly in an increase of the slight stammer that he never completely lost, a twitching of the corner of his mouth and of his eyebrows and a mounting colour . . . he was never awkward or ill-at-ease.

At about the same time one of Lister's Edinburgh house surgeons, F L Grasett, who now practised in Toronto, came to England for a visit. The Listers gave a small dinner for him and Mrs Grasett. 'His brown hair was heavily tinged with grey', Grasett recalled, 'spectacles were necessary for operating'.

In September 1886 Sir Joseph and Lady Lister went to Lake Constance for their holiday, and they spent Christmas that year with Arthur and his family at Lyme Regis. The next September they went again to Switzerland, having left Cheyne in charge at the Hospital and Fitzroy Square.

During the rest of 1887 and for long periods in the next two years Lister continued experiments with different antiseptic solutions in gauze dressings. It was at this time that his research was commemorated by a song sung by students at King's College Hospital:

> There is a worthy baronet who once took up the cause
> Of Antiseptic Surgery and Antiseptic Gauze.
> First there was a yellow one, then there was a blue;
> Then there was a red one and a white one, too.
> Next there was a violet one, so we thought he'd go
> Right through àll the colours of the bright rainbow.

Sal Alembroth gauze was blue, and the double cyanide of zinc and mercury, a lovely violet. Carbolic acid gives a typically yellow colour, and the red may have referred to the pink macintosh beneath the outer layer, but the others were no doubt invented for the occasion.

The song suggests that Lister had achieved not only respect but a certain fond sympathy amongst his students. His clinical lectures went on, and by their nature they could not have become standardized. In June, 1888, his clinical clerk, L W Gunn, noted that following an operation on a seventy-four-year-old man for kidney stones, 'Stone fragments shown in clinical lecture was uric acid showed laminated structure and nucleus was formed & looked harder than rest of fragments'.

Later that year Lister was asked by the Royal Society to referee a paper 'on some new and typical micro-organisms obtained from water and soil' by Grace C and Percy F Frankland. P F Frankland became a Fellow in 1891. The report, in Lady Lister's handwriting, painstakingly examines both the content and the illustrations:

... if we except the introduction, as a means of discriminating between different species of bacilli, and the fact, now established apparently for the first time, that the Nitric Acid in a solution of Nitrate is reduced to Nitrous Acid by some bacilli and not by others, there is nothing original in the methods of research ... Further, it seems to me matter of regret that the organisms isolated with so much pains have not been tested as to their pathogenic properties or otherwise by inoculation upon the lower animals.

He considered that the illustrations were 'somewhat disappointing'. Some were 'crude' and 'those which show the organisms highly magnified are not drawn accurately to the same scale, which seems to me a serious defect'. He seems to take it for granted that the paper, which has 'very distinct value', will be published, but he 'would suggest that the authors should be required to supply an "explanation of the plates", so that the reader who desires to know to what species any figure refers, need not be compelled, as he now is, to hunt for its description in the body of the paper'. Lister's judicious care, as well as his style, provide an insight into his manner during examinations.

The medical press had been completely won over to his side, or perhaps it is more accurate to say that with the virtual proof of the germ theory, the journals had nowhere else to go. Toward the end of 1888 the *British Medical Journal* published some details of the illness of the Emperor Frederick of Prussia, which were matters known only to the Emperor's doctor, Professor von Bergmann of Berlin, and certain medical men whom he had consulted. Publication involved a breach of faith on somebody's part, but it also violated professional secrecy. A meeting was held at Lister's house, and an apology was eventually made privately to von Bergmann. Lister's interest in the affair may have been stimulated in part by the award to him three years before of the German *Ordre pour la Mérite*, given by the Emperor Frederick. Lister's influence on Dawson Williams, the editor of the *British Medical Journal*, and on his colleagues illustrated the position he had achieved. Williams remained his devoted admirer.

Although he was now past sixty, he continued to operate. On June 6, 1888, two former house surgeons, Mr Carless and Mr Penny, were appointed to positions as Lister's assistant surgeons. By 1890 one of them always assisted at his operations. Nevertheless, when a man was brought in with severe concussion on March 16, 1889, Lister was called and arrived at 10.00 pm. He operated to relieve pressure on the patient's brain, and the man recovered.

Lister even performed occasional dental surgery. On May 11, 1889, he operated on the jaw of a forty-five-year-old man who had continued to have pain and swelling after the earlier removal of a tooth and a diseased bit of bone by another surgeon. Infection had not set in, and the patient showed no sign of tuberculosis. In the words of his clinical clerk Lister 'found embedded in the substance of the bone the root of a decayed molar tooth which had evidently caused all the mischief'. The patient was discharged, cured, on July 27.

Antiseptic procedures could still go wrong, and Lister always looked for a reason. On February 2, 1889, he wrote to a doctor whose patient had died after an operation: 'I feel sure the unusual course was the result of my trying a new dressing which I thought had been sufficiently tested, but which I afterwards found a flaw in'. His frankness must have been refreshing to the referring doctor, however distressing the circumstances.

He knew that he ran risks because of his ceaseless attempts to improve his dressings. He tried to minimize the risks by careful laboratory procedures, by providing safeguards against infection and as he grew older, by consultations, even during an operation.

On February 20, 1889, he operated to remove a tumour on the liver of a thirty-two-year-old woman. After making the initial incisions, he came to what appeared to be a much enlarged portion of intestine. The intestine could have been abscessed, in which case the abscess would have caused the swelling that he had diagnosed as a tumour. But if the intestine was abscessed, he dared not cut further because to open the intestine would almost certainly lead to peritonitis. He could only hope that the abscess would drain itself through the bowel, and was preparing to sew up the incision. 'While thus deliberating Mr Cheyne arrived,' wrote the clinical clerk in the ward journal. 'Sir Joseph and he deliberated together for some time'. They deduced that the tissue revealed by Lister's scalpel might not be intestine but part of the peritoneum, the gut lining. 'Sir Joseph therefore determined to make a small cut into it; being prepared to sew up if it should turn out to be intestine.' It was not. Lister's first diagnosis had been right. He removed the tumour, and the patient recovered.

His personal preparations for an operation were minimal. According to one of his later house surgeons, Arthur H Cheatle, Lister would 'button up his coat, turn up his collar and sleeves, and purify his hands. He never wore an overall, mask, or gloves.' Cheatle also described his ordinary dress in 1890. Lister wore a

broad cloth frock coat, always unbuttoned, except when he operated; the sleeves were quite long, reaching well below the wrist. His collar was a stand-up one, with the points turned backward. His tie was a small black satin bow and the trousers a dark-stripe cashmere. His boots . . . had thin soles . . . He wore a silk tall hat, slightly tilted forwards. In the winter he wore a thin dark great-coat, often carelessly put on with the collar sticking out behind. He never wore gloves . . .

Cheatle recalled Lister in relaxed moments. Once he declared, 'I wish germs were as obvious as green paint'. On another occasion after they had finished ward round, he turned to the house surgeon and said: 'Cheatle, you ought to be a very honest man'. Somewhat warily, his assistant asked why. 'Because you Cheat-ill!' Lister replied. John Stewart mentioned Lister's 'propensity... to indulge in *puns*... and the best of them was the half-apologetic, half mischievous smile with which he perpetrated his pun'.

His active professional life was nearing its end, but his mood remained limpid and optimistic despite his querulous insistence, on occasion, that he was not understood by his colleagues. He and Lady Lister went to the Iberian peninsula for a rest in December 1889, as they had the year before. They were at High Cliff for Christmas. On Boxing Day Lister wrote to Mary Godlee thanking her for the 'pretty card of good wishes, and recollections of by gone days'. 'It is a happy thing that while we look back fondly on the past, we may look forward to a brighter and better future.' Lister's Victorian faith in the inevitability of progress contrasts strikingly with the self-doubt and uncertainty reflected in his exaggeration of the opposition to antisepsis. While the private man was frustrated, sometimes embittered and suffered bouts of depression, the public man was safe, dependable, assured and gave testimony to the expanding horizon of public life.

In November 1889 Lister delivered two short public talks, the first in two years. On the 4th he spoke to the Medical Society 'on a New Antiseptic Dressing', displaying the gauze soaked in double cyanide of zinc and mercury. On the 27th he read a paper to the Hunterian Society on 'Two cases of long-standing Dislocation of both Shoulders treated by Operation, with further observations on the Cyanide of Zinc and Mercury'.

He was invited to give a major address to a plenary session of the International Medical Congress to be held in Berlin during August 1890. From Wiesbaden, where he and Lady Lister were taking the waters in April, he wrote to Arthur that he had begun to think about the paper. He intended to review antiseptic surgery. He tried to write the speech at Swanage and Lyme Regis over Whitsun and at St Margaret's Bay later in June: 'at St Margaret's'

15. *Lord Lister, aged about 70, probably taken while he was President of the Royal Society.*

16. A newspaper photograph of Lister when he received the Freedom of the City of London. Dated June 28, 1907. (See page 324.)

he wrote to Arthur from the Tyrol after the Congress:

I had really bitterness of anxiety as to what lay before me at Berlin. But on the other hand the full summer beauty of the cliff and cornfields 'did all my weary carking care beguile', & our walks were truly sweet. For the first few days I could'not rest satisfied without reading some articles regarding Metchnikoff's phagocyte theory, sufficient to make me feel sure that I was not going upon a false basis in making that theory a chief point in my address. The result was that I was much driven at the last. Part of my address was written in the train between Calais & Cologne, part in the garden of the Cologne hotel, more in the train between Cologne and Berlin, and last not least, although we arrived at our hotel at Berlin at 1 am, and had to take supper there, we were up at 5.30, and an important part of the affair was written that morning! Had I only known that the address announced to be given at 11 o'clock would not come off till about 3, I might have taken the matter rather more coolly.

And finished writing the paper at 2.45 rather than 10.45, no doubt!

Lister's paper followed one by Virchow, who was President of the Congress, and came just before Koch's dramatic but sadly premature announcement of a vaccine against tuberculosis. Sir James Paget, one of the English organizers of the meeting, wrote about Lister's 'excellent paper'. Lister said, 'it was delivered to a kind audience'. The entire occasion was another triumph for him. The day after his speech Lister went to a dinner of the German Society of Surgeons attended by some 500 of his fellows. In German he proposed the health of his old friend, Professor Thiersch, President of the Society; 'when Thiersch proposed my health in return', he wrote to his brother, 'there was such a storm of applause and such a coming up of surgeons from all parts of the world to touch glasses with me, as was almost overpowering'. He was elected one of the Presidents of the surgical section of the Congress, and the Empress Frederick, Queen Victoria's daughter, received him.

But enough of this, which begins to look like a dream. Yet I must add an amusing incident. Prof. Baccelli, the chief representative of Italy, and the main author of the great Clinical Institute in Rome, where my effigy is to appear in bas relief on the entrance to the surgical department, on taking leave of me as we came away from Berlin, insisted on embracing me and kissing both my cheeks: which at any rate showed that he did not repent of having given me a place of such distinguished honour in the Institute at Rome.

The 'effigy' appears in one of the tympana above a Roman hospital, the Policlinico Umberto I. A bad attempt at a classical representation, the bas relief shows Lister at the centre beside an operating table complete with patient, lecturing to an audience all of whom are draped, like the Surgeon, in flowing marble robes.

One more doubtful victory awaited Lister in Berlin, one which must have distressed him despite its apparent confirmation of his views. Professor von Bergmann had been converted to the new aseptic surgery. He invited Lister to the University Clinic, recalled Hector Cameron, to see 'some cases of breast amputation which von Bergmann had reserved for Lister's inspection'. Dramatically, he removed the dressings from each successive patient, only to find that every wound was infected. 'The master of us all,' Cameron told his son, 'said never a word of triumph or of comment on that striking vindication of his treatment, either then or later!'

There was a personal sequel to the Berlin Congress which stemmed from Koch's over-optimistic announcement. It is said that Koch had been pushed into premature revelation of the tuberculosis vaccine by the express command of the young Kaiser Wilhelm, who insisted that there must be a German medical breakthrough to launch appropriately the great gathering in his capital. But the responsibility for arousing hope where none could yet be justified must lie upon Koch. In any case Lister returned to Berlin for several days not long after the end of the Congress. He went to observe Koch's treatment, and he took with him a young niece, Jane Harrison's daughter, who had tuberculosis. According to Godlee, she 'was quickly passing, if she had not already passed, into the hopeless stage of a rapid decine'. Lister 'watched from day to day' as the poor girl died.

The incident may have caused a permanent break between Lister and his youngest sister. Her husband, Smith Harrison, had died in 1883. Jane continued to live in South Woodford, Essex, near Arthur Lister's home in Leytonstone. On February 7, 1891, she wrote to her nephew, R J Godlee, from Cannes:

It is strange to look back to the day we met last.—at Park Crescent, when we were going away!— . . . I should most certainly have blamed myself if I had used my influence against the visit to Berlin.—I cannot help wondering why it was that the doctors could not see that the treatment was making her very ill . . . I cannot tell thee how we miss her.—Our one comfort is that she was entirely satisfied with the result of the stay at Berlin!—

Evidently, Jane Harrison had agreed reluctantly to send her daughter to Berlin with Joseph. No further correspondence of any kind connects Lister with the Harrison family, though Jane was the only one of his brothers and sisters to survive him. His Godlee, Pim and Lister nieces and nephews have written about visits with Uncle Joseph and Aunt Agnes. Ten of them initialled the ornate, illustrated copy of *The Great Rift Valley* by J W Gregory as a Christmas present to 'Uncle Joseph', in 1900, but none of the initials could be that of a Harrison, though Jane had other children. If his sister had somehow blamed him for her daughter's death, Lister would have been devastated, but except only the one letter Jane wrote to Godlee, the evidence of a break is negative.

On December 3, 1890, Lister lectured at King's College Hospital on Koch's treatment. He characterized the results as 'simply astounding'. Tuberculin, the inoculum, did not affect the causative germs, he said, but he suggested that it might work by eliminating diseased tissue which is sloughed or absorbed. Bacilli left in healthy tissue cannot grow. So far, immunity to the disease was not bestowed by tuberculin, but new research was then in progress. Recurrences of the disease after inoculation, Lister explained, may be due to pockets of infection that remain. He pointed out that because tuberculin caused a rise in fever and other symptoms only in patients with tuberculosis, it has diagnostic value. Indeed, it is still used for diagnosis if tuberculosis is suspected.

Lister, and probably Koch too, were already well aware of the relapses that occurred after the brief remission often produced by tuberculin. Such was the power of publicity and wishful thinking, even amongst such sophisticated research workers, that the relapses were somehow seen as mere incidents in the recovery process. Much of the history of biological science during the last century has been occupied by the search for safeguards against such subjective misjudgements, but they still happen.

On December 18, 1890, for the first time at King's, Lister began the inoculation of a patient with 'Koch's lymph'. After an operation by Mr Carless to remove carious bone from the knee joint of a fourteen-year-old boy, the patient was given a series of nine injections over a period of eleven days in quantities rising from ·0006 grams to ·01 grams. Two more operations were performed on the knee, and in May the boy received a second series of shots. On June 3 the note, 'Left the hospital cured', appears in the ward journal. During these six months several more patients were treated with tuberculin, but by the middle of 1891 all the world knew of Koch's failure.

From Lyme Regis, where they spent Christmas 1890 Lister wrote to Godlee on 31st December, 'I hope you will not think that the addition in the enclosed to the "customary cheque" is in too mercenary a form for a wedding present. At all events it comes with our best wishes for you both & with the hope that you may lay it out in some way more acceptable than any that might occur to us.' Godlee was about to marry Juliet Seebohm, the daughter of another prominent Quaker family. It seems probable that the 'customary cheque' was Lister's annual Christmas present to his numerous nieces and nephews.

During April 1891 he and Lady Lister went to Swanage. He wrote to Arthur that he had first to decide on the subject of a talk for the Medical Society scheduled for May 4. Then he revised the obituary of their father that he had written for the *Monthly Microscopical Journal* in 1870. The Royal Society had requested a shortened version which 'Agnes is now engaged in copying'. He had also to decide the subjects for a short talk to be given in Edinburgh and a paper he had been asked to write for a *Festschrift*, a celebratory volume of essays, in honour of Virchow. Despite these demands, afternoons were devoted to 'expeditions'. 'Altogether we have seen fifty-six species of birds already.' On April 24 he wrote to Cargill that he would return to London on the 30th and 'visit the hospital at 2 o'clock on Friday, May 1st.

The new Clerks & Dressers will, I trust, be in attendance on that day.'

His address to the Medical Society 'On the Coagulation of the Blood in its practical Aspects' was his last visit to this well-trodden territory. It was, Lister said, his first paper without any new research, but that is not strictly the case. For more than a decade he had based addresses on the work of others. The fourth and last Common-place Book covers the years 1890 to 1899. Unlike earlier volumes it contains many references to published papers some of which are précised. Lister's talk to the Medical Society in 1891 draws more on his professional reminiscences, however, than on work by other men.

On May 15 he was in Lyme Regis, but a week later the University of Edinburgh awarded Lister the Cameron Prize in Therapeutics. He spoke on antiseptic surgery, 'A brief lesson', as he said. The *British Medical Journal* called it 'his favourite topic'.

In June he and Lady Lister went to Ilfracombe and Salisbury so that Lister could complete the paper for the Virchow volume. He had also to prepare an address for the forthcoming International Congress of Hygiene in London. The Virchow essay, 'On the Principles of Antiseptic Surgery', contains an important admission of error. He had taught since 1867 that pus in abscesses 'was caused by inflammation which, however it had originated, was kept up by the tension of the pent-up liquid operating through the nervous system'. Alexander Ogston, a Listerian surgeon at Aberdeen, had shown that micrococci always appeared in pus, and Koch had discovered the bacillus of tuberculosis in chronic abscesses, at last demonstrating the connection between the disease and these painful swellings. Lister also said that 'the 1 to 40 solution of carbolic acid . . . has been shown to be far more uniform in its action upon micrococci than corrosive sublimate', and referred to the work of Pasteur's colleague, Behring, on which the statement was based. His willingness to accept new research meant much to his younger contemporaries like Cameron and Godlee who saw the importance of scientific discovery to medicine. They could also see that he accepted work when it fitted into the antiseptic system, but that he rejected the new aseptic practices which stood outside it.

More than 3000 people attended the International Congress of Hygiene. The Prince of Wales was President of the Congress, and Lister presided over the bacteriological section. His Introductory Address contained little of note beyond his welcome to a remarkable assembly of talent. Professor A Laveran, discoverer of the malaria plasmodium, spoke on that disease, and Dr Hueppe of Prague described his cholera toxin. Roux, discoverer of the diphtheria antitoxin, Dr H Buchner of Munich and Dr Almroth Wright, the great British immunologist, introduced a debate on 'Immunity, acquired and natural'. Metchnikoff and Kitasato, Roux's colleagues at the Pasteur Institute, and Dr Joseph Ehrlich of Berlin contributed to the discussion. Without hyperbole Godlee called the debate 'a contest of giants'.

The Friday night before the Congress ended, the Listers gave a large dinner party for the scientists who had read papers before the bacteriological section. The guest list included Ehrlich, Hueppe and Kitasato, Dr Vaughn from Michigan and a number of English bacteriologists, among them Cheyne and Charles Sherrington.

On August 17, immediately after the meetings, Sir Joseph and Lady Lister left for Saas Fe and Pistoja. On the train he wrote to Arthur: 'So now all my tasks in the way of articles and addresses are accomplished and we hope to enjoy some real relaxation'. They were in Switzerland and Italy for seven weeks.

During the spring and summer of 1892 Lady Lister took her sister, Lucy, to Wiesbaden for treatment of 'her nervous susceptibility to noise', as Lister described the complaint in 1895. Lister stayed with them for the first month and returned to Wiesbaden over Whitsun. In late July at the end of his fifteenth academic year at King's, he delivered his last clinical lecture. He gave a résumé of the antiseptic system as it then stood. *The Lancet* noted the occasion of Lister's retirement with a compliment to his youthful manner. He was sixty-five, the retiring age at King's, but the Hospital Board asked him to stay on another year in his wards, chiefly as a consultant. He decided therefore to continue his private practice for another year; according to Godlee, he had determined to retire completely 'when he no longer had such opportunities of constant operating and gaining new experience as . . . are only afforded by the charge of wards in a hospital'.

The Listers went to the Isle of Skye during September and October. Water birds abounded. He described the sightings to Arthur: 'three hooded crows, two redshanks, one greenshank, with kittywakes and black-headed gulls: and just now immediately below the window we have been watching a curlew worriting the sand with its long bill and apparently pulling out sand worms. And we have got a *few* plants, most of them common enough, though new to me, and two or three rarities from Skye.' There were no lectures to draw him back to London.

His only public engagement during this retirement year came in December, and it was one which gave him genuine pleasure. Pasteur's seventieth birthday was celebrated with a special ceremony at the Sorbonne two days after Christmas. Though he was just five years older than Lister, Pasteur had never recovered from his stroke and found it more and more difficult to overcome his disabilities. On January 3, 1889, he had thanked Lister for a seasonal remembrance and for his good wishes. 'The impairment of my speech has become permanent,' Pasteur wrote, 'just as the partial paralysis of my left side has become permanent.' Although the rabies vaccine had now been accepted and provided a brilliant capstone to a career of unique significance to medicine and biology, Pasteur could no longer work. The birthday tribute had very much the air of an acknowledgement while there was still time. Lister represented the Royal Society and the Royal Society of Edinburgh. When he was called upon to speak, he was greeted with tremendous applause. He spoke in French briefly and with unusual grace, assisted by a sense of the indebtedness that he personally owed to this great man. 'Thanks to you, Surgery has undergone a complete revolution which has deprived it of its terrors and enlarged almost without limitations its power for good.' When Lister had finished, Pasteur rose from his seat on the platform to embrace him, according to the official record of the occasion, 'like the living picture of the brotherhood of science in the relief of humanity'.

Pasteur died in September 1895. There was a public funeral, and his body was placed temporarily in Notre-Dame. In January 1896, after a tomb had been built for him in the grounds of the Institut Pasteur, a second ceremony took place. Lister attended. Speaking in French again, he briefly conveyed the respects of the Royal Society, the Royal College of Surgeons, the Medico-Chirurgical Society of London and the British Institute of Preventive Medicine, as well as his own.

On January 18, 1893, Lister lectured at King's 'on the Antiseptic Management of Wounds'. The address defended the antiseptic system against the encroachments of aseptic surgeons. If you drop an instrument on the floor, he said, 'You could not boil it again before going on with the operation; but the bath of carbolic lotion at once puts it right.' If no chemical antiseptic was available, however, then sponges, ligatures and instruments could be boiled, towels could be dipped in boiling water and the surgeon's hands and the patient's skin thoroughly washed. On February 21, furthermore, a note in the Common-place Book indicates that with Lady Lister's assistance, Lister conducted an experiment which he labelled, 'Sponge, Effects of Boiling'. Evidently he had determined to confront the new system squarely, as he had always done, with research of his own.

That same week in Paris a review of Lister's work was read to the Académie des Sciences by M Charcot, the psychologist. On March 6 the Académie elected Lister a Foreign Associate Member to fill the place of his father's old friend, Sir Richard Owen, who had died recently. Two days later Sir James Paget wrote a note of congratulations and invited Lister to lunch with Virchow on March 18. He said that Mr Gladstone would also be present.

That spring the Listers decided again to desert Swanage, this time for the Italian Riviera. According to Lucy Syme, Lady Lister left home on April 2 or 3 with 'a severe cold, and was looking very ill'. Perhaps the warmer air had helped because Godlee said that after about a week of botanizing, she 'was in perfect health'. Lister described what followed in a letter to Hector Cameron dated 'Rapallo 12 Ap 1893'

My dear Cameron
I have this moment received your kind letter. But oh! what news I have to tell. My darling Agnes, after two days of enjoyment of this lovely place, took a shivering fit as

she was helping me to change the papers of some flowers we had collected. She had to go to bed, & soon ensued high temperature, but no definite other symptoms for awhile, till on Monday morning I discovered dullness of the base of one lung, in fact pneumonia. In the evening the other base was affected & from day to day the symptoms became more grave & this morning she left me, about 8.30 a.m. passing away painlessly in a fainting fit brought on by an effort in changing her night clothes. There she lies in the room next to that where I write, looking very sweet, with a beautiful wreath of flowers hung at the bed head, the gift of our landlord's mother. All here are very sympathetic & kind. The doctor (Piaggio) most devoted. My grief, bitter though it is, is sweetened by the extremely beautiful frame of mind in which Agnes was when & after I told her of her danger yesterday afternoon. I never saw her character so beautiful before, full of love for all, thinking almost more of others than herself, and, though very humble, relying in undoubting confidence on our Saviour. So I do not sorrow as those that have no hope! But oh how different life will be to me in the future!

I write to you in openess, as we know one another pretty well. She mentioned many persons to whom she wished messages of most kind regard to be sent; & you were one of them.

I hope to return to London by Saturday afternoon & to make arrangements for having the funeral at a place which she herself suggested!

Excuse hasty scrawl

Yours ever affecty

Joseph Lister

I am glad your thumb is well.

Cameron's thumb had been bitten by a parrot. The injury prevented his operating for several months.

Lister travelled home on the train with the coffin. An acquaintance, Y Stacey Wilson of Birmingham, recalled that he was having breakfast in a railway refreshment room somewhere between Basle and the Channel. 'While there we saw Lord Lister passing through to get his breakfast in another room. I went up and spoke to him but all he said on shaking hands was "I am in great trouble" and passed on'.

Paget too was one of those whom Lady Lister remembered in her last hours. On May 1 he wrote thanking Lister for conveying 'the kind thought of us which she expressed even while she was passing away'. Enclosed with the letter is a manuscript copy of a poem by Tennyson, dated January 14, 1892:

To the Mourners

The bridal garland falls upon the bier,
The shadow of a crown, that o'er him hung,
Has vanish'd in the shadow cast by Death.
So princely, tender, truthful, reverent, pure—
Mourn! That a world-wide Empire mourns with you,
That all the Thrones are clouded by your loss,
Were slender solace. Yet be comforted;
For if this earth be ruled by Perfect Love,
Then, after his brief range of blameless days,
The toll of funeral in an Angel ear

JOSEPH LISTER 1827–1912

Sounds happier than the merriest marriage-bell.
The face of Death is toward the Sun of Life,
His shadow darkens earth: his truer name
Is 'Onward.' no discordance in the roll
And march of that eternal Harmony
Whereto the worlds beat time, tho' faintly heard
Until the great thereafter. Mourn in hope!

12

'...PRETTY UNIVERSAL ACCEPTANCE.'

AGNES LISTER WAS FIFTY-SEVEN when she died, a young woman by the standards of her day. She had been married for thirty-seven years. Godlee said that when Lister's laboratory hours lengthened tediously, 'she showed no signs of impatience'. 'Though not accomplished as a musician or an artist, she was a good linguist, and her mind was stored with knowledge kept well up to date.' These are almost the only personal characteristics assigned to her by the nephew who had lived in the same house and worked closely with her. He stressed her motherly care of Lister, their mutual interests, respect and love, but he could not have been fond of his aunt. She was, it seems, not given to affectionate displays, neither gracious nor particularly elegant, but she must have been immensely practical, hard-headed and not averse to the sight of poverty or blood. Perhaps to Godlee Agnes Lister lacked those ideal traits of womankind implicit in the pre-Raphaelite image, but to her husband, brought up by pragmatic Quaker women, she *served* perfectly. Lister was positively afraid of emotional display. At the age of twenty excessive and conflicting emotional feelings had almost destroyed him. Agnes Lister had been a cool and brainy woman. They loved each other, and when she died so unexpectedly, 'Lister was a solitary man', as Godlee said.

Lucy Syme, Miss Syme as she was always known, stayed on as his housekeeper at Lister's 'urgent request', she said. 'It was not my *intention* to remain, but I could not refuse—after his GREAT kindness in having invited me, after my Father's death, to make his house my home.' Sentences with italics and capital letters were not Lister's usual style, but perhaps they both preferred the devil they knew. Excepting for occasional small dinner parties, his entertaining stopped, and his laboratory work all but came to a halt.

His career had ended, but he had nineteen lonely, dreary years to live. Still, it is too much to say that when Lady Lister died, 'the whole course of his life was altered', as Godlee wrote. The tendency toward existence on a single plane merely intensified. It is almost as though he had no further need for a mind or personality apart from the public image that he had constructed.

For the moment he went back to his practice as though for consolation. His letters were now written on note paper with such a wide black border—almost an inch—that there was scarcely room for the message. Naturally social engagements were abandoned. On April 20 Lord Leighton, President of the Royal Academy of Arts, wrote to him expressing sympathy for 'the terrible affliction which has befallen you so suddenly and which must deprive us of the pleasure of entertaining you on the 29th'. On the next day, however, Lister wrote to his house surgeon: 'I expect to be back at my duty in the Hospital in the middle of May'. The ward journal, now being kept by his nephew, Arthur Hugh Lister, as clinical clerk, shows that he performed an operation on May 16. But his final retirement was very near. On July 24, 1893, he performed two operations, the first to open an abscess and the second to remove a tumour. They were the last he did at King's.

Later in the year some of his friends who were Fellows of the Royal Society thought to lighten Lister's retreat into depression by electing him Foreign Secretary of the Royal Society. The idea seems to have originated with Dr T Lauder Brunton, Professor of Materia Medica at St Bartholomew's, at the end of October. The Council had already nominated Professor Edward Thorpe, a chemist at the Royal College of Science, but Brunton and three Council members, Michael Foster, Professor of Physiology at Cambridge, Sir Norman Lockyer, Professor of Astronomical Physics at the Royal College of Science, and Sir Archibald Geikie, the retiring Foreign Secretary, were able to have the nomination withdrawn. Brunton had meanwhile called on Lister, who at first refused, both because he had no heart for the job and because the whiff of politics did not much please him. On November 2, however, Geikie called 'with a message from the officers of the Royal Society expressing their desire that I should take the Foreign Secretaryship', he wrote to Brunton. Geikie put his mind at rest as to the amount of work there was to be done as well as making it clear that the Council wanted him in the job. Brunton acknowledged Lister's acceptance with 'very great pleasure' on the same day. He pointed out that Lister could help 'to heal . . . the breach that was forming and beginning to widen between the chemists and physicists on the one hand and the biologists, especially the physicians on the other'.

In May 1894 Lister went to Glasgow, this time to address the Medico-Chirurgical Society 'On the Simplification of the Antiseptic System'. The talk was devoted chiefly to the most recent work on immunity by Metchnikoff, which showed once more that excessive application of anti-septics might interfere with the body's normal defences. 'When the meeting ended,' he wrote to Arthur, 'the students must needs unyoke the horse and draw and push me by a circuitous route' to Hector Cameron's house where he was staying—'a distance of over a mile', according to *The Lancet*, whose correspondent also mentioned 'deafening cheers'.

Soon afterwards he suffered another severe loss, with the death of his eldest sister, Mary Godlee. On August 10 he wrote to one of her sons:

Your dear mother's departure is of course a different thing to me to what it is to her children. But in some respects her loss seems even greater to myself. Being 7 years older than I, she was associated with my earliest recollections & with her is gone a link with the dear past which I feel it very sad to lose.

In the autumn the Royal College of Surgeons commissioned W W Ouless, RA, to paint Lister's portrait. As was customary the artist was approved by Lister, and his fee was paid by subscription. The picture was presented on March 29, 1897, and copies were painted for the Lister Institute and the Royal College of Surgeons of Edinburgh. Meanwhile a second portrait by J H Lorimer, RA, was commissioned by King's College Hospital and presented on July 30, 1895, by Sir John Erichsen. It must have been completed very rapidly: Lister noted on July 17 that he left work that he was doing on catgut to go to a sitting. Copies now hang at Edinburgh and Glasgow Universities. These were the only portraits done during Lister's life. Godlee preferred the one by Ouless to that by Lorimer.

Lister agreed, in March 1895, to preside at the meeting of the British Association to be held in Liverpool during September 1896. In April the Prince of Wales presented him with the Albert Medal of the Society of Arts 'in recognition of his application of antiseptic methods to practical surgery'. From Swanage on April 17 he wrote to Hector Cameron, 'my knee is not yet <u>sound</u> though much better; I have not yet picked up my general strength completely'. Complaints about his health increase in number and seriousness from this time. During July he was in Harrogate chiefly because it was restful there for Lucy.

His friends in the Royal Society now proposed that he succeed Lord Kelvin as President. On July 20 Lister wrote to Cameron, who had been in London recently:

When you left I had, as it were half consented, or rather . . . I had endeavoured to escape on the score of my utter aversion to being pitted against Evans. Michael Foster afterwards wrote & told me that there was such an almost universal feeling in the Council against Evans being President . . . that there was no question whatever of my running in competition with him & that, at the informal meeting of the Council which Lord Kelvin called to talk the matter over, 'they had no difficulty in coming to the conclusion' that I ought to be President. I could wish most heartily that it had been otherwise.

Sir John Evans, an archaeologist, was Treasurer of the Royal Society. Thus in December Lister was elected, being only the second surgeon to fill the position. His predecessor, Sir Benjamin Collins Brodie, had been the first president of the General Medical Council. One of Lister's earliest uses of Presidential power led to the election of Elie Metchnikoff as a Fellow, an honour for which Metchnikoff thanked him at the time. He continued in the Presidency until 1901.

A new interest now manifested itself. In October 1895 Lister was listed for the first time as a Patron of the Howard Association, forerunner of the Howard League for Prison Reform. Though not officially allied to the Society of Friends, the Association had strong Quaker connections. John Howard, the prison reformer who had also taken an interest in hospital hygiene, was a Quaker. In 1895 Thomas Hodgkin, the brother of Lister's fellow lodger at University College, and J Gurney Barclay, the banker and an old friend of the Lister family, were members of the General Committee. Smith Harrison had been a subscriber, and his widow contributed her guinea each year. Arthur Lister was a member of the General Committee from 1882 to 1886, 1889 to 1891 and 1899 to 1901. Lister was evidently friendly with the Quaker Secretary of the Association, William Tallach. On November 11, 1901, he wrote to Tallach, who had recently had a lung removed, that 'a man may get on with only one lung'. Lister said his own health was good enough for 'a man nearer 75 than 74'. He was listed as a Patron of the Howard Association until 1905 and continued to pay his subscription at least until 1908.

On May 7, 1896, the magazine *Nature* carried an article on Lister as the 29th in a series called 'Scientific Worthies'. It was written by a German surgeon, H Tillmanns. In addition to the increasingly familiar details of Lister's biography, Tillmanns sought to place his work in the context of contemporary surgery:

... the technique of modern surgery is based on Lister's method, and takes for its watchword 'asepsis without the use of antiseptics'. Antisepsis has given place to asepsis, but the latter is just as surely based on the ground first broken by Lister.

Tillmanns's article helped contemporaries to overcome the apparent distinction between Lister's teachings and the new surgery. For a moment it looked as though he too might accept the role of asepsis. His lecture at King's early in 1893 and the speech to the Glasgow students in May 1894 stressed the importance of scrupulous cleanliness. He recognized 'that those surgeons who get such results of uniform success as ought to be got with antiseptic treatment are still but few in number', and he insisted that failure occurred only when general cleanliness was ignored. There was good reason for his argument. Even in Edinburgh there was evidence that some of his former colleagues who followed his method neither understood nor believed in his principles. The acceptance of the scientific foundations of Lister's work awaited the attainment by his students of positions of authority. Antiseptics *and* cleanliness were required to obtain asepsis.

In July 1903 Dr T D Griffiths delivered the Presidential Address to the British Medical Association on 'The Evolution of Antiseptic Surgery and Its Influence on the Progress and Advancement of Bacteriology and Therapeutics'. He cautioned against the abandonment of antiseptics, as Lister would have done, but he pointed out that Lister recognized the importance of the body's natural defences. 'It is therefore evident that the acme of safety is secured in open surgery by the judicious application of the two principles advocated and practised by Lister.' But the appearance of unity was chimerical as far as 'the master of us all' was concerned.

Three years later Lister wrote to Hector Cameron about the publication of Cameron's lectures on antiseptic surgery to which he was to add a note on the catgut ligature. He preferred *The Lancet* for publication, he said, because it was read more abroad although the *British Medical Journal* had a wider domestic readership.

Then I fancy the Lancet would give more whole-hearted support to the antiseptic doctrine than the Journal. After the meeting last year (if I recollect rightly) The B.M.L. adopted the word 'aseptic' instead of antiseptic in a leader on the subject. This the Lancet has never done.

So significant had the *word* become that Lister could overlook the bitter years after he first came to London, when the *BMJ* had been his only staunch ally. His disapproval of aseptic surgery reflected his paranoia more than his own rational grasp of the facts. At the end of 1908 he wrote to Cameron from Walmer, Kent, that he was 'greatly disappointed' because 'Cheyne had adopted gloves' for operations. 'I also regret that he advises sterilizing instruments by heat (boiling) without any reference to 1 to 20 solution.' One of his last letters, written by Lucy Syme to Lister's dictation on January 5, 1910, was addressed to Cheyne:

You must forgive me if I express my regret at what you say about the use of gloves because it may convey to some minds the idea that you distrust carbolic lotion for the disinfection of the hands—

That the argument was intellectually fruitless, Cameron, Godlee and others pointed out. Sadly, the new surgery eased the surgeon's lot rather more than that of the patient. Erysipelas and cellulitis continued to appear in hospitals and to figure in mortality rates. When Lister asked in his talk to the Glasgow students in 1894 why there were still failures, he knew the answer. Established infections could not always be extirpated nor could all bacteria, bacterial spores and viruses be excluded. To Lister, these facts made it all the more urgent to continue to use every weapon available. Yet he also knew that any excess of antiseptics only made matters worse by killing the cells capable of destroying the invaders.

It took the perverse wit of George Bernard Shaw to drive home the point. In 1898 he underwent an operation on his left foot by a Listerian surgeon. For eighteen months, he wrote after Lister had died, he went around on crutches while the wound was regularly dressed with carbolic acid. Once a new surgeon stopped the carbolic ritual, Shaw 'was well in a fortnight'. 'The *fin de siècle* stank of carbolic acid' he said. In Shaw's opinion 'Lister's antiseptic surgery' which 'won him a London statue and a shrine in the temples of medical science, proved a disastrous blunder'. Shaw *disliked* doctors, but he had *two* good feet.

He made another criticism though, that was closer to the mark:

... when war required prompt and speedy surgery wounded soldiers died while Listerious nurses were boiling water to sterilize everything. The Listerics had to be got rid of ...

Shaw knew nothing and would have cared less about the quarrel between boiling and carbolic acid, but he was right about wartime surgery. Godlee said during the First World War, 'with insignificant exceptions, attempts to carry out the antiseptic treatment of recent wounds have ended in failure'. The wounded lay too long in wet and filth. In Godlee's opinion aseptic surgery was even less satisfactory.

Two of Godlee's fellow medical officers drew much the same conclusion. Dr Almroth Wright of St Mary's, Paddington, published research from 1915 onwards demonstrating that antiseptics did not eliminate bacteria from contaminated wounds. In 1919, with his student, a young Captain named Alexander Fleming, Wright wrote in *The Lancet*:

The surgeon who treats wounds with antiseptics assumes the organism is unable to deal with the infecting microbes. The proper assumption would be that the organism must—for else there would be bacterial infections from which nobody could recover—be competent to deal with every species of microbe.

Yet they died under aseptic treatment too, and for the very reason—wound infection—that had led Lister to try carbolic acid in the first place. Not until the introduction of antibiotics, in 1935, was it possible to supplement the natural defences of the body with drugs that *selectively* destroyed bacteria. Even now many viruses are not sensitive to antibiotics, and there are bacteria which have acquired resistance to them. Surgery still opens the envelope of the body to potentially-inimical invaders. But today the risk is far greater that the patient will die of some process ancillary to the operation, such as shock. Lister lowered the death rate to about 5%, but he also vastly expanded both the number of operations and the complexity of those it was considered safe to try. The aseptic surgeon could do no better. Lister practised and taught surgery as safe as the technology and the drugs he knew could achieve.

By accepting the Presidency of the British Association, with the Presidential address that the position required, Lister accepted for the first time the obligation of speaking to a non-medical audience. The British Association 'excludes from her sections medicine in all its branches', he noted. Until 1896 his most popular audiences had consisted of students.

During July and August 1896 he and Miss Syme were at Malvern where, as he told Godlee, he hoped to get the 'address for Liverpool concocted'. He also congratulated his nephew on being appointed Surgeon to the Royal

Household in Ordinary, but denied that he had influenced the appointment in any way. Lister was then Surgeon Extraordinary to the Queen, a consultative rather than a practising position.

His address 'on the Interdependence of Science and the Healing Art' was delivered on September 16. The title made explicit Lister's role as he saw it, and as the medical profession had at last come to appreciate it. He had previously spoken only to 'my dearly loved profession', he said, because he had feared that any other course 'might seem to savour of self-advertisement'. Now that he had retired, that consideration no longer applied.

Almost at the start the speech introduced a new technological wonder. Roentgen's paper describing what were later identified as x-rays had been published on December 28, 1895, and a translation appeared in *Nature* a month later. Probably at its conversazione in May, Lister had shown the Royal Society a Roentgen-ray picture of a bullet embedded in a hand that had been sent to him by Oliver Lodge, Professor of Physics at University College. So far the rays were a curiosity, but Lister had asked his Royal Society audience whether they might not be used for diagnosis. He also wondered whether excessive use of the rays could affect the body, including the internal organs, 'with a sort of aggravating sunburn'! Later in the address to the British Association, he said: 'The improvements of the microscope, based on the principle established by my father . . . have apparently nearly reached the limits of what is possible'. Roentgen rays introduced a new science and brought new methods of diagnosis and treatment, as the microscope had done in the seventeenth century.

The greater part of the speech dealt with Pasteur's discovery of the germ theory and the subsequent development of bacteriology. He then turned briefly to the new science of immunology. Again he emphasized the role of these abstruse notions in the everyday lives of people. There had been an outbreak of smallpox earlier that year in Gloucester, but the Guardians should not be blamed, he said. They are 'not sanitary authorities, and had not the technical knowledge necessary to enable them to judge between the teachings of true science and the declamations of misguided, though well-meaning, enthusiasts' who oppose the use of vaccination. 'Would that the entire country and our legislature might take duly to heart this object-lesson'.

The address must rank as Lister's most important statement. No wonder *The Times* was complimentary the next day. He brilliantly described the bacteriology on which his discovery had been based, the antiseptic system that had evolved from that knowledge, and the most recent observations of phagocytes which showed why antiseptics had their limitations. 'On the Interdepencence of Science and the Healing Art' provides the evidence of Lister's greatness. He had not only made surgery safer, but he had sold the germ theory, indeed science itself, first to a resistant medical establishment and then to the public. With this talk Lister made it clear that he understood what he had accomplished.

Happily, whatever his personal Calvary, he was not one of those misunderstood geniuses like Semmelweis. Dr Dawson Williams, editor of the *British Medical Journal*, wrote to Sir Hector Cameron on February 13, 1907, proposing that a collection of Lister's papers be published as a fitting memorial on his eightieth birthday. He had already discussed the idea with C J Martin, Director of the Lister Institute:

Dr Martin thinks, and I have no doubt that he is right, that such a collection would show that Lord Lister did pioneer work with regard to our conception of infectious diseases over a wider field than is covered by the system of surgical practice identified with his name.

To mark the successful conclusion of the British Association meeting, a grand dinner was given in the Liverpool Philharmonic Hall. Of the 360 guests the most eminent included the Lord Mayor, who was the Earl of Derby, Lord Kelvin, Sir William Turner and Professor Burdon-Sanderson. Lister was in the Chair. John Beddoe, the friend with whom Lister had climbed the Salisbury Crags with near-disastrous results forty-two years before, had one memory of the dinner: 'Lord Derby made a good hit . . . when, in proposing the health of Lister, he said the toast would be received with enthusiasm by any audience in Europe, except it were an audience of bacilli'.

At the annual Fellows' dinner of the Royal Society in December, Lister gave the first of his five Presidential addresses. These talks reviewed outstanding work done by the Fellows during the year and named the winners of the Royal Society's various prizes. In addition to 'Roentgen's great discovery' Lister noted, in 1896, the identification of helium by Professor William Ramsay of University College, London. The next year Lister was able to announce the award of the Copley Medal to Rudolph Kölliker, the Professor of Physiology at Würzburg whose work on muscle tissue had formed a foundation for Lister's first research papers. Kölliker, who was then eighty, wrote a cordial letter of thanks. In the same address Lister reviewed the work of Yersin of the Pasteur Institute, whose plague vaccine had been tested in Bombay beginning in February. Yersin had discovered the microbe in Hongkong in 1894 and had first tried out the vaccine in China. It had been the Royal Society which induced the India Office to open the huge Indian seaport to him.

The next year Karl Pearson was awarded the Darwin Medal for applying probability statistics to evolutionary theory. In 1899 Lister reviewed Haffkine's preventive inoculation for cholera and Metchnikoff's 'anti-infective immunization'. He gave a further report on Yersin's trial of plague vaccine in Bombay. These Presidential addresses give a running history of science as new discoveries multiplied at the end of the last century. At the dinner in December 1900 Lister announced that he would retire the following year.

His culminating honour, though by no means his last, came in the New Year Jubilee Honours List of 1897. At the recommendation of the Prime Minister, the Conservative Lord Salisbury, the Queen created Lister a Baron. Cameron, who must have had advance notice from Lister, wrote his former Chief on New Year's Day suggesting the title which Lister took: Lord Lister of Lyme. His arms were based on arms which Joseph Jackson had taken the trouble to have copied from *The Peerage and Baronetage* when his eldest son was still alive. Lister's motto was *Malo mori quam foedari*. He was the first medical man to be elevated to the peerage, though Benjamin Brodie, the surgeon who had also served as President of the Royal Society, had been offered the honour. Brodie had refused because he considered himself too poor a man to support the title!

Of the dozens of congratulatory letters and telegrams that Lister received, four exemplify the variety of his well-wishers. Charles Sherrington, now a physiologist in Liverpool, wrote a very formal note. Sherrington became Britain's first great neurophysiologist, and his admiration for Lister may have been based in part on the operations to repair nerve trunks.

From the Office of the Chief Rabbi of Great Britain there came a brief informal note signed by the incumbent, H Adler. What connections Lister had with the Jewish community, if any, are unknown. It is probable that many of his patients and his principal suppliers of chemicals were Jewish. In June 1899, according to a letter Lister wrote to Hector Cameron's son, he attended a dinner given by a large Jewish club to honour Haffkine. Lister said: 'I was called upon to give the mixed company an account of Haffkine's work'. None of his dealings with Jews appear to have had any special significance, excepting possibly the fact that they took place. The medical profession seems to have been no less subject to anti-Semitism than any other major group in Britain. Lister's Quaker tolerance had evidently vaccinated him against it.

A third congratulatory letter was from Metchnikoff, who also thanked Lister for the reference to his work in the Liverpool address. 'I am sending you a copy of the number of the Bibliotheka medica which contains the paper by M Sautchenko on the cancer parasite', he added in French. The germ theory, like any other powerful theory of causation, produced observations of things that were not there.

Finally Lister received this brief note, also in French: 'Mme. Pasteur begs Lord Lister to pardon her unintentionally tardy congratulations on his new title. What joy M Pasteur would have had to send his most affectionate regards with hers'.

Lord Lister was introduced to the House of Lords by Lords Watson and Playfair on February 23, 1897. His maiden speech on May 17 supported a motion to reinstate the Contagious Diseases Act of 1869 which was subsequently withdrawn. At issue was the means of controlling the increasing incidence of venereal disease amongst British troops in India. The proposal of the Secretary of State for India did not go far enough, Lister felt, but the former act,

made special provision for chaplains to attend the women under treatment in hospital, with a view to their moral improvement. And I have been informed . . . that it was not a rare thing for them to be restored to a virtuous course of life; and this does not surprise me. I know as a hospital surgeon how very wholesome a moral influence residence in hospital does exert upon people of the lower classes . . .

He shared these attitudes with Florence Nightingale, who had reversed her original opposition to regulation of prostitution and medical inspection. *The Lancet* noted that, 'He spoke without undue nervousness', perhaps the kindest thing that could be said about the speech.

His second on August 4, 1898, supported the Government's Vaccination Bill. Several outbreaks of smallpox such as that in Gloucester had made it imperative to strengthen the existing law. The original Government Bill had dropped the conscience clause, but the House of Commons had restored it. Despite his opposition to the clause, Lister spoke for the Bill because it did introduce minimal administrative improvements in vaccination procedures. He made only one more statement in the House of Lords. In 1900 he supported the Early Closing Bill.

It was not a brilliant record. As Godlee said, 'he was . . . obliged, with evident reluctance, to look at his subject from the point of view of the politician, and to accept the second best because the very best was not obtainable'. That he spoke at all in so uncongenial a setting affords an insight into the strength of his sense of duty. In September 1898 after the debate on the Vaccination Bill, he went to Brecon alone. He was worn out, he wrote to Arthur, by 'the excessive heat, and . . . the real worry connected with the Vaccination Bill'.

On January 20, 1897, Lister spoke in Belfast at the opening of new laboratories at Queens College. His subject was 'the Value of Pathological Research'.

Early in February he accepted the Presidency of the General Lying-in Hospital where, according to *The Lancet*, he had been a consulting surgeon 'for many years'. He had one other hospital connection. In 1899 he became President of St Mary's Hospital for Women and Children in Plaistow, very near to Upton Park. He held the office until 1908 when he accepted the position of Patron instead.

In the early months of 1897, he also became chairman of the Distribution Committee of what came to be called King Edward's Hospital Fund for London, a charitable undertaking designed to provide London hospitals with money above the fees they charged so that they could continue to treat indigent patients. On March 16, 1898, following a discussion with the Prince of Wales at Marlborough House, his official residence, Lister wrote a letter to the Prince containing a long, useful analysis of the problem confronting the Fund and how it might best be resolved. He pointed out that without the support of the medical profession, the Fund could not prosper. Yet his lay Committee lacked the knowledge to judge whether 'the principles on which they are conducted' justified helping certain hospitals in preference to others. He gave three examples. The first concerned the so-called Mattei treatment for cancer, one of many nostrums that have been tried only to fail first in the eyes of the doctors and then slowly, after some years, in the hopeful heart of the general public. As early as 1892 Lister's clinical clerk noted in the King's College Hospital ward journal that a 'patient has had the "Mattei" treatment and got rapidly worse'. Lister told the Prince of Wales that 'persons moving in high circles' still favoured this fallacious system, but if money were to be granted to a hospital that practised it, the Fund would at once lose the support of medical opinion. Similarly, although the Temperance Hospital did 'excellent work' its refusal to allow practitioners the right to prescribe alcoholic drinks for their patients represented an unwarranted interference with the doctor's freedom to treat his patient solely on the basis of his technical knowledge and professional judgement.

The third example was evidently even more delicate because it appeared elsewhere in the letter though its admonitory effect was the same as the first two. In the discussion that preceded the writing of the letter the Prince of Wales had 'referred to the subject of homeopathy'. Homeopathy, Lister said, was based on the 'essential doctrine' of 'Like cures like', which 'as a dogma of universal application in the treatment of disease is perfectly untenable scientifically'. To grant money to hospitals that practised homeopathy would alienate the sympathy of the medical profession.

To avoid such pitfalls, Lister suggested that an existing body with medical members and hospital experience be regularly consulted by the Fund. The eleven leading London hospitals had recently established the Central Hospital Council to coordinate matters of policy and management. Lister recommended that this Council be asked to advise on distribution. The suggestion was accepted. Lister continued to chair the Committee until after Edward VII's accession in 1902.

In April 1897 Lister and Sir James Paget were given the Honorary Medal of the Royal College of Surgeons of Edinburgh. He went to Edinburgh to receive the award in June and was asked to become a member of the Council of the College. Although he had served on the Council until 1888, he now refused.

He had observed his seventieth birthday in April. To celebrate the occasion his former house surgeons, clerks and dressers, or as many of the 700 or so who had filled those offices as could be got together, organized a great banquet in his honour at the Café Royal. It was held on May 26, 1897, and St Clair Thomson, secretary of the organizing committee, said there were 130 guests, some from South Africa and South America. Professor Joseph Coats of Glasgow University presided. The address was presented by R Hamilton Ramsay, Lister's 'bouquet friend' of the early Edinburgh years and now his oldest surviving house surgeon. Reverend J E London, MRCS, presented a second address 'from the native practitioners of British Guiana'. Flowers were supplied by another former student who now practised in Guernsey. It was a typically Victorian celebration of speeches and reminiscences, a twelve-course meal and a magnificent selection of wines.

Two days later Lister was a guest of the Glasgow University Club at a dinner again held at the Café Royal. On this occasion, as sometimes in the past with more unfortunate results, he allowed the event to dictate his sentiments. *The Lancet* reported him as having said that he had spent the 'happiest years of his life at Glasgow'.

On June 2 he refused an invitation to preside at the Sanitary Institute Congress at Leeds that autumn. He had decided to attend the meetings of the British Association and the British Medical Association, both of which were held in Canada in 1897. The British Association met first, in August. Lister attended the zoological section but made no formal address. With Lord Kelvin, Lord Rayleigh and Sir John Evans he received the degree of Doctor of Laws from the University of Toronto.

The BMA met in Montreal. On August 31 Lister addressed the Medico-Chirurgical Society of Montreal, and the next day McGill University gave him an honorary degree. Lister did not speak to the BMA, but his name was frequently on the lips of speakers. The Cambridge physiologist, Michael Foster, said: 'In early life Lister belonged to a Society the members of which called all men Friends, and now in turn, because of his inestimable beneficence and service to mankind, all men the world over call him Friend'.

When the meeting ended, the Canadian Pacific Railway put a special car at Lister's disposal. With Arthur and two of his daughters, and Professor and Mrs Foster, he made a three-week tour of the West during which they spent several days in Yellowstone National Park.

In April 1898 the universal acclaim accorded Lister on every public occasion involving medicine suffered its last interruption. Lawson Tait, a student at Edinburgh during the 1860s now practising gynaecology in Birmingham, published an article on aseptic surgery. 'Let us hear no more', he wrote, 'of the nonsense about the bad results in surgery of pre-Listerian times as having been cured by Lister. It is not the truth'. Syme and Keith had demonstrated that cleanliness could produce successful surgery. Tait recognized the reality of germs, but said that it was only necessary to clean the surgeon's hands and instruments. The arguments for aseptic surgery were not new, and the personal attack on Lister after so many years was astonishing. Tait had expressed his antagonism to antiseptic surgery on three previous occasions in 1871, 1880 and 1891. In the latter article he said antiseptic doctrines were 'a mere perversion' and a 'strange phase of surgical eccentricity'. *The Lancet* published five replies to that outburst from various parts of the British Isles, all of them opposed to Tait. Whereas his opposition, even as late as 1891, reflected reasonable doubt, it is apparent that he never succeeded in understanding Lister's real contributions to surgery and to medicine. The language he used recalls the unrestrained disputations of the first half of the century and suggests that he bore Lister some personal animosity.

Yet to his contemporaries Lister was never a plaster saint. Despite his fame, lay reports could slight him. Alfred Russell Wallace devoted two pages of his book, *The Wonderful Century*, to antiseptic surgery at the end of a chapter on 'Popular Discoveries in Physiology'. He suggested in 1898 that the spray was still in use in operating theatres, but apart from that inaccuracy, his account is significant because it does not mention Lister's name!

He was beyond reach of this kind of casual neglect by this time. On June 15, 1898, in company with the Commander in Chief of the Army, Lord Wolseley, Lister received the Freedom of the City of Edinburgh. Wolseley delivered what Godlee called 'a soldierly speech'. Lister followed him. He recalled his 'best and happiest years' in Edinburgh, and then drew an analogy between his work and that of Wolseley. 'For the cure of ills in the body-politic he performs operations—bloody, painful, dangerous'. He then gracefully mentioned Sir James Simpson's role in eliminating pain from surgery. In a letter to Arthur he estimated the audience at 2500 and said the speech was well received.

The following day, after visiting a zoo belonging to a member of the Edinburgh faculty and lunching with his old friend, David Christison, Lister went to a reception in his honour at the College of Surgeons. That evening there was a dinner of former Infirmary Residents at which he presided. It was a very busy and tiring visit. Lister welcomed a few days in the Trossachs with Hector Cameron before returning to London and the Vaccination Bill.

In October 1898 Lister participated in two more grand public scientific functions. As President of the Royal Society he introduced Rudolph von Virchow, who delivered the second Huxley lecture at Charing Cross Hospital. Named for Thomas Huxley, who had died in 1895, the lectures permitted eminent scientific figures to describe their work. The first had been delivered by Michael Foster, and Lister was to deliver the third. Virchow was seventy-seven. His cellular hypothesis, first stated in 1858, that all organic matter consisted of distinctive living cells, had 'swept away the false and barren theory of a structureless blastema', Lister said. If all cells derived from pre-existing cells, furthermore, spontaneous generation was impossible.

Two days after the lecture Lister presided at a banquet given in Virchow's honour.

He delivered a speech on October 8 to mark the opening of laboratories which were to become part of the Liverpool School of Tropical Diseases. Victoria University took the occasion to give him a degree of Doctor of Science.

The Liverpool speech reflects Lister's interest in malaria research. He knew Sir Clement Markham who had brought the cinchona plant, the source of quinine, from Peru to India. Sir Donald Ross, Professor of Tropical Medicine at Liverpool, had discovered the mosquito vector of the disease. Ross wrote to Lister in January 1900 thanking him for having sent papers by Grassi, an Italian working in the field of malarial research. Lister devoted a part of his Presidential Address to the Royal Society in 1900 to malaria. It was considered of sufficient importance to be published separately by the *British Medical Journal*. He traced the history of malaria research and described the role played by Grassi, who was awarded the Royal Medal. At the British Association meeting in 1901 Lister again commended Ross, this time in the context of a squabble that had developed between Ross on the one hand and Grassi and some of his colleagues on the other over an issue of scientific precedence.

Malaria had all but disappeared in Britain, but it remained pandemic in the Empire. Lister's own research had ended with a last incomplete entry in the Common-place Book on July 22, 1899. It was timed at 1.20 pm and begins to describe the antiseptic properties of two kinds of catgut. Perhaps now, more than ever, he wished to associate himself with active scientific work.

In June 1899 the Council of the Royal Institute of Public Health awarded Lister its Harben Gold Medal for his contribution to *preventive* medicine. Of all of his honours and awards this was the only one that recognized how much his work underlay not only the acceptance of the germ theory, but its contributions to public health. He actively promoted vaccination, and by raising the general standards of hygiene, personal as well as public, he helped to reduce the incidence of communicable disease.

Lister now spent a large part of each year outside of London either travelling or resting in one of the watering places that he and Miss Syme found comfortable. They went to Swanage in April 1900, indicating that the old charm still lingered there, but in July they spent several weeks at Buxton in Derbyshire. Evidently it suited them, for this was the first of many visits to its fashionable hotels.

His last visit to Paris took place later that summer. In February 1899 he had been elected a special foreign member of the Paris Academy of Medicine. In 1900 another International Exhibition had been mounted and the *Conference Scientia* gave a dinner for Lister. On August 4 he wrote to Cameron: 'About 60 of the best men in the profession attended the banquet. . . . On the morning of the day (Wednesday), I took a steamer down the Seine to St Germain; and as there were very few passengers I had a quiet time for thinking what to say in the evening'. Lucas-Championnière and several other doctors spoke. Lister's reply, in French, was simple and direct: Pasteur had suggested a line which he had done his best to follow.

He returned to Buxton in September. There he was able to write what Godlee called 'the last of his great public addresses', the Huxley lecture. 'I did not wish to give this lecture and absolutely declined early in the year,' he wrote to Sir William Turner. 'But I was afterwards so pressed that I could hardly refuse . . . I am concocting a rechauffe of some of my observations of ancient days which may possibly have some interest for men of the present generation!'

Queen Victoria died in January 1901. Lister wrote to David Christison: 'What a terrible blow the Queen's death was. Yet it seemed to come at about the right time . . . I was in the St George's Chapel at Windsor at the funeral. It was a wonderful sight.' For the past two years he had been Serjeant-Surgeon to the Queen. When he had been offered the position, he had suggested that he should decline it in favour of a younger man. He was told that the Queen insisted. The new King confirmed Lister in the post, which he continued to hold until 1910, long past the time when he would have wished to be relieved of it. Lister was by no means indifferent to these formalities and the honours associated with them. On February 11 he moved the loyal address to Edward VII at the Royal Medical and Chirurgical Society. The report of the loyal address is the first in a batch of press clippings labelled 'Lord Lister', by Durrants Press Cuttings. It is possible that the service was taken by someone else, but there is no reason that the firm should not have been paid by Lister. He devoted at least one letter to Cameron and much thought to the most suitable selection of his titles and honours which he wished to have printed on the title page of his *Collected Papers*.

He was a political Conservative, a firm believer in the benefits that would accrue to those less fortunate than himself educationally as well as financially if he and his peers were acknowledged by the demos. Gladstone had proposed his knighthood tardily, but he had been created a peer at the recommendation of the Conservative Prime Minister. On July 14, 1902, he wrote to Cameron:

So Lord Salisbury has resigned! I attended today a great meeting of the Unionist Party, at which Mr Balfour was most enthusiastically received as the new Prime Minister. Although it is of course right for Lord Salisbury to take well-earned . . . relief from official burdens, I cannot but feel his departure as a heavy blow to the empire.

Lister had served as he believed his class should serve. Within days of the loyal address he spoke at the York Road, Lambeth, Hospital. The inmates of lying-in hospitals, he said, were now better off than private patients had been twenty years before because doctors had been convinced of the importance of antisepsis in combating puerperal fever. He had served as he had wished to when he had spoken in Quaker meeting. Then he had incurred his father's displeasure. Joseph Jackson had believed there was a better way for his son, that on balance his talents could be better used in surgery, and Joseph now knew with all his soul that he had proven his father right. Despite the difference in their political labels, Lister's politics were in the same mould as Joseph Jackson's, but Joseph had been able to rise higher and therefore held himself to be that much more responsible. Age had ended his usefulness as a surgeon, but he could still give practical advice and moral leadership.

His faith had been secularized. In his retirement the public platform—and the House of Lords—replaced the operating theatre as his church, and his religion tended toward the practical rather than the dogmatic. On March 31, 1901, he wrote to Evart Barter, vicar of the Grosvenor Chapel:

I trust you will not take it amiss if I suggest that a slightly longer interval might be allowed in presenting the elements in the service . . . so that the two solemn injunctions may not be sounding at the same time in the ears of the recipients.

The following year he sent £10 toward current Chapel expenses and wrote a month later commending changes in the time of service. His pew rental was paid regularly each year, and in 1907 he sent £5 toward repair of the organ. Lister's father had thought Joseph's faith was stronger than his own: 'that faith that cheers thee, a light on the path of life to which I do crave is weak indeed with me,' Joseph Jackson wrote on January 18, 1867. But he had allowed his memories to cloud his judgement. Unlike his father's, Joseph's faith could not protect him against the phantoms of self-doubt.

Like most nineteenth-century scientists in non-Catholic countries Lister believed in a remote, probably benign First Mover. John Stewart had returned to his native Nova Scotia to practise. In June 1894 a year after Lady Lister's death he came to London for a visit. On the 14th he wrote to his mother:

I had a very pleasant evening with my dear old Master, Lister . . . He asked me to dine with him on Thursday and not to trouble dressing, 'just come in any toggery you may have.' I don't think he is giving dinners now. Of course I was glad to go. There was no one there but myself and of course Miss Syme, who now keeps house for him. He had asked Cheyne to come but he was engaged. After dinner we talked of a great many things: of old Edinburgh days: of particular patients: of the career of some of his old students, of politics and religion . . . And went on to say that he really did not feel that he cared to live very long now. 'I would like to say with St Paul that I desire to depart and to be with Christ, which is far better, and I often feel this when I think of my dear wife', but 'then' he said 'we are not to choose these things' . . . We got talking of the curious phases of religious thought, the philosophy of some, that there is no individual immortality but that we only live eternally in the 'race' as it were. He thinks this is 'ridiculous'.

Stewart referred to men who practise 'all the Christian virtues' without 'acknowledging Christ . . . and he said "these men are better than their creed, look at such a man as Huxley for example. If it had not been for Christianity

Huxley would never have been what he is'''. In Britain the Church had acclimatized itself to the new ethos of material progress by maintaining that God had designed the British Empire. In so far as the Church sanctioned knowledge and research as a basis for service, Lister was right. In his judgement of Huxley he merely epitomized his culture, a culture he had helped to create.

The University of Glasgow celebrated its ninth jubilee in June 1901. Lister accepted an invitation, and he attended also as the delegate of the Royal Society. With Lord Kelvin and the American steel millionaire, Andrew Carnegie, who had been born in Dunfurmline, Lister received the degree of Doctor of Laws.

After a brief rest in Buxton he returned to London in order to attend the Tuberculosis Congress. On July 23 he chaired the second general meeting at which Koch read a paper. In it Koch announced that the weight of evidence supported the conclusion that bovine tuberculosis was not transmissible to humans. If this was true, there would be no danger from cows' milk or beef and no need to inspect herds, but unfortunately it is not. In his comment after the paper Lister pointed out that Koch himself had said the evidence was not yet conclusive. After the Congress the Government set up a Royal Commission to investigate. Lister was interested in the Commission's work and made an exception to the rule that he did not interfere directly in the work of the Lister Institute. According to Godlee, he initiated and directed two series of experiments. They were reported in August 1902 but were inconclusive.

Following the Tuberculosis Congress Lister returned to Glasgow for the meeting of the British Association. He took no active part, however. Afterwards he joined Arthur and three of his children 'on an expedition among the islands to Gairloch' in the Hebrides. His niece, Gulielma Lister, recalled that Uncle Joseph 'took a lively interest in trying to follow with us the geology of the coast'.

In mid-October he went to Berlin for the celebrations of Virchow's eightieth birthday. He represented the Royal Society, the anthropological section of the British Association, the Universities of London and Edinburgh, the Faculty of Physicians and Surgeons of Glasgow, the Medico-Chirurgical Society of Edinburgh and the Royal Academy of Medicine of Ireland. At the ceremony he began his short address: 'Revered Master'.

These journeyings and formal addresses began to take their toll. Lister's sense of obligation combined with the imperative that he must show the antiseptic flag, but he was nearing seventy-five. In December 1901 his old friend, Professor Tilanus of Amsterdam, asked him to intercede with the Secretary of War 'on behalf of the ambulance surgeons prisoners in Ceylon'.

Lister replied that the Secretary had made enquiries and had found 'that the circumstances of those prisoners were such that he feared an interview would be fruitless'. Tilanus pressed the matter, and on December 31 Lister replied: 'There must be circumstances which you do not know of that make it impossible to release the surgeons'. In a postscript he added sharply: 'I beg you to give me credit for no lack of good will in this matter'. This unusual display of impatience, indeed rudeness, may have reflected a tiredness that was not relieved by occasional trips to Buxton.

In January and February 1902 he was confined to bed by illness for several weeks. His family pressed him to take a long holiday. A voyage to South Africa via Madeira was proposed, and Isabella Lister, Arthur's eldest daughter, offered to accompany him. On February 24 he wrote to Arthur with some enthusiasm about his plans. He said that his health was making 'progress & have today been twice down to the drawing room & up again. Lucy has been kindness itself in acting as amanuensis, and doing all sorts of things for me'. Apparently she was not interested in the sea voyage, however, and the only other member of the party was Lister's butler, Henry Jones, who said he was 'delighted at the prospect'. On March 13 Lister wrote to his brother: 'Thanks for thy dear farewell greetings', and said he had made his will, utilizing the legal services of his nephew, Theodore Godlee.

According to Gulielma Lister, Isabella 'recalled how, every morning while they were at sea, they read together a chapter of the New Testament in Spanish, an ode of Horace and a canto from Dante's *Divina Commedia*, with Wickstead's translation. He entered into the social life on board, taking interest in the deck games and sometimes distributing the prizes to the successful competitors... In addition to the plants he and my sister collected, his faithful manservant... took long walks and brought back rich supplies.' They returned to London on June 1, 1902, the day the Boer War officially ended.

He returned from South Africa just in time to make the last important professional decision of his life. Edward VII's health had not been strong for some time. In June it became clear that he was suffering from appendicitis, and that the disease had entered the acute stage. The King's doctors felt a natural reluctance to operate until no alternative remained, and the King himself wished above all not to be required to postpone his coronation scheduled for the end of June. On June 24, however, Sir Frederick Treves, one of the three Serjeant Surgeons, along with the King's doctors, Francis H Laking and Thomas Barlow, decided that immediate surgery was imperative. Treves would not act without the advice of the other two Serjeant Surgeons, Sir Thomas Smith and Lord Lister. According to Treves:

The King objected. He did not see the necessity of any further consultation. He said that he was ready and wished the operation to be done at once. I pressed the need of such a consultation on public grounds and grounds of policy. He consented;

314

whereupon I at once sent off my carriage for the two gentlemen named. They were awaiting my message and came at once.

The King received them most kindly. After they had made their examination they agreed with me that there was an abscess and that it should be opened. Sir Thomas Smith was emphatically in favour of immediate operation. Lord Lister hesitated. While he did not oppose operation he said that the other alternative was to wait and to apply fomentations. I did not discuss this point with him but pressed him to say if he was prepared to *advise* delay and fomentation. He hesitated and at last said that he would not go to the length of *advising* that course. I then asked him did he sanction an immediate operation and, with some apparent reluctance, he said he did. Lord Lister did not appear to be at all well and I am confident that he was misled by the fact that the swelling was tympanitic . . .

Lord Lister, as the senior, communicated our decision to the King in the presence of us all. The King at once agreed and was only anxious to have the operation performed as soon as possible. I said that everything would be ready a little after 12. As to the operation itself the King did not exhibit the least anxiety. The operation had never troubled him: his sole concern was the postponement of the coronation.

Treves performed the operation after Lister and Smith had left the palace. The King responded well.

On July 14 Lister wrote to Cameron that healing 'is said to be well advanced. I have not myself seen the patient for a considerable time. What was the immediate cause of my ceasing to attend was a sharp and persistent attack of diarrhoea.' He had remained in London to be on call, however, but now that the King was about to leave, Lister felt that he could too. 'Of course the diarrhoea pulled me down a good deal, & I cannot say that the rheumatism is materially better.' He told Cameron that Professor Macewen of Glasgow was to be knighted in the coronation honours list and added: 'As for me, if his Majesty, instead of loading me with additional honours, could have restored to me something of the old vigour, it would have been more to the purpose!'

The first new honour had been the Order of Merit, instituted by Edward VII and limited to twenty-four members. Only twelve were appointed at the time of the creation of the Order. At the ceremony on August 8, according to a later account, Lister bowed his head so that the King could place the ribbon holding the Order around his neck, but it would not pass over his head. The jewelled medal rested on Lister's nose. The King tried again, but Lister said, 'I think, Sir, that I had better take it away in my hand'. Another observer reported that the King said: 'Lord Lister, I know that if it had not been for you and your work I would not have been here to-day'. Shortly after the ceremony the King admitted Lister to membership of the Privy Council.

After these ceremonies which had marked the postponed coronation, Lister returned to Buxton. He was chiefly afflicted with a 'new enemy', rheumatism. It is not surprising that he should have resented his loss of strength, but rather more so that he displayed no bitterness. Excepting such rare outbursts as the postscript in the letter to Tilanus, his temper appears to have remained benign, indeed resigned. He knew that his active life had

315

ended, and as early as 1894 he had told Stewart he wished it might not go on much longer. Yet here he was at seventy-five, doctor enough to know that his complaints accumulated too slowly to provide a swift release. His resentment turned down the avenue worn by years of struggle against opponents whom he perceived all too often to be merely perverse. Cameron's son, who had come down from Cambridge to become a student at Guy's, dined alone with Lister during 1902: 'I remember . . . that he felt that much of his teaching was still not fully understood and that he deplored his loss of strength'.

In November the Royal Society tendered him a great dinner and awarded him its Copley Medal. The American Ambassador, Mr Bayard, proposed Lister's health with a toast that ended: 'My Lord, it is not a profession, it is not a nation, it is humanity itself which with uncovered head salutes you'. In his response Lister said: 'I worked for years together with exceedingly little encouragement from my professional brethren. There were, however, two great exceptions, my father-in-law and my students'. Young Cameron called attention to Lister's appointments, first to Syme's chair at Edinburgh and then at King's, as evidence that he had enjoyed some additional, very powerful 'encouragement'. His complaint might be put down to the querulous self-pity of a tired old man except that it echoed so many like it, made while he was very much younger and stronger.

On December 9 he observed the fiftieth anniversary of his Fellowship of the Royal College of Surgeons. A telegram came from the King and Queen, and the *British Medical Journal* published a special 'Lister Jubilee' number. There were several foreign contributors as well as articles by Lister's former students. On the 14th he wrote to Cameron: 'Your own contribution is probably the most interesting of all'. He commented on some of the others too: Lucas-Championnière's 'is calculated to do real good; and so is Bloch's'. Bloch was Professor of Clinical Surgery at Copenhagen. Professor Thomas Annandale had been Syme's last assistant and succeeded to Lister's chair at Edinburgh. His 'reminiscences are interesting and kindly; but he is wrong in thinking that I was working at bacteriology before I went to Glasgow'. 'Chiene's is quite nice, and better than I expected,' he said about the paper by his former Edinburgh assistant. The German aseptic surgeon, von Bergmann's 'production is a little ridiculous'. On papers by Cheyne and several others he made no comment at all. Nor did he remark on praise from a young Russian physiologist named Pavlov, who had not written a paper but was quoted in the leader: 'I am convinced that it is only by the development of surgical operations on the alimentary canal that we can hope to understand the exquisite chemical work affected by it'. In a note of thanks to Dr Dawson Williams, Lister said: 'It pleases me not only because "dulce est laudari", but much more because it seems to me calculated . . . greatly to profit many of your readers'.

That Christmas of 1902 was the last he spent at Lyme Regis. The disruption caused by grand-nieces and nephews no longer suited him, and they may also have been a problem for Miss Syme. Early in 1903 they went to Bath. His rheumatism now evolved into what appears to have been arthritis of the hip joint and knee. 'The knee is now quite well,' he wrote to Cameron on February 24, 'and the limb generally much better, so that I can take a slow walk in the park here.' He had felt well enough to come up to London to attend the reception for Joseph Chamberlain at the Guildhall, and the lunch following it at Mansion House that celebrated the peace settlement worked out by the Foreign Secretary in South Africa. He told Cameron that he found the 'proceedings decidedly fatiguing'. Nevertheless he felt duty bound to continue to attend meetings of the Council of the Royal Society. In June he came up for the degree of Doctor of Science from the University of London.

Soon afterwards he and Miss Syme left Bath for Buxton. Early in August Lister suffered what he described as 'a slight paralytic stroke'. He told Cameron that it was 'slight as regards the amount of impairment of power . . . in my right leg, but by no means slight in the way of the nervous instability & general weakness which it occasioned'. Godlee thought the attack was not a stroke, but he made no attempt at an alternative diagnosis. Whatever it was, it momentarily accelerated Lister's slow decline. After it, he further restricted his activities. Not until December was he able to write his own letters again. Then, he and Lucy drove about four miles each morning, and he was able to walk 'a little in the house in the afternoon,' he told Cameron.

Lister's intellectual interest also began to revive. In the same letter he remarked on the biography of Dr John Brown which he had 'read . . . with much interest'. In January he wrote to Arthur that he had read a *Times* report of a speech by the physicist, Oliver Lodge:

Lodge's lecture . . . is indeed intensely interesting; though the reading of it was pretty trying to my poor brain.

I send the last 2 numbers of the Medical Journal, which speak of rays of a totally different description . . . They speak of the x-rays as of the same essential nature as the emanations from Radium, only differing in the length of the waves; whereas the x rays are (like those of light & heat) undulations; while the Radium rays are emanations of material particles. And altogether the reports make an odd mixty maxty . . .

In March Lister noted that Arthur's son, Arthur Hugh, had made successful use of 'radiography'. Later that month he asked Hector Cameron to try a piece of his tannic acid catgut as a ligature. Cameron appears to have misunderstood the request which was repeated in greater detail on May 10.

Among Lister's papers is a leader clipped from the popular *Daily Chronicle*, dated April 5, 1904, his seventy-seventh birthday:

But for the antiseptic and the aseptic surgery of which he is the founder, a multitude of men, alive today, would be dead or maimed. Put the figures at near a million among the white races, and one cannot be far above the mark . . . Lord Lister has made, on a large scale, our English manhood whole.

He had begun to make his own plans for the information of posterity. Before his stroke he had asked Arthur Hugh Lister to collect and publish his papers after his death, and he placed in his will a bequest to his nephew of £1000 for the purpose. On April 16, 1904, he wrote to Arthur: 'I have lately been trying to put down some words which may be of help to Arthur Hugh in the task that he has so kindly undertaken to execute. But it is as yet very slow work.' These notes were never finished.

Lister also realized that some kind of biography was inevitable, and he discussed with Arthur Hugh aspects of such a project that he disliked. Soon after Lister's death Arthur Hugh learned that R J Godlee was planning a biography and wrote to him:

As regards the Life, it would be splendid if you could see your way to undertake it . . . I feel that I ought to tell you that in the old days when he contemplated my preparing a collection of his papers, he was quite definite in expressing the wish that no formal life dealing with his private affairs should be written. He wished anything that was published concerning him . . . to be simply such a record as might give the sequence of his scientific work . . .

Godlee accepted the spirit of Lister's injunction, but he knew that it was impossible to accept the letter, and in consequence wrote a book that is both useful and readable.

Lister's rheumatism improved during the early spring of 1904 and by the end of April his letters were filled with a family problem. Arthur's youngest son, William T Lister, an ophthalmological surgeon, faced a crisis in his career. Lister was concerned 'that his powers should not be overtaxed and that he should have time not only for research but for publication of his results'. He urged that the young man protect himself against a 'break down'. 'I hope I shall not seem too meddlesome', he concluded. Two more letters dealt with William's career problems which were soon resolved satisfactorily. The second, on May 16, expressed Joseph's longing to be with Arthur and his family at Lyme 'were I in a state fitted for doing so!' He and Lucy planned to remain at Buxton with possibly a short trip to London 'on business'. They stayed at Buxton until Christmas time, changing only their hotel. On returning from London in July they went to 'this absurdly named house', the Maison Rouge.

In August Cameron planned to be in London. He appears to have been willing to test Lister's catgut on patients, a reasonably safe procedure which obviously gratified his former Chief. Lister was still in Buxton, and he asked Cameron to pick up the material from the laboratory at Park Crescent. He gave explicit instructions about the drawer and the place in the drawer where the gut was kept, but Cameron took the wrong sample:

. . . thanks apparently to the zealous attentions of my faithful servant Margaret, who changed some dirty newspapers for clean ones in the drawer containing the gut, and so changed also the relative positions of the various samples of gut in the drawer, the top most article (which you took, as requested) was not that which I intended you to try, but some prepared with twice the quantity of Tannin, and older by some ten years than what I wished to have tested!

Apologetically, Lister asked for results anyway.

In October he sent Cameron the right sort of gut, from Buxton. Early the next year he asked for the results of the trials, but then explained that he had really intended for the new gut to be tested in stitches, which were on the surface and could be watched, rather than as ligatures. He wanted to know 'the precise number of days' the material took to dissolve. 'I shall never be likely to make any more . . . In publishing, it would be very undesirable to say about so many days . . . if you knew the enormous amount of trouble I have expended on the mode of preparing this gut, you would have patience with me.' Three days later he explained that he had asked for the trial because of an article that said a similar gut had dissolved too slowly when used for sutures.

Cameron's patience can hardly be doubted. It reflected real friendship as well as affectionate respect. In his *Reminiscences* Cameron describes an incident that took place in Glasgow during the early days when he was Lister's assistant.

It can be dated to a winter afternoon in 1868 when Cameron drove with Lister to the Infirmary in Lister's brougham. The driver had been asked to wait.

We were . . . both busy in Ward 24 when suddenly we heard a scream of alarm outside, the galloping of horses, and immediately afterwards the terrible crash of horses, brougham, and coachman into the deep area which ran along the whole front of the Surgical Hospital. Lister rushed out immediately. It was a cold dark night, and from the stone bridge which spanned the area at the entrance of the main door of the Hospital, I saw the carriage lying on its side with the horses still attached to it; they were kicking violently against the stone wall and every blow with their hoofs emitted showers of sparks in the darkness . . . the coachman. . . was partially pinned under the carriage. Lister running down the grass slope had leapt into the area, when he found the kicking horses between him and the coachman. After most violent kicking they desisted for a minute or two from complete exhaustion. Lister seized the opportunity of jumping over their legs and reaching the coachman. In not more than another minute or two several hospital porters and others . . . got into the area on the other side of the entrance bridge to the hospital, and we raised the brougham a little, so as to enable Lister with some assistance to free the coachman.

The man was taken into the ward where Lister diagnosed a ruptured intestine, but he did nothing. It was still 'considered almost criminal' to open the abdomen surgically because of the danger of infection. Sadly, the coachman died of peritonitis, a victim of Lister's surgical conservatism, but the story reinforces the image of the selfless, fearless man whom Cameron so admired.

In 1879 Lister wrote to Cameron in the tortured prose that only he could create, especially if emotions were concerned, 'the first of three letters I have to thank you for gave me peculiar pleasure, inasmuch as it was simply the outcome of kindly feeling, such as, I assure you, is not wanting on my part towards yourself. I often think of you and wish you could drop in.' When he went to Glasgow to represent the Royal Society at Lord Kelvin's Jubilee in 1896, he asked 'whether it would be quite convenient for you to have me abide at your house at the time mentioned. I would rather be there than anywhere else in Glasgow'. Cameron was the recipient of more details about Lister's health than anyone other than Arthur. Perhaps the intimacy of Lister's correspondence, like his calls on Cameron's professional help, can be partly explained by the fact that Cameron had also lost his wife.

Lister's only other friend among his students was Sir William Watson Cheyne. When Cheyne received his knighthood, Lister wrote: 'I find Miss Syme much prefers Sir Watson to Sir William for you, as so much more distinctive. I thought I might as well let you know this. With renewed congratulations'. This was of course before Cheyne's aseptic apostasy. Amongst the few men of Lister's own generation whom he called friend, only Sir William Turner survived.

On February 1, 1905, Lister wrote to Turner from London. He was feeling stronger, he said, though he was 'far indeed from complete recovery'. His purpose was to arrange with Turner, now Principal of the University of Edinburgh, a gift of the memorabilia from Syme's waiting room.

Much of the rest of 1905 was spent at Wadhurst, Sussex. On December 14 because of his health he refused to represent the Royal Society at a University of Liverpool commemoration. The letter was written from London. He and Lucy lived at Buxton during most of the next year. The pattern of his life had become fixed. Excepting occasional visits to London, all but the winter months were spent in a quiet resort for the elderly. He seldom saw friends or family other than Miss Syme.

He had begun to read the scientific literature again, however. In April 1906 he was excited by an article 'on Vaccines in Surgery' by Mr Gray of Aberdeen. Gray suggested a vaccination against blood-poisoning, and Lister wrote to Cameron that the method might obviate antiseptics. On December 20 he wrote again on the subject: 'Although it must be allowed that the "vaccine treatment" is still in an inchoate condition, yet the evidence in its favour is such that it would hardly be right to pronounce it as valueless'. For physiological reasons the idea is impractical; too many different organisms can cause the hospital diseases so that inoculation against one is relatively useless. But it is interesting that Lister should respond with sympathy to a 'vaccine treatment' while aseptic surgery was anathema. There are probably two related reasons. Vaccination is a specific treatment against a known organism. Like an antiseptic, vaccination meant that a drug was to be added to the therapeutic regimen for a rational reason, whereas aseptic techniques implied the arbitrary withdrawal of agents of proven value.

That Lister should continue to press the case for strong antiseptics is not surprising, but that in his eightieth year he should pursue new ideas for research that could prove or disprove his contentions is indeed remarkable. 'With reference to your case of tetanus in a compound fracture of the jaw,' he wrote to Cameron on June 4, 1906:

a very interesting observation was made several years ago by two French bacteriologists Messrs Vaillard & Vincent, that tetanus bacilli are unable to develop when injected among the tissues of an animal, if they are in pure culture and washed of their toxin; though they grow with the utmost readiness if, while in pure culture, they have their toxin along with them.

He supposed that 'these facts may furnish an explanation of the efficacy of antiseptic treatment in preventing tetanus,' and went on to explain why. As he stated it, his hypothesis has not been demonstrated, but its great merit was that it suggested experiments by means of which the theory could be tested.

Dr Peter Paterson, a surgeon at the Glasgow Royal Infirmary, had published an article describing a new therapy for tuberculosis. In correspondence with Paterson during August and September 1906 Lister again made suggestions for further research, though he qualified them by admitting that he was 'so much out of the scientific world' that he found it hard to judge Paterson's results.

In January 1907 Lister returned to a project that he had thought about for some time, republication of his Huxley lecture on the development of the antiseptic method. At the time of its delivery in 1900 it had appeared in both the *British Medical Journal* and *The Lancet*. He wanted to correct 'various inaccuracies' and hoped that a pamphlet might be useful to doctors in America and on the continent. The pamphlet did appear in 1907, but the reason for it had been obviated by a larger project.

At the end of 1906 Dawson Williams had suggested to C J Martin, the Director of the Lister Institute, that a collection of Lister's papers might be an appropriate recognition for his forthcoming eightieth birthday. Martin agreed, but in light of the fact that the event was only four months away, it seems unlikely that either man could have been alive to the size of the undertaking. They certainly did not know that Lister had discussed posthumous publication of his papers with his nephew. Cheyne approached Lister about the Williams proposal, and learned that he was delighted to abandon his own plans in favour of the new scheme. The £1000 set aside in his will for Arthur Hugh Lister's expenses, he said, could be made available at once.

On February 14, 1907, Williams discussed the project with surgeons assembled for a dinner at the Hunterian Society and found universal approval. He suggested that a committee consisting of Godlee, Cheyne, Cameron and C J Martin undertake the task. In the end Williams too became a very active member. On February 23 Dr Martin wrote to Lister defining the project and Lister's relation to it, as the editors saw it. He said that there were about 450,000 words in the whole of Lister's papers. The committee thought there would be no problem about finding a publisher. The University of Glasgow Press seemed the most likely, but through the intercession of friends as the work slowly progressed, the Clarendon Press, Oxford, eventually brought out the two volume work. The committee would not permit Lister to share any of the financial responsibility, but they wanted his 'help', Martin wrote, 'in choosing and arranging papers and other little matters in which it is our desire to consult your wishes. Although to the outside world we will keep up the fiction that you are to be more or less innocent of our scheme.'

Largely because of Lister's 'help', there were delays. On January 23, 1908, Williams wrote to Godlee that the papers had been arranged under five headings 'approved by Lister'. 'But he still had some more notes which he wished to write for insertion at various points. I waited rather more than a fortnight and then, having heard nothing, wrote suggesting that Parts I, II, and III which are I believe complete—barring the Notes—should be sent to the Clarendon Press, & that the Notes should be inserted . . . in the proofs. He has acquiesced.'

At last, in May 1909, the work was ready for publication, when a fire at the Oxford University Press warehouse in Aldersgate Street damaged or destroyed the bound copies. Fortunately 1500 sets of unbound sheets remained at Oxford. The *Collected Papers* were published on June 5, 1909, more than two years after the occasion for which they had been intended.

Meanwhile, on Lister's eightieth birthday, April 6, 1907, the *BMJ* published two lectures that Cameron had given the previous July on 'Lord Lister and the evolution of Wound treatment during the last forty years'. To them Lister had added a signed Note on the double cyanide dressing. It is a brief review of work done twenty years before, the content of which could easily have been made a part of Cameron's papers. But it was the first item by Lister to be published in six years and his name still had an immense cachet. It is also possible that Cameron and Dawson Williams decided to make the Note a birthday present.

Lister suggested to Cameron that the lectures should be published as a pamphlet and proposed to pay half the cost. Cameron refused, and on May 17 Lister offered to pay the cost of mailing the pamphlet. He sent Cameron £8.9.6, 'which indeed seems very moderate'. It was in fact half the cost of the pamphlet.

If he was not a wealthy man, Lister was financially secure. The bequests in his will amounted to more than £30,000 exclusive of property. Much of his money must have accrued from the intelligent management of securities left to him by his father. For at least twenty years, after 1869, he probably lived on his professional income. To that he had added income from his securities, and possibly also the money that Lady Lister had inherited from her father.

The City of London made him a Freeman on June 28, 1907. A photograph of the ceremony shows Lister seated. He is wearing a top hat and coat. His full beard and thick hair are quite white. The face is thin, the mouth unusually drawn out by the moustache and beard, and he looks very tired. A month later he offered the casket containing the Freedom along with the Gold Casket given to him by the city of Edinburgh to the University of Edinburgh because of his 'sympathy' with a teaching university.

In July Lister wrote to his chemical suppliers, T Morson and Son of London, asking them for a sample of a chromium sulphate preparation. He questioned the formula Morson were using and offered them his own. They accepted it with thanks. He was preparing a paper on catgut. Both the *British Medical Journal* and *The Lancet* published it on January 18, 1908.

Three months later on April 11 both journals published 'Remarks on the Treatment of Fractures of the Patella of long standing', a letter that Lister had written in 1895 to Dr White of Philadelphia. In June they both published 'Remarks on some Points in the History of Antiseptic Surgery', an 'unfinished letter to Sir Hector Cameron written in early 1906 before his lectures, but never sent to him', as Lister wrote in a preface that appeared with the article.

His health had begun again to deteriorate in October 1907. He told Cameron that he had had shingles which had left him with 'very troublesome neuralgia'. The City of Glasgow wished to confer upon him its Freedom, but Lister felt that he was unable to make the journey. The Lord Provost offered to come to London to present the document. In the end Lister asked Cameron to accept it on his behalf at a ceremony on January 21, 1908. A few days later he wrote to Arthur that Cameron's 'eulogy is excessive', but he was pleased by it.

On the same day that he wrote to Arthur the Librarian at Windsor conveyed to Lister the King's wish to have a 'drawn portrait of every holder of the Order of Merit'. The request was never honoured.

It was also in January 1908, following the death of Lord Kelvin, that the General Council of the University of Glasgow informally asked Lister whether he would accept the Chancellorship. He wrote to Arthur:

I shall of course decline the proferred honour. It would be most undesirable in the interests of the University that the high office of Chancellor should be held by one who could take no part whatever in the University's business. Of course, considering the composition of the General Council, including graduates in all the Faculties, the kindness of the proposal is remarkable.

To the Principal of the University, he said: 'I am so very enfeebled by illness that there is no prospect of my ever being able to visit Glasgow & in my hands the high office of chancellor wd be an absolute sinecure'.

A week later in London he was given the Mary Kingsley Medal of the Liverpool School of Tropical Medicine. To his brother he wrote on February

323

10, 'The honours that have been heaped upon me of late have this that is satisfactory about them, that they may tend to give greater weight to my work in the past and promote its usefulness'. He echoed a remark that he had written to Cameron two years before: 'The applause that now greets me from my professional brethren has this satisfactory about it that it shews that the antiseptic principle has received pretty universal acceptance'. The devil of self-doubt pirouettes through the sad, irrelevant qualification.

Soon after his eighty-first birthday Lister received the last recognition of his life. The County Borough of West Ham in London's east end made him an Honorary Freeman. He had been born and had grown up within what were now its boundaries.

In mid-July 1908 Lister and Miss Syme went to Walmer on the Kent coast, where Lister had rented Brook Cottage. Then on July 19 the ultimate blow struck him. His beloved brother, Arthur, died. He was seventy-eight and had been ailing, so that his death was not unexpected. But Arthur had been closest to Joseph, and he was the last remaining member of the family whom Joseph saw. He was an accomplished amateur mycologist, moreover, whose work on fungi had paralleled and assisted Lister's own early bacteriological experiments. His family had grown up in an intimacy with Aunt Agnes and Uncle Joseph made possible by the joint ownership of the house at Lyme Regis. In October Lister acknowledged an account of Arthur's life written by his daughters, Isabella and Gulielma: 'I send, as usual, a most unworthy response which I know thee will excuse'. Only in letters to Arthur's family did he still use the Quaker pronoun.

Arthur's death seemed again to hasten Joseph's decline. Lucy wrote his letters with increasing regularity. On September 29 she wrote to Cameron at Lister's dictation: 'I am stronger as regards walking in my room; but in sight, hearing, memory and capacity for serious thought I have been losing ground'. For a time, that autumn, he was better again. He asked Cameron 'how many physicians there are at the Western Infirmary and also (quite roughly) how many beds each has charge of'. He wrote the letter himself evidently wishing to compare conditions in the new Infirmary to those that prevailed in his day.

In the same letter he revived a battle long since lost:

Another proposal which I could scarcely believe my eyes in reading, was that all medical students of the University of Glasgow were to be compelled to attend clinical teaching given to mixed classes of male & female students.

Lister returned to the theme in two letters during November, finally admitting that he and Cameron had to disagree on the subject.

On January 9, 1909, he submitted a note 'on sulpho-chromic Catgut' to the two medical journals, which dutifully published it on the 14th. He also wrote to Dr Martin asking if it could be added as a footnote in the *Collected Papers*. Martin replied that the volumes were being printed. It was his last publication. If the note showed no culminating insight, it demonstrated his persistent interest in this detail of the antiseptic system. Today catgut has been replaced by plastic material to which the body displays few of the defensive reactions such as inflammation which it was never possible to prevent after the use of catgut.

In March 1909 he remarked in a letter to Cameron on 'his failing sight'. Still, he kept his mind alert. The previous year Cameron had spoken on cancer of the breast, and Lister had read the speech. He disagreed that it is 'a disease which probably invades the body from without', as Cameron believed. The mystery is still unsolved.

In June the University of Glasgow asked him to agree to the creation of a 'Lister Surgical Chair', but the idea seemed almost as outlandish to him as the admission of women to clinical lectures. 'That the University authorities should desire that University Chairs should have the names of particular individuals seems to me an extraordinary idea, with which I cannot sympathize', he wrote to Cameron; 'and I should feel special objection to such an arrangement in the present instance considering the relations the new Chair will have to do with the teaching of women'. The time for flexibility had passed. Unbidden, his body focused on the avoidance of dissolution.

Cameron spoke at Guy's in September, and Lister asked him to call at Brook Cottage before he returned to Glasgow. He wanted Cameron's advice about his back pains. According to Cameron's son, 'My father returned saddened by the changes time had wrought'. Lister wrote to Cheyne in January 1910 about the 'feeble state' of his health. Despite growing blindness he could still 'see the sunset' from his window, Godlee told Stewart. In May 1910 Lister wrote to Cameron deploring the death of Edward VII, 'a terrible blow to the country' and the passing of another landmark in his life.

His last surviving letters were written in April and November 1911. In the first he thanked Cameron for birthday greetings adding, 'You will excuse my not saying more'. In November he asked Cheyne about the health of Sir Henry Butlin, James Paget's house surgeon in 1869, who had just retired.

Lister was now totally blind and almost deaf. No one saw him excepting the servants, Lucy, and occasionally Godlee and his wife. His doctor was Sir Richard D Powell, physician to the Middlesex Hospital, who had lived in Portland Place near Lister. He came regularly to Walmer. Lister remained conscious and capable of speech until a fortnight before the end. He died, at last, in the morning of February 10, 1912. Powell wrote to Godlee that day: 'What a merciful end to that later life of sorrow and misgivings!'

Lister refused to be buried at Westminster Abbey, wishing to lie beside Agnes in West Hampstead Cemetery. Nevertheless both the family ceremony on the 15th and the great public funeral the next day were conducted in the church that consecrates so many in Britain whose work survives.

ACKNOWLEDGEMENTS
AND BIBLIOGRAPHY

One grey November day my friend, Peter Buchman, and I strode vigorously down a muddy lane that opens across the road from his white hilltop house in Oxfordshire. He was finishing his biography of Lafayette, and I expressed a wish to write a biography too, which would bring my early training as an historian to the service of my recent interest in the biological sciences. He promptly suggested three names. One of them was Joseph Lister. I am grateful to him for the suggestion as well as the several comfortable visits with him and Rosemarie.

The bulk of the surviving family letters written by, to and about Joseph Lister are in the possession of Mrs David Dowrick. She also has photographs, drawings and a fascinating file of clippings kept by Joseph Jackson and Arthur Lister. I am grateful to Mrs Dowrick not only for her permission freely to use this wealth of material, but also because she made available to me a room in her house in which to use them, provided endless cups of tea, excellent homemade cakes and occasionally a full meal.

Letters relating to the Godlee family, pictures and correspondence between Sir Rickman J Godlee and Lister's friends and associates are now held by Dr Nicholas Godlee. Dr and Mrs Godlee also set aside a room in which I could work, and sometimes fed me. I thank them for their helpful kindness.

Mr A Michael Turton possesses diaries kept by John Lister and Mary Lister Godlee, letters from and to Joseph Lister, drawings, engravings and photographs. He housed and fed me for a weekend while I used the materials in his possession, and I am grateful.

I am also grateful to the Misses Mary and Anne Hay of Bishop's Stortford for papers relating to the Beck family and to Mrs Margaret Young of Blackheath for a genealogy of the Harris family.

Lister's Common-place Books, many of his manuscripts, the letters to him from Pasteur as well as other correspondence, laboratory notes and drawings, the huge brown paper 'barograph' recordings of blood pressure, and various presentation copies of addresses were given to the Library of the Royal College of Surgeons of England by Sir Rickman J Godlee. The Library also has the bulk of Lister's King's College Hospital ward journals. Mr Eustace Cornelius, Librarian, Mr Ian F Lyle, Senior Assistant Librarian and their associates made these rich materials available and allowed me to work on them in comfortable isolation.

In Glasgow Mrs Jean S A Robertson, Reference Librarian of the University of Glasgow Library, arranged appointments and accommodation and made available University Library material. Mr Michael S Moss, Archivist, and his assistant, Mrs Elspeth Simpson, helped me with records in the University of Glasgow Archives. Mr

Donald F Hay, Chief Technician, Department of Pathology, Glasgow Royal Infirmary, allowed me to use Lister's Glasgow ward journals and showed me the books from Lister's library held by the Infirmary.

Mrs P M Eaves-Walton, Archivist of the Edinburgh Royal Infirmary, provided without previous notice Minute Books, Nurses' Registers and other material. Mrs Dorothy H Wardle, Librarian of the Royal College of Surgeons of Edinburgh, made available the large collection of letters from Lister to Sir Hector Cameron and others and the remaining Edinburgh Royal Infirmary ward journals, also with very little notice. Mr J H McArdle of the Scottish Record Office arranged for me to see Glasgow Royal Infirmary ward journals and James Syme's will. Mr Charles P Finlayson, Keeper of Manuscripts, Edinburgh University Library, was also helpful. I wish to thank Mrs Charles Buchanan for the hospitality she and her late husband offered me in Edinburgh.

Mr Theodore Milligan, Librarian of the Society of Friends Library, London, provided helpful advice on Quaker attitudes as well as the minutes of relevant Meetings. Miss G M Pentelow, Librarian, made available ward journals and Minute Books in the possession of the King's College Hospital Library, London.

I wish also to acknowledge the assistance of Miss A M Young of the University of London Library, Mr N H Robinson, Librarian of the Royal Society, Mr G L E Lindow, Secretary of the Athenaeum, and the staff of the Passmore Edwards Museum, Newham, the Royal Society of Medicine Library, the Wellcome Institute for the History of Medicine Library and the British Museum.

The entry in Queen Victoria's diary for September 5, 1871, is published with the gracious permission of Her Majesty the Queen.

The quotation from Sir Frederick Treves is from a manuscript in the possession of the Royal College of Surgeons of England, but was supplied by The Librarian, Windsor Castle.

Quotations and certain other data are acknowledged in the text. The most important sources for this biography are letters, especially those written by Joseph Lister to members of his family and his closest associates, and those by Joseph Jackson Lister and Arthur Lister to Joseph. Perhaps the most unusual are the *Upton Journals* in the possession of Mrs Dowrick. Much of the new information about Lister's nervous breakdown comes from an unpublished memoir written by Thomas Hodgkin for Sir Rickman J Godlee. Lister's four Common-place Books, containing notes written by Lady Lister, Arthur Lister, Sir William Watson Cheyne, Godlee and Lister, are an invaluable source of information about his day-to-day research activities and give insights into his social life. They also provide one of the few sources of information about Lady Lister. The ward journals are for the most part routine, but they are the only source of data for Lister's hospital practice. Their existence underlines the lack of any equivalent documents describing his private practice. The ward journals are invaluable, moreover, for accounts of unusual operations, the first antiseptic cases and the non-antiseptic therapies Lister used.

They exist for most of the years of Lister's practice at the Glasgow Royal Infirmary and King's College Hospital, but of the Edinburgh Royal Infirmary journals only two have survived covering the periods 15.7.1854—8.1.1855 and 18.9.1870—17.1.1872. The Glasgow Royal Infirmary journal for Ward 24 for the crucial period, 1865 to May 1866, is also lost. Notes of some cases of wrist excisions performed in these months were copied, however, and are in the Royal College of Surgeons of England Library.

Lister, Joseph, Baron, *Collected Papers*, Oxford: Clarendon Press, 1909, contains in two volumes the major papers often with footnotes prepared by Lister for this collection. The introduction by Sir Hector Cameron contains useful data.

Le Fanu, William, *A List of the Original Writings of Joseph Lord Lister, O.M.*, Edinburgh and London: E and S Livingstone, 1965, was compiled by a former Librarian of the Royal College of Surgeons of England. It is complete but for two major groups of Lister's writings:

1. A large number of unpublished papers and lectures existing only in manuscript. With their location in brackets, this group includes:

'Notes of cases taken by Lister for the Fellowes Clinical Medal at UCH . . .' [1852] [RCS Eng]

'Introductory Lecture', Edinburgh, 1855 [RCS Eng]

'On the mode in which External Applications Act on Internal Parts'. Read to the Royal Medical Society, Edinburgh, 21.12.1855 [RCS Eng]

'Suppuration fm perculating Sore January 31 1866 John L Austin' [Mrs D Dowrick].

'Selected Lectures on Clinical Surgery. I On Granulations' [9.1.1871] [incomplete] [RCS Eng].

'On the healing of wounds without antiseptic treatment. An address delivered in Birmingham at the Opening of the Session of the Midland Medical Society' [30.10.1878] [incomplete] [RCS Eng].

2. A majority of Lister's letters to *The Lancet* and the *British Medical Journal*.

Power, H, *et al.*, editors, *A Biennial Retrospect of Medicine, Surgery, and Their Allied Sciences for 1865–6*, for The New Sydenham Society, London, 1867, contains the one-paragraph description of antiseptic surgery written by Lister in 1865, p. 219.

Power, H, *et al.*, editors, . . . *for 1873–4*, London, 1875, contains a report by R J Godlee on antiseptic surgery, pp. 261–3.

The Royal College of Surgeons of England has four sets of notes on Lister's lecture courses. They were taken by Dr Robert W Forrest (1863–1864), Mr P H McKellar (1864–1865), Alexander Logan Taylor (1867–1868) and William Watson Cheyne (1872–1873).

Godlee, Sir Rickman John, *Lord Lister*, 3rd edition, Oxford: Clarendon Press, 1924, is the only important biography. It was written by Lister's nephew and is based on family documents as well as the author's recollections. Godlee was himself a surgeon; both for this reason and because of Lister's desire that personal matters be omitted, the book is weighted on the professional side. It was nevertheless readably written by a humanist.

Anderson, J Ford, *Reminiscences of Lister*, from *National Medical Journal* (May 1927), is by a former house surgeon.

Cameron, Hector Charles, *Joseph Lister: The Friend of Man*, London: William Heinemann, 1948, is by the son of Lister's friend and assistant. Hector Charles was also a surgeon.

Cameron, Sir Hector Clare, *Reminiscences of Lister and of His Work in the Wards of The Glasgow Royal Infirmary 1860–1869*, Glasgow: Jackson, Wylie & Co, 1927, was written for the Lister centenary.

Cartwright, Frederick F, *Joseph Lister, the Man who made Surgery Safe*, London: Weidenfeld and Nicolson, 1963, used the King's College Hospital ward journals but is otherwise based on Godlee.

Cheyne, Sir William Watson, *Lister and His Achievement*, London: Longmans, Green, 1925; is a memoir by another house surgeon, assistant and friend.

Dukes, Cuthbert, *Lord Lister (1827–1912)*, Boston: Small, Maynard; London: Leonard Parsons, 1924, based on Godlee, was the first American biography.

Guthrie, Douglas, *Lord Lister: His Life and Doctrine*, Edinburgh: E and S Livingstone, 1949, is based on Godlee. The author wrote as a doctor.

ACKNOWLEDGEMENTS AND BIBLIOGRAPHY

Leeson, John Rudd, *Lister as I Knew Him*, London: Bailliere, Tindall and Cox, 1927, is a memoir by an Edinburgh house surgeon.

Thompson, C J S, *Lord Lister, the Discoverer of Antiseptic Surgery*, London: John Bale, Sons and Danielson, 1934, is based on Godlee.

Thomson, St Clair, *Lister 1827–1912, A House Surgeon's Memories*, from *King's College Hospital Gazette*, October 1937, is idiosyncratic, by a house surgeon at King's College.

Walker, Kenneth, *Joseph Lister*, London: Hutchinson, 1956, is based on Godlee.

Wallace, Abraham, MD, *Reminiscences of Lister*, Manchester: Two Worlds, 1928, also by a house surgeon.

Wangensteen, O H and S D Wangensteen, *Lister, His Books and Evolvement of His Antiseptic Wound Practices*, 46th anniversary meeting, American Association for the History of Medicine, Cincinnati, May 3, 1973 [privately printed], covers an unusual aspect of Lister's life.

Wangensteen, O H, S D Wangensteen, C F Klinger, *Some Pre-Listerian and Post-Listerian Antiseptic Wound Practices and the Emergence of Asepsis*, from *Surgery, Gynaecology and Obstetrics* (1973) 137: 677–702. I am grateful to the authors for sending me both titles.

Wrench, G T, *Lord Lister: His Life and Work*, London: T Fisher Unwin, 1913. The first biography, written entirely from published material.

Several celebratory volumes have been published. They include:

'Lister Jubilee Number', *British Medical Journal* (1902) 2189: 1817–1861.

'Lister Number', *Canadian Journal of Medicine and Surgery* (May 1912) XXXI, contains talks given to the Academy of Medicine, Toronto, April 2, 1912.

Royal College of Surgeons of England, *Lister Centenary Conference* 1967 . . . April 2–6, 1967.

Turner, A Logan, editor, *Joseph, Baron Lister, Centenary Volume, 1827–1927*, Edinburgh: Oliver and Boyd, 1927. Memoirs by house surgeons including Sir William Watson Cheyne, John Stewart and W Henry Dobie.

Amongst other useful secondary sources are:

Beck, William and T F Bell, *The London Friends' Meetings . . . Their History and General Associations*, London: F Boyer Kitto, 1869.

Beddoe, John, *Memories of Eighty Years*, Bristol: J W Arrowsmith; London: Simpkin, Marshall, Hamilton, Kent, 1910.

Brown, John, *Horae Subsecivae*, London: Adam and Charles Black, 1900. Essays on medical figures and subjects.

Brown, John, *Rab and His Friends and Other Papers and Essays*, London: J M Dent; New York: E P Dutton, 1906.

Bruce, Maurice, *The Coming of the Welfare State*, London: Batsford, 1961.

Cartwright, Frederick F, *The Development of Modern Surgery*, New York: T Y Crowell, 1968. Almost the only history of this subject.

Chick, H, M Hume, M MacFarlane, *War on Disease: A History of the Lister Institute*, London: Deutsch, 1971.

Chiene, John, *Looking Back, 1907–1860*, [University of Edinburgh], 1907. Chiene was Lister's assistant in the early 1870s.

Clark, Ronald W, *Einstein: The Life and Times*, London: Hodder and Stoughton, 1973.

Comrie, John D, *History of Scottish Medicine*, Vol II, London: Balliere, Tindall and Cox, 1932.

Cope, Zachary, *The Royal College of Surgeons of England: a History*, London: Blond, 1959.

Coutts, James, *A History of the University of Glasgow*, Glasgow: James Maclehose, 1909.

Dubos, René J, *Louis Pasteur: Free Lance of Science*, London: Gollancz, 1951. An excellent modern biography by a scientist.

Duns, J, *Memoir of Sir James Y Simpson*, Edinburgh: Edmonston and Douglas, 1873.

Forrest, D W, *Francis Galton: The Life and Works of a Victorian Genius*, London: Elek, 1974.

French, Richard D, *Antivivisection and Medical Science in Victorian Society*, Princeton University Press, 1975. An enjoyably sane and careful history.

Illingworth, Sir Charles, *A Short Textbook of Surgery*, 9th edition, Edinburgh and London: Churchill Livingstone,1972.

Lyle, H Willoughby, *King's and Some King's Men*, London: Oxford University Press, 1935.

Lyle, H Willoughby, *An Addendum to King's and Some King's Men (London)*, London, New York, Toronto: Oxford University Press, 1950.

Masson, Flora, *Victorians All*, London and Edinburgh; W and R Chambers, 1931. A delightful memoir by the girl whose maid said she had swallowed a pin.

Merrington, W R, *University College Hospital and its Medical School: a History*, London: Heinemann, 1976.

Paget, Stephen, editor, *Memoirs and Letters of Sir James Paget*, London: Longmans, Green, 1901.

Paterson, Robert, *Memorials of the Life of James Syme*, Edinburgh: Edmonston and Douglas, 1874. The only biography of a great surgeon.

Patrick, John, *A Short History of Glasgow Royal Infirmary*, Glasgow: [n.p.], 1940.

Saleeby, C W, *Modern Surgery and Its Making: A Tribute to Listerism*, London: Herbert and Daniel, 1911. Saleeby was an eugenicist and vivisectionist, and this curious book is as much concerned with these causes as it is with antisepsis.

Shaw, G B, *Everybody's Political What's What*, London: Constable, 1944, in which the Great Dramatist slays the Listerian dragon.

Thomson, Henry, *A History of Ackworth School During Its First Hundred Years*, London: Saml Harris, 1879.

Turner, A Logan, editor, *History of the University of Edinburgh, 1833–1933*, Edinburgh: Oliver and Boyd, 1933.

Victoria, Queen, *The Letters of* . . . Second Series, Vol II, 1870–1878, G E Buckle, editor, London: John Murray, 1926.

Woodham-Smith, Cecil, *Florence Nightingale, 1820–1910*, London: Constable, 1950. Easily the best post-war biography in English.

Woodward, John, *To do the sick no harm: A study of the British voluntary hospital system to 1875*, London and Boston: Routledge and Kegan Paul, 1974. Scholarly and immensely useful.

The following magazines contain articles and letters by and about Lister, antiseptic surgery and antiseptics. The dates indicate the years of greatest importance for this book:

British Medical Journal (1877–1909)
Edinburgh Medical Journal (1854–1875)
The Lancet (1867–1909)

ACKNOWLEDGEMENTS AND BIBLIOGRAPHY

Medical Examiner (1877)
Medical Times and Gazette (1879–1882)
Nature (1869–1900)

Most of this book was written on n.b. *Balthazar* on the Rivers Wey and Thames and the Grand Union Canal. It was typed in Canonbury, N1, above ground and below. Its merit, if any, was enhanced by these settings; its faults are of course my own.

London   September 1976

experiments with (1865–7) 130–1, 134–40, 146, 155, 156, (1880s) 260, 272–3; JL's use of 269, 272, 276; *and see* antiseptic methods, carbolic acid, ligatures, spray

anti-vivisection campaign, 218–202, 228–9; and legislation, 219, 220, 221–2, 247, 265; and British Institute of Preventive Medicine 282–3

Apothecaries Act (1815) 35

appendectomy, Edward VII's 315–16

Army Sanitary Commission 191

art: and JL's drawings 25, 30–1, 47, 51–2, 268; Lister family and 25

asepsis, and purpose of antiseptic methods 145, 146, 275, 300,

aseptic surgery: and new techniques 275; replaces antiseptic methods, 210, 260, 300, 301; support of 308–9; techniques of 260

Association for the Advancement of Medicine by Research 222

Athenaeum, JL elected to (1877) 242–3

Australian Medical Journal 158–9

Austria: medicine in 81–2, 126–7, 159, *and see* Semmelweiss, Tyrol, Vienna

Ayr Advertiser 229

Babbage, Charles, economist 21

bacteria: action of antiseptics on 272–3, 301, 302; and gangrene 122; and inflammation 89, 255, 270; JL's identification of 201, 202, 235; JL's researches into *see* bacteriology; JL's views on 144, 199, 200, 202, 204, 249; Pasteur and 133, 198, 201, 249, 263; and putrefaction 172, 235; relationship of to disease 198, 246, 255, 256, 263, 270; *and see* bacteriology, germ theory, infection

bacteriology: Cohn's work in 198, 203; development of 124, 198, 203, 263, 303; and International Congress of Hygiene (1891) 292–3; JL's experimental research in 21, 84, (1867) 151–7, 160, (1871–77) 195–204 *passim*, 209, 224, 232–3, 235–6, 245–6, 263, (1878) 247, (1879) 255, (1880) 264, 265, 271; JL gives up work on 265–6; JL lectures on (1877) 235–6, 245, (1878) 248–9, (1880) 263–5, (1896) 303, (1882–3) 265; JL's papers on (1873) 200, 202; and JL's proof of germ theory 235–6; Koch's work on 263, 265, 271–2; and tetanus 209, 322; *and see* bacteria, germ theory

Baker, Morrant 257

Bakewell, JL fishes at 243

Balfour, Isaac Bayley 225–6

Balmoral, JL attends Royal Family at 178, 193–4, 207

Baly, William 97

Bangor, family holiday at (1848) 46

Bantock, George 266

Barbauld, Anna Letitia 23

Barber-Surgeons, Company of 35

Barcelona: JL visits (1882–3) 274; rabies institute in 282

Barclay family 16, 17

Barclay, J. Gurney 300

Barclay, Rev. Thomas 167

Bardeleben, Professor 215

Barlow, Dr Thomas 315

Barrett, Elizabeth 101

Barter, Rev. Evart B 267–8

Bastian, Prof. Henry Charlton 181–2, 204, 245–6

Bath, JL at (1903) 318

Batt, William 18

Bayard, American Ambassador 317

Beck, Elizabeth (*née* Lister), aunt, 14, 21

Beck, Marcus, cousin: defends JL during antiseptic controversy 14, 163, 217; lives with Listers in Glasgow 14, 101–2, 112; on Franco-Prussian war 182; JL's advice to on medical education 46, 101, 149; on Lucy Syme 167; on UCH staff 163

Beck, Richard, cousin 14, 20, 29

Beddoe, John 63, 64, 128, 304

Belfast: JL visits (1848) 46; JL addresses Queen's College at (1897) 280, 306

Belhaven, Lord 94, 111

Bell, Joseph 58, 97, 163

Bennett, Prof J. Hughes 83; opposes admission of women 190; opposes germ theory 179, 181; prescribes cold liver oil 256

Berlin: JL visits (1856) 82, (1875) 214–15, (1890, and address to International Medical Congress) 186, 222, 288–9, (1902) 314; University Clinic at, 289–90

Bernard, Claude, chemist 53

Bert, Paul, surgeon 110

Beverley, Dr Michael 209–10

Bible Society 101

Bickersteth, E R, surgeon 165, 166, 167

Billroth, Theodore 212

Bingley, Yorks 13

bird watching, JL's interest in 243–4, 248, 274, 291, 293

Birmingham: General Hospital 202; JL speaks at (1878) 205, 249

Black Prince, warship 111

Blackie, John Stuart 229–30

Bloch, Professor 317

blood coagulation: eighteenth-century theories of 91; and JL's lectures 112, 116, 249, 292; JL's research into 91–3, 95, 97, 99, 112; and suppuration 121

blood flow; JL demonstrates 188, 247; and inflammation, JL's work on, 71, 84–9, 91, 180

blood hydraulics, JL's innovative work in 245, 247–8, 249

blood-letting 74–5, 117, 258

blood poisoning 122, 131; statistics on 257, 259; *and see* erysipelas, pyaemia

334

blood transfusions 142, 253
Boer War 183, 315, 318
Bologna medical schools 58, 81
Bombay, plague vaccine tested in 304
bone deformities, JL operates on 205–6,
253
Bonn, JL visits (1875) 215
botany: Arthur Lister's interest in 113,
142; JL's interest in 29, 33, 142, 234,
243, 248, 274, 315; JL studies at
University College 33, 48, 149, 176
Bottini, Professor 245
Bowman, Sir William 56, 225, 228, 239,
243
Bradford 69, 70, 135
brain surgery, JL performs (1885) 269
Brecon, JL holidays in (1898) 306
Brewster, Sir David 114
Bright, John, Corn Law reformer 18
Bristol: Medical School, JL gives prizes at
(1880) 261; Royal Infirmary 202, 261
British Association: JL's Presidency of
(1896) 302; JL represents (Berlin, 1902)
314; meetings of, JL at (1857, Dublin)
90, (1896, Liverpool) 37, 302, 303–4,
(1897, Canada) 308, (1901) 310, (1902,
Glasgow) 314
British Guiana 308
British Institute of Preventive Medicine
282–4, 294
British Medical Association: and antiseptic
surgery, 130, 168, 240, 215–6, 250, 251,
257–8, 259, 300–1; and anti-vivisection
campaign, 219, 221; and chloroform
109, 273; and germ theory 134, 168,
246; JL's addresses to (1867, Dublin)
135, 139, 149–50, (1871, Plymouth),
169, 179, 191–3; (1875, Edinburgh)
209, (1879, London) 257, (1880,
Cambridge) 262–5; JL attends Canada
meeting (1897) 308; JL presides at
meetings of (1870, 1875) 179; Paget
addresses 125, 258
British Medical Journal: and aseptic
surgery 301; and anti-vivisection
campaign 219; and death of Fergusson
224–5; and germ theory 181, 250; on
decline in hospital mortality (1902) 260;
on improvements in surgery (1880)
275; on JL's Amsterdam address (1879)
252; represents scientific medicine 228;
JL's contributions to: on antiseptic
surgery (1868) 162, (1870) 182–3,
(1871) 186, (1880) 258–9; on catgut
(1908) 324, (1909) 325; Huxley lecture
(1900) 322; on malarial research (1900)
309; on Sal Alembroth gauze (1907)
273
Brodie, Sir Benjamin Collins 299, 305
Brougham, Lord 114, 140
Brown, Isaac, Master, Hitchin School 28
Brown, Dr J: biography of 76; career of 76;
friendship of with Symes 76, 81, 176;
and JL's appointment to King's College

229, 231; 'Rab and His Friends' 76
Browning, Robert 219
Brown-Sequard, M, physiologist 87
Brown Square School, Edinburgh 59
Bruno, Giordano 117–18
Bruns, Professor 185
Brunton, Dr T Launder 298
Bryant, Thomas, surgeon 227
Buchanan, George 50, 114, 143
Buchner, Dr H 292
Budapest, Listers visit (1883) 127, 276
Bull, William and Mary, great-
grandparents 18
Burdon-Sanderson, Dr John S,
physiologist 195, 219, 222, 304;
experimental work of 228, 264; visits
JL's wards 245; on rabies vaccine
Commission 281
Burke and Hare murders (1827–8) 69
burns, treatment of 159, 165; and plastic
surgery 206
Burns, Jemima *see* Syme, Jemima
Busch, Professor 215
Butlin, Sir Henry, surgeon 166, 326
Buxton, Derbys, JL and Lucy Syme
holiday in (1900–5) 310, 311, 314, 315,
316, 319–20, 321

Café Royal, London 308
Caird, Francis M 177
Calcutta military hospital 246
Callendar, Dr 216
Calvert, Prof F Crace 134–5
Cambridge: BMA meeting at (1880)
263–5
Cambridge University 34, 61
camera lucida 25, 177
Cameron, Hector Charles 188, 285, 317,
326
Cameron, Sir Hector Clare, surgeon: on
aseptic surgery 274–5, 301; assists JL
102; and development of antiseptic
treatment 150, 157, 158, 159, 160, 163,
166, and catgut ligatures 269, 318,
319–20; and collection of JL's papers
304, 322; on Fitzroy Square nursing
home 244; friendship of with JL 177,
237, 272, 309, 320–1; on hospital
hygiene 126, 159; and JL's baronetcy
305; on JL in Berlin (1890) 289–90; on
JL and carbolic acid spray 185; and
JL's failing health (1909) 326; and JL's
Freedom of City of Glasgow 324; on
JL's dinners for French and Germans
(1881) 272; on JL's interest in botany
243; on JL's lecture style 100, 189; JL's
letters to 294–5, 299, 301, 310–11, 316,
317, 318, 319–22, 324, 325, 326; on JL's
life and career in Glasgow 99, 102, 103,
141, 173, 244, 320–1; on JL and
mastectomy operation 148–9; on JL's
opinions of London medical training
232; on JL's poor writing style 147; JL
stays with in Glasgow 298, 321; on JL's

335

and nieces 290; and JL's religious
enthusiasm 41–2; and letter writing 25,
29; origins of 13–14; and Quakerism 11,
13, 14–15, 16–18
Lister, Gulielma, niece 243, 280, 314, 325
Lister Institute of Preventive Medicine
284–5, 299, 304, 314
Lister, Isabella (*née* Harris), mother: and
family life 11, 12, 19–20, 23, 31, 46, 94,
111; and JL's courtship of Agnes 77;
death of (1864) 85, 115; JL's letters to
28, 29, 30, 31, 32, 37, 38, 39, 58, 85, 86;
letter of 11, 20, 25; marriage of 18, 19,
22; poor health of 19–20, 31, 41, 80,
111, 113; and Quakerism 17, 19, 33, 77;
teaches at Ackworth 19; visits Glasgow
(1860) 101, (1862) 111
Lister, Isabella, niece 315, 325
Lister, Isabella Sophie *see* Pim, Isabella
Sophie
Lister, Jane *see* Harrison, Jane
Lister, John, brother 11, 12, 22, 27, 30, 31;
illness and death of (1846) 21–2, 41, 43;
school days of 12, 28, 30
Lister, John, grandfather 13–16, 22
Lister, Joseph Jackson, father 11; death of
(1869) 169, 173; Delafour's portrait of
170; education and career of 15–16, 22;
and education of children 22, 23, 27, 28;
failing health of (1869) 168, 170; and
family holidays 31, 32–3, 141, 150, 170;
and family wine business 15–16, 20,
113; Fellow of Royal Society (1832) 21;
and Irish potato famine 22, 46; and
Isabella's death 115; investments of 16,
119, 231, 323; library of 242; and JL's
antiseptic system 138–9, 144–5, 155,
158, 166, 171; and JL's breakdown 41,
43–5, 47; and JL's career 58, 65, 67, 68,
69, 114, 115, 118, 141, 312; and JL's
choice of arms 305; and JL's courtship
and engagement 77, 78–9, 80; and JL's
departure from Edinburgh 100; and
JL's ear hook 115; and JL's election to
Royal Society 95; and JL's finances 69,
78–9, 98, 118–9; and JL's friendship
with Ramsay 94; and JL's health 144;
and JL's lectures in Edinburgh 72, 73,
74, 83; JL's letters to 30, 44, 47, 58, 90,
96, 97, 108, 112, 138, 139, 141, 144,
148, 154, 158, 161, 162, 169; and JL's
London lodgings (1847) 38; and JL's
marriage (1856) 80, 82; JL's obituary of
170, 291; JL's special relationship with
170–1; and JL's religious faith 312;
letters of, stylistic brilliance of 20, 147,
and references *passim*; on JL's
unpunctuality 244; and life at Upton
Park 11, 12, 13, 22–3, 25, 113; marriage
of 18, 19–20, 22; papers by 20–1, 71;
and Pritchard execution (1865) 120;
and Quakerism 15, 16, 17, 18, 22; on
snowball rioting 119; and Syme 64,
167; urges JL to publish 83, 90, 113,

115, 139; visits Edinburgh (1855) 80,
(1856) 84; visits Glasgow (1860) 101,
(1862) 111; visits Hastings (1864) 115;
visits London (1862) 111; visits Wales
and Ireland (1848) 46–7; work of on
lenses and microscopes 15, 20–1, 22, 51,
84
Lister, Joseph, ancestor 13
Lister, Joseph, great-grandfather 11, 13
Lister, Mary, aunt 14, 24, 27
Lister, Mary (*née* Jackson), grandmother
14–15, 16
Lister, Mary (*née* Gray), great-
grandmother 13
Lister, Mary, sister *see* Godlee, Mary
Lister, Susannah (*née* Tindall) 94–5, 111,
150, 199, 212, 213, 223; marriage of to
Arthur Lister 69
Lister, Thomas, of Bingley, ancestor 13
Lister, William Henry, brother 22; career
of 25–6; death of (1859) 25–6, 97; and
family holidays 31, 32, 33, 44–5, 46; and
JL's engagement 26, 78, 79; at JL's
wedding 81; letters of 25–6, 29, 78, 79;
and life at Upton Park 23–4, 25
Lister, William T, nephew 319
Liston, Prof Robert 37, 40, 59, 125
Liverpool 305; JL addresses BA meeting at
(1896) 299, 303–4, 305; Royal Infirmary
165; School of Tropical Diseases 310,
324–5; University 321
Livingstone, Dr David 63
Local Government Board 50, 219, 284
Loch Lomond, expeditions to (1860) 102,
(1864) 115
Loch Long, Syme's house at 64
Lockyer, Sir Norman 298
Lodge, Oliver, physicist 303, 318
London: and acceptance of JL's methods
164, 165–6, 179, 229, 246, 266, 276–7,
300–01; BMA meeting in (1879) and
antiseptic surgery 257–8, 259; division
among medical men of 228–9; growth
of JL's reputation in 252–3, 257, 266;
hospitals of *see under* hospitals, King's
College Hospital, University College
Hospital; International Congress of
Hygiene in (1891) 292–3; international
exhibition in (1862) 111; International
Medical Congress in (1881) 185, 270–2;
JL's desire to return to 64–5, 96, 114,
140–1; JL's 80th birthday in (1907)
324; JL's home in (1877–1909) *see* Park
Crescent; JL lectures in (1877) 236,
245, (1881) 270–1, (1882) 274, (1884)
280, (1889) 288, *and see* under King's
College Hospital; JL's life in (1844–8)
37–41, (1878–1908) 231, 241–5, 266,
267–8, 297–300, 312, 315, 316–17, 318,
324; JL's private practice in 244–5, 252,
252–3, 280, 293, 298; JL returns to
(1877) 210, 231–2, 233, 234; JL's 70th
birthday in (1897) 306–7; JL speaks at
rabies meeting in (1889) 282; JL's

344

348

Wolseley, Lord, 183, 309
Wonderful Country, The (Wallace) 309
Wood, John, surgeon 225, 227, 229, 230, 231; convert to antiseptic surgery 240, 257–8
Woodham-Smith, Cecil 43
Woodside Place, Glasgow, JL's home in 98, 100, 149, 160, 163, 169
Woolwich Military Medical Society 183, 280
workhouses 103, 128
World War I 302
wound dressings: and antiseptic surgery 100, 136, 137–40, 145, 149–50, 160, 161–2, 164, 176, 211; and aseptic surgery 274, 275; and hygiene 129–31;

JL's dissatisfaction with 160, 164; JL's experiments with 176, 182, 186, 260, 261, 273, 285–6, 287; JL lectures on (1888) 288; and JL's Note on cyanide dressing (1907) 323; and sealers 130, 136
Wright, Dr Almroth 292, 302
Wylie, Dr J R 163

x-rays, JL and 303, 318

Yeo, Dr Burney 240–1
Yersin, Alexandre, bacteriologist 304
York Road, Lambeth, Hospital 311–12
Young, Brigham, Mormon leader 226

351